The Reader
in the Text

Edited by
Susan R. Suleiman
and Inge Crosman

The Reader
in the Text

Essays on Audience
and Interpretation

Princeton
University
Press

Copyright © 1980 by
Princeton University Press

Published by Princeton University Press,
Princeton, New Jersey
In the United Kingdom:
Princeton University Press,
Guildford, Surrey

All Rights Reserved

Library of Congress Cataloging in
Publication Data will be found on the
last printed page of this book

Clothbound editions of Princeton
University Press books are printed on
acid-free paper, and binding materials are
chosen for strength and durability

Printed in the United States of America
by Princeton University Press,
Princeton, New Jersey

Contents

Preface   vii

Susan R. Suleiman Introduction: Varieties of Audience-Oriented Criticism   3

Jonathan Culler Prolegomena to a Theory of Reading   46

Tzvetan Todorov Reading as Construction   67

Karlheinz Stierle The Reading of Fictional Texts   83

Wolfgang Iser Interaction between Text and Reader   106

Christine Brooke-Rose The Readerhood of Man   120

Robert Crosman Do Readers Make Meaning?   149

Naomi Schor Fiction as Interpretation Interpretation as Fiction   165

Pierre Maranda The Dialectic of Metaphor: An Anthropological Essay on Hermeneutics   183

Jacques Leenhardt Toward a Sociology of Reading   205

Gerald Prince Notes on the Text as Reader   225

Peter J. Rabinowitz "What's Hecuba to Us?" The Audience's Experience of Literary Borrowing   241

Cathleen M. Bauschatz Montaigne's Conception of Reading in the Context of Renaissance Poetics and Modern Criticism   264

Louis Marin Toward a Theory of Reading in the Visual Arts: Poussin's *The Arcadian Shepherds*   293

Michel Beaujour Exemplary Pornography: Barrès, Loyola, and the Novel   325

Norman N. Holland Re-Covering "The Purloined Letter": Reading as a Personal Transaction   350

v

Contents

Vicki Mistacco	The Theory and Practice of Reading Nouveaux Romans: Robbe-Grillet's *Topologie d'une cité fantôme* 371
Inge Crosman	Annotated Bibliography of Audience-Oriented Criticism 401
	Notes on Contributors 425
	Subject Index 429
	Index of Names 435

Preface

The editors' aim in bringing together this group of original essays has been to examine, in the widest perspective possible, the theoretical and practical implications of the notion of *reader*—and more generally of *audience*—in literary texts and in other artistic forms that can be thought of by analogy as texts. The notion of the reader "in" the text seems sufficiently paradoxical to suggest the ambiguities inherent in the concept of audience. Artistic texts invariably contain clues as to how they are to be interpreted: audiences are evoked, or, often enough, represented in the text. But the actual audience, no matter how willingly it follows such clues, remains irreducibly itself, appropriating the text for its own tastes and purposes. If a reader may be "in" a text as a character is in a novel, he or she is certainly also in it as in a train of thought—both possessing it and possessed by it. A primary aim of this volume then is to explore fundamental questions about the status—be it semiotic, sociological, hermeneutic, subjective—of the audience in relation to the artistic text.

The idea for the volume grew out of a seminar organized by the editors at the 1975 Modern Language Association Convention, entitled "The Reader in Fiction." The unusually large attendance at this seminar convinced us that the time had come for a serious assessment and overview of the rapidly growing new field of audience-oriented criticism. We felt, however, that rather than presenting a mere collection of already published articles, we ought to seek original essays which, even while building on previous works, would represent new and significant contributions to the field. We therefore solicited essays from a group of scholars with varying research interests; some had already written distinguished

vii

Preface

works on the subject, and others were approaching it for the first time. The juxtaposition of their essays, diverse in scope and method but unified in their common focus on the "receiving end" of artistic texts, is itself an eloquent argument for the richness and novelty of audience-oriented criticism.

All the essays were written especially for the volume except that of Tzvetan Todorov, which appears here in English for the first time. The essay by Karlheinz Stierle appeared in a longer version in the German review *Poetica* but was revised and translated especially for inclusion here.

We have not tried to separate the contributions into theoretical or methodological categories. One of our purposes has been to suggest that the most interesting future works in this field will transcend strict categorization, combining several approaches, as many of the essays in this book already do. To orient the reader, we have included an introductory essay surveying the major contemporary approaches to audience-oriented criticism. Of course, the introduction expresses the personal views of its author, who alone is responsible for them.

The essays after the introduction are arranged in order of increasing specificity, going from broadly theoretical statements to readings of individual works from various national literatures, genres, and periods. Even the most specific essays, however, are set within a theoretical framework, and the general essays invariably cite specific works.

We would like to express our appreciation to all the authors of the volume, who have acquiesced to our editorial suggestions with admirable patience and graciousness, and who have demonstrated that the individualism of fine scholarship is not at odds with the spirit of cooperation. To our editor, Robert Brown of Princeton University Press, go our many thanks for his infinite care.

S.R.S.
I.C.
Los Angeles and Providence

The Reader
in the Text

Susan R. Suleiman | Introduction: Varieties of Audience-Oriented Criticism*

Some revolutions occur quietly: no manifestoes, no marching and singing, no tumult in the streets; simply a shift in perspective, a new way of seeing what had always been there. New words enter the vocabulary, old words suddenly take on new meaning: proletariat, ego, structure. Or they retain their meaning but their *position* changes: the peripheral becomes central, the walk-on becomes the hero of the play.

For the past few years, we have been witnessing just such a change in the field of literary theory and criticism. The words *reader* and *audience*, once relegated to the status of the unproblematic and obvious, have acceded to a starring role. A little over ten years ago, the authors of an influential study on the nature of narrative could self-confidently affirm that narrative literature was "distinguished by two characteristics: the presence of a story and a story-teller."[1] The fact that all stories are implicitly or explicitly addressed to an audience, whose presence is as variable and as problematic as that of the story-teller, escaped their notice or was considered too trivial to mention. Today, one rarely picks up a literary journal on either side of the Atlantic without finding articles (and often a

---

* This essay was written in part while I held a summer research grant from the National Endowment for the Humanities in 1977. I wish to thank the Endowment, as well as the following people, who read the essay in manuscript and from whose criticisms I benefited: Wayne C. Booth, Christine Brooke-Rose, Shlomith Rimmon-Kenan, and Ezra Suleiman.

[1] Robert Scholes and Robert Kellog, *The Nature of Narrative* (New York: Oxford Univ. Press, paperback ed., 1968), p. 4.

Susan R. Suleiman

whole special issue) devoted to the performance of reading, the role of feeling, the variability of individual response, the confrontation, transaction, or interrogation between texts and readers, the nature and limits of interpretation—questions whose very formulation depends on a new awareness of the audience as an entity indissociable from the notion of artistic texts.

One could adduce many reasons for this shift in perspective, and I shall discuss some of them in this essay. Even at first glance, however, it is obvious that the current interest in the interpretation, and more broadly in the reception, of artistic texts—including literary, filmic, pictorial, and musical ones—is part of a general trend in what the French call the human sciences (history, sociology, psychology, linguistics, anthropology) as well as in the traditional humanistic disciplines of philosophy, rhetoric, and aesthetics. The recent evolution of all these disciplines has been toward self-reflexiveness—questioning and making explicit the assumptions that ground the methods of the discipline, and concurrently the investigator's role in delimiting or even in constituting the object of study. Such self-reflexiveness, which has its analogue in the principles of relativity and uncertainty as they emerged in physics early in this century, necessarily shifts the focus of inquiry from the observed—be it defined as text, psyche, society, or language—to the interaction between observed and observer. Claude Lévi-Strauss's *Tristes Tropiques* is, like so many of his works, exemplary in this respect.

As concerns the increasingly interrelated disciplines of linguistics and literary theory, the general move toward self-reflexiveness has been accompanied by more specific or local evolutions tending toward the same results. In linguistics, generative grammar, with its emphasis on linguistic competence and performance, has tended to displace the older (and in its own day revolutionary) Saussurean linguistics, whose emphasis was primarily on the static system of language. The Chomskyan project is not to describe the system of relations that constitute a given language (*langue*), but to state the general rules that account for the production of the potentially

Introduction

infinite number of utterances (*parole*) considered grammatically acceptable by speakers of a language. Moreover, generative grammar has itself been challenged by generative semantics and by the theory of speech acts, which attempt to take into account not only the syntactic and phonological rules of sentence formation but also the semantic and contextual rules that govern actual speech situations.[2]

In literary theory, there has been a parallel movement away from the formalist and New Critical emphasis on the autonomy of "the text itself" toward a recognition (or a re-recognition) of the relevance of context, whether the latter be defined in terms of historical, cultural, ideological, or psychoanalytic categories.[3] This does not mean a return to traditional historical or biographical criticism, and it would be a pity if the current fashion of using the New Criticism as a whipping boy—or as a discredited father—made us forget the very significant contributions of both the New Critics and their predecessors, the Russian Formalists, to modern literary theory and criticism.[4] The same must be said of the Czech and French structuralists, whom it has become de rigueur in some circles to reject, either in the name of a newly discovered semiotics or in that of Derridean "post-structuralism." Semiotics has nothing to disdain in structuralism, for as I

[2] For a brief summary of the evolution of recent linguistic theory, especially the theory of speech acts, see Mary Louise Pratt, *Toward a Speech Act Theory of Literary Discourse* (Bloomington, 1977), chap. 3: "The Linguistics of Use." See also John R. Searle, *Speech Acts: An Essay in the Philosophy of Language* (Cambridge, 1969); and Searle, "Chomsky's Revolution in Linguistics," in G. Harman, ed., *On Noam Chomsky: Critical Essays* (New York, 1974).

[3] Among recent articles that argue for the relevance of context in interpretation are E. Wasiolek's "Wanted: A New Contextualism," *Critical Inquiry* 1 (1975), W. A. Levi's " 'De Interpretatione': Cognition and Context in the History of Ideas," *Critical Inquiry* 3 (1976), and Walter B. Michaels, "Against Formalism: the Autonomous Text in Legal and Literary Interpretation," *Poetics Today* 1 (fall 1979).

[4] Among today's "anti-New Critics," Paul de Man is one of those who temper their criticism with a sympathetic assessment of the New Critics' achievements. See his "Form and Intent in the American New Criticism," in *Blindness and Insight: Essays in the Rhetoric of Contemporary Criticism* (New York, 1971), pp. 20-35.

shall show later the two are continuous, often overlapping enterprises. As for "post-structuralism," the very term implies what its most distinguished exponents (beginning with Jacques Derrida himself) acknowledge: namely, that it could not have existed without structuralism and constitutes not so much a rejection of the latter as its *dépassement*.

If one may safely affirm that a preoccupation with audience and interpretation has become central to contemporary American and Continental theory and criticism, one encounters a major difficulty in citing names or examples. Even a partial list of American critics most closely associated with this mode must include names as apparently incompatible, for theoretical reasons, as Jonathan Culler and Norman Holland, Stanley Fish and Wayne C. Booth, E. D. Hirsch, Jr., and J. Hillis Miller, Walter J. Ong and Paul de Man; if one complicates the list by French and German additions—Roland Barthes, Gérard Genette, Jacques Derrida, Tzvetan Todorov, H. R. Jauss, Wolfgang Iser, to name only the most eminent—one fully realizes what one is up against. Audience-oriented criticism is not one field but many, not a single widely trodden path but a multiplicity of crisscrossing, often divergent tracks that cover a vast area of the critical landscape in a pattern whose complexity dismays the brave and confounds the faint of heart. I intend to map here, however tentatively, the principal tracks in the landscape—not in order to simplify them or minimize their diversity (although some simplification is inevitable because of the ordering and selection that the enterprise requires), but to help the reader through the essays in this book. Such a mapping of the ground—or rather the background—seems essential, since the volume itself is not a didactic anthology of previously published and therefore familiar texts. What unites these essays, aside from the common concern indicated by the title of the volume, is precisely their exploratory character, the authors' willingness to venture into little-traveled territories.

We may distinguish, for the sake of the exposition, six varieties of (or approaches to) audience-oriented criticism: rhetorical; semiotic and structuralist; phenomenological; subjective

Introduction

and psychoanalytic; sociological and historical; and hermeneutic. These approaches are not monolithic (there is more than one kind of rhetorical or hermeneutic criticism), nor do they necessarily exclude each other. As several of the essays in this volume show, a critic may have recourse to more than one approach. The vitality of audience-oriented criticism depends precisely on the realization that various dimensions of analysis or interpretation are possible, and that a combination of approaches is not a negative eclecticism but a positive necessity. This does not mean, of course, that one should overlook or attempt to eradicate real differences and incompatibilities between the theoretical assumptions of individual critics or critical schools. One of our aims must be to pinpoint those issues on which no theoretical consensus is possible, issues which, in W. B. Gallie's phase, designate the presence of "essentially contested concepts."[5]

I

One thing the rhetorical approach shares, even if only implicitly, with the semiotic and structuralist one is a model of the literary text as a form of communication. According to this model, whose most sophisticated formulation was proposed by Roman Jakobson,[6] the author and the reader of a text are related to each other as the sender and the receiver of

[5] See W. B. Gallie, *Philosophy and the Historical Understanding* (London, 1964), chap. 8, cited in Wayne C. Booth, " 'Preserving the Exemplar': Or, How Not to Dig Our Own Graves," *Critical Inquiry* 3 (1977), 410.

[6] See "Closing Statement: Linguistics and Poetics," in T. Sebeok, ed., *Style in Language* (Cambridge, Mass., 1960), pp. 353-59. Jakobson's model distinguishes six constitutive factors in any speech event, each one corresponding to a specific function of language: the addresser, corresponding to the emotive function; the addressee, corresponding to the conative function; the context, corresponding to the referential function; the code, corresponding to the metalinguistic function; the contact or material medium, corresponding to the phatic function; and the message, corresponding to the poetic function. Strictly speaking, the poetic function according to Jakobson is not "communicative." One need not accept all his conclusions, however, especially as regards the specificity of "poetic" versus "everyday" language, in order to make use of the model itself.

a message. The transmission and reception of any message depend on the presence of one or more shared codes of communication between sender and receiver. Reading consists, therefore, of a process of decoding what has by various means been encoded in the text.

The communicative model allows for a variety of different emphases in critical practice, and it is in terms of critical emphasis and vocabulary that the rhetorical critics may most readily be distinguished from the semioticians and structuralists. To the rhetorical critic—at least the kind of rhetorical critic who shall chiefly concern us here and of whom Wayne Booth may be considered an exemplary representative—what matters primarily is the ethical and ideological content of the message. He seeks not only to formulate the set of verbal meanings embedded in the text, but above all to discover the values and beliefs that make those meanings possible—or that those meanings imply. The values and beliefs that underlie and ultimately determine the meaning of a work are attributed to the "implied author," whom Booth defines as the actual author's "second self": the shadowy but overriding presence who is responsible for every aspect of the work and whose image must be constructed (or rather, reconstructed) in the act of reading.

The implied author in Booth's scheme has a counterpart in the "implied reader." Just as the former differs from the actual author in that he exists only in a given work and is coextensive with it, so the latter differs from an actual reader in that he is created by the work and functions, in a sense, as the work's ideal interpreter. Only by agreeing to play the role of this created audience for the duration of his/her reading can an actual reader correctly understand and fully appreciate the work. As Booth puts it: "Regardless of my real beliefs and practices, I must subordinate my mind and heart to the book if I am to enjoy it to the full. The author . . . makes his reader as he makes his second self, and the most successful reading is one in which the created selves, author and reader, can find complete agreement."[7]

[7] Booth, *The Rhetoric of Fiction* (Chicago, 1961), p. 138.

Introduction

Booth's notion of the implied reader has important consequences for the aims and practice of criticism. If a successful
reading experience requires (1) a correct identification of the
implied reader's values and beliefs—which are by definition
also those of the implied author—and (2) an identification
with the implied reader to the extent of "completely agreeing" with his values, then the critic's task must be not only to
show how such identifications are invited by the rhetoric of a
given work, but also to explore, in some problematic works,
why such identifications may be difficult or even impossible
to achieve by an actual reader. For example, a reader may be
unable to "agree," even for the duration of his/her reading,
with the values of the implied reader, and thus may refuse to
play the role that the work demands. Conversely, certain
modern texts make it impossible to identify (much less identify *with*) the role one is asked to play, because the implied
author refuses to give directions—in Booth's words, to "take
a stand." This happens in what he calls "infinitely unstable"
ironic texts like those of Beckett, where "the author . . . refuses to declare himself, however subtly, *for* any stable proposition, even the opposite of whatever proposition his irony
vigorously denies."[8] The result is that the implied reader's
image becomes itself unstable, and the actual reader is left
with "no secure ground to stand on" (p. 248). Texts that produce this kind of instability make Booth extremely uncomfortable, for he sees in them a sign of nihilism: "Since the
universe is empty, life is empty of meaning, and every reading experience can finally be shaken out into the same empty
and melancholy non-truth" (p. 269). At this point, rhetorical
criticism opens out onto the field of metaphysics and morals.
It also opens out, as we shall see, onto the most problematic
concepts of contemporary literary theory: validity, meaning,
authority, intention, text.[9]

[8] Booth, *A Rhetoric of Irony* (Chicago, 1974), p. 240. Other page references
to this work will be given in parentheses in the text.

[9] For a detailed discussion of *A Rhetoric of Irony* in this perspective, see
S. Suleiman, "Interpreting Ironies," *Diacritics* 6, no. 2 (1976), 15-21. Wayne
Booth replied in his "The Three Functions of Criticism at the Present Time,"
Bulletin of the Midwest Modern Language Association (spring 1978).

Susan R. Suleiman

I would not wish to suggest that Booth's kind of rhetorical criticism is the only pertinent one for audience-oriented critics, nor even that the notions of implied author and implied reader, which Booth's work has put into currency, need be tied to ethical and axiological considerations. Any criticism that conceives of the text as a message to be decoded, and that seeks to study the means whereby authors attempt to communicate certain intended meanings or to produce certain intended effects, is both rhetorical and audience-oriented. Stanley Fish's pioneering work on *Paradise Lost* fits into this category;[10] so does the recent application of speech-act theory to the study of literature, especially the study of literary genres, to which speech-act theory has given a new and welcome impetus.[11] Finally, one must mention the quasi-polemical extension of the term *rhetoric* in the work of French structuralist critics like Gérard Genette and Michel Charles, who have impressively argued against the tendency to consider rhetoric as a mere study of tropes,[12] and in that of the American critic Paul de Man, for whom rhetoric seems to

[10] See Fish, *Surprised by Sin: The Reader in Paradise Lost* (New York, 1967). Fish might object to being called a rhetorical critic, and certainly his most recent work does not fit into that category. *Surprised by Sin*, however, does. Fish is a brilliant and mercurial critic whose theoretical shifts make him difficult to "place" in any one category, even his own category of "affective stylistics." I shall refer to his most recent work later, but I will not attempt a complete account of his evolution. For a group of essays concerned specifically with Fish's theories, see the special section on "Reading, Interpretation, Response," in *Genre* 10 (1977).

[11] The most comprehensive attempt to apply speech-act theory to the analysis of literature is Mary Louise Pratt's *Toward a Speech Act Theory of Literary Discourse*, which includes a section on genre. Two important articles applying speech act theory to the study of genres are Elizabeth W. Bruss's "L'Autobiographie considérée comme acte littéraire," *Poétique*, no. 17 (1974), and Tzvetan Todorov's "The Origin of Genres," *New Literary History* 8 (1976). See also S. Suleiman, "Le récit exemplaire: parabole, fable, roman à thèse," *Poétique*, no. 32 (1977).

[12] See in particular Genette's essay, "La rhétorique restreinte," in *Figures III* (Paris, 1972), and Charles' book, *Rhétorique de la lecture* (Paris, 1977), in which he argues that "a rhetoric must be neither a set of precepts . . . nor a catalogue of curiosities, but *a system of possible questions*"—in fact, an "art of reading" (pp. 118-19). My translation.

Introduction

be synonymous with all self-reflective (that is, creative or artistic) use of language.[13]

As for Booth's notions of implied author and implied reader, it would be a mistake to overlook their continued relevance for audience-oriented criticism by associating them too closely with Booth's own ethical concerns as a critic. The fact that Booth emphasizes what he calls the moral interest of the communication between implied author and implied reader does not exclude the possibility of other emphases. The usefulness of these notions becomes especially clear if one considers a fact that Booth is aware of but whose implications he is perhaps unwilling to pursue: namely, that the implied author and the implied reader are *interpretive constructs* and, as such, participate in the circularity of all interpretation. I construct the images of the implied author and implied reader gradually as I read a work, and then use the images I have constructed to validate my reading. The full recognition of this circularity does not render the notions of implied author and implied reader superfluous, but it does relativize them. They become no more—and no less—than necessary fictions, guaranteeing the consistency of a specific reading without guaranteeing its validity in any absolute sense. Where specific readings are concerned, one can never escape the dilemmas and paradoxes of interpretation.

This may be one reason why semioticians and structuralists generally do not attempt to "read" texts in the sense of interpreting them or assigning them a meaning, but seek to analyze, rather, the multiple codes and conventions that make possible a text's *readability*. As Roland Barthes defined it in one of his early essays, the aim of "structuralist activity" (which is synonymous, in this context, with the activity of the semiotician) is not so much to assign "full meanings" to the objects it discovers as to understand "how meaning is possible—at what price and along what tracks."[14] The struc-

[13] See, for example, "The Rhetoric of Temporality," in Charles Singleton, ed., *Interpretation: Theory and Practice* (Baltimore, 1969); "Semiology and Rhetoric," *Diacritics* 3, no. 3 (1973), as well as *Blindness and Insight*.

[14] "L'Activité structuraliste," in *Essais critiques* (Paris, 1964), p. 218. Other

Susan R. Suleiman

turalist, according to Barthes, does not interpret a work; he describes it, in such a way as to make its rules of functioning—its system—manifest. His description is a simulacrum whose purpose is not to copy the original but to make it intelligible (p. 215). Barthes's own activity has evolved since he wrote those words, and if one considers them as a program for criticism it is doubtful that he would still fully subscribe to it.[15] That need not deter us, however, from using his formulation as a starting point, for it gives as succinct and accurate a definition of the aims and general method of semiotic and structural analysis as any that has been proposed.

Among the pertinent questions that the structural and semiotic variety of audience-oriented criticism allows one to formulate are the following: How (by what codes) is the audience inscribed within the system of a work? How does the inscribed audience contribute to the work's readability? What other aspects of the work, whether formal or thematic, determine readability or intelligibility? Finally, and in a slightly different perspective, what are the codes and conventions—whether aesthetic or cultural—to which actual readers refer in trying to make sense of texts and to which actual authors refer in facilitating or complicating, or perhaps even frustrating, the reader's sense-making activity?

These questions are all interrelated, and we may think of them as forming a series of concentric circles leading out from the text to its cultural and literary context. The first three questions involve the systematic study of a particular work or group of works (e.g., a genre) considered as a specifically literary or artistic entity—a set of interlocking structures and formal devices; the last question opens out onto potential considerations of the relation between the text and its con-

---

page references to this essay will be given in parentheses in the text. Translations are my own.

[15] This book was already in proof when Barthes died, after being hit by an automobile, in March 1980. It is a tribute to his work that he still seems so very much alive. We have not altered any other references to him in the present tense.

Introduction

text, or what the Soviet semiotician Juri Lotman calls the *hors-texte*.[16] Speaking rather schematically, we may say that the first set of questions is characteristic of "classical" structural analysis or the structuralist first wave. The work of structural semanticians like A. J. Greimas and J.-C. Coquet, of structural stylisticians like M. Riffaterre, of narratologists like Claude Bremond, Gérard Genette, Gerald Prince, and Tzvetan Todorov, as well as some of Roland Barthes's early work (in particular his important article, "Introduction à l'analyse structurale des récits"[17]) belong to this category. The last question—which was never entirely absent from the work of the structuralists, but which tended to remain in the background—has come to the fore in recent years in the work of Lotman and his group of Tartu semioticians, in Mikhail Bakhtin's studies (only recently made available) of Dostoevsky and Rabelais, as well as in the recent work of Umberto Eco, Stanley Fish, and Jonathan Culler. One may also mention, in this context, Barthes's *S/Z*, which marked not only a turning point in Barthes's own critical activity but indicated a new direction for structural analysis in general.

After this rapid enumeration, some more-specific observations are in order. Regarding the inscription of the audience in the system of a given work, the key notion, as first formulated by Gérard Genette and Gerald Prince, is that of the narratee.[18] A narratee is defined as the necessary counterpart of a given narrator, that is, the person or figure who receives a narrative. Narratees can be analyzed in terms of some of the same categories as narrators: they may be intrusive or discreet, dramatized or not, single or multiple, and they may be

[16] See Lotman, *La Structure du texte artistique*, trans. Anne Fournier et al. (Paris, 1973), pp. 89-91, 390-406; and "Le Hors-texte," *Change*, no. 6 (1970), 68-81.

[17] In *Communications*, no. 8 (1966), English translation in *New Literary History* 6 (1975). Works by other critics cited in this paragraph are listed in the bibliography at the end of the volume, which is organized according to the categories of audience-oriented criticism treated here.

[18] See G. Genette, *Figures III*, pp. 265-67; and G. Prince, "Introduction à l'étude du narrataire," *Poétique*, no. 14 (1973), 178-96.

present in a given narrative on several levels. In a narrative with more than one level of narration (e.g., a "frame" narrative), the levels are related to each other hierarchically, based on the comprehensiveness of the narrative information a given narrator sends and a given narratee receives. By analyzing the relationships between the various narrators and narratees—relationships that are indicated by linguistic markers in the text—one can not only make manifest the complex circuits of communication established in a given work, but also arrive at a typology of narratives based on the kinds of narrative situations they involve and on the place(s) they assign to the narratee(s).

Clearly, a first-level narratee (one who receives the whole narrative, not just a part) may be considered the inscribed or encoded reader of the work. How, then, does the notion of inscribed reader differ from Booth's notion of the implied reader? The difference is that the latter functions as an "ideal" interpreter of the text, whereas the former's place must be located somewhere this side of interpretation. An interpretation of the work necessarily takes account of the inscribed reader, as well as of narratees that may be present in the work on other levels, but it treats the inscribed reader as simply one element among other meaning-producing elements in the text (e.g., temporal organization, variations in point of view, system of characters, thematic structures). The inscribed reader thus has no privileged status as far as interpretation is concerned; a description of the inscribed reader in a work allows a variety of interpretations, or even the possibility of hazarding no global interpretation of the work at all. Booth's notion of implied reader, on the other hand, is indissociable from a global interpretation, for as we saw earlier, the implied reader is called upon to "agree" with the values of the implied author, values that ultimately determine the meaning of the work as a whole. An individual critic may rely on both notions in practice, using the inscribed reader to arrive at an image of the implied reader and at an interpretation of the work. This way of proceeding is a personal choice, however, rather than a methodological neces-

Introduction

sity; a structural analysis of the inscribed audience requires only the first step, not the second. Christine Brooke-Rose's essay in this volume is exemplary in this respect, for it clearly distinguishes between the analysis of the inscribed audience and the personal interpretation that may follow from such an analysis.

The next question, concerning the ways in which the inscribed audience contributes to a work's readability, is again not interpretive but analytic. A first analytic distinction may be made between texts that insistently evoke the presence of the inscribed audience, and correlatively of the narrator (these texts belong to the category of what E. Benveniste has called *discours*[19]), and texts that tend to efface the presence of both audience and narrator (Benveniste's category of *histoire*, where "no one is speaking and the events seem to narrate themselves"[20]). In the latter case, the quasi-absence of the inscribed audience is itself an index of the text's readability: the text designates itself as impassive, taciturn. Such autodesignation may in turn be analyzed as characteristic of a particular school or movement, that is, as a convention of writing; in that case the analysis moves from our second question to our fourth. As for texts that are heavily discursive (in Benveniste's sense), they constitute a rich lode for the semiotician, who can study the function of literary or cultural allusions, the use of deictics ("here," "now," etc.), the role of explanations and definitions formulated by the narrator. All are indexes of readability and all are intimately linked to the inscribed audience, to whom the allusions and explanations are addressed and who must be situated in relation to the deictics. Gerald Prince studies the role of one such index in his essay for this book. Here again, such indexes may be considered in terms of writing and reading conventions, thus opening the analysis to considerations of context.

As for the other aspects of a work that determine readability or intelligibility, structural analysis has called particular at-

---

[19] See "Les relations de temps dans le verbe français," in Benveniste, *Problèmes de linguistique générale* (Paris, 1966), pp. 237-50.

[20] "Les relations de temps dans le verbe français," p. 241.

tention to the role of *redundancy* in the sense that the term is used in linguistics and information theory—i.e., as a system of repetitions designed to insure optimum reception of a message. It has been suggested, for example, that the readability of realistic fiction is based on redundancies operating on multiple levels: verbal repetitions, recurrence of narrative structures, "doubling" of characters, thematic equivalences, etc.[21] One might also mention, among determinants of readability, Tzvetan Todorov's notion of construction as outlined in his essay here, especially his analysis of construction as a theme within fictional texts themselves.

With the final question in our series, concerning codes and conventions that actual readers and authors may deploy in the writing and reading of texts, we reach the point where structural and semiotic analysis meets the domain of hermeneutics, both traditional and modern. I use the terms *traditional* and *modern* in a somewhat special sense: traditional referring to the line of inquiry initiated by Schleiermacher, developed by Dilthey, and continued through today in the work of Emilio Betti in Europe and of E. D. Hirsch, Jr., in America; "modern" referring not so much to a period—although it could be traced historically from Nietzsche through Heidegger to Gadamer—as to a particular attitude toward, or theory of, interpretation.[22] Without anticipating too much our later discussion and at the risk of oversimplification, we may say that traditional hermeneutics seeks to arrive at an understanding (Dilthey's *Verstehen*, as opposed to *Erklären* or scientific explanation) of a human mind, as that mind manifests or manifested itself in written texts. The aim of traditional hermeneutics can be seen as an attempt to rid interpretation of subjectivist or romantic overtones and to establish the notion (in Dilthey's words) of "universally valid

[21] See Philippe Hamon, "Un discours contraint," *Poétique*, no. 16 (1974), 411-45, and Susan Suleiman, "Redundancy and the 'Readable' Text," *Poetics Today* 1 (April 1980), 119-42.

[22] For a useful account of the development of hermeneutic theory since Schleiermacher, see R. D. Palmer, *Hermeneutics: Interpretation Theory in Schleiermacher, Dilthey, Heidegger and Gadamer* (Evanston, Ill., 1969).

Introduction

interpretation, [which is] the basis of all historical certainty."[23] Modern hermeneutics—or what Paul Ricoeur and others have called "negative" hermeneutics—starts, on the other hand, from the assumption that the very notion of a universally valid interpretation is untenable. It cites, among other texts to support this view, Nietzsche's statement that "whatever exists . . . is again and again reinterpreted to new ends, taken over, transformed; all events in the organic world are a subduing, a becoming master, and all subduing and becoming master involves a fresh interpretation, an adaptation through which any previous 'meaning' and 'purpose' are necessarily obscured or even obliterated."[24] The issues at stake in the debate between "positive" and "negative" hermeneutics (to which I shall return later) are nothing less than the determinacy of meaning, the privilege of authority, and the ontological status of understanding; the acerbity of the debate is due not only to the essentially contested nature of the concepts involved, but also to the metaphysical, and sometimes political, implications that the advocates of each position discern in the arguments of their opponents.

Jonathan Culler has noted that although a structuralist poetics is not hermeneutic in the sense of proposing "startling interpretations" or resolving literary debates, "it is obvious that structuralism and even structuralist poetics . . . offer a theory of literature and a mode of interpretation, if only by focusing attention on certain aspects of literary works and particular qualities of literature."[25] But it may be too simple to suggest that structuralist poetics offers *a* mode of interpretation, for structuralist poetics is itself caught up in modern hermeneutic controversies. Even the fundamental notions of

[23] See W. Dilthey, "Die Entstehung der Hermeneutik" (1900), in *Gesammelte Schriften*, vol. 5 (Stuttgart and Göttingen, 1968), 317; quoted in Paul Ricoeur, "Qu'est-ce qu'un texte?," in *Hermeneutik und Dialektik*, vol. 2, ed. R. Bubner, K. Cramer, R. Wiehe (Tübingen, 1970), p. 18.

[24] *On the Genealogy of Morals*, trans. Walter Kaufman and R. J. Hollingdale (New York, 1969), pp. 77-78; quoted in Edward Said, *Beginnings: Intention and Method* (New York, 1975), p. 175.

[25] Culler, *Structuralist Poetics: Structuralism, Linguistics and the Study of Literature* (London 1975, paperback ed.), p. 259.

Susan R. Suleiman

code and of system are ultimately put to different uses depending on a critic's conception of the nature of texts, meaning, and the aims of interpretation. Riffaterre's conception of the poetic text, for example, as a totally self-sufficient system whose meaning is analyzable as a series of variations on (transcodings of) a single semantic invariant, dictates a kind of reading that will necessarily demonstrate the poem's unity, its closure, its antireferentiality, as well as the correctness of the interpretation that results and the insufficiency, even invalidity, of all other interpretations.[26] Barthes's conception of the literary text, as formulated in *S/Z* and *Le Plaisir du texte*, is entirely different (nor is the difference attributable to the fact that Barthes works on fictional texts whereas Riffaterre works mostly on poetry), whence his different use of the notion of code and his different way of reading.[27]

Given the importance of *S/Z* in Barthes's own development and its influence on contemporary critics, the theory it presents is worth examining in some detail. Barthes begins by distinguishing between two radically different kinds of texts, of which only one is properly speaking "readable" (*le texte lisible*); the other is not readable but "writable" (*scriptible*), and about this kind of modern text there is, according to Barthes, "perhaps nothing to say."[28] Certainly structural analysis can say nothing about such texts, for the very notion of system, code, or structure is foreign to them (pp. 11-12). Barthes's idealization of these "infinitely plural" texts that defy any attempt at systematization need not concern us for the moment. More to the point is the fact that even the kind of reading he proposes for *les textes lisibles* (of which Balzac's novella

[26] See, for example, Riffaterre, "The Self-Sufficient Text," *Diacritics* 3, no. 3 (1973), 39-45; *id.*, "Interpretation and Descriptive Poetry: A Reading of Wordsworth's 'Yew-Trees,' " *New Literary History* 4 (1973), 229-56; and *id.*, "Paragram and Significance," *Semiotext(e)* 1 (fall 1974), 72-87.

[27] *S/Z* (Paris, 1970); *Le Plaisir du texte* (Paris, 1973).

[28] *S/Z*, p. 11. Further page references will be given in parentheses in the text. All translations are my own. Richard Miller, in his translation of *S/Z* (New York, 1974), renders *lisible* as "readerly" and *scriptible* as "writerly." I prefer a more literal rendering of the French terms, for both linguistic and theoretical reasons.

Introduction

Sarrasine is his example) is founded on a valorization of all that is asystematic, nonunified, nonordered—in a word, on all those aspects of a "readable" text that tend to make it "unreadable." The text is seen as "a galaxy of signifiers, not a structure of signifieds" (p. 12), and the work of reading consists not of "respecting" the text, but of breaking it up, maltreating it, preventing it from speaking (*lui couper la parole*—p. 12). Consequently, although Barthes goes on to define five different codes through which the readable text constitutes itself, he refuses to treat these codes as forming an intelligible system, as structuring the text and allowing a reader to "make sense" of it. A code, he maintains, "is a perspective of quotations, a mirage of structures" (p. 27). The five codes coexist in the text as a tissue of voices, "an immense *fading* that assures both the overlapping and the loss of messages" (p. 27).

One could argue, on this basis, that *S/Z* is not a work of structuralism but is, rather, a critique of "structuralist poetics" and of Barthes's own earlier work on the structural analysis of narrative. It would be more accurate, however, to see *S/Z* as Janus-like, pointing in opposite directions, and to suggest that this very two-facedness accounts for its appeal, since a reader can emphasize one or the other direction according to his or her theoretical preferences. The notion that texts are constituted by a number of diverse, even overlapping, "voices" or codes (including a cultural or referential code that speaks the "truths" of a given society) is not, in itself, antistructuralist; what is anti- (or "post"-) structuralist is the contention that the codes do not form a coherent system. But in fact Barthes does not say that; he merely says that he himself refuses to "structure the codes, either individually or as they relate to each other" (p. 27). This refusal is perfectly consistent with Barthes's interpretive strategy (more precisely, his anti-interpretive strategy), which breaks up the text to prevent its "naturalization" or "recuperation" by traditional modes of reading. This strategy is simply one among others, however, and must not itself be "naturalized" by being treated as the only valid way of reading.

Susan R. Suleiman

We seem to have strayed from the question of reading and writing conventions, but only apparently so, for the notion of interpretive strategy is indissociable from the notion of convention. An interpretive strategy is never the result of a purely individual decision, whether by the reader or by the writer (who is also a reader of his own text); it can only be understood as a collective phenomenon, a set of shared conventions within a community of readers, which may, but does not necessarily, include the writer of the text being interpreted. If Barthes's reading of *Sarrasine* differs from Balzac's or an academic Balzac scholar's, it is because they belong to what Stanley Fish has called different interpretive communities.[29] Some would claim that the author's reading (identical to that of his immediate interpretive community) is by definition the best, and that Barthes's reading is by that standard aberrant. Such a claim is itself indicative of membership in a particular interpretive community—the community of author-centered critics, of hermeneutic absolutists, or whatever other name one might choose to give it—and as such carries no privilege of priority or authority.

It may be asked whether we are justified in discussing the notion of interpretive communities under the heading of structuralism and semiotics, since this notion (whatever the actual term used to designate it) has been taken up in recent years by critics with widely varying approaches, including

[29] See Fish, "Interpreting the *Variorum*," *Critical Inquiry* 2 (1976), esp. 473-85, and "Interpreting 'Interpreting the *Variorum*,' " *Critical Inquiry* 3 (1976). These articles represent a new direction in Fish's theory of reading; whereas his earlier work affirmed there was but one road to salvation where reading and criticism are concerned (see esp. "Literature in the Reader: Affective Stylistics," *New Literary History* 2 [1970]), here he argues that how one reads is entirely a matter of shared conventions or interpretive strategies, none of which is better than another. Concurrently, he has shifted his position about texts; whereas even in 1972 he spoke of reading a work "correctly," that is, as the author intended (*Self-Consuming Artifacts* [Berkeley and Los Angeles], p. 229), in "Interpreting the *Variorum*" he explicitly rejects the notion that there is a "correct" reading, or even that texts contain any "encoded" directions for how to interpret them. In this sense he belongs among the most radical of the "negative" hermeneuticians and not at all among the semioticians.

Introduction

subjectivists like David Bleich[30] and sociologists of literature like Jacques Leenhardt (see his essay in this volume). Although I shall return to the notion of interpretive communities, I introduce it here, for it is precisely around this notion that I believe a most fruitful combination of critical approaches to reading and interpretation can be realized. Interpretive communities may be studied in many different ways that have nothing to do with structural analysis—but they can, and must, be studied in terms of textual encoding as well. Every literary text, no matter how "modern" or "unconventional," contains some indication of the artistic and/or cultural codes it is affirming, reaffirming, or "playing" with (playing against).[31] To claim, as Barthes does in the opening pages of S/Z, that certain texts exist outside all conventions, in an ideal space which no coherent discourse can penetrate, is a form of extreme—and naive[32]—romanticism. Perhaps the most innovative and ambitious task that a structuralist poetics or a semiotics of literature can set itself is (as Jonathan Culler has suggested in somewhat different terms) to study the inscription of interpretive conventions—the inscription of "other" texts, individual or collective, written or unwritten—in specific works or genres.

II

If the rhetorical and the structural-semiotic approaches to literature both have a heavy investment in problems of audience and interpretation, these problems do not exhaust their

[30] See, for example, the section entitled "Interpretation as a Communal Act," in Bleich, *Readings and Feelings: An Introduction to Subjective Criticism* (Urbana, Ill., 1975). See also Bleich's more recent *Subjective Criticism* (Baltimore, 1978).

[31] This is shown by Vicki Mistacco in her essay in this volume; she studies the procedures of the *nouveau roman* as a set of new but increasingly codified conventions.

[32] I am aware that qualifying a supremely sophisticated critic like Roland Barthes as naive smacks of heresy, or worse still of naiveté. Despite these risks, I shall let the qualifier stand. The only feasible alternative would be Schiller's "sentimental," which he used in opposition to "naive," but which

concerns. A rhetorical or a structuralist critic may place the question of reading—and even of readability—into the background, and concentrate instead on describing techniques of persuasion, narrative or thematic structures, individual or collective styles, in short those aspects of literary works that have traditionally been regarded as the province of textual analysis.[33] The phenomenological approach, on the contrary, is necessarily centered on the question of reading, and more generally on that of aesthetic perception. Phenomenological critics are concerned with the experience whereby individual readers (or listeners or spectators) appropriate the work of art—or, to use the term proposed by Roman Ingarden, whereby they *realize* it. The act of realization (*Konkretisation*) is what transforms a text—i.e., a mere series of sentences—into a work of literature. As Wolfgang Iser, commenting on Ingarden, writes: "The work is more than the text, for the text only takes on life when it is realized, and furthermore the realization is by no means independent of the individual disposition of the reader. . . . The convergence of text and reader brings the literary work into existence."[34] A phenomenological approach to literature concentrates, therefore, on the convergence between text and reader; more exactly, it seeks to describe and account for the mental processes that occur as a reader advances through a text and derives from it—or imposes on it—a pattern. The act of reading is defined as essentially a sense-making activity, consisting of the complemen-

---

in fact designated (in his famous essay on "naive and sentimental poetry") the sensibility of the romantics. Such a substitution would not eliminate the risks, however: Roland Barthes a "sentimental" critic?

[33] I have tried to show in the preceding pages that all of these aspects can and should be studied by foregrounding the questions of reading and readability. This is not, however, what all rhetorical and structuralist critics do in practice, even if they all have implicit notions about what reading and readability involve.

[34] "The Reading Process: A Phenomenological Approach," in Iser, *The Implied Reader: Patterns of Communication in Prose Fiction from Bunyan to Beckett* (Baltimore, 1974), pp. 274-75. This essay first appeared in *New Literary History* 3 (1972), 279-99. Other page references to *The Implied Reader* will be given in parentheses in the text.

Introduction

tary activities of selection and organization, anticipation and retrospection, the formulation and modification of expectations in the course of the reading process. Although every reader performs these activities, exactly how they are performed varies from reader to reader and even within a single reader at different times; these variations account for different realizations of a given text. Iser (on whose work I shall concentrate in my discussion) uses the analogy of two people looking at the night sky, "who may both be looking at the same collection of stars, but one will see the image of a plough, and the other will make out a dipper." Variations in the readings of a text are thus attributable to variations in the activities of selection and organization: "The 'stars' in a literary text are fixed; the lines that join them are variable" (p. 282). This implies that "the potential text is infinitely richer than any of its individual realizations" (p. 280). It suggests, furthermore, that there is a wide spectrum of acceptable realizations for any one text.

Iser's analysis of the reading process, as formulated in the essay I have been quoting, is extremely interesting, not least because it raises certain questions that are left unanswered or that are answered ambiguously. Two such questions, central to any phenomenological approach to reading, are (1) the nature of the relationship between a text and an individual realization of it, especially as concerns "idiosyncratic" realizations; and (2) the status of the reading subject.

Although I have quoted several statements that seem to answer the first question, a more thorough reading suggests that Iser's answer is quite ambiguous. On the one hand, Iser asserts the primacy of the reader's creative role in realizing the text, thus allowing for a high degree of "free" variations; on the other hand, he suggests that it is ultimately the text itself which directs the reader's realization of it. Iser does not treat the question of idiosyncratic readings directly, but his discussion implies that only a limited number of patterns are realizable for a given text (in which case some readings must be considered idiosyncratic). And more importantly, his own readings of specific works (in the volume that includes "The

Reading Process") leave no doubt that he considers some realizations more correct, more true to the intentions of the text, than others. Writing about *Vanity Fair*, for example, he states: "The esthetic effect of *Vanity Fair* depends on activating the reader's critical faculties so that he may recognize the social reality of the novel as a confusing array of sham attitudes, and experience the exposure of this sham as the true reality. Instead of being expressly stated, the criteria for such judgments have to be inferred. They are the blanks which the reader is supposed to fill in, thus bringing his own criticism to bear" (p. 113). The notion of inference, as well as the clear formulation of the conclusion that the inference "is supposed" to lead to, render problematic the subsequent statement that texts are infinitely richer than any individual realization. The notion of reading implicit in Iser's analysis is here very close to Booth's notion; though one certainly need not object to this, it is important to realize that Iser's theoretical description of the reading process allows for a great deal more latitude in individual realization than does his actual critical practice.

It is true that *The Implied Reader* contains essays which were published at various times, so that even though the phenomenological essay occupies the place of a conclusion it may not have an organic relation to the essays preceding it. But even in a single essay explicitly devoted to the question of reader response, published shortly before the essay on "The Reading Process," one finds a similar ambiguity.[35] A key notion, mentioned in "The Reading Process" and elaborated in this earlier essay, is that of textual indeterminacy. According to Iser, it is because all texts contain elements of indeterminacy, or "gaps," that the reader's activity must be creative: in seeking to fill in the textual gaps—gaps that function on multiple levels, including the semantic level—the reader realizes the work. But here again, the question of how much freedom

[35] "Indeterminacy and the Reader's Response in Prose Fiction," in J. Hillis Miller, ed., *Aspects of Narrative: Selected Papers from the English Institute* (New York, 1971), pp. 1-46. Further page references to this essay will be given in the text.

Introduction

a reader has is eluded, or rather answered in contradictory ways. Iser's conclusion is that "the literary text makes no objectively real demands on its readers, it opens up a freedom that everyone can interpret in his own way" (p. 44). This conclusion is opposed, however, by the weight of numerous other statements which suggest that the reader's activity of filling in the gaps is "programmed" by the text itself, so that the kind of pattern the reader creates for the text is foreseen and intended by the author.[36] Although Iser criticizes Ingarden (who first formulated the notion of "gaps of indeterminacy") for his "classical conception of a work of art," which considers that "there are true and false realizations of a literary text" (p. 14n), his own conception turns out to be not very different.[37]

As for the status of the reading subject in Iser's theory, we have already answered the question. The reading subject who emerges from the essays we have been discussing is not a specific, historically situated individual but a transhistorical mind whose activities are, at least formally, everywhere the same. In his most recent work,[38] Iser has sought to introduce

[36] Cf. the following: "The text is constructed in such a way that it provokes the reader constantly to supplement what he is reading. . . . Whenever this occurs, it is clear that the author is not mobilizing his reader because he himself cannot finish off the work he has started: his motive is to bring about an intensified participation which will *compel* the reader to be that much more aware of *the intention of the text*" (pp. 32-33, my emphasis). Or again: "Literary texts differ from those which formulate a concrete meaning or truth. . . . *The meaning is conditioned by the text itself*, but only in a form that allows the reader himself to bring it out" (p. 43, my emphasis).

[37] Iser does defend, with great skill and vigor, certain highly indeterminate modern works, such as those of Joyce and Beckett, that Ingarden rejects *because* of their indeterminacy; but his defense entails a demonstration that even these works program their reading: the realization they "force" on the reader is that "his projected meanings can never fully cover the possibilities of the text" (p. 41). This conclusion in no way suggests that the reader is free in his "pattern-making" or in his "act of generating meaning." It simply ascribes to modern texts a different program, and a different kind of meaning (the meaning of *Ulysses* is that there are no simple meanings) from those of "classical" texts.

[38] See *The Act of Reading: A Theory of Aesthetic Response* (Baltimore, 1978).

Susan R. Suleiman

a historical dimension to his description of the reading process by distinguishing the response of contemporary readers from the response of later readers of a text. For the contemporary reader, or "participant," the text brings to light the deficiencies of the prevailing thought systems or systems of norms; for the later reader, or "observer," the text serves to "re-create that very social and cultural context that brought about the problems which the text itself is concerned with." Consequently, the contemporary reader will see, thanks to the work, "what he would not have seen in the course of his everyday life," while the later reader will "grasp something which has hitherto never been real for him."[39] Although such a historicization of the reader represents an attempt at specification, we are still dealing with implied, not actual, readers. The transhistorical reader has been divided into a "contemporary" and a "later" version, but the description of each one's response remains schematic and general.

Iser's essay in this volume, which represents his latest theoretical formulation of the reading process, suggests that his ideas are continuing to evolve, so that any assessment of his work is necessarily incomplete. I have merely sought to point out some of the unresolved tensions within the phenomenological approach to reading, of which Iser's work stands out as a particularly persuasive and influential example. Given that the phenomenological approach promises to take account of the experience of the individual reading subject, it is important to note that the individual subject it poses is often indistinguishable from an abstract and generalized "reader."

Whether the fault lies with phenomenological criticism or with the misguided commentator who expects from it something it cannot deliver is, in the last analysis, irrelevant. What is certain is that there must be room in audience-oriented criticism for descriptions of the reading process that go beyond the supposed experience of a generalized reader (whether "he" is defined as a contemporary of the author or as some-

[39] *The Act of Reading,* pp. 78-79.

Introduction

one who lived centuries later), and that focus on the actual reading experiences and responses of specific individuals to specific works. Until recently, there were very few attempts at such description, for reasons both practical and institutional. Over the past few years, however, partly in response to classroom pressures for "relevance" and partly in reaction to the scientific or objectivist claims of structuralism and New Criticism, there has arisen an unabashedly subjectivist criticism, which claims priority for the idiosyncratic over the typical, for the singular over the universal.

The American critics most closely associated with this approach are David Bleich and Norman Holland. Although some basic differences in method (and according to both sides, in epistemological assumptions) have surfaced recently between Bleich and Holland,[40] they are both essentially psychoanalytic critics interested in the influence of personality and personal history on literary interpretation and in the potential application of their theories to the classroom. I shall focus on Holland's work, for his theoretical evolution over the past ten years is particularly interesting. Before doing so, however, I should mention the work of a less systematic and nonpsychoanalytically oriented critic who has eloquently argued for the rights of "ordinary" (and extraordinary) readers—Walter Slatoff. Slatoff, like Iser, conceives of reading as a process that unfolds in time and in the space of a text, and of the literary work as something that takes shape "only in minds."[41] Unlike the phenomenologists, however, Slatoff does not attempt to give a theoretical—and therefore abstract, generalized—account of "*the* reading experience." What he pleads for is a teacher-critic who "would be sharply aware of what took place during his act of reading and might well describe changes in his experience in successive readings or dif-

[40] See especially the articles by Bleich ("The Subjective Paradigm") and by Holland ("The New Paradigm: Subjective or Transactive?") in *New Literary History* 7 (1976), and the exchange of letters in *College English* 38 (1976), 298-301.

[41] Slatoff, *With Respect to Readers: Dimensions of Literary Response* (Ithaca, 1970), p. 21. Other page references will be given in parentheses in the text.

Susan R. Suleiman

ferences between his experiences while reading and reflecting upon the work. . . . Such a critic would try to be aware of his biases and open about them, and he might well wonder aloud at times about their effect on his literary experience. . . . The main thing is that he would sound like *somebody*, and if not a particular somebody, at least a recognizably human creature" (p. 171).

To be sure, one could criticize Slatoff for his distrust of theoretical generalizations, his unquestioning belief in the value of individual experience, his faith in the power of introspection and in the power of ordinary language to express adequately the complexity of human responses—in a word, for his "old-fashioned" humanism. While these may indeed be limitations, they are also virtues of a sort, and perhaps too rarely acknowledged as such in modern literary theory and criticism.

The changes in Norman Holland's thinking about texts over the past ten years may be seen as symptomatic of a more general shift in American criticism. In *The Dynamics of Literary Response* (1968), Holland sought to reconcile the objectivist assumptions of New Criticism with an orthodox Freudianism. The basic question he addressed was "What is the relation between the patterns [the textual critic] finds objectively in the text and a reader's subjective experience of a text?"[42] His method consisted of three steps: first, a description of the text "objectively, as so many words on a piece of paper or spoken aloud"; second, a psychological description of his own response to the "objective stimulus"; finally, an identification of "points of correspondence between the text objectively understood and [his] subjective experience of the text" (p. xvi). The main point of correspondence lay in the Freudian notion of fantasy: according to Holland, the appeal of any literary text, no matter how stylized or abstract, was that it contained at its core an unconscious fantasy. The literary

[42] *The Dynamics of Literary Response*, paperback edition (New York, 1975), p. xv. Other page references to this edition will be given in parentheses in the text.

Introduction

work thus expressed the reader's most primitive (and by
definition pleasurable) fantasies, but transformed them in
such a way that the feelings of anxiety attendant upon such
fantasies in real life were minimized or eliminated. The transformations operated by the work were essentially formal;
whence the assertion that "form in a literary work corresponds to defense; content to fantasy or impulse" (p. 131).
"Great" literature deploys a wider array of defenses, and appeals to the ego at a higher level of consciousness, than "en-
tertainment" literature, and poetry in general deploys a
wider array of defenses than fiction. No work of literature,
however, would give pleasure without the central fantasy
that it allows the reader, in a disguised and sublimated way,
to gratify.

The originality of *The Dynamics of Literary Response*, which
distinguished it from earlier psychoanalytic works on reading
(such as Simon O. Lesser's *Fiction and the Unconscious*[43]), lay
in Holland's attempt to provide theoretical models for the
process whereby readers moved from the unconscious level
of fantasy to the level of conscious interpretation, and to
show that this kind of movement was parallel to the process
whereby the work itself transformed (or displaced) its primitive fantasy content into "meaning." As I noted earlier, Holland's underlying assumption here was that texts could be
described objectively and that it was possible to relate the
text's objective characteristics to a reader's subjective response. By the time he wrote *Poems in Persons* (1973) and *5
Readers Reading* (1975), Holland had abandoned this assumption; he had discovered, thanks to David Bleich's prompting
(according to Holland's own account) that "books do not
have fantasies or defenses or meanings—people do."[44] This
led him to study, in an experimental way, how individual
readers "re-created" texts according to their own personalities. His new model of reader response retained the
Freudian components of defense, transformation, and fan-

[43] Boston, 1957.
[44] "The New Paradigm: Subjective or Transactive?," p. 337.

Susan R. Suleiman

tasy, but added a new component of "expectation" and saw these as operating exclusively in a reader's encounter (Holland's term is "transaction") with a text rather than "in" the text itself. According to this model, "interpretation is a function of identity. . . . That is, all of us, as we read, use the literary work to symbolize and finally to replicate ourselves."[45]

Implicit in this model is the notion that individuals do have an unchanging essence, a central "identity theme" that remains constant throughout their lives and manifests itself in all their activities; consequently, "we can arrive at someone's identity by interpreting their behavior for an underlying thematic unity just as we would interpret a literary text for a centering theme."[46] There is a worm in the apple, however: "Naturally, one pursues this inquiry through one's own identity."[47] Holland does not seem to be fully aware of the implications this casual remark has for his model: if identity replicates itself in interpretation, and if identity itself can only be arrived at through interpretation, then the enterprise whereby the analyst seeks to demonstrate the validity of the first statement is hopelessly circular—it can never fail but it can never be proven either, for proof would require that the identity of the reader be definable independently of the interpreting identity of the analyst. Holland has admitted on various occasions that this is in fact the case; yet he speaks of his readers' identity themes as if they were objectively verifiable and stable entities rather than interpretive, and therefore necessarily relative, constructs. In his essay in this book, Jonathan Culler criticizes Holland harshly for this blind spot in his thinking. Having rejected the oversimplified notion of textual unity dear to American New Criticism, Holland has committed, according to Culler, the even graver error of accepting the notion of the unity of the self, dear to American ego psychology.[48]

[45] "Unity Identity Text Self," *PMLA* 90 (1975), 816. See also note 66.

[46] "The New Paradigm: Subjective or Transactive?," p. 337.

[47] Ibid., p. 343.

[48] Although coming from a different direction and expressed in more sympathetic terms, David Bleich's criticism of Holland makes a similar point. Ac-

Introduction

Does this mean, as Culler suggests, that Holland's enterprise has nothing to offer to theorists of reading? I do not think so, and Holland's own essay in this book shows otherwise. Reading is far too rich and many-faceted an activity to be exhausted by a single theory. Holland's work, whatever its philosophical foundations (and we should make no mistake about it—the issues *are* philosophical[49]), has provided some extremely interesting "case histories" of reader response, including his own; it has also reminded us, most salutarily, that reading is not only an institutionalized and interpersonal phenomenon, but one that involves daydreaming, private delusions and fantasies—what Donald Barthelme has aptly called, in the title of one of his works, "unspeakable practices, unnatural acts."

III

If subjective criticism takes us as far as we can go in the investigation of reading as private experience—an experience in which the determining factor is the individual "life history,"

---

cording to Bleich, Holland's mistake is that he has not entirely given up the "objective paradigm." On the one hand, his notion of transaction grants at least a partial role to the text in determining meanings rather than locating meaning entirely in the reader (see Bleich, "The Subjective Paradigm," p. 332). On the other hand, Holland's notion of identity, as well as his method (by projective tests) for determining it, imply an "objectivist" view: "Holland speaks as if defenses, expectations, fantasies, and transformations are discrete items perceivable by anyone studying a response. . . . But projective tests depend heavily on the leanings of the interpreter; for as long as these tests have been used there is still no good reason to suppose that they yield objective knowledge about the subject" (Bleich, "Pedagogical Directions in Subjective Criticism," *College English* 37 [1976], 462-63).

[49] To the extent that the issues are philosophical, it will hardly do to place them between parentheses. If indeed Holland's (and, for that matter, Bleich's) view of the self is essentially that of American ego psychology—the latter being but a particular, if particularly influential, reading of Freud—then one must unavoidably confront it with the view of the self presented by *the* "other" reading of Freud: Jacques Lacan's. Having recognized the need for such a confrontation, I will nevertheless beg out of staging it here. I will speak of Lacan in the last part of this essay; in the meantime, the reader may

Susan R. Suleiman

not the history of groups and nations—the sociological-historical variety of audience-oriented criticism seeks to investigate reading as essentially a collective phenomenon. The individual reader is seen, in this perspective, as part of a *reading public*; the relationship between specific reading publics (varying with time, place, and circumstances) and either specific works or genres, or else the whole body of works that make up the literary and artistic tradition of a given society, then becomes the focus of inquiry.

I purposely use the vague term *relationship* in formulating this definition, for there are many kinds of sociological and historical approaches to reading, and one of the things which distinguish them from each other is the way they conceive of the relationship between work and public and the particular aspects of that relationship they choose to study. One rather elementary question that sociologists of literature have asked, for example, is, Who reads what? In more formal terms, how does membership in a given social group at a given time influence, or even determine, one's reading habits and taste?[50] A considerably more sophisticated question that has preoccupied historically and sociologically minded critics is how changes in the composition (and consequently in the ideology and taste) of a national reading public have contributed

---

wish to ponder Jeffrey Mehlman's remark that "whereas the American theorists have retained the Freudian notion of the ego as an agent of synthesis, mastery, integration, and adaptation, Lacan's point of departure . . . has been to revive a far more worrisome conception of the ego, which is implicit in Freud's papers on narcissism and on mourning and melancholia: the ego as constituted by an identification with another as whole object, perpetually threatened by its own otherness to itself, essentially suicidal." ("The 'Float-·ing Signifer': From Lévi-Strauss to Lacan," in *French Freud: Structural Studies in Psychoanalysis, Yale French Studies*, no. 48 [1972], p. 19).

[50] See, for example, a study of the reading habits of young army recruits in France: *Le livre et le conscrit* (Université de Bordeaux, Institut de Littérature et de Techniques Artistiques de Masse, 1966). The Bordeaux Institute, headed by Robert Escarpit, has conducted a number of important statistical surveys on reading and other aspects of the sociology of literature. For an overview of their work and a detailed bibliography, see R. Escarpit et al., *Le Littéraire et le social: Eléments pour une sociologie de la littérature* (Paris, 1970).

Introduction

to the emergence of new literary forms. Ian Watt's classic study, *The Rise of the Novel*,[51] attempted to answer this question by examining the works of Defoe, Richardson and Fielding in light of the changing social conditions and ideology of the eighteenth-century English middle-class reading public. The rise of the realistic novel in England, according to Watt, was both a consequence and a direct expression of the values and aspirations (individualism, experience, originality) of a new class of readers, a large proportion of whom were women. Although Watt did not attempt to theorize the relationship between individual works and the public for which they were destined, his analyses suggest that a close correlation exists between the forms of the eighteenth-century English novel (e.g., the epistolary form, with its emphasis on private experience), its characteristic themes (e.g., courtship and marriage), and the changing expectations and interests of its readers.

Lucien Goldmann's *Le Dieu caché*,[52] published around the same time as Watt's book, posits a similarly close relationship between a writer, his works, and the latter's public. Goldmann went further than Watt, however, for he sought to give an explicit (essentially Marxist) theoretical account of this relationship, thus providing a general model that would apply to other periods and other works than those he studied. According to Goldmann's model, all great works of literature express the "vision of the world" of a specific social class—a class to which the writer himself belongs and which constitutes, therefore, both the source and the destination of his works.

Although Goldmann made brilliant use of this model in studying the "tragic vision" in the works of Pascal and Racine (a vision he traced to the political and social situation of the *noblesse de robe* under Louis XIV), some serious objections can be made to it. First, the model assumes a total and unproblematic homogeneity between the writer and "his" public; it is therefore inapplicable, as Jacques Leenhardt points out in

[51] London, 1957.   [52] Paris, 1959.

his essay in this book, to the situation of rupture that has characterized the relationship between "serious" writers and the bourgeois reading public (which is the only public they have had) in France since the mid-nineteenth century. This rupture and its consequences were analyzed by Sartre in *Qu'est-ce que la littérature*, and by Roland Barthes in *Le Degré zéro de l'écriture*.[53] Since Flaubert, modern writers of significance have all, in one way or another, written against the bourgeois public, and it is precisely this contradiction that accounts for what Sartre calls their bad faith and what Barthes calls their guilty conscience.

Goldmann himself recognized the inadequacy of his original model when he undertook, in *Pour une sociologie du roman* (1964), to study the rise and development of the novel. According to the model he elaborated in this later work, the novel as a genre (and Goldmann suggests that this is true of all forms of modern art) is characterized by a "search for values that no social group defends" but that have become implicit in all members of the society owing to the latter's economic organization.[54] By positing a direct homology between changes in economic organization and the evolution of artistic forms, Goldmann was able to bypass his earlier correlation between artistic "vision" and class consciousness, yet at the same time retain his central notion that artistic creation is always in the last instance collective. This new solution poses problems of its own, however. In particular, it runs the risk of extreme reductionism, for it requires that all the forms of modern art be seen as homologous to (determined by?) the evolution of capitalism from a liberal market economy to that of monopoly capitalism. While such an explanation is appealing in its simplicity, it seems inadequate to account for the variety of modern art forms and especially for changes in artistic form that have occurred since the advent of monopoly capitalism.[55]

[53] "Qu'est-ce que la littérature?" in *Situations* II (Paris, 1948), esp. chap. 3: "Pour qui écrit-on?"; *Le Degré zéro de l'écriture* (Paris, 1953).

[54] See *Pour une sociologie du roman* (Paris, 1965), p. 43, and more generally pp. 44-52.

[55] Both the appeal and the limitations of the "homology" model are appar-

Introduction

Finally, neither of Goldmann's models can account for an obvious fact of literary history: some works continue to be read by generations and in cultures different from those for which they were written, while others are forgotten for long periods only to be revived at a later time and place. In both cases, the explanation must rely on an analysis quite different from Goldmann's, which, being primarily concerned with the genetic link between a work and a given society, cannot account for the phenomena of literary continuity and discontinuity.

The attempt to account both for the dialectic of production and reception of literary works in a given culture at a given time, *and* for historical continuities and discontinuities in the reception of individual works or authors, is what characterizes the work of the group of contemporary German critics loosely united under the banner of *Rezeptionsgeschichte* or *Rezeptionsästhetik*. Hans-Robert Jauss, one of the most prolific and most persuasive members of this group (which includes, among others, Harald Weinrich, Wolfgang Iser, and Karlheinz Stierle), outlined the aims of the history of reception a few years ago in a programmatic article that is worth studying in some detail.[56] Jauss's central notion is that of the "horizon of expectations" (*Erwartungshorizont*), defined as the set of cultural, ethical, and literary (generic, stylistic, thematic) expectations of a work's readers "in the historical moment of its appearance" (p. 14). These expectations are the basis on which the work was both produced and received, for a writer necessarily writes in function of what he knows to be the previous experience—and hence the current expectations—of

---

ent in Goldman's essay on the *nouveau roman*; he finds in the "chosisme" of the *nouveau roman* a direct reflection of the depersonalized, mass-production economy of monopoly capitalism ("Nouveau roman et réalité," in *Pour une sociologie du roman*, pp. 281-324).

[56] "Literary History as a Challenge to Literary Theory," *New Literary History* 2 (1970). Page references to this article will be given in parentheses in the text. For a more recent theoretical essay by Jauss, devoted to the specific problem of the dialectic between production and reception, see "The Idealist Embarrassment: Observations on Marxist Aesthetics," *New Literary History* 7 (1975).

Susan R. Suleiman

the reading public, even if in his work he criticizes or acts against those expectations. The modern understanding of a literary work of the past necessarily differs from its first understanding, because today's horizon of expectations is itself different. One task of the history of reception, according to Jauss, is to reconstruct, using both extrinsic and intrinsic data, the horizon of expectations that existed when a given work first appeared (this involves finding "the questions to which the text originally answered"), and thereby to "bring out the hermeneutic difference between past and present ways of understanding a work" (p. 19).

The notion of horizon of expectations has a number of advantages, not the least of which is that it allows for a systematic study of the history of reception. Unlike traditional histories of a writer's reputation or influence, the method advocated by Jauss "not only follows the fame, image, and influence of a writer through history but also examines the historical conditions and changes in his understanding" (p. 19, n. 29). These changes in understanding are always functions of changes in the readers' horizon of expectations, changes which are themselves the result of both literary evolution and the evolution of cultural, political, and social conditions and norms in the society at large. Secondly, the notion of horizon of expectations allows Jauss to theorize the relationship between works appearing simultaneously but received in different ways—some as "fashionable," others as "outdated," still others as "before their time," and so on. Such labels are a way of designating the degree to which a given work meets, disappoints, or anticipates the reading public's horizon of expectations at a given time (p. 29).

Finally, the horizon of expectations is used by Jauss to set up critical or evaluative categories: according to him, "The distance between the horizon of expectations and the work, between the familiarity of previous aesthetic experiences and the 'horizon change' demanded by the response to new works, *determines the artistic nature of a literary work* . . . the smaller this distance, which means that no demands are

Introduction

made upon the receiving consciousness to make a change on the horizon of unknown experience, the closer the work comes to the realm of 'culinary' or light reading" (p. 15, my emphasis). Misunderstood or ignored masterpieces, by the same token, are works whose distance from the horizon of expectations of a given time is so great that it may take generations before they are incorporated into the literary canon.

The idea that a work's artistic value is directly proportional to its "negativity" with respect to the expectations of its first readers is especially appealing to modern theorists. It is not at all certain, however, that the rule holds in every case, and surely it does not hold with the mathematical precision that Jauss attributes to it. (He speaks of "measuring" the "artistic character" of a work, as if only a slide rule and a head for figures were needed; as if the "distance" between work and readers' expectations could be quantified.) It seems especially difficult to make such a claim without considering the possibility of *different* horizons of expectations co-existing among different publics in any one society. A work that appears totally unacceptable to one group of contemporary readers may appear as just the opposite to "the happy few." Jauss's notion of the public and its expectations does not allow for enough diversity in the *publics* of literary works at a given time.

This is not to suggest that the notion of horizon of expectations is invalid. On the contrary, what appears necessary is the "multiplication" of horizons of expectation, the realization that even in the distant past and in a single society there was no such thing as a single homogeneous reading (or listening) public. The audience of courtly love poems was not the same (although it may also have been the audience of some of the same works) as the audience of the *Chanson de Roland*; and even within the audience of courtly love poems, different "publics" may have existed. Obviously it is not easy to study variations within audiences and their reception of literary works in the distant past. The results of certain recent empirical sociological studies of reception, however, such as the study reported on by Jacques Leenhardt in this book,

Susan R. Suleiman

should make us more wary about our general theories, and more humble about what we can never know.

We come thus to the last of the varieties of audience-oriented criticism enumerated in the beginning of this essay: the hermeneutic variety, by which I mean a kind of criticism whose chief focus of inquiry is the nature and possibilities of reading and interpretation as such. To the extent that all critical activity implies the presence of acknowledged or un-acknowledged postulates about the ontological status of texts and of human understanding, such activity is always in the last instance hermeneutic. Every kind of criticism, no matter how resolutely "scientific" or "practical," implies a philo-sophical stance. Hermeneutics is not, by that token, some-thing one can do without (it is coextensive with all criticism), but merely something one can acknowledge or not. The great virtue of what has been called the current "crisis of criticism" is that it has forced critics of all persuasions to make explicit the philosophical postulates that ground their activity—to be-come self-conscious about what they are doing. What I call the hermeneutic variety of audience-oriented criticism is therefore, in a broader sense, the self-conscious moment of all criticism, when criticism turns to reflect on its own inten-tions, assumptions, and positions.

I spoke earlier about the debate between traditional and modern, or "positive" and "negative" hermeneutics. We must now return to that debate and to the issues underlying it, for these issues not only constitute the crux of contempo-rary literary theorizing, they also function as dividing lines within and between the varieties of audience-oriented criti-cism that we have been discussing.

We may begin with a statement by Geoffrey Hartman, one of the American critics most closely associated with the "negative" hermeneutics, who in fact proposed that term (borrowed from Paul Ricoeur) to describe his own and his col-leagues' activity. In a short article presented expressly as an apology for the work of the "new Yale critics,"[57] Hartman

[57] "Literary Criticism and Its Discontents," *Critical Inquiry* 3 (1976), 203-20.

Introduction

defined the project of negative hermeneutics as follows: "On its [i.e., hermeneutics'] older function of saving the text, of tying it once again to the life of the mind, is superimposed the new one of doubting, by a parodistic or playful movement, master theories that claim to have overcome the past, the dead, the false" (p. 212). That sentence, admirably concise, can be read not only as a program but as an indirect commentary on the last thirty years of American criticism. The New Criticism, by militantly rejecting the idea of authorial intention and emphasizing the autonomy of the poetic "object," ended up divorcing the text from the life of the mind; the same can be said, according to Hartman, about the newer brand of formalism recently imported from Europe and claiming the status of "a science of literature on the basis of semiotics" (p. 203). Traditional hermeneutics, particularly as it was presented to American readers in E. D. Hirsch's *Validity in Interpretation*, restored the primacy of intention and thereby contested the formalist notion that (in Hirsch's words) "linguistic signs can speak their own meaning."[58] However, Hirsch and the older hermeneutics are themselves, in Hartman's terms, open to strong criticism, for they believe in the possibility, indeed the necessity, of objectively valid interpretation—interpretation that can "overcome the dead and the false." All master theories which claim to speak the truth are to be distrusted, and it is the task of negative hermeneutics to give voice to that distrust. How? By focusing on those aspects of a text that reveal the vulnerability of any absolute statement about its meaning, and by making of the impossibility of a single interpretation the primary subject of criticism.

The critics Hartman cites are Paul de Man, Harold Bloom, and J. Hillis Miller of Yale; Joseph Riddel of UCLA and Edward Said of Columbia, whose conceptions make them "new Yale critics" by association; and Stanley Fish, Norman Holland, H. R. Jauss, and Fredric Jameson, who, although not part of the group, favor "a more 'dialogic,' 'dialectic' or transactive model for the interpretive activity" (p. 207). Further page references to this article will be given in parentheses in the text. For an informed but thoroughly hostile recent account of the Yale critics' work, see Gerald Graff, "Fear and Trembling at Yale," *The American Scholar* 46 (1977).

[58] *Validity in Interpretation* (New Haven, 1967), p. 23.

Susan R. Suleiman

My own commentary on Hartman's single sentence is, to be sure, not innocent. It is based on my understanding of the larger philosophical and theoretical context in which the sentence occurs, and of which it can be read as a sign. A full description of this context would require an essay in its own right, one that would show, among other things, the influence of Heideggerian ontology, of Lacanian psychoanalysis, and of Derrida's theory of textual deconstruction on a whole branch of contemporary American criticism—and that would show, as well, the reactions against this kind of criticism on the part of other American theorists. Here I shall have to be content with focusing on two of the most "essentially contested" concepts in the discussion: the text (with its attendant concepts of authority, intention, and meaning) and the writing—and reading—subject.

Perhaps no single idea has had as tenacious and influential a hold over the critical imagination in our century as that of textual unity or wholeness. Amidst the diversity of metaphors which critics have used to describe the literary text—as an organic whole, as a verbal icon, as a complex system of interlocking and hierarchically related "strata"—the one constant has been a belief in the text's existence as an autonomous, identifiable, and unique entity: the *text itself*. Under these conditions, critical controversies, no matter how heated, never concern anything more than the proper approach to, or the proper explication of, the text. Whatever their differences, rhetoricians, semioticians, psychologists, sociologists, philologists, and historians can all meet on common ground in their recognition of the text as a "full" object, all the more full and rich for its ability to accommodate a number of different readings, different approaches.

It is precisely this common ground that Derrida's theory of textual deconstruction seeks to undermine. The belief in the text as a full object, a set of signs used to communicate a meaning (or even a set of complex meanings) from one subject to another, is the real target of Derrida's deconstructive enterprise. For Derrida, a text can never be understood as a plenitude, an organization of elements present to themselves

Introduction

and pointing only to themselves (or to the "text itself"). On
the contrary: "every 'element'—phoneme or grapheme—is
constituted from the trace it bears in itself of the other elements in the chain or the system. This linking [enchaînement],
this tissue, is the *text*, which is only produced in the transformation of another text. Nothing, either in the elements or
in the system, is ever or anywhere simply present or absent.
Throughout there are only differences and traces of traces."[59]
By defining "difference" not as something that exists *outside*
the text, between its different readings, but *within* each element of the text and constitutive of the text *as text*, Derrida
not only subverts the cherished critical notion of textual
unity, but also challenges what he calls the "metaphysics of
presence," which he sees as the dominant mode of Western
thought since Plato, and of which the notion of textual unity
is but a specific manifestation.

The junction between Derrida's notion of the text and Lacan's notion of the self (and a fortiori of the writing and reading subject) is not difficult to place. If Derrida sees internal
difference and the continual deferring of presence as constitutive of the literary text, that is precisely how Lacan sees
the human subject. As Anthony Wilden has noted in his masterful exposition of Lacan's theory of the self, Lacan views the
subject as the " 'empty subject'—a subject defined only as a
locus of relationships" and hence impossible to totalize, to
define in any way but as a place of intersection of multiple
functions, of "other voices."[60]

That there exists a strong correlation between theories of
the self and theories of the text has not escaped the more
perspicacious of today's literary critics;[61] nor has the correlation between both theories and self *and* of text and larger

[59] J. Derrida, "Sémiologie et grammatologie," in *Positions* (Paris, 1972), p.
38. My translation.

[60] See Anthony Wilden, "Lacan and the Discourse of the Other," in J. Lacan, *The Language of the Self*, ed. and trans. Anthony Wilden (New York:
Delta paperback ed., 1975), p. 182 and *passim*.

[61] For a marvelously suggestive discussion of this correlation, see Walter B.
Michaels, "The Interpreter's Self: Peirce on the Cartesian 'Subject,' " *The
Georgia Review* 31 (1977), 383-402. As far as Derrida and Lacan are concerned,

41

philosophical issues. Indeed, I think it is the recognition of these correlations and of their consequences that accounts for the passionately polemical tone in the debate between "positive" and "negative" theorists of interpretation. At the 1976 Modern Language Association convention, one of the most heavily attended meetings was the Forum on "The Limits of Pluralism," featuring papers by Wayne Booth, M. H. Abrams, and J. Hillis Miller. Their papers, published subsequently in a single issue of *Critical Inquiry*,[62] defined the issues that separate the "positive" from the "negative" hermeneutics with particular clarity. According to Booth, "A critic who denies the authority either of author or text is trying to fly without a supporting medium" (p. 422). According to Abrams, the theorist chiefly responsible for the elimination of textual and authorial authority is Derrida, who denies recourse "to a speaking or writing subject, or ego, or cogito, or consciousness, and so to any possible agency for the intention of meaning something ('vouloir dire')" (p. 429). The re-

---

the most recent and in many ways the most exciting work of the Yale critics (as exemplified in particular by some of the articles in the special issue of *Yale French Studies* [*YFS*] on "Literature and Psychoanalysis," tellingly subtitled "The Question of Reading: Otherwise") has sought to make explicit the links between them by producing readings which, in Shoshana Felman's words, "concentrate . . . not only on what psychoanalytical theory has to say about the literary text, but also on what literature has to say about psychoanalysis" ("Turning the Screw of Interpretation," *YFS*, nos. 55-56 [1978], 102). In the same issue, Barbara Johnson pits Derrida's and Lacan's readings of "The Purloined Letter" against each other, only to conclude that in her discussion of "the letter as what prevents me from knowing whether Lacan and Derrida are really saying the same thing or only enacting their own differences from themselves, my own theoretical 'frame of reference' is precisely, to a very large extent, the writings of Lacan and Derrida" ("The Frame of Reference: Poe, Lacan, Derrida," *YFS*, nos. 55-56, p. 505). This combined "frame of reference" is also evident in Barbara Johnson's essay on "The Critical Difference," where she notes: "Difference is not engendered in the space between identities; it is what makes all totalization of the *identity of a self or the meaning of a text* impossible" (*Diacritics* 8, no. 2 [1978], 3; my emphasis).

[62] Booth, "Preserving the Exemplar"; M. H. Abrams, "The Deconstructive Angel"; J. Hillis Miller, "The Critic as Host," all in *Critical Inquiry* 3 (1977). Page references will be given in parentheses in the text.

Introduction

sult is a notion of the text as "a sealed echo-chamber in which meanings are reduced to a ceaseless echolalia, a vertical and lateral reverberation from sign to sign of ghostly nonpresence emanating from no voice, intended by no one, referring to nothing, bombinating in a void" (p. 431).

As their criticisms make clear, for Booth and Abrams the real danger of deconstructive criticism lies in its metaphysical and epistemological implications: eliminating textual authority, and with it the unicity of the writing subject, leads straight to nihilism. Miller counters this accusation not by denying but by triumphantly proclaiming its accuracy: "Nihilism is an inalienable alien presence within Occidental metaphysics, both in poems and in the criticism of poems" (p. 447). The notion of the unified text, like that of the unified self, is an illusion, and the virtue of deconstructive criticism is that it places this potentially tragic insight at the center of its activity. Far from recoiling in horror at the void, deconstructive critics gaze at it with Sisyphean impassivity. They show over and over again that "The poem, like all texts, is 'unreadable,' if by 'readable' one means open to a single, definitive, univocal interpretation" (p. 447). Or as Miller wrote in an earlier essay: "Deconstruction is not a dismantling of the structure of a text but a demonstration that it has already dismantled itself. Its apparently solid ground is no rock but thin air."[63]

There can be no question, here or elsewhere, of resolving the debate between positive and negative theorists of interpretation. To the extent that the debate has formulated itself as a conflict between diametrically opposed views about the ontological status of texts and of the self, it is irresolvable and potentially endless. For the negative hermeneuticians, "the ability of the mind to set up, by means of acts of judgment, formally coherent structures is never denied, but the ontological or epistemological authority of the resulting systems, like that of texts, escapes determination."[64] For the

[63] "Stevens' Rock and Criticism as Cure, II," *The Georgia Review* 30 (summer 1976), 341.

[64] Paul de Man, "The Timid God," *The Georgia Review* 29 (1975), 550.

Susan R. Suleiman

positivists, it is precisely that authority whose determination must be affirmed.[65]

Rather than seeking resolution or simply declaring a stale-mate, it may be useful to see in the debate itself a phenome-non that invites explanation and commentary. When the best critical minds of a period expend so much energy and passion on self-reflection and self-justification, that fact is itself of primary significance. We might see, in the self-reflexive turn of contemporary criticism, a slightly displaced (because tem-porally delayed) homologue of the self-reflexive turn in mod-ern literature. As Naomi Schor notes in her essay in this book: "the vicissitudes of hermeneutics in our time redupli-cate, with an inevitable time-lag, the vicissitudes of the inter-pretant [Schor's term for the interpreting protagonist in fic-tion] around the turn of the century."

Concurrently, we might find in today's hermeneutic con-troversies support for an idea which is gaining ground in both linguistics and literary study and which I discussed earlier—namely, that interpretation is a communal, context-

---

[65] By a somewhat curious twist, a critique of Derrida has surfaced recently from among the ranks of "anti-authoritarian" critics and his own admirers as well. This critique—which essentially reproaches Derrida for his lack of polit-ical *engagement*—is stated with great subtlety in Edward Said's essay on Der-rida and Foucault, "The Problem of Textuality: Two Exemplary Positions," *Critical Inquiry* 4 (1978), 673-714. Said ultimately chooses Foucault over Der-rida because Derrida "has chosen the lucidity of the undecidable in a text . . . over the identifiable *power of a text*" (p. 703), whereas Foucault is concerned with analyzing discourse as a means of exercising power and social control. The weak point of Derrida's work is thus seen, paradoxically, in terms that are formally similar to (even if their content is different from) those used by Derrida's "authoritarian" critics. Said finds Derrida's theory of textuality wanting because it has "not demanded from its disciples any binding en-gagement on matters pertaining to discovery and knowledge, freedom, op-pression, or injustice." Booth would say that it refuses to "take a stand." Al-though Said's definition of the stand to be taken places him at quite a remove from Booth or Abrams, on a formal level there is a definite family re-semblance: "For if everything in a text is always open equally to suspicion and to affirmation, then the differences between one class interest and another, one ideology and another are virtual in—but never crucial in mak-ing decisions about—the finally reconciling element of textuality" (p. 703).

Introduction

specific act, the result of what Stanley Fish calls shared interpretive strategies and what Jonathan Culler calls reading conventions. By this view, what separates the positive from the negative hermeneuticians is what separates any community of readers from any other—whether the separation be defined in terms of history, culture, ideology, or simply temperament. And by this view, one common task that each variety of audience-oriented criticism might fruitfully assign itself would be to study, by its own methods and in its own terms, the multiplicity of contexts, the shared horizons of belief, knowledge, and expectation, that make any understanding, however fleeting, of minds or of texts, possible.[66]

[66] To my regret, Louise M. Rosenblatt's pioneering work in the field of subjective criticism came to my attention only after this essay was in proof. A footnote will therefore have to replace the discussion her work deserved in an earlier section. Rosenblatt's book, *Literature as Exploration* (New York, 1938), challenged the objectivist assumptions of the New Criticism as they affected the teaching of literature in high schools and colleges. Rosenblatt first proposed the term *transaction* to designate the relationship between text and reader (*Literature as Exploration*, paperback edition, p. 27). Although her work was influential among those most concerned with questions of pedagogy, its relevance for literary theory was recognized only recently, when it was rediscovered by Bleich and others. *Literature as Exploration* was reissued in a paperback edition in 1976. See also Rosenblatt's recent book, *The Reader, the Text, the Poem: The Transactional Theory of the Literary Work* (Carbondale, Ill., 1978).

Jonathan Culler | Prolegomena to a
Theory of Reading

The fact that people engaged in
the study of literature are willing to read works of criticism or
articles like this one tells us something important about the
nature of our discipline. Few people, one imagines, open
these pages in the belief that this is the most relaxing and en-
tertaining way to spend an hour. We attend to criticism and
discussions of criticism because we hope to hear worthwhile
proposals, arguments, and discussions. We believe, it would
seem, that what is said about literature can matter; that it can
affect our own and other's dealings with literature and thus
help to advance an enterprise in which many members of a
profession are engaged. Our assumption that significant
things will be said in critical writings may be an expectation
more frequently defeated than fulfilled, but its presence, indeed its extraordinary persistence in the face of defeat, shows
that we see literary criticism as a discipline which aims at
knowledge.

One could, of course, argue that those engaged in the
study of literature are deluded about the nature of their activity. Norman Holland, for example, would say that in our pur-
suits we attain no knowledge of literature but only exercise
the self, as we sit in our studies hour after hour recreating our
identity themes in one masterpiece after another.[1] The notion
of a progressive, interpersonal body of knowledge would, by
these lights, be pure obfuscation. But I think we are not deluded about the fundamental nature of our enterprise. The
assumption thet we are investigating something other than

[1] See Holland, *5 Readers Reading* (New Haven, 1975) and my remarks below. This paper was written for a session of The English Institute (1976) at
which Holland also spoke.

46

Prolegomena to a Theory of Reading

ourselves, that we are dealing with a public institution which can to various degrees be known, does not seem to me a defensive and self-serving delusion, though admittedly the recent history of criticism does make it difficult to explain exactly in what way our discipline moves toward knowledge. Ever since literary studies turned from erudition to interpretation it has been easy to question the notion of literary criticism as a cumulative discipline. Each act of interpretation does not, alas, move us closer to a goal such as interpretive criticism might espouse: a more accurate understanding of all the major works of English (or French, or any other) literature. The accumulation of interpretations provokes, rather, a questioning of cumulative knowledge; it makes us unable to imagine progress except as dialectical transumption. Indeed, the cynic might say that criticism does not move toward better interpretations and fuller understanding but toward what Schoenberg achieved in his *Erwartung*: a chromatic plenitude, a playing of all possible notes in all possible registers, a saturation of musical space.

Some of us doubtless would be willing to abandon the notion of criticism as a discipline if this were the necessary consequence of interpretive criticism, the price we must pay if we are to make criticism an enterprise of interpretation. But unfortunately this is not a price one can pay; no such easy exchange is possible, for this consequence would paralyze the activity that engenders it. Interpretation cannot take place unless one assumes that a reading can constitute an advance in knowledge and that there are standards of adequacy which will enable others to see why the reading one proposes is superior to others. Interpretation is inseparable from notions of method and validity. It offers no escape from the conception of criticism as a discipline oriented toward knowledge. What one must ask is what shape such an enterprise might take and what problems it should address.

It is important to be clear from the outset about the nature and goals of criticism, for otherwise the most promising and energetic efforts miscarry. Northrop Frye once made bold proposals for criticism, seeking to make it a poetics, a system-

47

Jonathan Culler

atic account of forms, modes, themes, and genres. But because he was not explicit about the methodological status of his proposals or the criteria for their success, his efforts failed. Interpretive criticism simply assimilated Frye, and instead of a cumulative enterprise of poetics there arose yet another strain of interpretive criticism: myth criticism or archetypal criticism, which interprets works by labelling their parts with the names of Frye's categories. It is important to ensure that promising reorientations are not emasculated in this way, and I stress the point because the work of Stanley Fish, which urges us to attend to readers and to reading, constantly exposes itself to this danger. Though Fish has firm views about the nature of literary experience, he seems to have no explicit program for literary studies and he thus surrenders without a struggle to interpretive criticism, which always has waiting a program of sorts. Affective stylistics provides just another interpretation: a description of the reader's sequential experience of the text.[2]

If we are to avoid this kind of deflection and deflation we must from the beginning make our requirements clear, even if they should prove unattainable. We must know what we are trying to explain, what facts or problems our discipline addresses. This is, no doubt, the most difficult question for the study of literature: What are we trying to account for? It is not the existence of literary works that we are trying to explain, though we should want our discipline to provide some indication of their nature and function. What requires explanation is, above all, facts about form and meaning. In our dealings with literary works we treat them as objects or acts endowed with form and meaning; and here, in the properties which literary works have for us, are the facts that need to be explained: that *King Lear* is a tragedy, that Marvell's "Horation Ode" can be read as praise or blame, that *The Waste Land* can be unified by thematizing its formal discontinuities. There are facts aplenty to choose from; those who prize dif-

[2] For further discussion, see my article, "Stanley Fish and the Righting of the Reader," *Diacritics* 5, no. 1 (1975). Fish's recent work, however, no longer aims at interpretation.

Prolegomena to a Theory of Reading

ferences of interpretation can take the fact of disagreement about particular works as the fact to be explained. Criticism can address itself to the facts one selects and construct hypotheses to account for them.

Indeed, I contend that only in this way can literary criticism sustain the claims we might wish to make for it. More important for my present purposes, however, is the fact that this reorientation leads one to think about reading, because form and meaning are not *in* the text itself. Just as sequences of sound have meaning only in relation to the grammar of a language, so literary works may be quite baffling to those with no knowledge of the special conventions of literary discourse, no knowledge of literature as an institution. To account for the form and meaning of literary works is to make explicit the special conventions and procedures of interpretation that enable readers to move from the linguistic meaning of sentences to the literary meaning of works. To explain facts about the form and meaning works have for readers is to construct hypotheses about the conditions of meaning, and hypotheses about the conditions of meaning are claims about the conventions and interpretive operations applied in reading. In brief, I am arguing that if the study of literature is a discipline, it must become a poetics: a study of the conditions of meaning and thus a study of reading.

To anyone who questioned whether this methodological reorientation could really be as crucial as I claim, one might cite the example of linguistics. The decisive step in postwar linguistics is not the suggestion that there might be two levels of linguistic structure—deep structure and surface structure—but a change in focus, a redefinition of the task of linguistics. Structural linguistics conceived of its goal as the description of a body of data: a corpus of sentences. But with the recognition that a natural language consists of an infinite set of sentences, linguistics must change its focus. Description of a finite set of sentences is no longer adequate; linguistics must instead describe the ability of native speakers, what they know when they know a language. The shift from corpus to competence, which makes one's task the representation of competence, is crucial because it gives linguistics a goal and a principle of relevance, leading to new hypotheses and new modes of argument. It becomes clear what the linguist is trying to do: he is trying to explain facts about the competence of native speakers (that they recognize the synonymy of active and passive sentences, that they grasp very different logical relations in two apparently similar sentences, etc.). Focus on the description of competence gives the linguist a large array of facts to explain—facts about judgments, intuitions, etc.—and creates a viable discipline.

In the case of literary criticism it is also true that once we are no longer attempting to analyze a corpus of works but are seeking to describe the ability or competence of readers, we shall find our methodological situation considerably improved. Interpretive criticism has no facts to explain nor any explicit standard of success; its goal is to produce interpretations that are new enough to be interesting but not so radically new as to prove unacceptable. But once we see as our task the analyzing of literary competence as manifested in the interpretive strategies of readers, then the activities of readers—their judgments, interpretations, hesitations—present us with a host of facts to explain, and the methodological clarity of our situation encourages thought. It is a boon to know what one is trying to do, even though the task itself may prove extremely difficult.

The immediate accessibility of facts requiring explanation is one of the great virtues of this reorientation and one of the reasons for focusing on reading rather than writing. In principle the notion of literary competence ought to be indifferent to the distinction between reading and writing, since the conditions of meaning, the conventions which make literature possible, are the same whether one adopts the reader's or the writer's point of view. It is his experience of reading, his notion of what readers can and will do, that enables the author to write, for to intend meanings is to assume a system of conventions and to create signs within the perspective of that system. Indeed, writing can itself be viewed as an act of critical reading, in which an author takes up a literary past and directs it toward a future.

Prolegomena to a Theory of Reading

In principle, then, one could look at the activities of either writers or readers for evidence about the conventions and conditions of meaning; but in practice it is very much easier to concentrate on the competence of readers, for the assumptions of writers are of difficult access and their statements about their own works are motivated by such varied factors that one is continually led astray if one tries to infer from them the conventions assumed. This is to say that in concentrating on the reader one is not attempting to strip the author of all his glory, suggesting that he does nothing and that the reader does all; one is simply recognizing that the activities of readers provide more and better evidence about the conditions of meaning. As a reader oneself, one can perform all the experiments one needs, and one has access to what numerous other readers have said about a given text, while the statements of its one author are few and problematical.

But generally when people object to thinking about reading they are objecting to phrases like "the meaning a work has for readers" or "the operations performed by the reader," phrases that seem to presuppose a convergence of perceptions which, they would claim, is not to be found among actual readers. Now any theory of reading will of course be very interested in the variations in procedure and conclusions among readers; in particular, a theory of reading will want to know how different their procedures of reading actually are. But the reorientation, as I have proposed it, leaves this question entirely open; it does not assume agreement of any kind among readers. It asserts that the facts to be explained are facts about readers' judgments, intuitions, and interpretations; so if we should decide that every reading of a text is markedly and unpredictably idiosyncratic, that would be the fact requiring explanation. The study of reading is a way of investigating how works have the meaning they do, and it leaves entirely open the question of what kinds of meanings or what range of meanings works have.

Indeed, far from assuming unanimity, the study of reading is interesting precisely because there is not agreement among readers. A theory of reading is an attempt to come to terms with the single most salient and puzzling fact about literature:

that a literary work can have a range of meanings, but not just any meaning. After all, if we believed that a work could have but a single true meaning, then we would expect that meaning to be there in the work itself, and a theory of reading would have only incidental interest, as an account of perceptual disturbances and failures to grasp that meaning. But since we believe that for any work there is a range of possible readings, and that this is an open rather than a closed set of meanings, we need to explain how these meanings arise. What conventions and procedures of reading enable one to produce new meanings which are plausible, defensible, and yet which contradict other defensible readings? Far from discrediting a poetics focused on literary competence, disagreements among readers make the need for it more apparent.

Moreover, the daily experience of our professional lives throws up facts which need explanation, which seem to call for something very like an account of literary competence. It is, alas, only too clear that knowledge of English and a certain experience of the world do not suffice to make someone a skilled and perceptive reader of literature. Something more is required, something teachers of literature are employed to provide. Either teachers of literature have brought off an unprecedented confidence trick or else there is knowledge and skill involved in reading literature: skill which can be imparted. It is, to say the least, surprising that those who do not hesitate to grade their students on the competence of their reading and on their progress in learning the art of reading should be prepared to deny the existence of literary competence and should make no effort to describe explicitly the skills they are supposed to teach. To characterize this competence may be extremely difficult, but one can scarcely doubt its existence without rejecting the whole institutionalized teaching process, which does seem to work.

Any theory of literature ought to account for, or at least square with, the facts as we know them, and the enterprise of literary education does provide some indubitable facts: that works remain opaque to those who have not assimilated the

Prolegomena to a Theory of Reading

appropriate conventions, that someone who has read a lot of literature is better equipped to understand a work than someone who has read none, that one can often be brought to see the superiority of one interpretation to another. Sometimes, of course, this may be a simple yielding to authority, but it does happen that one is convinced by argument, a process which testifies to the existence of common ground: shared notions of how to read, of what sort of inferences are permitted, of what counts as evidence and what must be explicitly argued for. Reading and interpretation may be carried out in solitude, but they are highly social activities, which cannot be separated from the interpersonal and institutional conventions that are explicitly manifested in literary journals, critical discussion, and literary education. Someone like Norman Holland might argue that these things are the result of a mass delusion, but communal delusion on this scale is a social fact in its own right, more interesting and significant than the supposed reality it is said to conceal.

What would happen if criticism did follow the program I have been defending and became a poetics investigating the conditions of meaning? Suppose that, resisting the current notion that criticism is justified only by its interpretations of individual works, one set out to study reading as a cultural practice or institution, as a manifestation of an interpersonal literary competence. What difficulties would one encounter?

The first obstacle would doubtless be the problem of the relationship between reading and readers. How do the conventions of reading, in which one is interested, relate to the behavior and thoughts of actual readers? It is no solution to say that one is concerned with an ideal reader or a super-reader rather than actual readers, for as I have already insisted, a major advantage of concentrating on reading is that the practice of actual readers (oneself, one's students, colleagues, and other critics) provides evidence: facts to be explained.[3]

[3] To speak of an ideal reader is to forget that reading has a history. There is no reason to suggest that the perfect master of today's interpretive techniques would be the ideal reader or that any trans-historic ideal could be conceived.

53

Jonathan Culler

Moreover, notions of an ideal reader suggest that there is an ideal reading for a poem, and it is doubtless better for a theory of reading to adopt a terminology and a focus which leave such questions open and allow it to study and exploit the different strategies and different conclusions that actual readers employ. Since the possibility of a range of meanings is a major fact that one is trying to explain, it is better to avoid notions which imply the desirability of selecting an "ideal" reading. This does not mean, though, that one should rush out armed with questionnaires to interview the reader in the street. We can see why not from the example of Norman Holland's *5 Readers Reading.* Interested in how personality might affect the reading process, Mr. Holland found five undergraduates who could read, gave them personality tests to determine their five personalities, and then discussed with them several stories they had read, asking them "how they felt" about a particular character, event, or situation, or asking them to imagine what a character might have done in various circumstances. "By so informal a procedure," he reports, "I was hoping to get out free associations to the stories."[4] ("Get out," one might add, does not mean "eliminate" but "elicit.") Mr. Holland discovered a significant correlation between their free associations to the stories they had read and their personalities, as determined by free-association tests.

The example is instructive, not because it tells us anything about reading but because it illustrates a temptation to which the unwary can easily succumb, especially since they can convince themselves that they are being virtuously humanistic. If one begins to study a series of individual readers, one will tend to ask them about matters on which they might conceivably have individual views; one may even go so far as to seek free associations, for the simple reason that it is not very interesting to ask each of one's readers to recount the plot of a given novel or to indicate whether there is a thematic shift in the sestet of a particular sonnet. Moreover, the theorist will probably have difficulty publishing his book or paper if he

---

[4] *5 Readers Reading*, p. 44.

Prolegomena to a Theory of Reading

demonstrates that ninety-three out of a hundred readers agreed about the plot of *Macbeth* and similar matters. Free association may not be central to the reading process, but it can come to preoccupy the undiscriminating student of readers.

However, since Mr. Holland's writing is often grouped with more effective investigations of reading, such as the work of Stanley Fish, Michael Riffaterre, and Gerald Prince, it is perhaps worth indicating one of the ways in which his approach goes wrong. Mr. Holland begins with the claim that a work does not have a unity: it is unified in different ways by the activity of readers. But then he argues that the unity produced by readers is the projection onto the work of the reader's own "identity theme," which is the constant and unifying center of the reader's personality. It is not difficult to see what has happened here: finding texts extremely complex and ambiguous, Mr. Holland has transferred the concept of unity from text to person. But what is involved in locating this unity in the individual, as an "identity theme" which persists in all his behavior? A person can have an identity theme only if his behavior is read and interpreted in precisely the unifying way that Mr. Holland had rejected when applied to texts. He speaks of personal identity as if it were something given, but of course it is precisely a thematic, even a literary, construct: to discover an identity theme is to treat a person's behavior as a text, to interpret it as one would the accounts of a character in a traditional novel. Rejecting as a fallacious oversimplification the notion of a literary work as a harmonious whole in which everything expresses a central theme, Mr. Holland proceeds blithely to treat the behavior of an individual as the expression of a consistent central essence. This is, of course, the way of American ego psychology, which can be shown to be a vulgarized and sentimentalized version of the New Criticism.

In brief, Mr. Holland fails to study reading as a process with its own operations and goals. He leaps from text to reader, calling upon a simplified notion of personal identity that is much more problematic than the notion of thematic unity which he thought oversimplified literature. But people,

55

especially readers, are at least as complicated as texts. They are not harmonious wholes whose every action expresses their essence or is determined by their ruling "identity theme." A person is a place of intersecting roles, forces, languages, none of which belong to him alone, all of which are interpersonal. Indeed, the behavior of Mr. Holland's five readers illustrates very nicely how much the activity of interpretation is determined by the codified commonplaces of a culture: his five undergraduates are most unlike one another at the moment when they proffer the clichés and codes of different subcultures.

Rather than the model of a center that commands and informs every moment, rather than a transcendental signified for which every action is a signifier, one might think of the way in which one thing leads to another, so that people end up doing, thinking, or saying things which are not in themselves surprising but which one would not have expected of them, as they move from one role or discursive activity to another. Indeed, any psychoanalytic model would be more useful and accurate than the ego psychology on which Mr. Holland draws: my language is not mine, just as my unconscious is not mine; it is a set of processes and possibilities, where one thing leads to another, often through chains of signifiers rather than under the direction of a dominant signified. One reads as a reader, becomes a reader for the time of reading, and is caught up in a social activity that one does not wholly control. In the study of reading, as in most areas of what the French call the "human sciences," there is a central axiom which modern research has established: that the individuality of the individual cannot function as a principle of explanation, for it is itself a highly complex cultural construct—a result rather than a cause.

A first priority, then, if one is to study reading rather than readers, is to avoid experimental situations that seek free associations and to focus rather on public interpretive processes. Here the very nature of the act of writing provides some assistance. If one sets out to write an explicit account of one's own literary competence—to explain, step by step, what assumptions, conventions, and interpretive moves make possi-

Prolegomena to a Theory of Reading

ble one's perceptions and interpretations of various literary works—the act of writing this out, of communicating the grounds of interpretation, stresses everything that is public and explicable in the reading process. In any case, since one's notions of how to read and of what is involved in interpretation are acquired in commerce with others, a model of one's own literary competence would be extremely valuable and doubtless have much general validity. Moreover, to ensure awareness of the range of interpretive possibilities contained within the system of literary conventions, one need only consult the spectrum of interpretations that literary history records for almost every major work. These considered reactions of readers are more than adequate to ensure the breadth of an investigation into conditions of meaning. To inquire what conventions and interpretive moves must be postulated to connect text to interpretation is the best way to begin a study of reading.

My discussion so far has consisted entirely of preliminary considerations—considerations preliminary to a theoretical project—but I want to take up one example to illustrate what I have so far been taking for granted without explicit argument: the artificiality of special conventions that readers call upon in producing even very ordinary interpretations. By looking at various readings of Blake's "London," one can both show that the interpretation of literary works is based on special conventions which ought to be described and learn something about how critical disagreements are related to conventions of interpretation.

The poem is presented as a list of things seen and heard:

I wander thro' each charter'd street,
Near where the charter'd Thames does flow,
And mark in every face I meet
Marks of weakness, marks of woe.

In every cry of every Man,
In every Infant's cry of fear,
In every voice, in every ban,
The mind-forg'd manacles I hear.

Jonathan Culler

How the Chimney-sweeper's cry
Every black'ning Church appalls;
And the hapless Soldier's sigh
Runs in blood down Palace walls.

But most thro' midnight streets I hear
How the youthful Harlot's curse
Blasts the new-born Infant's tear
And blights with plagues the Marriage hearse.[5]

What the various interpretations of this poem demonstrate most emphatically is the importance of the convention of unity. If I were to tell you what I have seen and heard while wandering through the streets of New York, you might be appalled, but you would feel no compulsion to transform these heterogeneous experiences into versions of the same thing. Readers of poems, however, do. The various interpretations of this poem show that the reading process involves the attempt to bring together the sights and sounds according to one of our models of wholeness, and one can classify interpretations according to the model they appear to use. In this case, the most common is the model of the synecdochic series, where a series of particulars is taken to represent a general class of which the particulars are all members. This class can be, and is, named in various ways: the real social evils of eighteenth-century urban life; the woes which result from the artificial and repressive institutions that human reason has created; or, simply, distant generalized cases of suffering. The other model of wholeness used here is the basic aletheic reversal: first an inadequate vision, then its true or adequate counterpart. By this model, there is a shift in the third stanza: "a release from the repetitiveness of the preceding stanzas," writes Heather Glen. "The abstracting sameness of 'every . . . every . . . every,' the dimly realized cries and voices, give way to specifically realized human situations."[6]

[5] William Blake, *Complete Writings*, ed. Geoffrey Keynes (London, 1966), p. 216.

[6] Glen, "The Poet in Society: Blake and Wordsworth on London," *Literature and History* 2 (May 1976), 10.

Prolegomena to a Theory of Reading

Interpretations of "London" are more frequently based on the former model of unity, though the latter produces a dramatic structure that students of poetry generally value. Whichever model is used, however, the subsequent interpretive operations are very similar: the reader performs imaginative transformations on the various things seen and heard so as to relate them in a way that fits the model: he treats the poem's statements as figural notations that require interpretation.

The complexity of the interpretive process is clearest in the operations performed on the last two stanzas. The fact that every critic finds the third stanza a vision of misery and oppression testifies once again to the power of the convention of unity, but the different paths to this conclusion are wondrous to behold. The chimney sweep, of course, is for our culture the very type of the oppressed innocent, but his cry is said to "appall" the church. How can one explain the fact that no critic accepts this statement at face value, that each finds a way around it? If the literal statement is inadmissible, this is for reasons that have nothing to do with language or thought in general but only with conventions of literary structure; and one can only explain why "appall" is interpreted as it is by guessing what are the conventions at work here. First, we seem to have no model of unity that would permit at this point a note of institutional outrage, which is neither carried on in the fourth stanza nor explicitly denied or explained. Either of those developments might give us a new structure, but in their absence the convention of unity rules out a literal reading of "appalled." Secondly, the parallelism between

	sweeper	cry	church
and			
	soldier	sigh	palace

brings into play the convention that parallelism of expression creates parallelism of thought: the structure brings together church and palace in such a way that their roles must be either opposed (which, as I suggested, would be ruled out by the demands of unity at this point) or equivalent. The conventions thus give the reader a goal that governs his interpre-

59

tation of the third stanza: find a common relationship between institution and individual in the two cases.

Though critics say very different things about the church, they all seem to be following the same underlying conventions, performing very much the same operations. The one exception is D. G. Gillham, who reads "appalls" literally: "The Church is horrified," he writes, "at the evil of the sweeper's condition," but then, as if recognizing the inappropriateness of this reading, he quickly tells us a little story about churches so as to neutralize "appalls" and get us to the kind of conclusion that unity demands: "The Church is horrified . . . , but it is helpless to do much about it—no vigourous remedy may be undertaken because institutions are, by nature, conservative."[7] The sympathetic institution cannot or will not do anything and thus, in effect, sides with the oppressors.

Another way of transforming "appalls" is to call it ironic. This is a major interpretive operation, a powerful tool for making what seems deviant accord with various structural demands and conventions. Thus, Hazard Adams treats "appalls" as an ironic indication of the church's hypocritical attitude: "The church is once again a symbol of complacency and blindness. It is 'appalled' at the conditions it observes, but its histrionic reaction is clearly hypocritical."[8] As this example shows, one must think of irony not just as a technique available to authors but as a trope or interpretive operation available to readers whenever they encounter problems which it might help to solve.

However, a more common strategy in this particular case is based on a special convention that allows puns or lexical de-

[7] Gillham, *Blake's Contrary States* (Cambridge, 1966), p. 12. E. D. Hirsch also appears to take "appall" literally but then to cancel that reading in a remark I find extremely obscure: "The cry appalls (dismays, horrifies) the church, not because the church pities the plight of the chimney sweeps, nor because what blackens chimneys blackens churches, but because it is the church that has caused chimney-sweepers to exist." *Innocence and Experience* (New Haven, 1964), p. 264.

[8] Adams, *William Blake: A Reading of the Shorter Poems* (Seattle, 1963), p. 282.

Prolegomena to a Theory of Reading

composition in cases where they contribute to coherence and do not displace a satisfactory literal reading. In *The Visionary Company*, Harold Bloom argues that the cry "appalls" in the sense that "it makes the church pale and so exposes the church as a whited sepulchre."[9] Other critics, while striving toward the same interpretive conclusion, disagree about the figural route: "appall" means to cast a pall over or so to blacken rather than whiten, "blackening with the guilt of its indifference far more than with soot," argues Martin Price.[10] To appall is here to darken, writes Thomas Edwards, stressing that "the church itself is not horrified."[11] This reading, which plays with the metaphorical soot of guilt, is doubtless reinforced by the fact that chimney sweeps are supposed to remove soot, not apply it. An observer who knew nothing of literature might expect this fact to work against the reading: it is appropriate for sweeps metaphorically to cleanse the church since their job is to remove literal soot, but it is absurd to have "appall" mean "make dirty." There is much to be said for such a line of reasoning, and it indicates just how peculiar the properties of literary language are. It is a fact about the conventions of literary interpretation that such reversals or paradoxes work as a kind of proof of the poem, a demonstration of logical and semantic density. As we see here, conventions of interpretation let us perform quite radical acts of semantic transference, moving blackness and soot around from chimneys to sweeps to the church to its moral authority.

The critics I have cited may disagree about what the lines mean, but they are all following the same convention of unity, performing interpretive operations to fill, in their different ways, a structure they have all posited. And, as I have emphasized, the interpretive operations or semantic transformations that they employ are not in any sense personal and idiosyncratic acts of free association; they are very common and acceptable formal strategies.

[9] Bloom, *The Visionary Company* (Garden City, N.Y., 1961), p. 42.
[10] Price, *To the Palace of Wisdom* (Carbondale, Ill., 1964), p. 401.
[11] Edwards, *Imagination and Power* (London, 1971), p. 143.

Jonathan Culler

What I want to stress here are the interpretive operations at work in producing perfectly ordinary interpretations. It is often difficult to see what kinds of moves lead from text to interpretation, but that does not mean that these moves are in any way unique or even idiosyncratic. For example, the poem tells us that "the hapless Soldier's sigh / Runs in blood down Palace walls." It is very difficult to explain what figures, what interpretive moves and semantic shifts, are employed when a reader transforms this statement to something like, "The despair and pain of the soldier brands the people and institutions he has been defending with the guilt of causing his suffering." But no matter how difficult it is to make explicit the interpretive operations responsible for this reading, we admit that they are not idiosyncratic moves when we recognize that the poem's statement could very well mean this. In granting the plausibility of this interpretation we are in effect identifying as public, reproducible operations the interpretive strategies we find hard to describe. A primary task of the study of reading is to describe the operations responsible for interpretations we find plausible. Questions such as to what extent individual readers perform the same operations or how far these operations are confined to a tiny community of professional critics cannot really be answered until we are rather better at describing the operations in question.

The full complexity of these operations is revealed in readings of the last stanza of "London." Of course, it requires some imagination to see how a harlot's curse blasts an infant's tear and blights the marriage hearse, but this difficulty does not in itself explain the amount of interpretive labor which readers and critics have expended on the stanza. It would, after all, be quite plausible to say that the speaker hears a harlot both curse her child for crying and, in shouting at a wedding procession, curse the institution of marriage. But those who attempt to interpret this poem are never content with such readings and the reason seems to depend once again on conventions of literary structure. The final stanza must bring the poem to a close, must produce unity. There

Prolegomena to a Theory of Reading

are, of course, various ways of doing this.[12] But in a poem organized as a series of perceptions, the reader seeking unity attempts to read the final stanza as the climax of the vision, its most intense and typical moment. This leads to large claims. The harlot, says Edwards, "blasts the prospects of innocent children . . . and blights the healthful possibilities of marriage," because her existence is "a gross parody of sanctified mutuality in love."[13] Others see in this stanza a critique of the institution of marriage: "If there were no marriage there would be no ungratified desires, and therefore no harlots. Thus it is ultimately the marriage hearse itself and not the youthful harlot which breeds the pestilence that blights the marriage hearse."[14]

How do such conclusions emerge from the statement that the harlot's curse blasts an infant's tear and blights the marriage hearse? There are, certainly, a great many interpretive moves involved, all of which are attempts to transform this bizarre sentence into a causal scheme that includes harlots, children, and marriage and produces at least one victim. The child, of course, is a victim in all readings, but views of the harlot differ radically, depending on which interpretive moves are followed. The convention of unity allows the reader to place the harlot in the series established by chimney sweep and soldier: the sweep cries, the soldier sighs, and the harlot curses. Since every cry speaks of mind-forged manacles and reveals a victim, the harlot's "curse" may be reduced to her "cry" and the semantic force of "curse" applied to the harlot herself, who becomes a victim cursed. On the other hand, if one starts with infant as cursed victim, the syntax allows one to group married couples with the infant as victims of a curse, and one justifies this move by a reference to venereal disease.

So far these schematic readings are quite different, though

[12] See Barbara H. Smith's excellent *Poetic Closure: A Study of How Poems End* (Chicago, 1968).

[13] *Imagination and Power*, p. 143.

[14] Hirsch, *Innocence and Experience*, p. 265.

Jonathan Culler

based on similar operations, but a further interpretive move, provoked by the need to find in the final stanza a more comprehensive climax, brings the two readings much closer to one another. The earlier victims, sweep and soldier, affect by their cries the social institutions of which they are the victims. Reading "marriage hearse" as a complex figure for the social institution of matrimony, one can place it in the series with church and palace, and, moving synecdochically from part to whole, speak of the harlot as victim of a social system. If, on the other hand, one makes married couples and children victims cursed by the harlot and wishes the poem to conclude with a broad vision rather than with a condemnation of venereal disease, one stresses that "the harlot's curse is, therefore, something more than simply a figure for the venereal disease that 'blasts . . . and blights.' "[15] The innocent are blighted not just by specific diseases, nor even by the presence of prostitutes on the street, but by a social system based on exploitation and of which the harlot is merely a provocative and garish part.

In both cases, it seems, the final semantic transformation takes the form of a synecdoche, a move from part to whole, which makes the poem a political statement. The accounts different readers offer of what is wrong with the social system will, of course, differ, but the formal interpretive operations that give them a structure to fill in seem very similar in the two cases.

This attempt to make explicit some of the conventions and interpretive operations that make possible the various readings of this poem should illustrate two things. First, it shows that reading is not an innocent activity nor a moment of unanalyzable communion between a self and a text. It involves a complex series of operations which ought to be described. Second, this example illustrates the peculiar status of interpretive differences for any study of reading. Against anyone who maintains that studies of reading are otiose because no two people read and interpret in the same way, one can

[15] Adams, *William Blake*, p. 285.

Prolegomena to a Theory of Reading

say that even when readers come to very different conclusions about the meaning of a line or a work, they employ interpretive moves and rely on interpretive conventions which can be formally defined. Interpretation is not a random process, and it is quite possible to explain how disagreements are produced by the application of common though complex displacements.

More generally, it is important to stress that if we want to understand the nature of literature and of our adventures in language we will have to recognize that the "openness" and "ambiguity" of literary works result not from vagueness nor from each reader's desire to project himself into the work, but from the potential reversibility of every figure. Any figure can be read referentially or rhetorically. "My love is a red, red rose" tells us, referentially, of desirable qualities that the beloved possesses. Read rhetorically, in its figurality, it indicates a desire to see her as she is not: as a rose. "Chartered street" in the first stanza of "London" tells us, referentially, of an ordered city, its streets full of chartered institutions. Rhetorically, it is hyperbole: to speak as if even the streets had royal charters is excessive, ironic. One can, of course, go on to read this irony referentially, as a suggestion that too many charters enslave: London is so restrictive that even streets need charters to exist. But one could also in turn reverse this figure and, reading the irony in its figurality, say that the act of seeing streets as if they were chartered is an example of another kind of enslavement: enslavement to one's own fiction. These four readings are generated by two elementary operations which, as a pair, constitute the possibility of figural reading.

On a larger scale, for example, the repetitive movement of "London" 's opening stanzas can, referentially, tell us of a visionary power to perceive the common misery beneath the variety of outward appearances: "Only the poet hears what is *in* each cry or sees *how* it looks and acts—in short, what it means," writes Martin Price.[16] But, rhetorically, to hear man-

---

[16] Price, *To the Palace of Wisdom*, p. 401.

Jonathan Culler

acles in every cry of every person, to connect through a figure of repetition all surfaces and sounds, is itself an obsession, a mind-forged manacle, the danger always courted by the visionary poet.

This kind of reversal is inherent in the possibilities of reading, in the possibilities of literary language as we know it. The opposing, even contradictory, readings engendered in this way depend not on prior "opinions" of the subject but on formal operations that constitute the activity of interpretation. Opposed readings which stand in the same relation to one another can be produced for most texts: the interpretive move that treats a linguistic sequence as figurative opens the possibility of a series of reversals, which will produce other readings. The content of these readings will differ according to the nature of the text, but their formal properties will be a result of definable operations of reading. To understand interpretive disagreements, to understand the ambiguity or openness of literary meaning, one must study the reading process. No other area of literary criticism offers such an interesting and valuable program.

Tzvetan Todorov | Reading as
Construction

What is omnipresent is imperceptible. Nothing is more commonplace than the reading experience, and yet nothing is more unknown. Reading is such a matter of course that, at first glance, it seems there is nothing to say about it.

In literary studies, the problem of reading has been posed from two opposite perspectives. The first concerns itself with readers, their social, historical, collective, or individual variability. The second deals with the image of the reader as it is represented in certain texts: the reader as character or as "narratee." There is, however, an unexplored area situated between the two: the domain of the logic of reading. Although it is not represented in the text, it is nonetheless anterior to individual variation.

There are several types of reading. I shall pause here to discuss one of the more important ones: the one we usually practice when we read classical fiction or, rather, the so-called representative texts. This particular type of reading, and only this type, unfolds as a construction.

Although we no longer refer to literature in terms of imitation, we still have trouble getting rid of a certain way of looking at fiction; inscribed in our speech habits, it is a vision through which we perceive the novel in terms of representation, or the transposition of a reality that exists prior to it. This attitude would be problematic even if it did not attempt to describe the creative process. When it refers to the text itself, it is sheer distortion. What exists first and foremost is the text itself, and nothing but the text. Only by subjecting the text to a particular type of reading do we construct, from our reading, an imaginary universe. Novels do not imitate reality;

67

they create it. The formula of the pre-Romantics is not a simple terminological innovation; only the perspective of construction allows us to understand thoroughly how the so-called representative text functions.

Given our framework, the question of reading can be restated as follows: How does a text get us to construct an imaginary world? Which aspects of the text determine the construction we produce as we read? And in what way? Let us begin with basics.

REFERENTIAL DISCOURSE

Only referential sentences allow construction to take place; not all sentences, however, are referential. This fact is well known to linguists and logicians, and we need not dwell on it.

Comprehension is a process different from construction. Take for example the following two sentences from *Adolphe*: "Je la sentais meilleure que moi; je me méprisais d'être indigne d'elle. C'est un affreux malheur que de n'être aimé quand on aime; mais c'en est un bien grand d'être aimé avec passion quand on n'aime plus."[1] The first sentence is referential: it evokes an event (Adolphe's feelings); the second sentence is not referential; it is a maxim. The difference between the two is marked by grammatical indices: the maxim requires a third-person present-tense verb, and contains no anaphores (words referring to preceding segments of the same discourse).

A sentence is either referential or nonreferential; there are no intermediary stages. However, the words that make up a sentence are not all alike in this respect; depending on the lexical choice, the results will be very different. Two independent oppositions seem pertinent here: the affective versus the nonaffective, and the particular versus the general. For

[1] "I felt that she was better than I; I scorned myself for being unworthy of her. It is a terrible misfortune not to be loved when one loves; but it is a far greater misfortune to be loved passionately when one no longer loves." All translations from *Adolphe* and *Armance* by Susan Suleiman.

example, Adolphe refers to his past as "au milieu d'une vie très dissipée." This remark evokes perceptible events but in an extremely general way. One could easily imagine hundreds of pages describing this very same fact. Whereas in the other sentence, "Je trouvais dans mon père, non pas un censeur, mais un observateur froid et caustique, qui souriait d'abord de pitié, et qui finissait bientôt la conversation avec impatience,"[2] we have a juxtaposition of affective versus nonaffective events: a smile, a moment of silence, are observable facts; pity and impatience are suppositions (justified, no doubt) about feelings to which we are denied direct access.

Normally, a given fictional text will contain examples of all these speech registers (although we know that their distribution varies according to period, schools of thought, or even as a function of the text's global organization). We do not retain nonreferential sentences in the kind of reading I call reading as construction (they belong to another kind of reading). Referential sentences lead to different types of construction depending on their degree of generality and on the affectivity of the events they evoke.

Narrative Filters

The characteristics of discourse mentioned thus far can be identified outside of any context: they are inherent in the sentences themselves. But in reading, we read whole texts, not just sentences. If we compare sentences from the point of view of the imaginary world which they help to construct, we find that they differ in several ways or, rather, according to several parameters. In narrative analysis, it has been agreed to retain three parameters: time, point of view, and mode. Here again, we are on relatively familiar ground (which I have already dealt with in my book, *Poétique*); now it is simply a question of looking at the problems from the point of view of reading.

___

[2] "I found in my father not a censor, but a cold and caustic observer who would first smile in pity and soon finish the conversation with impatience."

Mode. Direct discourse is the only way to eliminate the differences between narrative discourse and the world which it evokes: words are identical to words, and construction is direct and immediate. This is not the case with nonverbal events, nor with transposed discourse. At one point, the "editor" in *Adolphe* states: "Notre hôte, qui avait causé avec un domestique napolitain, qui servait cet étranger [i.e., Adolphe] sans savoir son nom, me dit qu'il ne voyageait point par curiosité, car il ne visitait ni les ruines, ni les sites, ni les monuments, ni les hommes."[3] We can imagine the conversation between the editor-narrator and the host, even though it is unlikely that the former used words (be it in Italian) identical to those which follow the "he told me that" formula. The construction of the conversation between the host and the servant, which is also evoked, is far less determined; thus we have more freedom if we want to construct it in detail. Finally, the conversations and the other activities common to Adolphe and the servant are completely vague; only a general impression is given.

The remarks of a fictional narrator can also be considered as direct discourse, although on a different (higher) level. This is especially the case if, as in *Adolphe*, the narrator is represented in the text. The maxim, which we previously excluded from reading as construction, becomes pertinent here—not for its value as an "énoncé" (i.e., a statement) but as "énonciation" (i.e., an utterance, implying a speaker and his circumstances). The fact that Adolphe as narrator formulates a maxim on the misery of being loved tells us something about his character, and therefore about the imaginary universe of which he is a part.

Time. The time of the fictional world ("story" time) is ordered chronologically. However, the sentences in the text do not, and as a rule cannot, absolutely respect this order; the reader undertakes therefore, unconsciously, the task of

[3] "Our host, who had chatted with a Neapolitan servant who attended on that stranger [i.e., Adolphe] without knowing his name, told me that he was not at all traveling out of curiosity, for he visited neither the ruins, nor the natural sites, nor the monuments, nor his fellow-men."

chronological reordering. Similarly, certain sentences evoke several events which are distinct yet similar ("iterative narrative"); in these instances we reestablish the plurality of the events as we construct.

Point of view. The "vision" we have of the events evoked by the text clearly determines our work of construction. For example, in the case of a positively slanted vision, we take into consideration (1) the event recounted, and (2) the attitude of the person who "sees" the event.

Furthermore, we know how to distinguish between information that a sentence gives concerning its object, and the information it gives concerning its subject; thus the "editor" of *Adolphe* can only think of the latter, as he comments on the story we have just read: "Je hais cette vanité qui s'occupe d'elle-même en racontant le mal qu'elle a fait, qui a la prétention de sa faire plaindre en se décrivant, et qui, planant indestructible au milieu des ruines, s'analyse au lieu de se repentir."[4] The editor constructs the subject of the narrative (Adolphe the narrator), and not its object (Adolphe the character, and Ellénore).

We usually do not realize just how repetitive, or rather how redundant, fiction is; we could, in fact, state almost categorically that each event is narrated at least twice. For the most part, these repetitions are modulated by the filters mentioned above: at one point a conversation may be reproduced in its entirety; at another, it may be alluded to briefly; action may be observed from several different points of view; it can be recounted in the future, in the present, and in the past. In addition, all these parameters can be combined.

Repetition plays an important role in the process of construction. We must construct *one* event from *many* accounts of it. The relationship between these different accounts varies, ranging from total agreement to downright contradiction. Even two identical accounts do not necessarily produce the

[4] "I hate that vanity which is preoccupied only with recounting the evil it has done, which has the pretention of inspiring pity by describing itself, and which, hovering indestructibly above the ruins, analyzes itself instead of repenting."

Tzvetan Todorov

same meaning (a good example of this is seen in Coppola's film *The Conversation*). The functions of these repetitions are equally varied: they help to establish the facts as in a police investigation, or to disprove the facts. Thus in *Adolphe*, the fact that the same character expresses contradictory views on the same subject at two different times which are quite close to each other, helps us to understand that states of mind do not exist in and of themselves, but rather in relationship to an interlocutor, to a partner. Constant himself expressed the law of this universe in the following manner: "L'objet qui nous échappe est nécessairement tout différent de celui qui nous poursuit."[5]

Therefore, if the reader is to construct an imaginary universe through his reading of the text, the text itself must be referential; in the course of reading, we let our imagination go to work, filtering the information we receive through the following types of questions: To what extent is the description of this universe accurate (mode)? When did the events take place (time)? To what extent is the story distorted by the various "centers of consciousness" through whom it is told (vision)? At this point, however, the job of reading has only begun.

SIGNIFICATION AND
SYMBOLIZATION

How do we know what happens as we read? Through introspection; and if we want to confirm our own impressions, we can always have recourse to other readers' accounts of their own reading. Nevertheless, two accounts of the same text will never be identical. How do we explain this diversity? By the fact that these accounts describe, not the universe of the book itself, but this universe as it is transformed by the psyche of each individual reader. The stages of this transformation can be diagrammed as follows:

---

[5] "The object that escapes us is of necessity altogether different from the one that pursues us."

1. The author's account   4. The reader's account

    ↓   ↑

2. The imaginary universe   3. The imaginary universe
   evoked by the author   →   constructed by the reader

We could question whether there really is a difference between stage 2 and 3, as is suggested by the diagram. Is there such a thing as a nonindividual construction? It is easy to show that the answer must be positive. Everyone who reads *Adolphe* knows that Ellénore first lived with the Comte de P^xxx, that she left him, and went to live with Adolphe; they separated; she later joined him in Paris, etc. On the other hand, there is no way to establish with the same certainty whether Adolphe is weak or merely sincere.

The reason for this duality is that the text evokes facts according to two different modes, which I shall call signification and symbolization. Ellénore's trip to Paris is *signified* by the words in the text. Adolphe's (ultimate) weakness is *symbolized* by other factors in the imaginary universe, which are themselves signified by words. For example, Adolphe's inability to defend Ellénore in social situations is signified; this in turn symbolizes his inability to love. Signified facts are *understood*: all we need is knowledge of the language in which the text is written. Symbolized facts are *interpreted*; and interpretations vary from one subject to another.

Consequently, the relationship between stages 2 and 3, as indicated above, is one of symbolization (whereas the relationship between stages 1 and 2, or 3 and 4, is one of signification). In any case, we are not dealing with a single or unique relationship, but rather a heterogeneous ensemble. First, we always abbreviate as we read: stage 4 is (almost) always shorter than stage 1, whence stage 2 is richer than stage 3. Secondly, we often make mistakes. In both cases, studying the relationship between stages 2 and 3 leads to psychological projection: the transformations tell us about the reading subject. Why does he remember (or even add) certain facts and not others? But there are other transformations which provide information about the reading process itself, and these are the ones that will be our main concern here.

It is hard for me to say whether the situation I observe in the most varied kinds of fiction is universal or whether it is historically and culturally determined. Nevertheless, it is a fact that in every case, symbolization and interpretation (the movement from stage 2 to stage 3) imply the determinism of action. Would reading other texts, lyrical poems for example, require an effort of symbolization based on other presuppositions (e.g., universal analogy)? I do not know; the fact remains that in fiction, symbolization is based on the acknowledgment, either implicit or explicit, of the principle of causality. The questions we address, therefore, to the events that constitute the mental image of stage 2 are the following: What is their cause? What is their effect? We then add their answers to the mental image that constitutes stage 3.

Let us admit that this determinism is universal; what is certainly not universal is the form it takes in a given case. The simplest form, although one that we rarely find in our culture as a reading norm, consists in constructing another fact of the same type. A reader might say to himself, "If John killed Peter (a fact present in the story), it's because Peter slept with John's wife (a fact absent from the story)." This type of reasoning, characteristic of courtroom procedures, is not applied seriously to the novel; we assume that the author has not cheated and that he has provided (has signified) all the information we need to understand the story (*Armance* is an exception). The same is true as concerns effects or aftereffects: many books are sequels to others and tell the consequences of events in the imaginary universe represented in the first text; nevertheless, the content of the second book is generally not considered inherent in the first. Here again, reading practices differ from everyday habits.

When we read, we usually base our constructions upon another kind of causal logic; we look for the causes and consequences of a particular event elsewhere, in elements unlike the event itself. Two types of causal construction seem most frequent (as Aristotle already noted): the event is perceived as

Reading as Construction

the consequence (and/or the cause) either of a character trait or of an impersonal or universal law. *Adolphe* contains numerous examples of both types of interpretation, and they are integrated into the text itself. Here is how Adolphe describes his father: "Je ne me souviens pas, pendant mes dix-huit premières années, d'avoir eu jamais un entretien d'une heure avec lui. . . . Je ne savais pas alors ce que c'était que la timidité."[6] The first sentence signifies a fact (the absence of lengthy conversations). The second makes us consider this fact as symbolic of a character trait—timidity: if the father behaves in this way, it is because he is timid. The character trait is the cause of the action. Here is an example of the second case: "Je me dis qu'il ne fallait rien précipiter, qu'Ellénore était trop peu préparée à l'aveu que je méditais, et qu'il valait mieux attendre encore. Presque toujours, pour vivre en repos avec nous-mêmes, nous travestissons en calculs et en systèmes nos impuissances ou nos faiblesses: cela satisfait cette portion de nous qui est, pour ainsi dire, spectatrice de l'autre."[7] Here, the first sentence describes the event, and the second provides the reason—a universal law of human behavior, not an individual character trait. We might add that this second type of causality is dominant in *Adolphe*: the novel illustrates psychological laws, not individual psychologies.

After we have constructed the events that compose a story, we begin the task of reinterpretation. This enables us to construct not only the "personalities" of the characters but also the novel's underlying system of values and ideas. A reinterpretation of this type is not arbitrary; it is controlled by two series of constraints. The first is contained in the text itself: the author need but take a few moments to teach us how to

---

[6] "I cannot recall, during the first eighteen years of my life, ever having had an hour's conversation with him. . . . I did not know then what timidity was."

[7] "I told myself that I mustn't be overhasty, that Ellenore was not sufficiently prepared for the confession I was planning and that it was better to wait some more. Almost always, to live in peace with ourselves, we hide our weaknesses and impotence beneath the guise of calculations and systems: this satisfies the part of ourselves which is, as it were, the spectator of the other."

interpret the events he evokes. This was the case in the passages from *Adolphe* cited earlier: once he has established a few deterministic interpretations, Constant can forgo naming the cause of the subsequent events; we have learned his lesson, and we shall continue to interpret in the way he has taught us. Such explicit interpretations have a double function: on the one hand, they tell us the reason behind a particular fact (exegetic function); on the other hand, they initiate us into the author's own system of interpretation, the one that will operate throughout the course of the text (meta-exegetic function).

The second series of constraints comes from the cultural context. If we read that so-and-so has cut his wife up into little pieces, we do not need textual indications to conclude that this is truly a cruel deed. These cultural constraints, which are nothing but the commonplaces of a society (its "set" of probabilities), change with time. These changes permit us to explain why interpretations differ from one period to another. For example, since extramarital love is no longer considered proof of moral corruption, we have trouble understanding the condemnations heaped upon so many fictional heroines of the past.

Human character and ideas: such entities are symbolized through action, but they can be signified as well. This was precisely the case in the passages from *Adolphe* quoted earlier: action symbolized shyness in Adolphe's father. Later, however, Adolphe signified the same thing, saying: My father was shy; that is also true of the general maxim. Human character and ideas can thus be evoked in two ways: directly and indirectly. During the course of his construction, the reader will compare the various bits of information obtained from each source and will find that they either tally or do not. The relative proportion of these two types of information has varied greatly during the course of literary history, as goes without saying: Hemingway did not write like Constant.

We must, however, differentiate between human character constructed in this way and the characters in a novel as such: not every character has a character, so to speak. The fictional character is a segment of the spatio-temporal universe represented in the text, nothing more; he/she comes into existence the moment referential linguistic forms (proper names, certain nominal syntagms, personal pronouns) appear in the text regarding an anthropormorphic being. In and of itself the fictional character has no content: someone is identified without being described. We can imagine—and there exist—texts where the fictional character is limited to just that: being the agent of a series of actions. But, as soon as psychological determinism appears in the text, the fictional character becomes endowed with character: he acts in a certain way, *because* he is shy, weak, courageous, etc. There is no such thing as character without determinism of this type.

The construction of character is a compromise between difference and repetition. On the one hand, we must have continuity: the reader must construct the *same* character. This continuity is already given in the identity of the proper name, which is its principal function. At this point, any and all combinations become possible: all actions might illustrate the same character trait, or the behavior of a particular character might be contradictory, or he might change the circumstances of his life, or he might undergo profound character modification . . . So many examples come to mind that it is not necessary to mention them. Here again the choices are more a function of the history of styles than of the idiosyncracies of individual authors.

Character, then, can be an effect of reading; there exists a kind of reading to which every text can be subjected. But in fact, the effect is not arbitrary; it is no accident that character exists in the eighteenth- and nineteenth-century novel and not in Greek tragedy or the folktale. A text always contains within itself directions for its own consumption.

Construction as Theme

One of the difficulties in studying reading is due to the fact that reading is so hard to observe: introspection is uncertain, psycho-sociological investigation is tedious. It is therefore with a kind of relief that we find the work of construction represented in fiction itself, a much more convenient place for study.

Construction appears as a theme in fiction simply because it is impossible to refer to human life without mentioning such an essential activity. Based on the information he receives, every character must construct the facts and the characters around him; thus, he parallels exactly the reader who is constructing the imaginary universe from his own information (the text, and his sense of what is probable); thus, reading becomes (inevitably) one of the themes of the book.

The thematics of reading can, however, be more or less emphasized, more or less exploited as a technique in a given text. In *Adolphe*, it is only partially the case: only the ethical undecidability of action is emphasized. If we want to use fiction to study construction, we must choose a text where construction appears as one of the principal themes. Stendhal's *Armance* is a perfect example.

The entire plot of the novel is, in fact, subjugated to the search for knowledge. Octave's erroneous construction functions as the novel's point of departure: based upon Armance's behavior (an interpretation deducing a character trait from an action), Octave believes that Armance is too concerned with money. This initial misunderstanding is barely settled when it is followed by a second one, symmetrical to but the reverse of the first: Armance now believes that Octave is too concerned with money. This initial mix-up establishes the pattern of the constructions that follow. Next, Armance correctly constructs her feelings for Octave, but it takes Octave ten chapters before he discovers that his feelings for Armance are called *love*, not *friendship*. For five chapters Armance believes that Octave doesn't love her; Octave believes that Armance doesn't love him during the book's fifteen main chapters; the same misunderstanding is repeated toward the end of the novel. The characters spend all their time searching for the truth, in other words, constructing the facts and the events around them. The tragic ending of the love relationship is not caused by impotence, as has often been said,

Reading as Construction

but by ignorance. Octave commits suicide because of an erroneous construction: he believes that Armance doesn't love him anymore. As Stendhal says suggestively, "Il manquait de pénétration et non pas de caractère."[8]

We can see from this brief summary that several aspects of the construction process can vary. One can be agent or patient, a sender or receiver of information; one can even be both. Octave is an agent when he pretends or reveals, a patient when he learns or is mistaken. It is also possible to construct a fact ("first-level" construction), or someone else's construction of that same fact ("second-level" construction). Thus, Armance rejects the idea of marrying Octave when she contemplates what others might think of her. "Je passerais dans le monde pour une dame de compagnie qui a séduit le fils de la maison. J'entends d'ici ce que dirait Mme la duchesse d'Ancre et même les femmes les plus respectables, par exemple la marquise de Seyssins qui voit dans Octave un époux pour l'une de ses filles."[9] Octave likewise rejects the idea of suicide when he envisions the possible constructions of others. "Si je me tue, Armance sera compromise; toute la société recherchera curieusement pendant huit jours les plus petites circonstances de cette soirée; et chacun de ces messieurs qui étaient présents sera autorisé à faire un récit différent."[10]

What we learn above all in *Armance* is the fact that a construction can be either right or wrong; if all right constructions are alike (they are the "truth"), wrong constructions vary, as do the reasons behind them: flaws in the transmitted information. The simplest type is the case of total ignorance: until a certain point in the plot, Octave hides the very exist-

[8] "He lacked penetration, not character."

[9] "The world would regard me as a lady's companion who seduced the son of the house. I can already hear what the Duchesse d'Ancre would say, or even more respectable women like the Marquise de Seyssins, who sees in Octave a husband for one of her daughters."

[10] "If I kill myself, Armance will be compromised. All of society will spend a week in tracking down the most minute circumstances of this evening; and every one of these gentlemen who were present will be authorized to give a different account of what happened."

ence of a secret concerning him (active role); Armance is also unaware of its existence (passive role). Afterwards, the existence of the secret may be learned, but without any additional information; the receiver may then react by inventing his own "truth" (Armance suspects Octave of having killed someone). Illusion constitutes yet a further degree of faulty information: the agent does not dissemble, but misrepresents; the patient is not ignorant or unknowing, but is in error. This is the most prevalent situation in the novel: Armance camouflages her love for Octave, claiming she will marry someone else; Octave thinks that Armance feels only friendship toward him. One may be both agent and victim of the travesty; thus Octave hides from himself the fact that he loves Armance. Finally, the agent can reveal the truth, and the patient can apprehend it.

Ignorance, imagination, illusion, and truth: here are at least three stages through which the search for knowledge passes before leading a character to a definitive construction. Obviously, the same stages are possible in the reading process. Normally, the construction represented in the text is isomorphic to the one that takes the text as its point of departure. What the characters don't know, the reader doesn't know either; of course, other combinations are possible as well. In the detective novel, a Watson figure constructs like the reader, but a Sherlock Holmes constructs better: the two roles are equally necessary.

Other Readings

The flaws in the reading construction do not in any way undermine its existence: we do not stop constructing because of insufficient or erroneous information. On the contrary, defects such as these only intensify the construction process. Nevertheless, it is possible that construction does not occur, and that other types of reading supersede it.

Discrepancies between readings are not necessarily found where we might expect. For example, there does not seem to be a big difference between construction based on a literary text and construction based on a referential but nonliterary text. This resemblance was implied in the propositions I advanced in the previous section; in other words, the construction of characters (from nonliterary material) is analogous to the reader's construction (from the text of a novel). "Fiction" is not constructed any differently from "reality." Both the historian and the judge, the former on the basis of written documents, the latter on that of oral testimony, reconstitute the facts; in principle, they do not proceed differently from the reader of *Armance*; this does not mean there are no differences as far as details are concerned.

A more difficult question, beyond the scope of this study, concerns the relationship between construction based on verbal information and construction based on other perceptions. From the smell of roast lamb, we construct the roast; similarly for a sound, a view, etc. Piaget calls this phenomenon "the construction of reality." In these instances the differences may be much greater.

We do not have to stray very far from the novel to find material requiring another type of reading. There are many literary texts, nonrepresentative texts, that do not lead to any construction at all. Several types can be distinguished here. The most obvious is a specific type of poetry, generally called lyric poetry, which does not describe events, which evokes nothing exterior to it. The modern novel, in turn, requires a different reading; the text is still referential, but construction does not occur because, in a certain sense, it is undecidable. This effect is obtained by a dismantling of any one of the mechanisms necessary for construction as we have described them. To take just one example: we have seen that a character's identity was a function of the identity and inambiguity of his name. Suppose now that, in a text, the same character is evoked successively by several different names, first "John," then "Peter," then "the man with the black hair," then "the man with the blue eyes," without any indication of co-reference between the two expressions; or, suppose again that "John" designates not one, but three or four characters; each time, the result is the same: construction is no longer

Tzvetan Todorov

possible because the text is representatively undecidable. We see the difference here between such impossibility of construction and the defective constructions mentioned earlier: we shift from the misunderstood to the unknowable. This modern literary practice has its counterpart outside of literature: schizophrenic discourse. Schizophrenic discourse preserves its representative intention, yet through a series of inappropriate procedures (which I have tried to classify elsewhere) it renders construction impossible.

This is not the place to study other types of reading; noting their place beside reading as construction will suffice. To perceive and describe reading as construction is all the more necessary, given that the individual reader, far from being aware of the theoretical nuances it exemplifies, reads the same text in several ways at the same time, or at different times. His activity is so natural to him that it remains imperceptible. Therefore, it is necessary to learn how to construct reading—whether it be as construction or as deconstruction.

Translated from the French
by Marilyn A. August

Karlheinz Stierle | # The Reading of Fictional Texts

To understand how readers deal with fictional texts we must first consider the status of fiction as such.[1] Despite all potential references to reality, a fictional text is characterized by being a nonreferential composition. Thus references to reality in fiction have their function in a poetics of fiction that might aim at reality and the collective experience of reality to a greater or lesser degree. While a pragmatic referential text can be corrected by our knowledge of reality, a fictional text—in its potential deviation from facts—cannot be corrected but only interpreted or criticized.[2] However, this license, which distinguishes fictional texts from a mere depiction of reality, entails a motivation that is closely linked to the character of fiction itself. By definition, fiction means difference from and not congruity with a given state of affairs. Supposing that a particular deviation is not simply an error, its perception by the reader may very well provide him with the key to understanding the text's constructive intention and its poetic motivation. In fictional as well as in pragmatic texts the elementary task of the reader

[1] This essay is a revised, translated version of an essay first published in *Poetica* 7 (1975), 345-87, under the title "Was heisst Rezeption bei fiktionalen Texten?" ("What Is 'Reception' in the Case of Fictional Texts?"). In the original, it is preceded by an analysis of the reading of pragmatic texts, and followed by an argument on fiction being the horizon of life-world, and life-world being the horizon of fiction. The term *Rezeption* ("reception") refers to the activity of reading, the construction of meaning, and the reader's response to what he is reading. [The translators.]

[2] See my articles, "Fiktion, Negation und Wirklichkeit" (pp. 522-24) and "Der Gebrauch der Negation in fiktionalen Texten" (pp. 235-40), in *Positionen der Negativität*, Harald Weinrich, ed., Poetik und Hermeneutik VI (Munich, 1975).

consists in grasping the proposition and the perspective from which it is presented. But contrary to pragmatic texts, the relationship between proposition and state of affairs is not strictly fixed in fictional texts; moreover, the fictional situation is presented in such a manner that it has no real consequences for the reader: the reader plays a role which is unrelated to the context of his personal life. The same is true for the author, whose role is equally bound to the text. This role playing does not, however, take place in a void but is based on an implied communicative situation, which is a distinctive feature of all fiction. A particularly good example of fictional situation building is science fiction. According to Käte Hamburger's theory, science fiction, being written in the past tense, reveals that under certain fictional conditions the past tense loses its temporal function. However, it retains this conventional function when we presuppose a fictional situation that, from the reader's perspective, lies in the future, but one that is conceived from the implied fictional perspective as a post-future from which the future may appear as past.[3]

Although fictional and pragmatic speech differ in status, this difference does not necessarily influence the actual reception of fictional texts. There is a form of reception with regard to fictional texts that one could call quasi-pragmatic. In quasi-pragmatic reception the boundaries of the fictional text are transcended through an illusion created by the reader himself. This illusion may be compared to pragmatic reception, which is always overstepping the boundaries of the text in an attempt to fill the gap between word and world. In quasi-pragmatic reception fiction is removed from its verbal base without, however, having a position in the actual reader's field of action beyond the text.

The reading of fiction in terms of mimetic illusion is an elementary form of reception that has a relative right of its own. Depending on the vividness of the illusion, the reader may be compelled to identify with fictional roles.[4] Take, for

---

[3] See *Die Logik der Dichtung*, 2nd ed. (Stuttgart, 1968), p. 94. In English, *The Logic of Literature*, trans. M. J. Rose (Bloomington, 1973).

[4] For a theory on fictional identification, see H. R. Jauss, "Negativität und

The Reading of Fictional Texts

example, the child's experience of the imaginary, which is the purest and least restricted form of this type of reception. For him the imaginary world of the fairy tale is real presence, its verbal mediation is still unperceived. That is why the imaginary, though fixed in language, may have such a powerful impact on the child. In reading fairy tales the child is mainly confronted with embodiments of preconceptual forms of experience like fear, hope, happiness, unhappiness, wonder, and horror. Yet the child's pleasure in repetition reveals his desire to gain control over these experiences transformed into a world of strange disguise. Instead of simply surrendering to the imaginary, he sets it deliberately into motion. Sartre's *The Words* strikingly illustrates how he, as a child, experienced without reservation an imaginary world verbally created and how, at the same time, by experiencing this illusory world, he acquired a consciousness of language and its power to produce illusion.[5] The illusory character of fictional communication—not yet recognized by the child—would remain meaningless, however, if it were not sustained by a certain conceptual coherence created within the specific articulation of the fictional text itself. Though the child can still ignore this relationship between illusion and conceptual coherence, its recognition is a prerequisite to aesthetic experience once the referential illusion has seriously been questioned. Only illusion that is sustained by fiction can turn into aesthetic experience that lasts and does not spend itself with illusion.

Though every fictional text is open to a naive reading—an elementary form of reception that has been learned in everyday communication—there are specific forms of fiction that count on an exclusively quasi-pragmatic reception. In such cases the verbal structure of narration is veiled in order to make the passage from fiction to referential illusion as easy as possible. We find this particularly in the kind of trivial literature whose sole function is to encourage the reader to create

---

Identifikation: Versuch zur Theorie der ästhetischen Erfahrung," in *Positionen der Negativität*, pp. 263-339.

[5] (Paris, 1964), p. 37. In English, *The Words*, trans. Bernard Frechtman (New York, 1964).

Karlheinz Stierle

an illusory reality.[6] Such literature is produced with the intention to provoke stereotypes of imagination and emotion while it tries to disguise the effect of language at the origin of such illusion making. This illusion, which is built upon stereotypes of perception, behavior, and judgment set in motion by the text, is usually characterized by a strong emotional component. The emotional tension of the text takes the reader outside the text itself and puts him into an illusory state of expectations and fulfillments. The expectations resulting from still unfulfilled illusions are conditioned by hope and fear, emotions that one could call the vectors of the illusory tension. This tension, which gives a certain coherence to the illusory world beyond the text, is reinforced on the level of narrative discourse by a system of affirmations that stabilize the produced illusion: the narrator affirms the story by vouching for it, the story affirms itself through recurrences, the narrative concepts affirm each other by their obvious interrelationships, the expectations provoked by the imaginary world are affirmed by their fulfillment, and finally the reader's view of the world is affirmed, since the text only stimulates those stereotypes that he has produced himself. This system of affirmations gives a clear orientation to the reader, filling all the gaps for him while he transforms fiction into illusion (the illusion of the "real"). This type of quasi-pragmatic reading tends to dissolve the distinct contours of the text into an illusory continuum. The reader responds to the stimuli of the text with stereotypes from his own experience. Since he is unaware of this process, these self-created illusions seem all the more probable and real. The reader thus turns the improbability of narrative fiction into the probability of a self-produced illusion. The relationship between quasi-pragmatic reception and a form of fiction that counts on it corresponds to a similar phenomenon in the fine arts. The viewer of a painting who is not aware of the depiction but only of the depicted is thus lead into an illusory realm beyond

[6] For an analysis of the history and the decline of reading in bourgeois society, see Q. D. Leavis's thorough study, *Fiction and the Reading Public*, 2nd ed. (London, 1968).

The Reading of Fictional Texts

the picture itself. More precisely, however, this illusory realm is not located beyond the picture but in front of it, since the viewer has substituted his own imaginary stereotypes for the pictorial signs. In this case, the picture, like trivial literature, can restrict itself to immersing the viewer in his own self-produced illusion, which can be attained without very complex aesthetic procedures. The trivial painting and its pictorial vagueness, which can easily be replaced by stereotypes, is a good illustration of how reception can lead from the work of art into a purely imaginary world.

The popular novel, in particular, is a form of fiction that presupposes a quasi-pragmatic reception. Here the act of reading is only a means to an end: illusion building. The reading of such literature, to which sociology of literature pays specific attention, could legitimately be called an act of non-reading insofar as it is separated from higher forms of conscious reception. Competent reading of fiction has to pass from quasi-pragmatic reception to higher forms of reception, which alone can do justice to the specific status of fiction. Only if the reader is aware of the great variety of activities entailed in "reading" does he have a chance to perform the skills demanded by the text, and to approach it with the right attitude. A competent reading of literature requires a versatility that can be analyzed. Though it could never be completely accounted for by any theory, such a reading can only be achieved if the act of reading is accompanied by theoretical reflection.

The quasi-pragmatic reception of fictional texts is most strikingly illustrated by the literary figure of Don Quixote. Don Quixote represents a reader for whom fiction changes into illusion to such a powerful degree that it finally replaces reality. As the hero of the first modern antinovel, Don Quixote represents the classic paradigm of a reader overwhelmed by the illusory power of the text, for whom the stereotypes of his reading turn into stereotypes of his practical and verbal actions because he has lost all awareness of the text as such. The fact that the "lost text" transforms reality itself into a text is the ironic result of a reading which has surrendered to the centrifugal power of reception.

Karlheinz Stierle

The quasi-pragmatic reading of fictional texts deprives them of their concrete verbal structure. This concrete articulation of the text can only be apprehended by a manner of reading that could be called centripetal, since it turns its attention to fictionality itself instead of surrendering to the centrifugal power of fiction, its illusion making. In working out frames of reference for this manner of reading, literary theory can indicate possibilities of reception that have only partly been realized in the histories of reception of the single works themselves. Thus literary theory can provide us with new ways of reading which, in turn, could give reading a new place in society.

If the communicative function of literature is to be preserved, a formal theory of reception and the proper reading competence are needed. The mode of reception that each fictional text demands cannot sufficiently be grasped through the description of how this text has actually been received by its readers. The fixed accounts of how a specific literary work has been read are always merely partial accounts whose particularity never entirely reflects the complex experience of reception. They are marked by contemporary concepts, conventions, and prejudices, as well as by the particular interests of the critic. Hence, what is relevant to any particular reading at a given time and place does not necessarily coincide with the predominant scheme thematically realized in the work. By isolating and emphasizing a particular aspect of the work, reception can constitute a new system of perspectives. Since different readings do not necessarily follow the same thematic scheme, it seems difficult to derive from the history of readings the meaning of a specific work. Although the study of the history of reception is important for the actual interpretation of a text and for its position in relation to other texts, it cannot reach the complexity of meaning organized by the text itself. That is why we need a complementary formal theory of reading that derives its specific criteria for the reception of fictional texts from the very concept of fictionality. Even if in the realm of fiction the relationship between the production of a text and its reception is not as stable as in the pragmatic

The Reading of Fictional Texts

realm, fictional communication presupposes a consensus about the status of fictionality. The analysis of this consensus will demonstrate that the type of reading demanded by the "fictional contract" has to be the most sophisticated form of reading. The history of fiction is the history of its rising complexity, always indicating increasingly complex skills of realization. Concurrently, the history of reading competence shows a tendency toward a growing complexity. Thus forms of reception have been established that go far beyond a "naive" pragmatic reading.

The determination of criteria for the specific reading conventions of fictional texts requires a more profound analysis of the predominant features of fiction. We have seen that fictions as "free" compositions cannot be corrected by contradictory information from the realm of experience, since they enjoy an autonomous existence, independent from the universe of knowledge. Thus what belongs to the sphere of fiction cannot simply be removed from it and transferred to the general context of knowledge. We have also seen that fiction presupposes its own form of communication, which preconstitutes the implied role of the reader. We have now to discuss the concept of fiction in detail.

In principle, language can be used in two different ways: it can either have a referential function, as in description or narration, or an autoreferential function. In "systematic texts" language acquires an autoreferential function, whose aim is to clarify the use of language in referential texts. But there is another possible use of language, which could be called pseudoreferential. In the pseudoreferential use of language the conditions of reference are not to be found outside the text, they are produced by the text itself. In texts using language pseudoreferentially—that is, in fictional texts—there is no way to distinguish what the author intended to say from what he actually said. The pseudoreferential use of language is but a specific variation of the autoreferential use of language, whose characteristics have still to be defined. It is important to emphasize, however, that the quasi-pragmatic attitude toward fictional texts and the pseudoreferential function of language in fictional texts are not directly related. The quasi-pragmatic reception has to be transcended in order for us to perceive the pseudoreferential function of language in fiction. Basically, the pseudoreferential function of language is nothing but autoreferentiality in the guise of a pseudoreferential form. Thus narrative fictional texts turn out to be a variation of systematic texts, if *systematic* denotes texts that are concerned with the conditions of usage of their inherent terms.

This seeming paradox needs further consideration. First we must inquire into the relationship between experience and concept, which is crucial to an understanding of the referential, the autoreferential, and the pseudoreferential usage of verbally expressed concepts. Concepts are instruments for organizing and communicating our experience. In phenomenological terms they are aspects under which experience appears and can be ordered into classes of experience. Such concepts constituted in language can be removed from their referential context in order to be considered for their own sake. The concept thus becomes self-reflexive, since it is referred back to itself. Under this condition, which is the condition of systematic texts, concepts serve to structure the organizing schemes for experience. This is only feasible, however, at the price of abstraction, which necessitates leaving aside any considerations of the particular situation in which concepts are used, as well as their specific referential function within that situation. This deficiency of the systematic self-referential use of concepts is compensated for by the pseudoreferential use of concepts in fictional texts. Certainly the correlation of concepts in fiction is not as rigid as in systematic texts. But it offers, in a tentative way, possibilities for using concepts and for organizing schemes for the classification of experience. The tentative relationship between different concepts, however, is compensated for by the closed and unifying structure of the fictional work. Even referential elements that appear in this pseudoreferential context are part of this unity. For instance, by linking a reference to a real landscape with a fictional story it is possible to integrate the real landscape into the closed mythical framework of the story. The works of Baudelaire, Proust, and Garcia Marquez are examples of how actual landscapes may be transformed into mythic ones by integrating them into a unifying fictional context. In turn, the fictionalized landscape may very well become part of our experience of the real landscape. Thus, to a reality drawn into fiction corresponds a fiction drawn into reality.

The closed framework of fiction is not the result of a systematic consistency but of a system of schematized views—a predominant scheme or structural matrix [*Relevanzfigur*] that stands as an equivalent for experience. Fiction, with its pseudoreferential use of language, can organize obvious relationships between concepts, as well as new relationships far removed from the stereotypes of experience. And finally, fiction can create forms of experience that have not yet been conceptually fixed. Thus fiction represents concepts, it modifies them by depicting them in a tentative or experimental way, and it presents preconceptual experience. Each concept of the fictional text is primarily determined by its interrelationship with all the other concepts of the text. The fictional determination of a concept by a limited number of other concepts corresponds to the pragmatic use of each concept. Thus fiction provides a framework for the use of its vocabulary, which thereby gains a kind of normative background. It is revealing that standard French dictionaries prefer fictional paradigms to illustrate the normative usage of a term. Furthermore, fictional texts allow for the thematic elaboration—within a possible conceptual framework—of preconceptual experiences. This possibility arises from the particular conceptual status of fictional texts. If we think of the systematic relationships between concepts as habitual relationships, then we can regard referential relationships as occasional relationships. In fiction we have the unique possibility of witnessing the interplay between them. Thus in fiction, habitual relationships may tentatively be presented as occasional ones, and occasional relationships as habitual ones.

If systematic texts and fictional texts are both self-referential, fictional texts are different from systematic texts in one decisive aspect. In fictional texts, autoreferentiality not only plays on the level of concepts; it is all-inclusive. This particular quality has now to be examined.

While reading pragmatic texts the reader must be able to reconstruct the propositional state of affairs, be aware of the perspective from which it is presented, and grasp the pertinent realm of discourse as well as the underlying pragmatic intention. Only the pragmatic intention transcending the boundaries of the text provides its predominant scheme [*Relevanzfigur*]. While the quasi-pragmatic reception of fictional texts entails the same process as the act of pragmatic reception, there is one essential difference: in fictional texts the conditions of the communicative situation have to be derived from the text itself.

The reading of fictional texts as fictional texts, then, does not demand an entirely different form of reception, but rather one that asks the reader to take an additional step, which is made necessary by the very status of fiction itself. In order to apprehend fiction, the reader first has to receive it as mimesis in the type of quasi-pragmatic reading that I have described. Therefore, the new dimension of reception, which characterizes adequate reading of fiction, is based on the general reversal of the relationship between "theme" and "horizon" as we find it in the "natural," that is the pragmatic and the quasi-pragmatic movement of reception.[7] While in the latter the *signifiant* merely represents the horizon for the thematic *signifié*, in the decoding of fictional texts—by a movement that is known as the hermeneutic circle—this *signifié* can become the horizon for the thematic *signifiant* and the constitutive processes between the first *signifiant* of the concrete sign and the last *signifié* of the referential illusion.

---

[7] "Theme" and "horizon" are central terms of E. Husserl's phenomenology. See *Erfahrung und Urteil*, ed. L. Landgrebe (Hamburg, 1948) (In English, *Experience and Judgment*, ed. Landgrebe, trans. J. S. Churchill and K. Ameriks, [Evanston, Ill., 1973]), and A. Schütz, *Reflections on the Problem of Relevance* (New Haven, 1970), where Husserl's theory of theme and horizon is further elaborated. For the German edition see, *Das Problem der Relevanz* (Frankfurt am Main, 1971).

The Reading of Fictional Texts

While in pragmatic reading the centrifugal movement of the text toward the construction of its meaning proceeds more or less automatically and without effort, the converse centripetal movement, which is the characteristic feature of fiction, proves to be unusual, painstaking, and methodically demanding, all the more when the fictional text is the result of textual procedures outside the boundaries of normal and everyday communication.

The reversal of theme and horizon can disclose the concrete fictional structure of the text in two different ways: on the one hand, through a "vertical" reversal that concentrates the attention on the verbal strata and articulatory levels, thus giving them a relative aesthetic autonomy beyond mere aesthetic function; on the other hand, by a "horizontal" reversal within the sphere of meaning. Since the very principle of fiction is the possibility of reversing theme and horizon, all levels of fictional structure are not merely the means but also the very moments of fiction. Yet it is the level of meaning that is most decisive for fictional constructions. Only with regard to meaning or—from a reverse perspective—only with regard to the horizon of meaning do all levels of fictional structure attain their function. Furthermore, it is this level which explains the emotional tensions and feelings that the reader experiences and to which all textual levels contribute. The conceptual level of fiction is the "prosaic" basis for even the most exuberant transformations into referential illusion. Only by keeping in mind the conceptual level of fiction are we able to assess adequately its emotional dimension. That is why nothing is more detrimental to the kind of fiction that relies on quasi-pragmatic reception than the reversal of focus from the subjective illusion created by the reader to a sobering conceptual decoding. This reversal discloses a surplus of reception that is not sustained by the construction and the articulation of the work, and which, therefore, reveals the poverty of the conceptual construction that the reader had covered with his own stereotypes. The reversal of the perspective from thematic illusion and horizontal conceptuality to thematic concept and horizontal illusion entails, first of all, the reader's awareness of language's quasi-referential use as self-referential, and secondly, his understanding of fiction as a particular organization of schemes for the organization of experience. The specific skill needed for this kind of reception, which consists of relating the particular fictional detail to a conceptual scheme, has been described in detail in Kant's *Critique of Judgment.* In fictional texts the power of judgment—which enables us to apprehend the particular as a manifestation of the universal (what Kant calls the "reflecting judgment")—undergoes a continuous training.[8] That is what could give fiction reading a relevancy reaching beyond the domains of fiction and aesthetics.

Judgment is also required in order to discover the relationships between scheme and realization, given by the text itself, and to discover the implicit concepts that direct the linear structure of the text. To orient ourselves in a text is to be able to situate the material we encounter in the act of reading in relation to the concepts that organize the given context. Only a reading of the text with respect to its organizing concepts permits us to translate the linear structure of the text into a multilayered one, and to see the fictional text as a continuum and a hierarchy of dispositions for experience. Thus the text can be perceived as a multitude of overlapping structures, which follow both an elementary linear order and an infinitely complex one. The perception of this dual order constitutes the basis for what could be called the immanent poetics of the text.

The manifestation of the particular in fiction is always subject to a conceptual reversal: on the one hand, the salient concepts orient our view of the particular; on the other hand, the particular reveals these concepts in a certain light, set against the specific background of our reading experience. It is the text in its linear structure that first shapes our understanding of the conceptual relationships given by, and implied by, the

---

[8] *Kritik der Urteilskraft,* ed. K. Vorländer (Hamburg, 1959) p. 15: "Judgment is the ability to apprehend the particular as comprised by the universal. If the universal (the rule, the principle, the law) is given, then the judgment, which subsumes the particular . . . , is *determining.* But if the particular for which the universal has to be found is given, the judgment is merely *reflecting*" [author's translation].

The Reading of Fictional Texts

text. But the judgment of the reader has to surpass this linear structure. The textual linearity has to be viewed in relation to the hierarchic conceptual organization of the text as a whole. The text interprets itself by verbalizing its hierarchic structure, and by supplying the reader with a mode of reading. The cognitive dimension of the text is based on different layers of meaning, and the conceptual structure is organized as a conceptual hierarchy of meanings.[9] This conceptual organization may be intuited by the reader during the linear unfolding of the text, while the linear structure for its part may determine the interpretation and focalization of the conceptual structure. This focalization, already an important factor in pragmatic texts where it throws light on a given state of affairs, discloses the conceptual orientation of the fictional text. Only after a second reading, however, is it possible to reverse our perspective on the text: while we first saw it as a text moving toward the gradual revelation of its system, we now see it in a retrospective view within the framework of the system. Only when the opening clauses of a text have been reinforced by corresponding terminal clauses can the perspective leading from fiction to illusion be reversed in such a way that now fiction itself becomes visible against the background of referential illusion. While reading the text for a second time, the reader at any moment of the act of reading is able to situate the given part of the text not only with regard to its context *to the left*—that is, to that section of the text which has already been perused—but also with regard to its context *to the right*—the section which has not yet been covered. Only when both contexts are united can the isolated part be seen within its integral context and located within the conceptual hierarchy. The second reading thus leads from the quasi-pragmatic reception producing illusion to a reception of fiction as such, since it is only then that the fabricated character of fiction is subjected to the reader's critical judgment.[10]

[9] Ingarden was the first to develop this idea in detail. See *Das literarische Kunstwerk*, 3rd ed. (Tübingen, 1965), especially chapter 2: "Der Aufbau des literarischen Werks," pp. 25ff; in English, *The Literary Work of Art*, trans. George Grabowicz (Evanston, Ill., 1973).

[10] Only this second reading fulfills the demands of what Nietzsche called

Karlheinz Stierle

While pragmatic texts have to be understood with respect to the intention beyond the text, autoreferential fictional texts require analysis of the text as such. The step from the reception of pragmatic texts to the study of fictional texts could be described metaphorically as a step from a two-dimensional plane to three-dimensional space. Using the metaphor of Euclidian geometry, which is based on a rising sequence of new dimensions from point to line, from line to plane, and from plane to three-dimensional and then to multidimensional space, one could roughly consider words as textual points, their linkage to sentences as textual line, and their combination on the level of meaning as textual plane. Seen in this light, the fictional text appears as a textual space where each textual element is related to all others, since the pseudoreferential nature of fictional texts presupposes that each concept be seen against the background of all the others.[11] The text as textual space where potential relationships infinitely multiply is, from the reader's perspective, a space or a medium for reflection,[12] which he may explore fur-

---

the philological art of slow reading. In his introduction to *Morgenröte* he writes: "Philology teaches us how to read well, meaning slowly, thoroughly, thoughtfully, and carefully, leaving the backdoors open, reading with afterthoughts, with sensitive fingers and eyes . . ." (*Friedrich Nietzsche: Werke in drei Bänden*, ed. K. Schlechta [Munich, 1954], 1:1016) [author's translation].

[11] This complex interrelationship of all textual elements grows the more problematic for the author the more he is aware of it. In his comments about the writing of *Madame Bovary*, Flaubert describes the problem of the author becoming the reader of his own text, while he is still producing it: "Je suis en train de recopier, de corriger et raturer toute ma première partie de Bovary. Les yeux m'en piquent. Je voudrais d'un seul coup d'oeil lire ces cent-cinquante-huit pages et les saisir avec tous leurs détails dans une seule pensée" (Letter to Louise Colet, dated July 22, 1852, in *Extraits de la Correspondance ou Préface à la vie d'écrivain*, ed. G. Bollème [Paris, 1963] p. 83). The author as well as the reader have only a limited hold on the work of fiction.

[12] In his doctoral thesis, *Der Begriff der Kunstkritik in der deutschen Romantik* (Bern, 1920), Walter Benjamin introduces this term to characterize Friedrich Schlegel's theory of reception. Though the impact of this dissertation has been overshadowed by later works, its thorough and profound analysis of Romantic theories of reception provides still an invaluable basis for the development of a modern theory of reading.

The Reading of Fictional Texts

ther and further, but without exhausting it.[13] That is why the apprehension of fictional texts can never be brought to an end. What Valéry said about the process of writing poetic texts, i.e., that it can never be ended but only interrupted, applies to the process of reception as well. The process of reception is only restricted by the reader's ability to apprehend the infinite relationships constituting the integral meaning of a fictional text. The limitations to which reception is subject are, on the one hand, limitations due to the reader's subjective perception and judgment, and on the other hand, restrictions imposed by the historical situation under which the text is read.

Although the work of reception can never come to an end, it is not necessarily subject to arbitrariness. The reception of a fictional text has to follow some method if we are to grasp the wealth of relationships organized in it. There are aspects of fictional texts that can only be accounted for by a methodical process of reception based on a theory of fiction, and not by a pretheoretical pragmatic approach. The number and type of relationships that can be found in a fictional text are restricted; they are subject to the distinct boundaries of fiction and its structural matrix. Though the reader exploring the text discovers a multitude of thematic relationships and possibilities for nonthematic relationships, the boundaries of fiction are clearly determined. What basically distinguishes fiction from the experience of real life is the fact that in everyday life the "theme" is perceived against a horizon of outer contingencies that have to be coped with, whereas in the fictional world, to which the reader contributes by participating in a fictional situation, the relationship between theme and horizon is predetermined by the relevant textual structure. While participating in the world of fiction and the illusion it provokes, the reader is living in a world of relevancy which, contrary to his daily experience, is not disrupted by irrelevant

[13] See the special edition of *Esprit* 12 (1974), entitled *Lecture I: L'Espace du texte*. Jean Ricardou's essay "La Révolution textuelle" (pp. 927-45) shows how new forms of literature may provoke new forms of reading.

Karlheinz Stierle

pects of reality. In fiction, even contingency contributes to the overall scheme. When contingency destroys illusions it is in the interest of provoking secondary illusions. The reader of fiction must acknowledge that fictional texts have a theoretical basis. Under this condition everything in fiction has a claim to relevancy.

The shift between determinacy and indeterminacy determines the very form of the text and constitutes its predominant scheme [*Relevanzfigur*], which in turn predetermines the process of reception, and more specifically, the part of the implied reader.[14] The text provides, however, infinite secondary schemes aside from those that are determined by its main structural design. The reader can construct an infinite number of these from his own reading perspective; however, they must always be related to the structural matrix of the text. The claim that the text prescribes its own predominant scheme has as a consequence that the ambiguous or non-determined parts of a text can no longer be taken as pretexts for the creativity of the reader. They have to be seen in their function as modifications of the overall scheme. The reader must grasp these modifications as he follows the textual relationships between determinacy and indeterminacy. This is the point where our argument differs from Wolfgang Iser's aesthetics of reception, which he developed in his essays "The Reading Process" and "The Reality of Fiction."[15] As

[14] For the relationship between determinacy and indeterminacy see my essay "Der Gebrauch der Negation in fiktionalen Texten," p. 240.

[15] See Wolfgang Iser, "The Reading Process: A Phenomenological Approach," in *The Implied Reader* (Baltimore, 1974), p. 285: "The text provokes certain expectations which in turn we project onto the text in such a way that we reduce the polysemantic possibilities to a single interpretation in keeping with the expectations aroused, thus extracting an individual configurative meaning. The polysemantic nature of the text and the illusion-making of the reader are opposed factors." Thus the construction of meaning is part of the formation of illusions through reading. In this context, however, it is important to point out that the reduction of the text's semantic potential is already part of the elementary process of pragmatic reception. The ability to reduce this semantic potential is presupposed by all communication. See also, Iser's "The Reality of Fiction: A Functionalist Approach to Literature," *New Literary History* 7 (1975), 7-38.

The Reading of Fictional Texts

opposed to the large number of studies on the historical and sociological aspects of reader response, Iser's phenomenological approach concentrates on the act of reception as such, thereby adding a new dimension to the aesthetics of reception. In this respect, my argument, as it is presented here, follows Iser. Where I differ is in my concept of the text as constituting for itself a structural matrix to which all secondary structures have to be referred. Iser, on the other hand, considers the construction of meaning to be an original achievement of the reader.[16] He describes it as an essentially creative act in which the reader fills the gaps and blanks of indeterminacy, relying on the power of his imagination. Fulfilling the text by creating ever-changing constellations, the reader is drawn into fiction and experiences it as a kind of complex "reality." For Iser, the aesthetic experience of fiction consists in the process of creating and destroying illusions, and at the same time of forming and dissolving "figures" of meaning. Thus starting from moments of indeterminacy or ambiguity, the reader simultaneously experiences his own productive reception as well as a "textual reality" that never coincides with a given meaning but evolves within the framework of constantly changing perspectives.[17]

Iser's argument is most suggestive and impressive in its precision and its phenomenological perspicacity, yet it seems to give too much weight to the reader's own creative activity. Iser's theory is a theory of the variables of reception, counting on constants only on the side of the text. Since Iser does not

[16] See *The Implied Reader*, p. 290: "The moment we try to impose a consistent pattern on the text, discrepancies are bound to arise. These are, as it were, the reverse side of the interpretative coin, an involuntary product of the process that creates discrepancies by trying to avoid them. And it is their very presence that draws us into the text, compelling us to conduct a creative examination not only of the text but also of ourselves."

[17] The process of reception differs considerably, depending on whether the text is quietly read or whether it is read aloud to an audience. While a quiet reading relies solely on written language, reading aloud adds a certain stress and intonation. It thereby reduces the configurative meaning to a specific shape. But it is this reduction, restricting the possibilities of interpretation, that draws attention to the very existence of other possibilities.

discuss the problem of the possible relationships between constants and variables in the process of reception itself, his theory leaves us with a spot of indeterminacy, which accounts for its oscillation between formal and material theory. A theory that considers only the variable factors of reception cannot go beyond the statement that reception, each time, is the result of a complex of variables. Iser's preferred paradigms are the novels of Joyce, where indeed those constants of reception that had been the basis for traditional fictional texts are eliminated. Here the isolation of the hero corresponds to the isolated position of the narrator and the reader. Even if in this case a theory of the variables of reception seems adequate to illuminate the conditions of aesthetic experience, this theory seems to be insufficient insofar as traditional fiction is concerned.

Iser's theory camouflages what for me is the distinctive feature of fiction: its ability to articulate a system of perspectives, which provides an experience radically different from the experience of daily life. While in real life the "theme" can only be attained by abstracting it always anew from a context that serves as a background for what is the focus of interest, the reader of fiction experiences a preestablished relationship of theme and horizon that is set up by the text itself. This relationship constitutes the very "subject" or "theme" of the work. Not as reality, but as nonreality does fiction provide its own possibility for ordering experience or, more precisely, for prestructuring potential paradigms of experience. That is why the quasi-pragmatic reading, which creates illusions, has to be corrected not only by a different reading but also by a form of reception that acknowledges the autoreferential character of fiction. Only then does the text disclose its dimension of self-interpretation, to which the reader's interpretation should primarily be bound, and display its intended imbalance of determinacy and indeterminacy, which is destroyed when the textual gaps are filled by the reader's own creativity. It is this imbalance inherent in the text that directs the implied reader's interest in the fictional situation of communication.

The Reading of Fictional Texts

What I have called the text's "predominant scheme" [*Relevanzfigur*] is the manifestation of a thematic dynamics through the gradual unfolding of a certain number of successive contexts, as in the extensive dynamics of the novel, or through the coexistence of simultaneous contexts, as in the intensive dynamics of poetry. By articulating a predominant scheme, and only through this articulation, the fictional text provides us with an experience that does not have to be derived from some extratextual reality, but which is contained in the aesthetic, meaningfully constructed world of the work itself. It should be emphasized that the schematized views of fictional texts do not correspond to those of everyday life: they have to be worked out in the text where they have their specific textual functions. Creative fiction writing establishes, or at least experiments with, new systems of perspectives.[18] The world of fiction is a competitive world of new views and new ways of presenting them. We may thus think of fiction as shaping the horizon of our everyday life by providing us with new models for the organization of our experience.

We can fully understand the predominant scheme of a fictional text only by paying close attention to textual structures, and by keeping in mind its autoreferential nature. Iser, too, stresses the self-referential character of fictional discourse. To him, however, this is not the goal of fictional discourse but its point of departure: "The auto-reflexive character of fictional discourse provides the imagination with the necessary conditions for producing an imaginary object."[19] Iser considers "the evocation of nonpresent or absent phenomena" the specific achievement of autoreferentiality.[20] But this particular feature is not unique to fictional texts, because historiog-

[18] Flaubert's new definition of style as "manière absolue de voir les choses" (Letter to Louise Colet, dated January 16, 1852, in *Extraits de la Correspondance*, p. 63) could be exempted from any metaphysical meaning and interpreted as the intention to liberate writing from stereotyped systems of perspectives and their corresponding verbal clichés.

[19] "Die Wirklichkeit der Fiktion," in R. Warning, ed., *Rezeptionsästhetik: Theorie und Praxis* (Munich, 1975), p. 292 [author's translation]. For a translated and revised version of this article see "The Reality of Fiction."

[20] "Die Wirklichkeit der Fiktion," p. 291.

101

raphy, too, evokes "absent" phenomena. This concept of self-referentiality, which for Iser is only of interest insofar as it provides the necessary conditions for creative reception, is of major importance in understanding fictional texts. Thus fiction can no longer be regarded as an "event" that has to be ordered and given a meaning by the reader. On the contrary, it should be thought of as the unique manifestation of a more or less complex organization of concepts that constitute its overall design [*Relevanzfigur*], and that present it as a paradigm for experience. Under this condition the indeterminacy, the incompleteness, and the fragmentary nature of fiction acquire a theoretical status they could never have if we only considered the reader's own creativity.[21] The *opera aperta* can only get its proper reading when it is not prematurely transformed by a quasi-pragmatic reading into what might appear to be a *completed* "figure of meaning." Only by changing the quasi-pragmatic reading into a reflexive one can all aspects of the work, as well as its potential openness, be taken into consideration. In his study *Pour une théorie de la production littéraire*, Pierre Macherey has criticized, from the perspective of literary production, Umberto Eco's theory of the *opera aperta* and the role it attributes to the reader's creative completion.[22] It seems that even Iser's much more sophisticated approach does not escape this criticism: "What is unstated in a book is not to be taken as a void to be filled, a loss that should be recovered. We are not dealing with a temporary lack that might definitely be taken care of. We must acknowledge the necessary status of all that is 'unsaid' in a given work."[23]

The reception of fictional texts has to be sustained by a

[21] In this context, Karl Maurer suggested a relevant distinction between "gaps of information" and "empty spaces" that have to be filled by the reader ("Formen des Lesens," paper presented at the Tagung des Deutschen Romanistenverbandes, October 1975, in Mannheim). However, it should be pointed out that even fictional "openness" presupposes the principle of fictional "completeness."

[22] *Pour une théorie de la production littéraire* (Paris, 1970); *Opera aperta* (Milan, 1962).

[23] *Pour une théorie de la production littéraire*, p. 103 [editor's translation].

theoretical orientation that allows us to see the implications of textual gaps and inconsistencies. Fictional texts ask the reader to construct experimental schematized views that exceed the horizon of his everyday life, and that open new experiences to him.

The self-referential nature of a fictional text requires the reader to see its formal structures against the horizon of its content structures. While reading a fictional text, the reader has to consider the pseudoreferential character of its content, and to refer content back to the concepts that manifest it. Thus form plays a dominant role in fictional texts, since it determines their structure and the type of response they elicit. In order to avoid possible misunderstandings, this argument has to be further explained. The formal aspect of fiction can be reduced neither to an aesthetics of form following the doctrine of *l'art pour l'art* nor to the idea of a strictly immanent structural order. The character of fictional form is determined by its particular function of organizing concepts as potential schemes for the organization of experience. Fictional representation, and here I agree with Iser, is not representation of the world but representation of possible forms of organization for experience.

The *signifié* of the fictional text is the *signifiant* of its form. This neither includes nor excludes the mimetic relation of the *signifié* to reality. Fictional texts are broader in scope than referential texts, since they project forms of "possible" experience, which they concretize as schematized views. Only the reflexive turning back from mimetic illusion—produced by a quasi-pragmatic reading—to fiction and its pseudoreferential articulation discloses the formal aspect of fiction.

While there are fictional texts that presuppose a straightforward, quasi-pragmatic reading, there are texts whose very form requires a reflexive reading. Novels like Flaubert's *L'Education sentimentale*, Proust's *A la recherche du temps perdu*, and Thomas Mann's *Der Zauberberg* disclose their meaning only against the horizon of a second reading, thus turning their composition into their very theme. In these novels, the reader's customary first impulse to be carried along by the

Karlheinz Stierle

centrifugal movement of reception is held in check by the manner of composition itself. This procedure applies above all to poets like Mallarmé, who organized his fiction in such a way that it excluded any quasi-pragmatic reading. He considered quasi-pragmatic readings entirely insufficient, and deliberately composed his poems as fictions by following a highly developed concept of fictionality that is still valid today. For him, fiction and reflexion are inseparably related, and the poetics of his poems corresponds to this concept. In his poems, a syntactic technique of suspense combined with semantic ambiguity delays the transition from *signifiant* to *signifié* and draws the attention to language itself as the poetic medium. His poems are paradigms for what we have called the reversal of the relationship between theme and horizon. The theme, which in Mallarmé's poems appears against the horizon of meaning, is the concreteness of the verbal act as such. Only then, in a process of continuous reversal, does a contextual meaning emerge, which cannot, however, be detached from its verbal structure. Besides syntactic suspense and semantic ambiguity, which has to be eliminated in the process of constructing a context of meaning, negation is another device essential to Mallarmé's poetics of autoreferentiality. Instead of stimulating referential illusion, negation in fiction leads back to the pure scheme of a conceptual configuration without any referential status.[24]

Mallarmé's theory marks the beginning of a tradition that considers autoreferentiality an essential feature of fiction, thereby excluding every possibility of a quasi-pragmatic reading. The fact that modern fiction cannot be transformed anymore into mere illusion is not to be taken as an act of provocation that is to encourage the reader to come up with a quasi-referential reading through his own creative efforts. Instead, his role is to perform the reflexive movement of reception that is prestructured by the very form of fiction. Only a mode of reading that transcends quasi-pragmatic reception

[24] For a more detailed discussion, see my essay "Position and Negation in Mallarmé's 'Prose pour des Esseintes,' " in *Yale French Studies*, no. 54 (1977), 96-117.

The Reading of Fictional Texts

will enable us to comprehend this particularly modern form of fiction. Francis Ponge's descriptive texts—in which the experience of objects converges with the experience of language—as well as the verbal games of the most recent novels of Claude Simon, Jean Ricardou, and Philippe Sollers, follow this tradition and would have been inconceivable without Mallarmé's theory of fiction. But already Gertrude Stein, before Joyce, follows this idea of fiction. In the enigmatic short texts of *Tender Buttons*, for instance, meaning cannot be construed by establishing references but only by considering the referential openness as the horizon of a formal syntactic organization of concepts, which is the text's very poetic theme. The semantic material is purposefully disconnected in order to emphasize the organizational power of language on the syntactic level and its primary role in shaping the text.

By exploring the possibilities of fiction, experimental literature challenges the reader to new modes of reading, thereby increasing the given repertoire of reception. The new reading procedures required by modern experimental fiction, as well as progress in the field of theory, provide us with new approaches to past fiction as well, thus enabling us to broaden our experience with literary texts.

Translated by Inge Crosman
and Thekla Zachrau

Wolfgang Iser | # Interaction between Text and Reader

Central to the reading of every literary work is the interaction between its structure and its recipient. This is why the phenomenological theory of art has emphatically drawn attention to the fact that the study of a literary work should concern not only the actual text but also, and in equal measure, the actions involved in responding to that text. The text itself simply offers "schematized aspects"[1] through which the aesthetic object of the work can be produced.

From this we may conclude that the literary work has two poles, which we might call the artistic and the aesthetic: the artistic pole is the author's text, and the aesthetic is the realization accomplished by the reader. In view of this polarity, it is clear that the work itself cannot be identical with the text or with its actualization but must be situated somewhere between the two. It must inevitably be virtual in character, as it cannot be reduced to the reality of the text or to the subjectivity of the reader, and it is from this virtuality that it derives its dynamism. As the reader passes through the various perspectives offered by the text, and relates the different views and patterns to one another, he sets the work in motion, and so sets himself in motion, too.

If the virtual position of the work is between text and reader, its actualization is clearly the result of an interaction between the two, and so exclusive concentration on either the

---

* This essay contains a few ideas which are dealt with more comprehensively in my book *The Act of Reading: A Theory of Aesthetic Response* (The Johns Hopkins University Press: Baltimore, 1978).

[1] See Roman Ingarden, *The Literary Work of Art*, trans. George G. Grabowicz (Evanston, Ill., 1973), pp. 276ff.

Interaction between Text and Reader

author's techniques or the reader's psychology will tell us little about the reading process itself. This is not to deny the
vital importance of each of the two poles—it is simply that if
one loses sight of the relationship, one loses sight of the virtual work. Despite its uses, separate analysis would only be
conclusive if the relationship were that of transmitter and receiver, for this would presuppose a common code, ensuring
accurate communication since the message would only be
traveling one way. In literary works, however, the message is
transmitted in two ways, in that the reader "receives" it by
composing it. There is no common code—at best one could
say that a common code may arise in the course of the process. Starting out from this assumption, we must search for
structures that will enable us to describe basic conditions of
interaction, for only then shall we be able to gain some insight into the potential effects inherent in the work.

It is difficult to describe this interaction, not least because
literary criticism has very little to go on in the way of guide-
lines, and, of course, the two partners in the communication
process, namely, the text and the reader, are far easier to
analyze than is the event that takes place between them.
However, there are discernible conditions that govern interaction generally, and some of these will certainly apply to
the special reader-text relationship. The differences and
similarities may become clear if we briefly examine types of
interaction that have emerged from psychoanalytical research
into the structure of communication. The findings of the
Tavistock School will serve us as a model in order to move the
problem into focus.[2]

In assessing interpersonal relationships R. D. Laing writes:
"I may not actually be able to see myself as others see me, but
I am constantly supposing them to be seeing me in particular
ways, and I am constantly acting in the light of the actual or
supposed attitudes, opinions, needs, and so on the other has
in respect of me."[3] Now, the views that others have of me

[2] R. D. Laing, H. Phillipson, A. R. Lee, *Interpersonal Perception: A Theory
and a Method of Research* (New York, 1966).
[3] Ibid., p. 4.

Wolfgang Iser

cannot be called "pure" perception; they are the result of interpretation. And this need for interpretation arises from the structure of interpersonal experience. We have experience of one another insofar as we know one another's conduct; but we have no experience of how others experience us.

In his book, *The Politics of Experience*, Laing pursues this line of thought by saying: *"your experience of me is invisible to me and my experience of you is invisible to you.* I cannot experience your experience. You cannot experience my experience. We are both invisible men. All men are invisible to one another. Experience is man's invisibility to man."[4] It is this invisibility, however, that forms the basis of interpersonal relations—a basis which Laing calls "no-thing."[5] "That which is really 'between' cannot be named by any things that come between. The between is itself no-thing."[6] In all our interpersonal relations we build upon this "no-thing," for we react as if we knew how our partners experienced us; we continually form views of their views, and then act as if our views of their views were realities. Contact therefore depends upon our continually filling in a central gap in our experience. Thus, dyadic and dynamic interaction comes about only because we are unable to experience how we experience one another, which in turn proves to be a propellant to interaction. Out of this fact arises the basic need for interpretation, which regulates the whole process of interaction. As we cannot perceive without preconception, each percept, in turn, only makes sense to us if it is processed, for pure perception is quite impossible. Hence dyadic interaction is not given by nature but arises out of an interpretative activity, which will contain a view of others and, unavoidably, an image of ourselves.

An obvious and major difference between reading and all forms of social interaction is the fact that with reading there is

---

[4] Laing, *The Politics of Experience* (Harmondsworth, 1968), p. 16. Laing's italics.

[5] Ibid., p. 34.

[6] Ibid.

Interaction between Text and Reader

no *face-to-face-situation*.[7] A text cannot adapt itself to each reader it comes into contact with. The partners in dyadic interaction can ask each other questions in order to ascertain how far their images have bridged the gap of the inexperienceability of one another's experiences. The reader, however, can never learn from the text how accurate or inaccurate are his views of it. Furthermore, dyadic interaction serves specific purposes, so that the interaction always has a regulative context, which often serves as a *tertium comparationis*. There is no such frame of reference governing the text-reader relationship; on the contrary, the codes which might regulate this interaction are fragmented in the text, and must first be reassembled or, in most cases, restructured before any frame of reference *can* be established. Here, then, in conditions and intention, we find two basic differences between the text-reader relationship and the dyadic interaction between social partners.

Now, it is the very lack of ascertainability and defined intention that brings about the text-reader interaction, and here there is a vital link with dyadic interaction. Social communication, as we have seen, arises out of the fact that people cannot experience how others experience them, and not out of the common situation or out of the conventions that join both partners together. The situations and conventions regulate the manner in which gaps are filled, but the gaps in turn arise out of the inexperienceability and, consequently, function as a basic inducement to communication. Similarly, it is the gaps, the fundamental asymmetry between text and reader, that give rise to communication in the reading process; the lack of a common situation and a common frame of reference corresponds to the "no-thing," which brings about the interaction between persons. Asymmetry and the "no-thing" are all different forms of an indeterminate, constitutive blank, which underlies all processes of interaction. With dyadic in-

[7] See also E. Goffman, *Interaction Ritual: Essays on Face-to-Face Behavior* (New York, 1967).

Wolfgang Iser

teraction, the imbalance is removed by the establishment of pragmatic connections resulting in an action, which is why the preconditions are always clearly defined in relation to situations and common frames of reference. The imbalance between text and reader, however, is undefined, and it is this very indeterminacy that increases the variety of communication possible.

Now, if communication between text and reader is to be successful, clearly the reader's activity must also be controlled in some way by the text. The control cannot be as specific as in a *face-to-face-situation*, equally it cannot be as determinate as a social code, which regulates social interaction. However, the guiding devices operative in the reading process have to initiate communication and to control it. This control cannot be understood as a tangible entity occurring independently of the process of communication. Athough exercised *by* the text, it is not *in* the text. This is well illustrated by a comment Virginia Woolf made on the novels of Jane Austen:

> Jane Austen is thus a mistress of much deeper emotion than appears upon the surface. She stimulates us to supply what is not there. What she offers is, apparently, a trifle, yet is composed of something that expands in the reader's mind and endows with the most enduring form of life scenes which are outwardly trivial. Always the stress is laid upon character. . . . The turns and twists of the dialogue keep us on the tenterhooks of suspense. Our attention is half upon the present moment, half upon the future. . . . Here, indeed, in this unfinished and in the main inferior story, are all the elements of Jane Austen's greatness.[8]

What is missing from the apparently trivial scenes, the gaps arising out of the dialogue—this is what stimulates the

[8] Virginia Woolf, *The Common Reader: First Series* (London, 1957), p. 174. In this context, it is well worth considering Virginia Woolf's comments on the composition of her own fictional characters. She remarks in her diary: "I'm

Interaction between Text and Reader

reader into filling the blanks with projections. He is drawn into the events and made to supply what is meant from what is not said. What is said only appears to take on significance as a reference to what is not said; it is the implications and not the statements that give shape and weight to the meaning. But as the unsaid comes to life in the reader's imagination, so the said "expands" to take on greater significance than might have been supposed: even trivial scenes can seem surprisingly profound. The "enduring form of life" which Virginia Woolf speaks of is not manifested on the printed page; it is a product arising out of the interaction between text and reader.

Communication in literature, then, is a process set in motion and regulated, not by a given code, but by a mutually restrictive and magnifying interaction between the explicit and the implicit, between revelation and concealment. What is concealed spurs the reader into action, but this action is also controlled by what is revealed; the explicit in its turn is transformed when the implicit has been brought to light. Whenever the reader bridges the gaps, communication begins. The gaps function as a kind of pivot on which the whole text-reader relationship revolves. Hence, the structured blanks of the text stimulate the process of ideation to be per-

---

thinking furiously about Reading and Writing. I have no time to describe my plans. I should say a good deal about *The Hours* and my discovery: how I dig out beautiful caves behind my characters: I think that gives exactly what I want; humanity, humour, depth. The idea is that the caves shall connect and each comes to daylight at the present moment." *A Writer's Diary: Being Extracts from the Diary of Virginia Woolf*, ed. Leonard Woolf (London, 1953), p. 60. The suggestive effect of the "beautiful caves" is continued in her work through what she leaves out. On this subject, T. S. Eliot once observed: "Her observation, which operates in a continuous way, implies a vast and sustained work of organization. She does not illumine with sudden bright flashes but diffuses a soft and placid light. Instead of looking for the primitive, she looks rather for the civilized, the highly civilized, where nevertheless something is found to be *left out*. And this something is deliberately left out, by what could be called a moral effort of the will. And, being left out, this something is, in a sense, in a melancholy sense, present." "T. S. Eliot 'Places' Virginia Woolf for French Readers," in *Virginia Woolf: The Critical Heritage*, ed. Robin Majumdar and Allen McLaurin (London, 1975), p. 192.

Wolfgang Iser

formed by the reader on terms set by the text. There is, however, another place in the textual system where text and reader converge, and that is marked by the various types of negation which arise in the course of the reading. Blanks and negations both control the process of communication in their own different ways: the blanks leave open the connection between textual perspectives, and so spur the reader into coordinating these perspectives and patterns—in other words, they induce the reader to perform basic operations *within* the text. The various types of negation invoke familiar and determinate elements or knowledge only to cancel them out. What is cancelled, however, remains in view, and thus brings about modifications in the reader's attitude toward what is familiar or determinate—in other words, he is guided to adopt a position *in relation* to the text.

In order to spotlight the communication process we shall confine our consideration to how the blanks trigger off and simultaneously control the reader's activity. Blanks indicate that the different segments and patterns of the text are to be connected even though the text itself does not say so. They are the unseen joints of the text, and as they mark off schemata and textual perspectives from one another, they simultaneously prompt acts of ideation on the reader's part. Consequently when the schemata and perspectives have been linked together, the blanks "disappear."

If we are to grasp the unseen structure that regulates but does not formulate the connection or even the meaning, we must bear in mind the various forms in which the textual segments are presented to the reader's viewpoint in the reading process. Their most elementary form is to be seen on the level of the story. The threads of the plot are suddenly broken off, or continued in unexpected directions. One narrative section centers on a particular character and is then continued by the abrupt introduction of new characters. These sudden changes are often denoted by new chapters and so are clearly distinguished; the object of this distinction, however, is not separation so much as a tacit invitation to find the missing link. Furthermore, in each articulated reading moment, only

Interaction between Text and Reader

segments of textual perspectives are present to the reader's wandering viewpoint.

In order to become fully aware of the implication, we must bear in mind that a narrative text, for instance, is composed of a variety of perspectives, which outline the author's view and also provide access to what the reader is meant to visualize. As a rule, there are four main perspectives in narration: those of the narrator, the characters, the plot, and the fictitious reader. Although these may differ in order of importance, none of them on its own is identical to the meaning of the text, which is to be brought about by their constant intertwining through the reader in the reading process. An increase in the number of blanks is bound to occur through the frequent subdivisions of each of the textual perspectives; thus the narrator's perspective is often split into that of the implied author's set against that of the author as narrator. The hero's perspective may be set against that of the minor characters. The fictitious reader's perspective may be divided between the explicit position ascribed to him and the implicit attitude he must adopt to that position.

As the reader's wandering viewpoint travels between all these segments, its constant switching during the time flow of reading intertwines them, thus bringing forth a network of perspectives, within which each perspective opens a view not only of others, but also of the intended imaginary object. Hence no single textual perspective can be equated with this imaginary object, of which it forms only one aspect. The object itself is a product of interconnection, the structuring of which is to a great extent regulated and controlled by blanks.

In order to explain this operation, we shall first give a schematic description of how the blanks function, and then we shall try to illustrate this function with an example. In the time flow of reading, segments of the various perspectives move into focus and are set off against preceding segments. Thus the segments of characters, narrator, plot, and fictitious reader perspectives are not only marshaled into a graduated sequence but are also transformed into reciprocal reflectors. The blank as an empty space between segments enables them

Wolfgang Iser

to be joined together, thus constituting a field of vision for the wandering viewpoint. A referential field is always formed when there are at least two positions related to and influencing one another—it is the minimal organizational unit in all processes of comprehension,[9] and it is also the basic organizational unit of the wandering viewpoint.

The first structural quality of the blank, then, is that it makes possible the organization of a referential field of interacting textual segments projecting themselves one upon another. Now, the segments present in the field are structurally of equal value, and the fact that they are brought together highlights their affinities and their differences. This relationship gives rise to a tension that has to be resolved, for, as Arnheim has observed in a more general context: "It is one of the functions of the third dimension to come to the rescue when things get uncomfortable in the second."[10] The third dimension comes about when the segments of the referential field are given a common framework, which allows the reader to relate affinities and differences and so to grasp the patterns underlying the connections. But this framework is also a blank, which requires an act of ideation in order to be filled. It is as if the blank in the field of the reader's viewpoint had changed its position. It began as the empty space between perspective segments, indicating their connectability, and so organizing them into projections of reciprocal influence. But with the establishment of this connectability the blank, as the unformulated framework of these interacting segments, now enables the reader to produce a determinate relationship between them. We may infer already from this change in position that the blank exercises significant control over all the operations that occur within the referential field of the wandering viewpoint.

Now we come to the third and most decisive function of the blank. Once the segments have been connected and a

[9] See Aron Gurwitsch, *The Field of Consciousness* (Pittsburgh, 1964), pp. 309-75.

[10] Rudolf Arnheim, *Toward a Psychology of Art* (Berkeley and Los Angeles, 1967), p. 239.

Interaction between Text and Reader

determinate relationship established, a referential field is formed which constitutes a particular reading moment, and which in turn has a discernible structure. The grouping of segments within the referential field comes about, as we have seen, by making the viewpoint switch between the perspective segments. The segment on which the viewpoint focuses in each particular moment becomes the theme. The theme of one moment becomes the background against which the next segment takes on its actuality, and so on. Whenever a segment becomes a theme, the previous one must lose its thematic relevance[11] and be turned into a marginal, thematically vacant position, which can be and usually is occupied by the reader so that he may focus on the new thematic segment.

In this connection it might be more appropriate to designate the marginal or horizontal position as a vacancy and not as a blank; blanks refer to suspended connectability in the text, vacancies refer to nonthematic segments within the referential field of the wandering viewpoint. Vacancies, then, are important guiding devices for building up the aesthetic object, because they condition the reader's view of the new theme, which in turn conditions his view of previous themes. These modifications, however, are not formulated in the text—they are to be implemented by the reader's ideational activity. And so these vacancies enable the reader to combine segments into a field by reciprocal modification, to form positions from those fields, and then to adapt each position to its successor and predecessors in a process that ultimately transforms the textual perspectives, through a whole range of alternating themes and background relationships, into the aesthetic object of the text.

Let us turn now to an example in order to illustrate the operations sparked off and governed by the vacancies in the referential field of the wandering viewpoint. For this reason we shall have a brief look at Fielding's *Tom Jones* and again, in particular, at the characters' perspective: that of the hero and

[11] For a discussion of the problem of changing relevance and abandoned thematic relevance, see Alfred Schütz, *Das Problem der Relevanz*, trans. A. v. Baeyer (Frankfurt am Main, 1970), pp. 104ff., 145ff.

115

Wolfgang Iser

that of the minor characters. Fielding's aim of depicting human nature is fulfilled by way of a repertoire that incorporates the prevailing norms of eighteenth-century thought systems and social systems and represents them as governing the conduct of the most important characters. In general, these norms are arranged in more or less explicitly contrasting patterns; Allworthy (*benevolence*) is set against Squire Western (*ruling passion*); the same applies to the two pedagogues, Square (*the eternal fitness of things*) and Thwackum (*the human mind as a sink of iniquity*), who in turn are also contrasted with Allworthy and so forth.

Thus in the individual situations, the hero is linked up with the norms of latitudinarian morality, orthodox theology, deistic philosophy, eighteenth-century anthropology, and eighteenth-century aristocracy. Contrasts and discrepancies within the perspective of the characters give rise to the missing links, which enable the hero and the norms to shed light upon one another, and through which the individual situations may combine into a referential field. The hero's conduct cannot be subsumed under the norms, and through the sequence of situations the norms shrink to a reified manifestation of human nature. This, however, is already an observation which the reader must make for himself, because such syntheses are rarely given in the text, even though they are prefigured in the theme-and-background structure. The discrepancies continually arising between the perspectives of hero and minor characters bring about a series of changing positions, with each theme losing its relevance but remaining in the background to influence and condition its successor. Whenever the hero violates the norms—as he does most of the time—the resultant situation may be judged in one or two different ways: either the norm appears as a drastic reduction of human nature, in which case we view the theme from the standpoint of the hero, or the violation shows the imperfections of human nature, in which case it is the norm that conditions our view.

In both cases, we have the same structure of interacting positions being transformed into a determinate meaning. For those characters that represent a norm—in particular Allwor-

Interaction between Text and Reader

thy, Squire Western, Square, and Thwackum—human nature is defined in terms of one principle, so that all those possibilities which are not in harmony with the principle are given a negative slant. But when the negated possibilities exert their influence upon the course of events, and so show up the limitations of the principle concerned, the norms begin to appear in a different light. The apparently negative aspects of human nature fight back, as it were, against the principle itself and cast doubt upon it in proportion to its limitations.

In this way, the negation of other possibilities by the norm in question gives rise to a virtual diversification of human nature, which takes on a definite form to the extent that the norm is revealed as a restriction on human nature. The reader's attention is now fixed, not upon what the norms represent, but upon what their representation excludes, and so the aesthetic object—which is the whole spectrum of human nature—begins to arise out of what is adumbrated by the negated possibilities. In this way, the function of the norms themselves has changed: they no longer represent the social regulators prevalent in the thought systems of the eighteenth century, but instead they indicate the amount of human experience which they suppress because, as rigid principles, they cannot tolerate any modifications.

Transformations of this kind take place whenever the norms are the foregrounded theme and the perspective of the hero remains the background conditioning the reader's viewpoint. But whenever the hero becomes the theme, and the norms of the minor characters shape the viewpoint, his well-intentioned spontaneity turns into the depravity of an impulsive nature. Thus the position of the hero is also transformed, for it is no longer the standpoint from which we are to judge the norms; instead we see that even the best of intentions may come to nought if they are not guided by *circumspection*, and spontaneity must be controlled by *prudence*[12] if it is to allow a possibility of self-preservation.

The transformations brought about by the theme-and-

[12] See Henry Fielding, *Tom Jones*, iii.7 and xviii, Chapter the Last (London, 1962), pp. 92, 427.

Wolfgang Iser

background interaction are closely connected with the changing position of the vacancy within the referential field. Once a theme has been grasped, conditioned by the marginal position of the preceding segment, a feedback is bound to occur, thus retroactively modifying the shaping influence of the reader's viewpoint. This reciprocal transformation is hermeneutic by nature, even though we may not be aware of the processes of interpretation resulting from the switching and reciprocal conditioning of our viewpoints. In this sense, the vacancy transforms the referential field of the moving viewpoint into a self-regulating structure, which proves to be one of the most important links in the interaction between text and reader, and which prevents the reciprocal transformation of textual segments from being arbitrary.

To sum up, then, the blank in the fictional text induces and guides the reader's constitutive activity. As a suspension of connectability between textual perspective and perspective segments, it marks the need for an equivalence, thus transforming the segments into reciprocal projections, which in turn organize the reader's wandering viewpoint as a referential field. The tension that occurs within the field between heterogeneous perspective segments is resolved by the theme-and-background structure, which makes the viewpoint focus on one segment as the theme, to be grasped from the thematically vacant position now occupied by the reader as his standpoint. Thematically vacant positions remain present in the background against which new themes occur; they condition and influence those themes and are also retroactively influenced by them, for as each theme recedes into the background of its successor, the vacancy shifts, allowing for a reciprocal transformation to take place. As the vacancy is structured by the sequence of positions in the time flow of reading, the reader's viewpoint cannot proceed arbitrarily; the thematically vacant position always acts as the angle from which a selective interpretation is to be made.

Two points need to be emphasized: (1) we have described the structure of the blank in an abstract, somewhat idealized way in order to explain the pivot on which the interaction between text and reader turns; (2) the blank has different struc-

Interaction between Text and Reader

tural qualities, which appear to dovetail. The reader fills in the blank in the text, thereby bringing about a referential field; the blank arising in turn out of the referential field is filled in by way of the theme-and-background structure; and the vacancy arising from juxtaposed themes and backgrounds is occupied by the reader's standpoint, from which the various reciprocal transformations lead to the emergence of the aesthetic object. The structural qualities outlined make the blank shift, so that the changing positions of the empty space mark out a definite need for determination, which the constitutive activity of the reader is to fulfill. In this sense, the shifting blank maps out the path along which the wandering viewpoint is to travel, guided by the self-regulatory sequence in which the structural qualities of the blank interlock.

Now we are in a position to qualify more precisely what is actually meant by reader participation in the text. If the blank is largely responsible for the activities described, then participation means that the reader is not simply called upon to "internalize" the positions given in the text, but he is induced to make them act upon and so transform each other, as a result of which the aesthetic object begins to emerge. The structure of the blank organizes this participation, revealing simultaneously the intimate connection between this structure and the reading subject. This interconnection completely conforms to a remark made by Piaget: "In a word, the subject is there and alive, because the basic quality of each structure is the structuring process itself."[13] The blank in the fictional text appears to be a paradigmatic structure; its function consists in initiating structured operations in the reader, the execution of which transmits the reciprocal interaction of textual positions into consciousness. The shifting blank is responsible for a sequence of colliding images, which condition each other in the time flow of reading. The discarded image imprints itself on its successor, even though the latter is meant to resolve the deficiencies of the former. In this respect the images hang together in a sequence, and it is by this sequence that the meaning of the text comes alive in the reader's imagination.

[13] Jean Piaget, *Der Strukturalismus*, trans. L. Häfliger (Olten, 1973), p. 134.

Christine Brooke-Rose | # The Readerhood of Man

Hypocrite lecteur, mon semblable, mon frère.

After a long period when the Real (I prefer Actual) Author had been enthroned by criticism, his every "laundry-list" (as Pound called biography) scrutinized, he was, in true carnivalesque fashion, unthroned, the wild and happy crowd of Actual Readers taking over—but, as is the way with carnival, only for a time. Extremes bring natural reactions, and the two polarities, called at the time the Intentional and the Affective Fallacies, seem to have compromised on a safe buffer state called The Text as Object, an apparently autonomous unit that encodes both its author (implied), or addresser, and its reader (implied), or addressee.

Buffer states, however, rarely remain safe or buffer, and wars (or carnivals) continue. Curiously enough, it is from a one-time actual buffer state, Poland, that there emerged the most interesting theory of the literary work of art as an "intentional" object:[1] that is, a product of acts of consciousness, different from "ideal" objects in that it is subject to contingencies and is not eternal as, say, a triangle is eternal, and different from "real" objects in that it transcends itself by designating something other than itself, as does a word or a sentence. Analysis, according to Roman Ingarden, must therefore eschew both psychologism and empiricism, to be replaced by "eidetic" (*eidos*, "essence") reduction.

---

[1] Roman Ingarden, *O dziele literackim* (Warsaw, 1931), in English *The Literary Work of Art*, trans. George Grabowicz (Evanston, Ill., 1973).

The Readerhood of Man

Ingarden is extremely complex and I shall not attempt to describe him here,[2] but I shall merely stress the fact that, to quote Earl Miner, we should "postulate four entities: an original creator of aesthetic knowledge, aesthetic knowledge about the world, a physical means of expression, and via the physical means of expression a re-knowing of the created knowledge by those who are capable of reading the expression. We must recognize what literary history shows us with irrefutable fact: that we readers are incapable of knowing *Hamlet* exactly as Shakespeare knew it or exactly as other readers have known and will know it another time. These differences are real but do not destroy the integrity of the work." Or again: "no scientist would consider his knowledge of an object to be itself an object."[3] But we literary people find it very difficult not to confuse "our" reading, enriched by those of others, with the text. As a literary critic, I shall restrict myself to the reader as encoded in the text, although this again is bound to be "my" reading of the reader as so encoded—nor do I claim to escape professional deformation any more than others have, though many try.

Some critics explicitly revive and defend the author's intention as not a fallacy,[4] and some harken back to it, talking of the author's "will."[5] On the other hand, the terminology of some well-known critics who do in practice deal with the reader as encoded in the text continues to suggest actual readers, from Fish's "informed reader" to Culler's "ideal" or

[2] For recent discussions of Ingarden's work, see Earl Miner, "The Objective Fallacy," *PTL* (*Poetics and Theory of Literature*), 1 (1976), 11-31; and Olga Scherer, "Ontologie de l'oeuvre littéraire d'après Roman Ingarden," paper read at the *Colloque sur la théorie de la littérature*, Université de Paris, III, 1974, to appear in the publications of the colloquium.

[3] Miner, "The Objective Fallacy," pp. 27 and 25.

[4] See, for example, Alex Preminger et al., *The Princeton Encyclopaedia of Poetry and Poetics*, revised and enlarged ed. (Princeton, 1975); and John R. Searle, "The Logical Status of Fictional Discourse," *New Literary History* 6 (1975), 319-32.

[5] E. D. Hirsch, Jr., *Validity in Interpretation* (New Haven, 1967). For a recent discussion of Hirsch's position, see Susan Suleiman, "Interpreting Ironies," *Diacritics* 6, no. 2 (1976), 16-17.

Christine Brooke-Rose

"qualified reader" or Riffaterre's "super-reader," defined, in the famous case of Baudelaire's "Les chats," as everyone from Baudelaire to Riffaterre.[6] Culler equates "literary competence" with "linguistic competence," but he has considerably to qualify his qualified reader in order to cope with the huge relativity of literary competence as opposed to the almost absolute quality of linguistic competence that a mere child or even an illiterate person possesses once he has learned his language; nor does Culler touch on the question of whether there could in theory be an "unacceptable" text in the same sense that there are "unacceptable" (ungrammatical) sentences in language, even for an illiterate person. In a brilliant paper read at the English Institute (Cambridge, Mass., 1976),[7] he goes so far as to suggest a transformational grammar of actual readings, without, however, proposing to do it himself.

All of which makes me retreat into what the French call *le ludique*, wondering if readerhood could in theory include a hooded reader, or if the addresser is not an addressair and the addressee an addressea, or the narrataire a narratair, a narr-a-terre or a Riffaterre. I am not sure that I can now contribute more than this frivolity to the discussion. As an author (real) who wants peace-above-all, I have no objection to being unthroned and to not having my laundry lists scrutinized. However, my contribution here is as a critic, teacher, and (real) reader.

First, I shall retain the more neutral term *encoded reader*, which makes my option for the textual buffer state clear. Second, I shall stick to very simple problems in simple narratives, on the grounds that these reveal encoded structures more easily than do complex poems or even complex narratives. Finally, I shall divide my material into three broad categories: texts in which a code is overdetermined, texts in which it is underdetermined, and texts in which it is non-

[6] Stanley Fish, "Literature in the Reader: Affective Stylistics," *New Literary History* 2 (1970); Jonathan Culler, *Structuralist Poetics* (Ithaca, 1975); Michael Riffaterre, "Describing Poetic Structures," *Yale French Studies*, nos. 36-37 (1966), reprinted in French in *Essais de stylistique structurale* (Paris, 1971).

[7] A revised version of the paper appears in this book; see pp. 46-66.

The Readerhood of Man

determined or so haphazardly determined as to be in effect nondetermined. These are operational terms: the contrast needed to reveal the first category will automatically touch on the second (so that the first section will be longer); and the last may turn out to be a transient category.

A CODE OVERDETERMINED:
Hypocrite Lecteur

A code is overdetermined when its information (narrative, ironic, hermeneutic, symbolic, etc.) is too clear, overencoded, recurring beyond purely informational need. The reader is then in one sense also overencoded, and does in fact sometimes appear in the text, dramatized, like an extra character: the Dear Reader. But in another sense he is treated as a kind of fool who has to be told everything, a subcritical (*hypocrite*) reader.

I shall start with an ultrasimple example from an American short story very like a folk tale, in which narrative information, both proaieretic and hermeneutic,[8] is overdetermined.

In Washington Irving's "Rip Van Winkle," Rip wakes up from his adventure on the mountain, and the reader naturally supposes that this happens the next morning. No indexes suggest otherwise, or rather, the time indexes are carefully unspecified, underdetermined, although this could escape a first reading (my italics): "*On waking*, he found himself on the green knoll whence he had first seen the old man of the glen [reader assumes he was transported there after drinking from the flagon]. He rubbed his eyes—*it was a bright sunny morning*. . . . 'Surely,' thought Rip, 'I have not slept here *all night*' [counterindex 1 = one night, but in character's viewpoint]. He recalled the occurrences *before he fell asleep.*"[9]

And he gives (like the reader), a "natural" explanation:

---

[8] I shall use Roland Barthes's codes as a kind of shorthand for types of information, but clearly any other procedure would do in this particular context, nor does this represent a full use of Barthes's methods (See *S/Z* [Paris, 1970]; English trans. Richard Miller [New York, 1974]).

[9] All quotations from Irving's "Rip Van Winkle" are as printed in *Great American Short Stories*, ed. Wallace and Mary Stegner (New York, 1957).

Christine Brooke-Rose

"Oh, that flagon! That wicked flagon!" From narrator to reader, Rip's "all night" is a false clue (Barthes' *leurre*), but, on second reading, a character-error.

There follows a long series of thirty indexes, all partaking of both the proaieretic and hermeneutic codes, and upon any one of which any actual reader may guess the truth, long before Rip.

In the mountains

Index 1:	his gun is rusty	⎫	
Index 2:	his dog, Wolf, is gone	⎬ could all receive natural explanation (one night)	
Index 3:	he is stiff in joints	⎭	
Index 4:	he can't find amphitheatre	⎫ s.t.s.p. 1 (suggestion of time supernaturally passed, no. 1), but could still have natural explanation	
Index 5:	the landscape has changed (stream, where none before, etc.)	⎬⎭	

In the village

Index 6:	he meets people he does not know	s.t.s.p. 2
Index 7:	they stare at him in surprise and stroke their chins	s.t.s.p. 3
Index 8:	stroking his chin, he finds his beard is a foot long	s.t.s.p. 4
Index 9:	(change to external viewpoint) strange children hoot at him and point to his gray beard	s.t.s.p. 5
Index 10:	the dogs are unfamiliar	s.t.s.p. 6
Index 11:	the village is altered (more populous, old	

s.t.s.p. 4 ⎫
⎬ see later for implausibility
s.t.s.p. 5 ⎭

The Readerhood of Man

	haunts gone, new houses built)	s.t.s.p. 7
Counter-index 2:	the mountains and river are unaltered	provokes both natural explanation (flagon) and supernatural (bewitched)
Index 12:	his own house is decayed	s.t.s.p. 8
Index 13:	"A half-starved dog, that looked like Wolf," shows his teeth. " 'My very dog,' sighed poor Rip, 'has forgotten me.' "	clearly presented as other dog, hence character-error. As such, no s.t.s.p., but within context: s.t.s.p. 9
Index 14:	the village inn (his refuge) is different	s.t.s.p. 10
Index 15:	it has a different name and owner: "The Union Hotel, by Jonathan Doolittle."	s.t.s.p. 11. Here a specific time code s.t.c. is added (post Revolutionary War): s.t.c. 1
Index 16:	it has a different flag (descr.)	s.t.s.p. 12 + s.t.c. 2
Index 17:	the sign has changed, from King George in red coat and scepter to same face but in buff and blue coat with sword (etc.), legend General Washington	s.t.s.p. 13 + s.t.c. 3
Index 18:	the drowsy tranquillity has become bustling disputation	as such no s.t.s.p. or s.t.c., but within context: s.t.s.p. 14 + s.t.c. 4
Index 19:	his old friends (named) gone	s.t.s.p. 15
Index 20:	people speak in a	

Christine Brooke-Rose

	"Babylonish jargon"	s.t.s.p. 16 (later revealed as election talk but no s.t.c. here)
Index 21:	"The appearance of Rip, with his long grizzled beard, his rusty fowling-piece, his uncouth dress"	repeat of Indices 8 and 9 (also with external viewpoint) and of Index 1
Index 22:	questions about how he voted, Federal or Democrat, and why he brings a gun to an election	s.t.s.p. 17 + s.t.c. 5
Index 23:	accused of being a spy and threatened	as such no s.t.s.p., but within context: s.t.s.p. 18 + s.t.c. 6
Index 24:	Rip protests, only looking for neighbors, names them and himself, asks questions: where are they?	
	a) Nicholas Vedder (dead 18 years)	
	b) Brom Dutcher (killed at war)	s.t.s.p. 19
	c) Van Brummel	s.t.s.p. 20 + s.t.c. 7
	(now in Congress)	s.t.s.p. 21 + s.t.c. 8
Index 25:	"Does nobody here know Rip Van Winkle?" They point to a counterpart of himself (identity crisis for Rip, who still clings to his one-night supposition)	s.t.s.p. 22
Index 26:	young woman appears with child in her arms, whom she calls Rip	s.t.s.p. 23

The Readerhood of Man

Index 27: Rip's memories
aroused, asks her
name (Judith
Gardenier), then her
father's name (Rip
Van Winkle, who
left home twenty
years ago)   s.t.s.p. 24

Index 28: Rip has tumbled to
the truth, and only
asks: "Where is your
mother?" (dead,
though recently)   s.t.s.p. 25

Index 29: Rip embraces his
daughter and
reveals himself as
her father, much to
general amazement   s.t.s.p. 26

Index 30: an old woman
recognizes him:
"Why, where have
you been all these
twenty long years?"   s.t.s.p. 27

Then comes the "explanation," by an old inhabitant who
turns up and tells the legend of Hendrick Hudson in the
Kaatskill Mountains. The explanation is supernatural.

Clearly any actual reader, first identifying with Rip in his
puzzlement, must quickly disidentify (probably at Index 8,
and possibly before); without knowing the exact explanation,
he knows that time has mysteriously elapsed and starts
watching Rip's puzzlement instead of sharing it. The encoded reader, however, is encoded throughout the thirty
indexes, in an overdetermined way.[10]

[10] Cf. Michael Riffaterre's definition: "The effect of over-determination is
to transfer the meaning of one word to several, as if it were saturating the
sentence with that meaning, so that the reader feels the sentence keeps on
confirming overtly what he gathered from a single word." ("Semantic
Over-Determination in Poetry," *PTL* 2 [1977], 1-19.)

Christine Brooke-Rose

Interestingly, it is at Index 8 that the narrator "cheats," as it were, in the *vraisemblable* necessary to the supernatural, with the implausibly late realization by Rip about the length of his beard (one must surely *see* one's own beard if it is a foot long, especially if one is picking up a gun from the ground, looking for a dog, a path, etc.; but I am ready to be corrected by any long-bearded man). And at Index 9 the narrator switches to an external view of the beard for its color, repeating the procedure at Index 21. Such a change of viewpoint, justified only by the need to delay Rip's recognition, is like an extra encoded wink, which increases the distance between hero and encoded reader. And of course the specific time codes (s.t.c.) about the Revolutionary War, which belong to Barthes's referential code, are overclear examples of what Wayne Booth calls stable irony.[11]

This overdetermination of the hermeneutic and proaieretic codes inevitably shifts the actual reader's interpretative powers onto other codes: the semic (Rip's character) slightly, the referential (interpretations about the American virago, etc.), and the symbolic.

I realize that this sounds like the desperate teacher or critic who, unable to excuse the "bad" aspects of a classic, takes refuge in the symbolic, a sin also besetting critics of contemporary fiction in those innumerable studies of the symbolism, allegory, and thematics of otherwise mediocre works (see "Codes Nondetermined," below). But that is only the abuse of a theoretically valid procedure. As Barthes (and Frye) have shown, a work, genre, or period can exploit one code (or mode) more than others, but can be read in each or all of them, the dominance of any one or more becoming highly relevant to generic expectation. Realistic fiction tended to overdetermine the referential and the semic codes, and could, but might not, underdetermine the proaieretic and/or the hermeneutic and/or the symbolic. A folk tale will overdetermine the proaieretic and sometimes (as here) the hermeneutic, but underdetermine (or not code at all) the referential, the semic, the symbolic.

[11] See *A Rhetoric of Irony* (Chicago, 1974).

The Readerhood of Man

"Rip Van Winkle" is a relatively sophisticated folk tale, for all its overdetermination, and it appeals to us as a folk tale with sophisticated variants. Without using any complex (Greimasian or other) analysis, we can recognize most of Propp's functions,[12] occasionally displaced (e.g., *pursuit* and *rescue* shifted to the beginning as Rip's wife chases him from home and then from his refuge, the inn; *interrogation* shifted to the end and fused with *task*; *victory* shifted to the end); or if not displaced, transmuted.

There is first an exposition of the initial situation, in the iterative mode, made up in fact of all the elements that turn up later (reversed) as indexes. The *transgression* is transmuted as not serious, a charming transgression of an implicit (social) injunction to work. Dame Van Winkle is a wicked-step-mother figure indirectly responsible for Rip's escape into the mountains. Rip's "transgression" does not cause an explicit *misdeed* by a villain, or a *lack*, but his indolent nature does create a lack of marital happiness. The *mediation* (call for help) is not the king's but is assumed by the hero and motivated by his own reaction to that unhappiness. The hero *departs*, is *tested* by a "donor" (call for help by the old man of the glen), *reacts*, indirectly receives a *magic auxiliary* (the drink, albeit taken surreptitiously), which *translocates* him, it seems only in space (back to the knoll), but actually in time. The *struggle* is shifted to a more metaphysical level, but is first presented as a physical struggle with the situation and only later becomes a struggle with his own identity. There is naturally no immediate *victory*, as in Propp, but there is a physical *marking* (of age), and there is an *arrival incognito*, a *false hero's claim* (society threatening him, in his identity), a *task*, assimilated to the struggle with identity in time (he solves the task and wins the struggle by asking questions himself), a *solution*, first for himself then for others (though the encoded reader knows the answer, as in the folk tale), followed by *recognition*, through his daughter in the role of the princess whose "marking" of

[12] Vladimir Propp, *Morfologija skazki* (Moscow, 1928), in English, *Morphology of the Folk-Tale*, trans. Laurence Scott, rev. Louis A. Wagner (Austin, Tex., 1968).

Christine Brooke-Rose

the hero (identity through name and blood) leads to the identification and is the more metaphysical counterpart to the
physical marking of age.

Above all there is an (ironic) *transfiguration*: Rip is no longer
the reckless young fellow but a respected patriarch; and an
(ironic) *reward* (Propp's "wedding" function): he goes to live
with his daughter and, as a respected patriarch, is not required to work. This is also his victory: he has all the peace
and comfort of marriage (albeit incestuous) without the responsibility and the nagging. He has paid a heavy price for it,
that of his youth and lived experience, but he is evidently
happy to pay it.

Even the actual reader who has not read Propp will, from a
general as opposed to a skilled literary competence (and this
general competence is the closest analogy to linguistic competence), be familiar with and recognize these folklore elements. But they are underdetermined; they have, as it were,
shifted into the symbolic code. The "villain," in fact, is really
Time, itself ambiguous: (1) working time (society versus laziness); and (2) free time (society and Rip's good relations with
it—he helps everyone except himself). His wife, often
thought to be the villain, is merely a specific manifestation of
the real villain, society in its bad aspect. She is punished by
death (Time). He is rewarded by the free time of old age, but
is also punished by the loss of youth (Time). Good society
(for him) has won, even if bad society (for others) goes on
(wars, political disputations). What we have is not, as some
critics have argued, an attack on the American Woman, but a
typical American story of the hero opting out of society. And
all this, including the carefully balanced rhetorical structure,
belongs to the symbolic code, which is underdetermined.

I have spent some time on a simple narrative in order to
overdetermine my point about overdetermination. With or
without a Proppian (or any other) analysis, and even if this
reading can be disputed, it is clear that overdetermination in
one area does not alter our feeling of something else being
there, less immediately accessible, which gives the story its
charm and quality (to use evaluative words), or (to avoid
them) its underlying structure and coherence.

The Readerhood of Man

If this is true, we can only conclude that whatever over-determination may occur in any one work or genre, some underdetermination is necessary for it to retain its hold over us, its peculiar mixture of recognition-pleasure and mystery.

In other words, the function of the overdetermined part of a text is to make things clear to the Dear Reader who is encoded as hypo-critical, while the function of the underdetermined part is to blur, to keep something back (and it may be much more in a complex text), so as not to insult the Dear Reader's intelligence enough to alienate him.

So I shall turn to a very different kind of text, Flann O'Brien's *At Swim-Two-Birds* (1939), which uses a very sophisticated form of overdetermination, in the best Sterne tradition.

The novel opens with the I-narrator disagreeing that one beginning is sufficient for a novel, and giving examples of three separate beginnings: the first about "the Pooka Mac Phellimey, a member of the devil class"; the second about Mr. John Furriskey, who "had one distinction that is rarely encountered—he was born at the age of twenty-five and entered the world with a memory but without a personal experience to account for it"; and the third about Finn Mac Cool, "a legendary hero of old Ireland."[13]

The I-narrator then takes over again in an extremely episodic narrative about himself (a lazy student), his uncle, his friends, his uncle's friends: a nonnarrative, in fact, that is frequently broken into by, and frequently breaks back into, other narratives produced by the student while he pretends to work in his room; these narratives are often discussed with his friends, and concern, among others, the above three personages.

The first of the narratives, however, is about a Mr. Dermot Trellis, author, who lives at the Red Swan Hotel with the characters he creates, and who locks them up at night so that they will not be up to any mischief while he sleeps. Mr. Trellis, like the narrator, writes in bed, and creates characters fully grown (such as Mr. Furriskey, and as does any novelist),

---

[13] All quotations are from the Penguin Modern Classics edition (London, 1967).

131

Christine Brooke-Rose

which amazing scientific feat calls for extracts from the press, including a medical correspondent, who claims, however, that some of the research was done by a Mr. William Tracy, another author. It turns out that most of the characters in the book (except those at the narrator's level) have been created by Mr. Trellis (himself created by the narrator), and that some of them also remember episodes experienced in Mr. Tracy's books. The narrator had earlier expressed certain views of the novel according to which "characters should be interchangeable as between one book and another. . . . The modern novel should be largely a work of reference. Most authors spend their time saying what has been said before—usually said much better." Characters are not only said to be "used" or "employed" by an author, but "hired."

Mr. Dermot Trellis creates the Pooka, Finn, Mr. Furriskey, and his friends, some of whom tell stories about other characters or quote poets who then appear in the "story" (such as it is). Finn tells ambling and incoherent legends, mostly about Sweeney, a traveling, outcast bird-creature who utters poems. At one point Finn appears to be Mr. Trellis, half asleep in the same room. Mr. Trellis also makes an indecent assault on one of his own characters (to protect whose virtue he had created her brother), the result of which is Orlick Trellis, to whose birth at the Red Swan all the other characters travel, coming across each other on the way. Orlick Trellis is, of course, also born adult, and Furriskey and his friends, perceiving that Dermot Trellis is becoming immune to the drugs they give him to keep him asleep while they act independently, induce Orlick to write a narrative against his father. After various false starts this narrative gets going, and poor Dermot is beaten about, tortured, and finally tried by all the other characters, including twelve judges acting also as witnesses and jury, the evidence against him being produced from their past "employment" in other books.

What we have, then, is constant and deliberate transgression of diegetic levels—a procedure not in itself new,[14] but so

[14] For a discussion of diegetic levels, see Gérard Genette, *Figures III* (Paris, 1972), pp. 238-51.

The Readerhood of Man

complicated, with so many levels (stories within stories and transgressions of narrators from one level to another) that it would be almost impossible to follow if the procedure itself, as part of a symbolic code superencoded, were not thoroughly overdetermined.

Thus we are given, at the mere level of the student-narrator's narrative, constant rhetorical headings followed by colons, such as: *"Description of my uncle*: Red-faced, bead-eyed, ball-bellied . . ."*; "Quality of rasher in use in the household*: Inferior, one and two the pound"; *"The two senses referred to*: Vision and Smell"; *"Nature of chuckle*: quiet, private, averted"; *"Name of figure of speech: Litotes"*; etc. There are, as well, marked transitions to other levels: *"Extract from my typescript descriptive of Finn Mac Cool and his people, being a humorous or quasi-humorous incursion into ancient mythology"* (this notwithstanding the fact that Trellis is later said, in a synopsis for the late-coming reader, to have created Finn); *"Further extract from MS, Oratio Recta"*; or, for returning to the student-narrator level: *"Biographical Reminiscence, Part the first . . . the second . . . the final"; "Conclusion of the book antepenultimate . . . penultimate. . . ."* And all the interruptions at all the levels end with a similar marking, such as *"End of foregoing."*

The book is funny in much the same way that *Tristram Shandy* is funny, each being in different ways concerned with the difficulty and absurdity of writing fiction. A "real" reader (Dylan Thomas) recommended it to a "fictionally real" reader in these terms: "Just the book to give to your sister, if she's a loud, dirty, boozy girl." But for the loud, dirty, boozy girl to follow there is a heavy overcoding on the rhetorical level, which does not detract from the book (as the overdetermination of the hermeneutic code in *Rip* does not), and is, in fact, necessary to its comprehension. More important, it also constitutes its chief delight. It is an integral part of the delight in the constant transgressions, transgression being delightful only if the rules are both clear and firm. Once again, but in a very different way, overdetermination is counterbalanced by underdetermination, but here it is the proaieretic code that is underdetermined, not only by the carnivalesque structure

133

Christine Brooke-Rose

(society turned upside down, insertion of other genres, etc.)[15] and by the constant transgression of levels, but also by its ambling, nonproaieretic nature at every level, including the narrator's. The transgression of diegetic levels, calling attention to diegetic procedure, is then itself thoroughly overdetermined rhetorically, as well as in the symbolic code (which is about the practice of *écriture*), and by the same token "unconfuses" the proaieretic code, so as not to alienate the Dear Reader (the very much encoded reader), with the result that he is flattered by his own understanding. Without the underdetermined area, the overdetermined one would alienate him as an insult to his intelligence.

A CODE UNDERDETERMINED:
Hypercrite Lecteur

In order to emphasize the balance needed by overcoding, I have necessarily and unhermeneutically encroached on this second category (though as we shall see the two are inversely linked), and so will analyze only one example and give more space to theoretical discussion.

Just as the function of overdetermination is to make clear, so the function of underdetermination is to blur. The encoded reader is then required to cooperate actively, to be hypercritical. This indeed was one of the avowed purposes of the *nouveau roman*. A more popular and obvious example is the detective story, in which the whole art is to give all the clues but in such a way that the important ones pass unnoticed. Here, too, there must be a careful balance between overdetermination and underdetermination, but the underdetermination is stronger, either remaining so throughout or remaining so till the last few pages. And of course when a narrator cheats, as in the much-cited instance of Agatha

[15] For the notion of carnivalesque structure, see M. Bakhtin, *Problems of Dostoevsky's Poetics*, English trans. R. W. Rotsel (Ann Arbor, 1973) (original ed. *Problemy tvorchestva Dostoievskogo* [Leningrad, 1929]), and Bakhtin, *Rabelais and His World*, English trans. Helen Iswolsky (Cambridge, Mass., 1968) (original ed. *Tvortchestvo François Rabelais* [Moscow, 1965]).

The Readerhood of Man

Christie's *The Murder of Roger Ackroyd*, where the reader is allowed inside the detective's thoughts throughout and then finds that the detective "dunit," he feels this not only as a transgression (a joke transgression) of viewpoint, but also as a transgression of the implicit contract to keep the fair balance: the viewpoint is overdetermined for wrong clues, but underdetermined for the truth.

The clearest type is the truly ambiguous text, such as, among others, the *nouveau roman*. There seems, however, to be an important difference: the detective story in general blurs by simply overdetermining false clues and underdetermining true ones (a code within the hermeneutic code, which the adept soon learns to look for); the ambiguous text, on the contrary, *seems* to overdetermine one code, usually the hermeneutic, and even to overencode the reader, but in fact the overdetermination consists of repetitions and variations that give us little or no further information. The overdetermination functions, paradoxically, as underdetermination, provided there is also a strong element of underdetermination within the same code.

The classic example is James's *The Turn of the Screw* (1898), in which the overdetermination of the enigma (ghosts versus hallucinations) is constant yet unresolved and can be read both ways each time; but this has been so overanalyzed that I shall not treat it here.[16] I shall take instead Poe's "The Black Cat" (1843), which Todorov places "perhaps" in the generic category of the Pure Fantastic (wholly undecidable as to whether the supernatural is indeed supernatural or can receive a natural explanation), even though he places Poe's tales as a whole in the category of the uncanny (natural explanation).[17] I shall look only at the hermeneutic code, since

[16] See my three essays, "The Squirm of the True," in which I (1) analyze other critics; (2) propose my own analysis of the general structure; and (3) examine the surface structure (*PTL* 1 [1976], 265-94, 513-46, *PTL* 2 [1977], 517-62).

[17] See T. Todorov, *Introduction à la littérature fantastique* (Paris, 1970), in English, *The Fantastic: A Structural Approach to a Literary Genre*, trans. Richard Howard (Cleveland, 1973).

Christine Brooke-Rose

the ambiguity depends on this code alone, the other codes being clear and relatively unexploited.[18]

There are, throughout most of the text, only three enigmas (E) introduced from the start, but three more are introduced at the end. Here is the first paragraph:

Title: THE BLACK CAT (E1: what—or later which—black cat?)

For the most wild, yet most homely narrative which I am about to pen,	E2ª: is it wild or homely? (supernatural/natural)
I neither expect nor solicit belief.	E2ª: wild (+ reader encoded)
Mad indeed would I be to expect it,	E2ᵇ: (2ª reversed): is *he* wild mad? = natural explanation (+ reader encoded)
in a case where my very senses reject their own evidence.	E2ᵇ: reversed: supernatural
Yet, mad I am not—and very surely I do not dream.	E2ᵇ: still reversed: madness denied, so supernatural
But to-morrow I die,	E3: why?
and to-day I would unburthen my soul.	E2ᵇ: from madness? (natural explanation) or from supernatural?
My immediate purpose is to place before the world, plainly, succinctly, and without comment,	(reader encoded)
a series of mere household events.	E2ª: homely
In their consequences, these events have terrified—have tortured—have destroyed me.	E2ª: homely—wild; E2ᵇ: mad? E3: how destroyed?
Yet I will not attempt to expound them.	(reader encoded)

[18] Quotations from "The Black Cat" are from *Great Short Works of Edgar Allan Poe* (New York, 1970).

136

The Readerhood of Man

To me, they have presented little but Horror—	$E2^a$: homely—wild; $E2^b$: mad?
to many they will seem less terrible than "barroques."	$E2^a$: homely (+ reader encoded)
Hereafter, perhaps, some intellect may be found which will reduce my phantasm to the commonplace—	$E2^b$: mad; $E2^a$: homely (+ reader encoded)
some intellect more calm, more logical and far less excitable than my own,	$E2^b$: mad; or $E2^a$: events are wild (supernatural) and have merely horrified him (+ reader encoded)
which will perceive, in the circumstances I detail with awe,	$E2^a$: wild (+ reader encoded)
nothing more than an ordinary succession of very natural causes and effects.	$E2^a$: homely; therefore $E2^b$: mad (+ reader encoded)

$E2^a$ and $E2^b$ are not two separate enigmas but merely the narrative/narrator aspects of the same enigma: are the events supernatural (wild) or has the narrator (mad) imagined natural events as supernatural? This and Enigma 1 (which black cat? Are there two or one?) will not be resolved. Enigma 3 will be reposed only twice, once clearly ("even in this felon's cell"), and once soon after as a contextually clear premonition, the white splotch on Cat 2 that grows to the shape of the gallows. Enigma 1 is apparently solved at the beginning with the introduction of *a cat* (in italics), called Pluto, and does not recur till after the murder of Pluto and the appearance of the second cat.

Enigma 2 is very much overdetermined, as we can see here, since it is the basis of the pure fantastic. In seminar work[19] we have discovered that, in general, the short story uses few semes of any one code (and of the semic and hermeneutic in particular), but that they recur often, a form of

---

[19] At the University of Paris VIII, in collaboration with my colleague Olga Scherer, to whom I owe this observation.

Christine Brooke-Rose

semantic overdetermination also found in poetry.[20] But over-determination also seems to apply to the pure-fantastic text, whether long or short (and most tend to be short, in order to sustain the ambiguity to the end). Obviously a pure-fantastic short story will be particularly marked in this way.

The reader, too, is overencoded. But contrary to the example of *Rip Van Winkle*, he is overencoded not for overclarity, but for further confusion. Far from being ahead of the protagonist, he lags behind, the enigmas being merely repeated, reversed, and rereversed. Nevertheless he is flattered ("some intellect . . . etc."), and has to be thus flattered, rather grossly, since he is not allowed, as in *Rip*, to feel more clever than the protagonist.

The story will continue to repeat Enigma 2, from the wife's superstititon that all black cats are witches in disguise to the narrator-protagonist's "wild" and dual behavior and his constant comment upon it in terms of split personality ("the Fiend Intemperance"; "the fury of a demon seized me"; "the spirit of PERVERSENESS"; "half horror, half remorse," etc.). The first clear suggestion of the supernatural does not occur until after the hanging of Pluto, with the image of a gigantic cat, a rope around its neck, impressed on the wall after the (fortuitous?) fire; but a "natural" explanation, wholly implausible, is immediately given, to be followed by ambiguous phrases about "fancy," "the phantasm of the cat," and so on.

It is with the appearance of the second cat, its splotch of white on the breast (unlike Pluto) gradually growing to the shape of the gallows (E1, E2, and E3) and, like Pluto after the narrator's first cruelty, deprived of one eye, that the element of the supernatural makes itself felt. Here it is worth noting that the narrator cheats a little (as in *Rip*, with the beard), in not giving us the highly visible detail of the cat's missing eye either at the moment when he sees, strokes, and describes the cat in the "den of more than infamy" (though this is justified later, and the den appears to be dark), or in his account of their later relationship; rather, it is after these two passages that he states: "What added, no doubt, to my hatred of the

[20] See note 10 above.

138

beast, was the discovery, on the morning after I brought it home [justification], that, like Pluto, it also had been deprived of one of its eyes." The ellipse (underdetermination) functions as a *leurre* (two cats) for the reader, but the subsequent *analepse* draws his attention (overdetermination) to the possibility of the second cat (who is never named) being the ghost of Pluto. It is, however, the only example of overdetermination for E1, and only as a possibility.

E3 (why must he die?) is solved the moment the narrator, tripped by Cat 2 in the cellar and prevented by his wife from venting his rage on the beast, buries his axe in her brain. And, because E3 is introduced at the outset, we also know, *un*hermeneutically, that he will be caught, but not how. A sick calm invades him as he entombs the body in the wall. Enigma 4 is then introduced: where is the cat? It has disappeared, and the narrator expresses his profound relief. Four days later the police arrive (E5—why?—this is never answered: it can be regarded as either hermeneutically obvious, from unstated local gossip, or as a hint of supernatural action by the cat), and search the house. In the cellar the narrator is hideously calm (E2^b) but, as they are about to leave, a manic madness seizes him (E2^b) and he praises the solid walls, tapping on them, whereupon:

But may God shield and deliver me	E2^b: split personality
from the fangs of the Arch-fiend!	E1: THE CAT
No sooner had the reverberation of my blows sunk into the silence; than I was answered by a voice from within the tomb!—	E6: whose voice? wife's? or cat's?
by a cry, at first muffled and broken, like the sobbing of a child,	E2^a: wild
and then finally swelling into one long, loud and continuous scream,	E2^a: wild

Christine Brooke-Rose

utterly anomalous and inhuman—	E6: inhuman=ghost, dead human? or animal?
a howl—a wailing shriek, half of horror and half of triumph,	E6: cat's triumph?
such as might have arisen only out of hell, conjointly from the throats of the damned in their agony and of the demons that exult in the damnation.	$E2^b$: mad? $E2^a$: wild E1: IF CAT (E6) = ghost of Pluto?
Of my own thoughts it is folly to speak . . .	$E2^b$: mad (+ encoded reader)
a dozen stout arms were toiling at the wall. It fell bodily. The corpse, already greatly decayed and clotted with gore, stood before the eyes of the spectators.	$E2^a$: wild
Upon its head, with red extended mouth and solitary eye of fire,	$E2^a$: wild
sat the hideous beast	E4: resolved; E6: resolved
whose craft had seduced me into murder,	$E2^b$: split (mad)
and whose informing voice had consigned me to the hangman.	E3: solution repeated; E5: supernatural strengthened
I had walled the monster up within the tomb!	E4: explained; $E2^{a,b}$: wild, mad.

What we get ostensibly is a "natural" explanation: Cat 2 (fortuitous), hated by the narrator out of his guilt for (madly) murdering Cat 1, got walled up by mistake in the further madness of the murderer and entombment of his wife. It remained half alive and screamed when the wall was (madly) tapped. E2 (madness and horror) is continuously encoded, E4 (where is the cat?) and E6 (whose voice?) are simultaneously solved, E3 (why does he have to die?) having been solved at the moment of the murder and being merely repeated here in the final chord. E5 (why does policeman arrive?) is resolved

140

either by obviousness or by a momentary hint of the supernatural, strengthened by "informing voice."

There remains E1: which black cat? And E1, unlike E2, has been underdetermined, with mere suggestions that Cat 2 is the ghost of Cat 1 (the noosed impression on the wall after the hanging of Cat 1, the weird appearance of Cat 2 in the den, the gallows mark, the one eye, his oppressively haunting behavior). All these elements, of course, could receive natural explanations, and also belong to E2 (madness), which is overdetermined but is itself in the end unresolved: either the narrator is mad and the events are "natural" or he is not mad, merely unbalanced and cruel, the latter traits being exacerbated by "supernatural" events.

In other words, the balance of overdetermination and underdetermination is once again essential. But whereas in the folk tale the balance was between two or more codes (hermeneutic and proaieretic overdetermined, symbolic underdetermined), and similarly in Flann O'Brien (proaieretic underdetermined, symbolic overdetermined), here the balance operates within one code (the hermeneutic), but between enigmas: the first two remain unresolved, E1 being underdetermined, E2 overdetermined; the third, introduced with the first two, is underdetermined but is clearly resolved toward the end; the fourth and sixth, undetermined, are introduced only in the last paragraph, and are immediately resolved; the fifth, introduced just before the last paragraph, is underdetermined, half-resolved (natural explanation, obvious/supernatural explanation, hinted):

Beginning	E1	underdetermined		unresolved
	E2	overdetermined		unresolved
	E3	underdetermined	resolved	
End	E4	underdetermined	resolved	
	E5	underdetermined	resolved	unresolved
	E6	underdetermined	resolved	

This difference in the balance of over- and underdetermination (between codes for the first category, between enig-

Christine Brooke-Rose

mas of one code for the second) may be a fortuitous and empirical result of the texts analyzed, and only further research can show whether the hypothesis is correct. The main difference is, as I have said, one of relative dominance in the final result: for the overdetermined code of the first type of text, the underdetermined area lies *in the reader's interpretation* (if he wishes); for the underdetermined code of the second type of text, an area seems to be overdetermined but in fact remains underdetermined *within the text* (unless, as in the detective story, it is neatly overdetermined right at the end).

The ambiguous text is essentially "dialogical":[21] in the dialogical novel (e.g., Dostoevsky, according to Bakhtin, as opposed to Tolstoy), the author has a constant metatextual dialogue with his characters, and the characters with each other; above all, the character has a dialogue with himself as against an imagined other.[22] The author in practice refuses to "delimit" his character, to have the last word on him (as in the monological novel), and for that matter he refuses to delimit himself. No man ever "coincides with himself," let alone with another's "word" on him. The character revolts, as it were, against his own author's tendency to delimit him, and Flann O'Brien's comic treatment of this in *At Swim-Two-Birds* is a dramatized (explicit, overdetermined) version of what is done more metatextually (or with an overdetermined enigma unresolved, as here) in the dialogical novel.

Since I have analyzed types of metatext in detail in my third essay on *The Turn of the Screw*, as has Olga Scherer for other texts,[23] I will say no more about it here. But in the case of the ambiguity that must remain unresolved in the pure fantastic, this dialogical metatext is clearly generated by

[21] For the notion of dialogical texts, see M. Bakhtin, *Problems of Dostoevsky's Poetics.*

[22] The clearest example is Dostoevsky's *Notes from the Underground*, which has strongly influenced modern fiction and, in America, explicitly, Ellison's *Invisible Man.*

[23] See "Absalon et Absalon," *Lettres Modernes*, vol. 1 (Paris, 1974), 1-24, and "La Contestation du jugement sur pièces chez Dostoievski et Faulkner," *Delta* 3 (1976), 47-62 (Université de Montpellier). Cf. also Scherer's forthcoming book, *Le Contre-courant de la conscience: Faulkner et Dostoievski.*

The Readerhood of Man

the underlying balance of the overdetermined and under-determined, unresolved enigmas; whereas the marvelous (supernatural accepted, as in *Rip*), in which this particular ambiguity does not exist, will contain only a minor (and overdetermined) hermeneutic code, which can generate only a monological and minor metatext, although the underde-termined other codes, often symbolic, can generate other metatexts. In this respect the marvelous is often more akin (*apart* from the element of the accepted supernatural) to realistic fiction: witness the heavy overdetermination of the referential and symbolic codes in Tolkien's trilogy, which has all the trappings of the realistic novel, and encourages sym-bolic, thematic, historical, etymological criticism of a tradi-tional kind.

The pure fantastic is not, of course, the only type of am-biguous text. The novels of Robbe-Grillet function, though differently, on a similar balance of apparent overdetermina-tion and underdetermination, as do other types of *nouveau* and *nouveau nouveau roman*. Or again, in Alphonse Allais' *Un drame bien parisien*, for instance, the joke-ambiguity does not depend on a supernatural/natural enigma but on an over-determination, followed by a sudden underdetermination (based on noncoreference, as Eco has shown)[24] within the ul-trasimple proaieretic code. And no doubt other codes are similarly exploitable.

The monological narrative, which delimits its characters and its ideological position, is the only type that, by over-determining a stance, say "unpleasant," to an actual reader, produces the question, Where does the author stand? This question simply cannot be asked of a dialogical text. In the case of Poe's "unpleasantness," the fact that the question cannot (or should not) be asked is often attributed to his "irony." No doubt. And irony has been much discussed and thoroughly analyzed, especially in America.[25] But few critics

[24] Eco, "Lector in Fabula: Pragmatic Strategy in a Meta-Narrative Text," in *The Role of the Reader: Explorations in the Semiotics of Texts* (Bloomington, 1979).

[25] In France, this is less the case. Barthes, for example, dismisses irony as part of his referential code, as another stereotype that destroys multivalence

seem to take Bakhtin's theory into account when discussing irony, and some dismiss it.[26] I think, however, that it is essential to any consideration, not only of the encoded reader, but of the ways in which the reader is encoded as I have tried to examine them here.[27]

CODES NONDETERMINED:
Hypnocrite Lecteur

I really do not have a great deal to say about this category, nor do I propose to analyze examples. It not only must exist theoretically, once the two previous categories have been posed, but does exist, in the effects we know; namely, that the reader, not being properly encoded, is or feels free to read everything, anything, and therefore also nothing, into the text.

Theoretically, this type of reading should only occur with

---

by affirming the ownership of a message, the power of one discourse over another (see *S/Z*, French ed., pp. 52 and 212).

[26] See, for example, Wolf Schmid, *Der Textaufbau in den Erzählungen Dostoevkijs* (Munich, 1973). Schmid not only disagrees that Dostoevsky is dialogical, but argues that such a structure (of autonomous voices emancipated from the creative author) is ontologically inconceivable, and prefers to characterize Dostoevsky's technique as text-interference. This, in my view, is to fall into the very trap that Bakhtin analyzes in his first chapter, namely his predecessors' and contemporaries' "monological" reading of Dostoevsky. Bakhtin of course admits that there are large monological chunks in Dostoevsky, but his purpose is to bring out the extraordinary nature of the technique in its incipient stage. And even if he were wrong about Dostoevsky, this would not alter the validity of his theory as theory, so original and requiring such a change (an Ingardian change) in our ontological view of a work of art as an "intentional" object that many are bound to fall back, as Schmid does, on more traditional concepts.

[27] An extreme example of the code underdetermined, though not relevant here, would be anagrammatical poetry, which also depends on a balance between the overdetermined (the sort of places where anagrams are most likely to occur or to begin, such as the first line, or word, or letter; and sufficient recurrence for the anagrams to be perceived at all) and the underdetermined ("hidden" anagrams). For a theory of anagrammatism, see Jean Starobinski, *Les Mots sous les mots* (Paris, 1971) and Anthony L. Johnson, "Anagrammatism in Poetry: Theoretical Preliminaries," *PTL* 2 (1977), 89-117.

The Readerhood of Man

texts in which the balance of overdetermination and underdetermination is apparently (but see below) not respected or structured, some codes being overdetermined here, underdetermined there, with no other reason than the author's whim.[28] In other words, it is not necessarily a *non*determination of codes which makes this kind of text; on the contrary, *all* the codes may be overdetermined (or under), therefore producing no structured metatextual tension for an encoded reader, hence no encoded reader. It is haphazard determination rather than a total absence of determination that results in nondetermination, so that the actual reader then takes over, with his feelings and ideology, his period-bound enthusiasms and limitations, his fashionable prejudices and his moral alienation.

I know that this is a thorny topic, many critics having in various ways, from damnation to reticence, condemned an author for his "views" not sufficiently "distanced" from those of the hero, for "not making it clear where he stands" or, on the contrary, for making it too clear. I should like briefly to digress on this actual reader in the light of my analysis and previous remarks, this in response to a particularly interesting essay by Susan Suleiman,[29] devoted to Drieu de la Rochelle's novel *Gilles*, in which she analyzes specific manipulating devices that negate certain values such as foreignness, Jewishness, psychoanalysis, Marxism, and portray them as decadent and sinister. She frankly (and honestly) analyzes her *own* process of "dissent" from the values posited by the text and comes to the conclusion that

1. Ideological dissent from works of fiction is a reading experience involving the "perception" of certain formal devices as masks for the novelist in his role as manipulator of values.

[28] Unfortunately this unrigorous kind of reading is so easy and so popular that it is all too frequently used on texts belonging to the first two categories, often missing much of their structure or hitting it by chance or through parasitical criticism.

[29] "Ideological Dissent from Works of Fiction: Toward a Rhetoric of the *roman à thèse*," *Neophilologus* 60 (1976), 162-77.

145

Christine Brooke-Rose

    2. A formal device of this type (i.e. identifiable . . . as a
    mask . . .) is a device of ideological manipulation.

She at once puts forward the objection that a reader might
share those values *and* be aware of the manipulating devices,
but counterobjects that since the "perception" of a device "is
a quasi-willful *act of non-cooperation with the text* on the part of
the reader," a reader who shared the values embodied in
Gilles, though aware of the devices, "would not find it difficult to cooperate with the text" and to "act as if" he were
unaware of them, "as if" he did not perceive them.

This may well be true, since political manipulation is so
easy, but the circularity of the argument makes that ease even
more depressing (perception of device = noncooperation;
cooperation can occur despite perception of device). And
what bothers me is that it seems to be true only of certain
texts (i.e., those belonging to this third category), this in two
ways: (1) It is perfectly possible to disagree totally with a *past*
author's ideology (say Dante's religious and political beliefs,
or Langland's, or Milton's, or even Shakespeare's violence)
and to perceive the devices of overdetermination, and *yet* not
to "dissent" in the way described. After all we may perceive
the devices of all literary works. Can a Catholic really not read
Du Bartas or a Methodist Donne? This could be due to the
passage of time since the Guelfs and the Ghibellines, the
Papal Schism or the Religious Wars; but (2) the same is mysteriously (though more complexly) true of, say, Pound's political views, or Eliot's, or Wyndham Lewis's, or for that matter
Neruda's, or Lawrence's extravagant (overdetermined)
treatment of sex. Pound's overdetermination is at times extremely unpleasant, and we perceive it, yet we do not have
that same easy reaction as the one Susan Suleiman describes
with *Gilles*. Why?

I should like to suggest that it is after all a question of the
balance of encoding I have described, and of the metatextual
(dialogical) tension produced for the encoded reader by this
balance. The text overdetermines certain codes, but must
compensate either by underdetermining others (as I have

146

The Readerhood of Man

shown, in easier terms, with "Rip Van Winkle" and *At Swim-Two-Birds*), or by over- and underdetermining within the same code but in such a way that the final result is underdetermined ("The Black Cat"). Drieu's devices, which amount to an overdetermination of the semic code, are not only "patent" (Suleiman), they are also uncounterbalanced by nondetermination in any other codes that would open up areas of mystery and above all dialogize the characters. The referential code that backs the semic code is, if anything, less underdetermined than simply taken for granted, and hence cannot allow for ideological dissent or evolution of ideas. I would suggest that Susan Suleiman reacted not only from ideological dissent, but also, or even chiefly, from intelligence: the actual reader could not coincide with the encoded reader, who is either overencoded as hypocrite, or haphazardly encoded, if at all, as hypnocrite (which in a sense is what she means by his not perceiving the devices he does perceive). In fact, the encoded reader, insulted in his intelligence, is so alienated that he withdraws, becomes passive, and leaves a great gap for the actual reader to take over— from the contemporary reader whom the author takes for granted as sharing his prejudices, to the adverse or later reader who will dissent because of these prejudices, and in between them the critic Suleiman quotes who regards Drieu's portrait of *Gilles* as "one of the most damning documents about French fascism of our time." The implied or encoded author, by the same token, tends to be eliminated and to leave a gap for the actual author of traditional criticism.

Contemporary hypnosis, however, leads me to close this digression on the actual reader and return to my nondetermined category. I said above that in this case the balance of overdetermination and underdetermination is "apparently" not respected or structured. It is clear, however, that an "apparent" nondetermination of codes (i.e., an apparent unbalance, producing no metatextual tension) may in some instances turn out to be a mere contemporary blindness to an unfamiliar form of this necessary balance, the encoded reader being, as it were, invisible for a while to the actual reader,

Christine Brooke-Rose

until later actual readers discover him: whence a lack of comprehension, a lack of reaction, or on the contrary, sometimes, overreaction, but for the wrong reasons.

The category of the nondetermined code is, in other words, a transient category: either the text dissolves, after a fashionable success, into limbo because of its unstructured or nonexistent balance between over- and underdetermination; or the apparent nonexistent balance turns out to be a structured balance, in which case the text will rejoin one of the first two categories, and keep critics happy for generations.

Students often ask me, Are all these things you read into a text, or that we read, applying this or that theory or method, really there, or are they in the mind of the analyzer? An epistemological question indeed, on which we should all read at least Ingarden, and if not Ingarden, then Barthes and many others. I suppose in the end there is no answer, and that I can only insist, rightly or wrongly, on (e.g.) these categories as presented here, which are naturally the result of "my" analysis of the encoded reader. Maybe the encoded reader is a character out of one of my own fictions, *mon semblable, mon frère, hypocrite, hypercrite, hypnocrite,* hooded, and merely hired by me for this essay on the Readerhood of Man.

Robert Crosman | Do Readers
Make Meaning?

The question is itself annoyingly
vague and ambiguous, yet it is as close as I can get to expressing what seems to me the central issue of literary theory today. When Jonathan Culler calls for a "theory of reading,"
when Stanley Fish speaks of "reading communities" and
"reading strategies," when Jacques Derrida announces that
"the reader writes the text," they are all, in varying degrees,
answering in the affirmative. And when other theorists—
Wayne Booth, E. D. Hirsch, and a host of others—see solip-
sism and moral chaos in such an answer, they too are testify-
ing to the importance of the issue for contemporary critical
theorists.[1] In the classroom as well, the kind and extent of a
teacher's authority in matters of interpretation hang on
whether or not readers make literary meaning. The question,
however puzzling, insists on being asked.

If we cannot immediately answer it, the problem lies
chiefly, I think, in the word *meaning*, which has several conflicting senses. First, we often use the word as a synonym for
intention—"if you take my meaning," "what I *meant* was. . . ."
Clearly, the speaker or writer of words is their maker and
hence the source of the intention that preceded or accompanied their making. But, second, we often attribute "meaning" to words themselves, and say that verbose "means"
wordy, or ice "means" frozen water. Here the sense of the

[1] See Culler, *Structuralist Poetics* (Ithaca, 1975) especially chap. 6, "Literary
Competence," pp. 113-30, and his essay in the present volume; Fish, "Interpreting the *Variorum*," *Critical Inquiry* 2 (1976), 465-85; Derrida, *Of Grammatology*, trans. Gayatri C. Spivak (Baltimore, 1976); Booth, "In Defense of Authors," *Novel* 11, no. 1 (1977). E. D. Hirsch is discussed at length later in this
essay.

word *meaning* seems not to be what a particular speaker intends, but what the mass of people understand by a word. Finally, *meaning* can mean the value we attribute to something—"it means a lot to me." The word can, in short, stand for a speaker's intention, the common understanding, or an individual's subjective valuing of something. Depending on how we use or understand the word, we will have different answers to the question of whether readers make meaning.

The quandary is not confined to the layman. When C. K. Ogden and I. A. Richards wrote *The Meaning of Meaning* in 1923, the issue already had a long history, and among language philosophers like H. P. Grice, P. F. Strawson, John Searle, and Max Black the controversy still rages, or seethes.[2] E. D. Hirsch, who has done more than anyone in the literary community to identify the word *meaning* with the author's intention, suggests calling meaning-to-the-reader by another word, *significance*:

> Verbal meaning is whatever someone has willed to convey by a particular sequence of linguistic signs and which can be conveyed (shared) by means of those linguistic signs.[3]

> In the present book . . . the term "meaning" refers to the whole verbal meaning of a text, and "significance" to textual meaning in relation to a larger context, i.e., another mind, another era, a wider subject-matter, an alien system of values, and so on. In other words, "significance" is textual meaning as related to some context, indeed any context, beyond itself.[4]

---

[2] Ogden and Richards, *The Meaning of Meaning* (New York, 1923); Grice, "Utterer's Meaning, Sentence-Meaning, and Word-Meaning," in *Foundations of Language* 4 (1968), 225-42; Strawson, "Intention and Convention in Speech-Acts," *Philosophical Review* 73 (1964), 439-60; J. R. Searle, *Speech Acts* (Cambridge, 1969); Max Black, "Meaning and Intention: An Examination of Grice's Views," *New Literary History* 4 (1973), 257-79.

[3] Hirsch, *Validity in Interpretation* (New Haven, 1967), p. 31.

[4] Hirsch, *The Aims of Interpretation* (Chicago, 1976), pp. 2-3.

Do Readers Make Meaning?

Naturally, if we stipulate in advance that by "meaning" we shall understand "authorial intention," then it follows logically that readers don't make meaning. Yet in these two definitions of meaning Hirsch has contradicted himself, affirming in the first that words mean something only in the context of an intending mind ("verbal meaning is whatever someone has willed to convey"), and claiming in the second that they mean something *apart* from any "larger context" (since their meaning in any larger context is not meaning but "significance").

In this essay I want to answer Hirsch's assertion that authors make meaning by standing his argument on its head. Any word or text, I shall argue, has "meaning" only when it is fitted into some larger context. Thus the act of understanding a poet's words by placing them in the context of his intentions is only one of a number of possible ways of understanding them. This way of arriving at their "meaning" is privileged both by long tradition and by our common interest in authors' minds, but it in no way supersedes or precedes other methods of interpretation which are, equally, contextualizing procedures. Thus I hope to show that the statement "authors make meaning," though not of course untrue, is merely a special case of the more universal truth that readers make meaning.

But let us start with an example. In 1914 Ezra Pound wrote what has become the most famous two-line poem in the language:

In a Station of the Metro

The apparition of these faces in the crowd;
Petals on a wet, black bough.[5]

How do we go about deciding what it means? Outside of college literature classes, I do not suppose that readers will be looking for meaning at all here, at least not for the kind of

[5] *Personae.* Copyright 1926 by Ezra Pound. Reprinted by permission of New Directions and Faber & Faber, Ltd.

Robert Crosman

meaning that can be put into words. They will imagine petals on a wet, black bough, and faces in a crowded Metro station, and derive some feeling from the surprising juxtapostion. But affective literary responses are commonly allowed to be free and subjective, so let us look for the poem's propositional force, if any.

We start by paraphrasing the poem: the poet went down into a subway station in Paris, and saw certain faces in the crowd that reminded him of, or made him see, or struck him with the force of, a tree-branch wet with rain and covered with flower petals. Now although this is too close to what the poem *says* to qualify as its meaning, we are already engaged in the interpretive process—providing contexts ("the poet went down"), filling in gaps ("that reminded him"), translating ("a tree branch wet with rain and covered with flower petals"). *Translating* is in fact a good word for the whole process: by adding to Pound's text, by subtracting from it, by rearranging it, changing it from verse to prose and so on, I make it mine. Even if I don't translate it into words at all, I still make it mine by the pictures it calls to my mind, by whether they melt together or replace one another or stand side by side in my imagination, and by what I make of abstract words like "apparition"—a ghostly event, a Platonic vision, or just a sudden appearance? The text, in other words, supplies me with words, ideas, images, sounds, rhythms, but I make the poem's meaning by a process of translation. That is what reading is, in fact: translation.

Meaning does not stop here, of course; the resolute meaning hunter will go on until he distills a philosophical proposition. Remembering Wordsworth's habit, imitated by poets down to our day, of prowling around the city until he found beauty amidst the ugliness, a reader may conclude that the meaning of Pound's poem is that even in the infernal surroundings of technological society mankind remains beautiful. Or, if he knows enough about Pound's theory of poetry in 1914, or about imagism generally, he may decode the poem into a proposition about poetry itself: the poet's task is to record precisely the moment when his creative imagination

Do Readers Make Meaning?

changes sensation into a poetic image. Or he may read the poem as a statement that poems should be brief.

As it happens, all three of these "meanings" are supplied by Pound himself in his book *Gaudier-Brzeska*,[6] where he also says that the poem is meant to reproduce an emotion, and is "meaningless unless one has drifted into a certain vein of thought." Obviously, Pound himself found three or four different "meanings" for the poem, and even imagined it as potentially "meaningless," which I suppose is a fifth meaning. Having done so well in finding plural meanings, Pound could have added a good many more if he had set his mind to it, and other readers could raise (and have raised) the number of meanings indefinitely.

But perhaps we can discover in all of these meanings a "family resemblance," some common thread that runs through them, and this could be called the invariable "meaning" that Pound has put into his poem—a sort of *ur*-meaning with no clearly discernible limits, but that nonetheless excludes many possible interpretations. Does Pound's text exclude certain meanings? The easiest way to answer is to invent arbitrarily an "eccentric" meaning and see if it can possibly be derived from Pound's text. Suppose . . . suppose a dairy farmer reads Pound's poem as a statement that we should drink milk regularly. Does something in Pound's poem refute this interpretation?

Surprisingly enough, nothing does. The interpretation is no more radical a translation of Pound's words than is a standard reading like "in the midst of technological ugliness mankind is still beautiful." We can only ask our hypothetical dairyman to provide the contexts that led to his interpretation, which he obligingly does: like us, he understood that the poet saw beautiful faces in the subway, but the image of petals on a bough reminded him of an apple orchard where his cows like to forage. Since milch cows have been brought into the picture, it is only a small and logical leap to remember that beautiful faces require a healthy diet, of which milk is

[6] (London, 1916), pp. 100-103.

an essential part. Since "meaning" is a translation into our own words of the words of the poem, there is no way of excluding some translations as invalid, as long as a context can be discovered in which they fit by ordinary rules of logic. And, as my example of the dairyman suggests, a little ingenuity can always discover such a context.

The conclusion is as inevitable as it is startling: since finding meanings for Pound's poem consists in translating it into other words or symbols, and building it into our own mental contexts, there is no such thing as *the* meaning of Pound's poem—not even for Pound himself. Hypothetical readers like my dairyman, and their readings, need not concern us (except for illustrative purposes), but there are real readers out there with interpretations as eccentric as the one I imagined. This being so, it follows that a poem really means whatever any reader seriously believes it to mean. Just as the number of mental contexts into which Pound's poem can be translated is infinite, so is the number of possible meanings of the poem itself infinite. And it is clear who is making these meanings—the reader, whether he be the author himself or anyone else.[7]

Before turning to the other side of the case, to the contention that authors make meaning, let us dally with the usual compromise notion that the text itself means something. In this view the reader "makes" meaning only in the sense that he actualizes a potential meaning latent in the text. The reader is necessary to the production of meaning (in this view) but he is constrained by the text, just as hot water is necessary to the production of tea, but a mixture of tea leaves

[7] It will seem arbitrary at this point to call the author simply one more reader, since the hypothesis being examined is that readers rather than authors make meaning. Even as reader of his own finished work, the poet has what no other reader has: direct knowledge of his intentions at the time he wrote the poem. All the same, it is curious that Pound should come up with four or five distinct meanings for his poem. This not only leaves the reader with the job of picking the right one, but suggests that for the author the number of intentions for this brief poem is indeterminate: it means different things to Pound as he moves it from one mental context to another.

Do Readers Make Meaning?

and water will produce only tea, never coffee or chocolate milk.

E. D. Hirsch has written with such devastating effect upon the modern (New Critical) heresy that meaning exists in the printed words, independent of any intention, that I can save considerable space here merely by summarizing his argument. Ridiculing the modern notion of textual autonomy, Hirsch begins by saying: "What had not been noticed in the earliest enthusiasm for going back to 'what the text says' was that the text had to represent *somebody's* meaning—if not the author's, then the critic's."[8] In other words, "meaning is an affair of consciousness, and not of physical signs or things" (p. 23). Words, Hirsch points out, are universally ambiguous, and since no word means one thing exclusively, understanding a speaker's meaning involves a guess about his intention. The word *bank*, for example, can mean (among other things) the side of a river, or a place where money is kept. When I say "I keep my money in the bank," then, it is your guess as to the relative probabilities of someone depositing money in a savings account versus burying it beside a river that enables you to decide what I probably mean (all understanding, Hirsch argues, is an affair of probabilities, not of certainties). The word *bank* means nothing definite, *even in context*, until a mind construes it.

Since neither words nor the utterances built up out of them can be made unambiguous, except by an act of reading, "meaning" is not inherent in words or utterances but is an inference drawn by the construing mind, based upon probabilities—this is Hirsch's point. When we get to utterances as long, as complex, or (in the case of the Pound couplet) as elliptical as literary texts, no two readers will ever agree entirely on a single meaning. If we wish to think of a literary work as having a definite and discernible meaning, he says, we must agree that this is the meaning the author intended.

[8] *Validity in Interpretation*, p. 3. All future page references to this book will be given in parentheses after quotations.

Robert Crosman

And so we encounter the true alternative to the proposition that readers make meaning, the very common-sensical and widely accepted belief that authors make meaning. It is this view that Hirsch has so ably and forcefully argued, and I will begin by making two observations about the nature of his argument. The first is that he does not demonstrate directly that authors make meaning, but rather he eliminates the other possibilities. That is, Hirsch never presents us with an ambiguous literary text whose meaning is cleared up by its author's extratextual explanation. Such explanations, even when one can find them, are usually (as the Pound quotation illustrates) unsatisfactory. Rather, Hirsch "proves" his contention by eliminating the reader and the text itself as possible loci of meaning: texts themselves cannot "mean," readers' interpretations differ, and only the author is left as the source of meaning. Clearly Hirsch's argument rests upon the unstated assumption that *a text can have only one meaning.*

Like all primary assumptions, like the axioms in Euclidian geometry, this assumption is unproved and unprovable. On the face of it, it seems improbable—after all, not even single words have just one meaning. Hirsch is really saying that a text *ought* to have only one meaning, a statement that he supports the way all ethical propositions are supported: with an essentially *political* argument. This is my second observation; grant Hirsch his premise that there is only *one* right interpretation of any literary text and the rest follows quite sensibly: who has a greater right than the author himself to say what his text means? If (as is usually the case) the author did not say, or said different things at different times, then it is up to the literary historian, the biographer, etc., to make informed guesses as to what he probably meant at the moment when he wrote. Where Hirsch is vulnerable is not in the chain of reasoning that hangs from this axiom but in the axiom itself, his premise that texts have only one meaning.

That premise is, as I have said, unstated in his book, hence unexamined. But Hirsch does give it some unobtrusive support: "If the meaning of a text is not the author's, then no interpretation can possibly correspond to *the* meaning of the

Do Readers Make Meaning?

text, since the text can have no determinate or determinable meaning" (p. 5). Hirsch hopes here we will agree that there should be "*the* meaning of a text." But suppose we ask why. Why must a text have only one meaning? Hirsch's only answer is a vision of political anarchy in the profession of literary study:

> When critics deliberately banished the original author, they themselves usurped his place, and this led unerringly to some of our present-day theoretical confusions. Where before there had been but one author, there now arose a multiplicity of them, each carrying as much authority as the next. . . . If a theorist wants to save the ideal of validity he has to save the author as well, and, in the present-day context, his first task will be to show that the prevailing arguments against the author are questionable (pp. 5-6).

As the imagery of banishment and usurpation makes clear, Hirsch is a latter-day Hobbes, arguing that meaning is either absolute and single (author=king), or it does not exist: without authorial authority there is no validity, hence no meaning, and mere anarchy is loosed upon the world:

> When disagreements occur, how are they resolved? Under the theory of semantic autonomy they cannot be resolved, since the meaning is not what the author meant, but "what the poem means to different sensitive readers" [T. S. Eliot]. One interpretation is as valid as another, so long as it is "sensitive" or "plausible." Yet the teacher of literature who adheres to Eliot's theory is also by profession the preserver of a heritage and the conveyor of knowledge. On what ground does he claim that his "reading" is more valid than that of any pupil? On no very firm ground (p. 4).

The choice Hirsch offers us here is between two visions, not of literature, but of society. In one the young rise up against the old, the ignorant are arrogant, degree is taken away and mark what discord follows. In the other, a decent regard for hierarchy and order is maintained, and the state is at peace.

That Hirsch's argument for authorial intention is basically a political one is a fact of the greatest significance, and one to which we must return. But for the moment let us do what Hirsch failed to do, and ask what we mean by "what the author intended it to mean." How does an author mean? Insofar as I have seen poets' accounts of how they write, the process does not seem to be particularly rational: images, lines, rhyme schemes, "come" to them, and they work at these until the poem seems "right." In *Paradise Lost* Milton claims that the poem was dictated to him while he slept. Hirsch assumes, on the contrary, that a poet writes with some philosophic proposition in mind. One of his chief examples is Wordsworth's "Lucy," part v, "A slumber did my spirit seal."

> A slumber did my spirit seal;
>   I had no human fears:
> She seemed a thing that could not feel
>   The touch of earthly years.
>
> No motion has she now, no force;
>   She neither hears nor sees;
> Rolled round in earth's diurnal course,
>   With rocks, and stones, and trees.

Hirsch's procedure is to quote two diametrically opposed interpretations of the poem, to show that they are fundamentally incompatible, and then to argue that the only possible way to settle the disagreement is to determine which more probably reflects Wordsworth's own outlook at the time he wrote the poem. To a pantheist, "Lucy's" death is cause for rejoicing; to the rest of us, it is cause for sorrow. But since Wordsworth was a pantheist in 1799, Hirsch argues, the poem is probably "meant" to be affirmative, and is to be read in that way—if, that is, we care about its meaning.

Do Readers Make Meaning?

I must say that this line of argument strikes me as extraordinary. I am asked to think that Wordsworth's motive in writing the poem was to communicate an affirmative attitude toward death, but that he was so indirect in his method of communication that he wrote a poem which communicates to many readers precisely the opposite message. Now, while I can't absolutely rule out such a motive a priori, I can legitimately object to a theory of poetic meaning that makes intimate knowledge of this poet's extratextual views so essential that only his personal friends during his lifetime, and biographical experts after his death, could possibly know his true meaning. If we were to accept Hirsch's view of poetic meaning, we would have to convict Wordsworth of inability to say what he meant.

The flaw rests, as usual, in Hirsch's assumptions. He confronts us with two interpretations of the poem and asks us to pick the right one. The assumption is that there *is* a "right one," or, more accurately, there *must be* a right one. Why must there be a right one? Because the alternative is "subjectivism and relativism" (p. 226), which Hirsch equates with political anarchy. Amazingly enough, all we need do to rigorously disprove the entire argument of Hirsch's book is to demonstrate that anarchy does not necessarily result from "subjectivism and relativism."

This is of course only too easy to do. Imagine, if you will, a group of friends discussing Wordsworth's poem. Each has an interpretation that is in some respects at variance with the others, and some of their interpretations are diametrically opposed. They discuss the poem long enough to be aware of the exact nature of the differences among them; each is made aware of the premises upon which his interpretation rests (A's reading rests quite heavily upon the negatives of "No motion has she now, no force; / She neither hears nor sees," for example, while B stresses the hopeful progression of "rocks, and stones, and trees"); minds are changed on a point here and there, but by and large each is confirmed in his own view of the poem. Now: is the result of this failure to

159

Robert Crosman

agree a battle royal, a war of all against all, in which furniture is smashed and bodily injury sustained?

Of course not. Depending upon the degree of respect these people have for each other, they may part on more friendly terms than they began, or they may separate inwardly seething with resentment, but they will hardly come to blows. And *if* they part resentfully, it is likely to be because one or more of them refuses to tolerate a difference in opinion, and is intent upon forcing the others to recognize *his* meaning as *the* meaning of the poem. In other words, Hirsch's principle is conducive not to social harmony but to discord. The more firmly these people believe in "the one right reading," the less civil they are apt to be to one another. Since readers spontaneously differ in their interpretations of texts, there will be many occasions on which only coercion can make them agree. I am not saying that we never change our minds about what a poem means, or that we are never persuaded to take another's view of it, but only that such changes should not and ordinarily do not take place as the result of coercion.[9]

Hirsch's model of the literary community is, of course, not the easy equality of friends, but the hierarchical structure of students, teachers, departments of literature, of less and more prestigious universities, journals, critical reputations. His idea of how to determine validity in meaning is based upon the analogy of a case being tried in the courts, rising through higher levels of jurisdiction until a final "adjudication" is performed by the literary equivalent of a Supreme Court. But even if it could actually be brought into being, such a system would result in the enthronement not of authors, but of a sacerdotal càste of critic-judges, who are after all only readers like ourselves. Better far, I think, to recognize

[9] Coercion may seem a strong word for what Hirsch advocates, but if his "adjudication" process means anything, it means that of all the interpretations made of a particular text, one would be judged "correct" and the others "mistaken." Anyone who continued to voice the "mistaken" view in public would be subject to correction or ridicule. That such a state of affairs could not actually come to pass is merely one more demonstration of how unsuited to a modern democracy is Hirsch's theory of meaning.

160

Do Readers Make Meaning?

that our nearest approach to an author not present in the room where we are reading is in the words of the text he wrote. Any "expert" guidance we get from critics should be accepted on the basis of its usefulness, not its authority.

The final refutation of Hirsch's claim that tolerating a plurality of meanings produces anarchy is that we presently tolerate such a plurality without experiencing anarchy. Nor do "subjectivism and relativism" even *tend* toward anarchy. As we have seen, it is not mutual tolerance and respect for differences of opinion but an aggressive belief in the exclusive rightness of one's own opinion that leads to a physical or intellectual "war of all against all."

The idea that as readers we are constrained in our interpretations by the author's own interpretation is shot through with insuperable difficulties. For most texts we simply do not have a statement from the author on its meaning. If we *do* have such a statement, it is apt to be ambiguous or contradictory, and *it* must be subjected to the same process of reader interpretation that we were trying to avoid in the first place. If we have to infer an intention from the facts of the author's life, then we will have to study his biography, and of course different biographers will infer different intentions. Whichever biographer we decide to trust, his opinion will again be a text that we will have to interpret. This leads logically to an infinite regress, which can be stopped only by an act of will. That is, we arrive at the "author's meaning" precisely when we decide we have arrived there: we *make* the author's meaning!

This is not to deny that readers generally believe, whatever interpretation they make of a text, that they have discovered the author's intended meaning. Their belief is perhaps the single most successful instance of what Stanley Fish calls an "interpretive strategy"—that is, a convention of reading.[10] Despite the manifest empirical fact that different readers interpret differently, this convention maintains that there is a correct interpretation (mine, naturally!). Readers frequently

[10] "Interpreting the *Variorum*," pp. 480-85.

believe (like Hirsch) that in order to mean at all, a text can only mean one thing; that communication, order, and ultimately life itself depend upon a univocality of texts, in theory if not, alas, in practice. The price of such a belief is, of course, the recognition that Truth is in a sorry state nowadays, that few possess it, and that the mass of our fellow men are stupid or perverse. Depending on our temperaments, we can then turn our backs on them in cynical contempt, or try to force them to see the light.

The idea that Truth is One—unambiguous, self-consistent, and knowable—has a long and venerable history in the West. The intellectual equivalent of aggressiveness and a wish to dominate, it has been an important part of the ideology of Hebrew, Athenian, Roman, Christian, European, and finally American and Russian imperialism.[11] Such a successful idea cannot have been all bad, but it may now have outlived its usefulness. In every area of human activity today the ability to see several points of view seems to be at a premium, and every intellectual discipline exhibits more and more of the attributes of paradox rather than of logical self-consistency. In this context, the hope for a univocality of literary texts appears not only naive but misguided. In order to serve the various needs and desires of various readers, texts *ought* to have plural meanings.

This is not to deny the extraordinary interest that an author's interpretation (or interpretations) of his own work may have for us but to put it in a new light. Do authors make meaning? Yes, of course they do, in exactly the same way that we all make meaning: as interpreters, as readers. Because we have all been taught to believe in Imperial Truth we have imagined the process of writing as antithetical to the process

[11] This is, I realize, a tendentious way to put it. The benign side of, say, Christian intolerance was a belief in the brotherhood of man. Imperial Christianity welded disparate peoples and cultures together first by conquest, but in the long run by common concerns and beliefs as well. The bloodiness and repressiveness of this way of achieving "brotherhood" should not be ignored, however. Tolerance and mutual respect seem today a more hopeful means to peace and harmony among peoples and nations than does the path of Imperial Truth.

Do Readers Make Meaning?

of reading: the writer, in contact with the wordless realm of Truth, somehow embodies his ineffable vision of reality in words and sends it to the reader, who (if all goes well) removes the "meaning" from its verbal envelope. I suggest that this accords rather badly with our own experience as writers. As a writer I begin with a jumble of purposes, ideas, and words that can only be examined by the activity of putting them on paper and reading them off. The physical acts of pushing my pencil over the paper, and of casting my eye over the markings thus made, may be called by different names, but in practice they are inseparable. The very act of writing includes reading.

It is impossible, I suppose, to deny categorically the existence somewhere of authors who imagine they know precisely what they will write before they set pen to paper, or who insist (however quixotically) that we understand by every word precisely what they *intend* us to understand. "When I say 'religion' I mean the Church of England," says Reverend Thwackum, thereby making it impossible for us either to misunderstand or to agree with him. But whether to take such hypothetical writers as either the rule or the norm is ineluctably *our* choice. The "facts" about writers—even about ourselves as writers—are far too vague and conflicting to support unequivocally either the view that writers encode a preexistent, nonverbal meaning when they write, or the view that they discover their own meaning only in the act of reading what they have written.

"Nature," says Whitehead, "is patient of interpretation in terms of laws that happen to interest us." We don't build up our laws out of neutral, innocent facts; "the facts," rather, are constituted by us when we examine nature through the grid of a hypothesis that suits our purposes—purposes that are not arbitrary or fortuitous, of course, but consistent with our ethical, social, or political needs and wants. The convention that authors make meaning arose from a desire to think of truth as single and unequivocal, and is part of an ideology of society that is authoritarian and hierarchical. It is true—to the extent that it is true—as all conventions are: by the consent of

Robert Crosman

the members of that society. My impression is that this consent is being withdrawn today at an accelerating rate, as people perceive that freedom is not incompatible with order, and that order is not necessarily hierarchical. Once we decide that readers *can* make meaning, and *ought* to be doing so, we begin to see it happening all around us—that is what reading is, after all. Meaning is made precisely as we *want* it to be made, and as usual we want different things. Unanimity is neither possible nor desirable, and reality is never unequivocal. Yes, authors do make meaning (since we go on insisting that they must) but—many of us are finding it increasingly necessary to say—yes, readers make meaning.

Naomi Schor | Fiction as Interpretation /
Interpretation as Fiction

In her 1964 essay, "Against Interpretation," Susan Sontag sounded the keynote of a
neoformalism, a new wave of French criticism that was about
to sweep over modern language departments, wreaking
havoc with the traditional interpretive positions standing in
its path. In order to assess the current state and status of interpretation, that is of hermeneutics in the wake of structuralism, I should like to recall very briefly the main points of
Sontag's essay, for they retain even today their polemical
freshness. What must first be noted is Sontag's definition of
interpretation, for her assault on hermeneutics is grounded in
this definition: "The task of interpretation is virtually one of
translation. The interpreter says, Look, don't you see that X is
really—or, really means—A? That Y is really B? That Z is really C?"[1] Having thus reduced interpretation to only one of
its acceptations, Sontag then proceeds to charge it with reductionism (ironically the very accusation most frequently
leveled at the structuralists and their algebraic equations and
algorithms): "To interpret is to impoverish, to deplete the
world—in order to set up a shadow world of 'meanings.' "[2]

As a prime example of the ravages of interpretation, Sontag
cites the fate of one of its most spectacular victims, Kafka,
whose work "has been subjected to a mass ravishment by no
less than three armies of interpreters,"[3] and these armies of
the night are the Marxists, the Freudians, and the Christians.
That Sontag should single out Kafka is almost inevitable, for

[1] In Sontag, *Against Interpretation* (New York: paperback, 1969), p. 15. Cf.
Tzvetan Todorov, *Poétique de la prose* (Paris, 1971), p. 245.

[2] Sontag, *Against Interpretation*, p. 17.

[3] Ibid., p. 18.

165

Naomi Schor

Kafka is unquestionably the touchstone for any future history or sociology of hermeneutics in the age of criticism. The peculiar solicitations of Kafka's "hysterical" texts (hysterical in the sense that they seem to invite rape, while denying penetration) have led to the critics' wonderment, if not the "commentators' despair"[4]: "Each sentence of Kafka's says 'interpret me,' "[5] writes Theodore Adorno; similarly Erich Heller remarks: "In the case of Kafka, and *The Trial* in particular, the compulsion to interpret is at its most compelling, and is as great as the compulsion to continue reading once one has begun. . . . There is only one way to save oneself the trouble of interpreting *The Trial*: not to read it."[6] Any account of interpretive strategies today must reckon with the Kafka "case," and this study is no exception.

That interpretation need not be equated with translation, need not result in an impoverishment of the text, has been the position consistently held by Roland Barthes, a position I would qualify as "ecumenical hermeneutics." Thus, in *S/Z* he proposes a definition of interpretation at complete odds with the definition quoted above: "Interpréter un texte, ce n'est pas lui donner un sens (plus ou moins fondé, plus ou moins libre), c'est au contraire apprécier de quel pluriel il est fait."[7] If polysemy is the relatively simple answer to the reductionist argument, the hermeneutician must still respond to the second and more constructive part of Sontag's essay, which calls for the elaboration of a "poetics of the novel": "The function of criticism should be to show *how it is what it is*, even *that it is what it is*, rather than to show *what it means*."[8] The question

---

[4] Franz Kafka, *The Trial*, trans. Willa and Edwin Muir (New York: Schocken paperback, 1968), p. 217.

[5] Adorno, "Notes on Kafka," in *Prisms*, trans. S. and S. Weber (London, 1967), p. 246; as quoted by Stanley Corngold in "The Hermeneutic of 'The Judgment,' " in Angel Flores, ed., *The Problem of 'The Judgment': Eleven Approaches to Kafka's Story* (Staten Island, N.Y., 1977), p. 139. This paper owes more to Professor Corngold than a mere footnote can convey; it has benefited overall from his generous and learned commentary.

[6] Heller, *Franz Kafka* (New York, 1974), pp. 72 and 71.

[7] Barthes, *S/Z* (Paris, 1970), p. 11. Cf. his *Critique et Vérité* (Paris, 1966), p. 50 and "La réponse de Kafka," in *Essais critiques* (Paris, 1964), pp. 141-42.

[8] Sontag, *Against Interpretation*, p. 23.

Fiction as Interpretation

then arises, On the basis of what we know now, after the revolution, as it were, are poetics and hermeneutics, description and interpretation, mutually exclusive? Is the pursuit of the "how" irreconcilable with the quest for the "what"? Furthermore, has the structuralists' emphasis on the "literariness" of the text, on the priority of the linguistic model in our apprehension of fiction, spelled the end of hermeneutics? In the face of a constantly growing body of evidence, my answer is unhesitatingly no. Almost paradoxically, a critical orthodoxy whose tenets are anti- or an-interpretive has provided a new impetus for latter-day hermeneutics. This apparent paradox is resolved if one considers the structuralists' praxis, and not merely their *theoria*: in their actual readings of texts, such bona fide poeticians as Gérard Genette and Tzvetan Todorov have repeatedly focused their attention on metalinguistic commentary incorporated in the texts themselves, tending thereby to make the authors they examine (e.g., Proust in Genette's "Proust et le langage indirect" or Constant in Todorov's "La parole selon Constant"[9]) appear to be (Saussurian) linguists before the letter.

Now, from the notion that fiction is self-conscious and reflects upon its own representation of speech acts, to the notion—which seems to be gaining ground today[10]—that novels also represent and reflect upon interpretation as performance, there is not such a very far way to go. In short, it

[9] Gérard Genette, "Proust et le langage indirect," *Figures II* (Paris, 1969); Tzvetan Todorov, "La parole selon Constant," in *Poétique de la prose.*

[10] In addition to the critics cited throughout this essay, others might be mentioned. Several recent examples of this trend: Paul de Man, "Proust et l'allégorie de la lecture," in *Mouvements premiers: Etudes critiques offertes à Georges Poulet* (Paris, 1972): Max Byrd, "Reading in *Great Expectations,*" *PMLA* 91 (1976), 259-65; and Philippe Hamon, "Texte littéraire et métalangage," *Poétique*, no. 31 (1977), 261-84. In an altogether different paradigm: Algirdas Julien Greimas, *Maupassant: La Sémiotique du texte* (Paris, 1976), in particular pp. 175-89 ("La Réinterprétation"). In this work Greimas introduces a new descriptive term, "le faire interprétatif," which, while not synonymous with our notion of "interpretation as performance" (the differences being one of scale—sentence versus novel—and methodological preoccupations—narratology versus hermeneutics), is to be retained for dealing with interpretation as manifested in microunits of the text.

has taken the importation of semiotics into the field of literary criticism for us to discover and turn to account a rather simple fact: novels are not only about speaking and writing (*encoding*), but also about reading, and by reading I mean the *decoding* of all manner of signs and signals. If, as I am suggesting, interpretation is viewed not as something that is done *to* fiction but rather as something that is done *in* fiction, then to be against interpretation becomes an untenable position, for it is tantamount to rejecting a considerable body of (modern) fiction that is explicitly, indeed insistently, concerned with interpretation: its scope and its limits, its necessity and its frustration. In dealing with what I call fictions of interpretation, the critic finds himself in somewhat the same situation as Joseph K.: "He hardly had the choice now to accept the trial or reject it, he was in the middle of it, and must fend for himself."[11] Indeed, long before Joseph K. came into the picture, the critic was already "embarked" on the Good Ship *Hermeneutic Enterprise*; according to the French psychoanalyst André Green, the necessity of interpretation is *the* lesson of the Oedipus myth: "l'interprétation n'est pas seulement champ du possible mais obligation, nécessité. La relation du sujet à son géniteur fonde le champ de la *contrainte interprétative*."[12]

The shift away from the illusion of an *interpretive option* toward a recognition of the *interpretive constraint* requires the introduction of a term which, while not strictly new (it is used by Charles Sanders Peirce in a very different context), will serve to distinguish between two types of interpreters: the interpreting critic, for whom I reserve the term *interpreter*, and the interpreting character, whom I will refer to henceforth as the *interpretant*.[13] That this term evokes the term *analysand* is

[11] Kafka, *The Trial*, p. 126.

[12] Green, *Un Oeil en trop* (Paris, 1969), p. 282.

[13] See Charles Sanders Peirce, *Collected Papers*, ed. Charles Hartshorne and Paul Weiss, vols. 1-2 (Cambridge, Mass., 1960): "A sign stands *for* something *to* the idea which it produces, or modifies. Or, it is a vehicle conveying into the mind something from without. That for which it stands is called its *object*; that which it conveys, its *meaning*; and the idea to which it gives rise, its *inter-*

Fiction as Interpretation

not coincidental, for the analytic situation is analogous to the one we have been outlining: both involve (at least) a double interpretive activity, interpretation in the second power or "en abyme." Hierarchically the interpretant "ranks" above the "narratee,"[14] the "fictionalized audience,"[15] or any other variety of "implied reader,"[16] in that he is neither supporting actor, nor theoretical construct, nor intaglio figure, but instead coextensive with the first-person narrator or main protagonist of the fiction.[17] If there existed a barometer capable of measuring the narcissistic gratification afforded by literary works, then fictions of interpretation would push the needle way over, for what could comfort and delight the interpreter more than to find the interpretant, his specular image, shimmering on the printed page, mirroring his confusions as well as his triumphs? And yet, the interpreter/interpretant relationship is not an easy one: the lure of narcissistic identification only makes it more difficult for the interpreter to keep his distance from the interpretant. My concern here is not, however, with the (impossible/fatal) coincidence of interpretant and interpreter (the interpreter's "countertransference," to

---

pretant" (1: 171). It might be, indeed it already has been suggested, that I would do better to develop a new terminology and leave the interpretant to the linguists. If I have chosen to maintain the term it is partly because of the interpretant/analysand homophony, and partly because, as I hope to show in my conclusion, my meaning and Peirce's are not so far apart as they at first appear.

[14] See Gerald Prince, "Introduction à l'étude du narrataire," *Poétique*, no. 14 (1973), 178-96.

[15] See Walter J. Ong, S. J., "The Writer's Audience is Always a Fiction," *PMLA* 90 (1975), 9-21.

[16] See Wolfgang Iser, *The Implied Reader* (Baltimore, 1974).

[17] This formulation is not restrictive: secondary characters can and do perform important interpretive functions; indeed, there are novels where the main protagonist, because he is either an "innocent" or an enigma or both, while not ceasing all interpretive activities, plays a largely passive role in the hermeneutic script. Two examples that come to mind, Balzac's *Le Cousin Pons* and Zola's *Le Ventre de Paris*, share a common feature: interpretation as practiced by the secondary characters is a form of persecution, the hermeneutic object is a scapegoat.

Naomi Schor

borrow a concept from Serge Doubrovsky[18] and pursue the analytic analogy), but rather with a simple proposition: via the interpretant the author is trying to tell the interpreter something *about* interpretation and the interpreter would do well to listen and take note.

Interpretants are so widespread in modern fiction that it is imperative from the outset to establish some sort of taxonomy to deal with them; what follows is an attempt in that direction. My approach is diachronic: the three interpretants I propose to examine represent three generations of protagonists, and they have been selected to demonstrate that the vicissitudes of hermeneutics in our time reduplicate, with an inevitable time-lag, the vicissitudes of the interpretant around the turn of the century. Two criteria govern my classification, quantity and quality. In other words, how much or how little interpretation the interpretant engages in, and with what results, what degree of success. For convenience' sake, the authors whose works I will draw upon offer impeccable interpretive credentials: James, Proust, and, of course, Kafka.

JAMES, OR THE INTERPRETANT AS YOUNG ARTIST

That his central or "focusing-characters"[19] are perpetually, indeed obsessively, involved in interpretive ventures should come as no surprise to even the most casual reader of James's fictions and prefaces. To single out any one novel or short story as representative of James's fictions of interpretation might seem arbitrary; however, I feel my choice of the "minor—but important"[20] novella, *In the Cage*, is warranted by the fact that in it all actions have been reduced to one: interpretation. *In the Cage* is the story of an anonymous

---

[18] Doubrovsky, *La Place de la madeleine* (Paris, 1974), p. 153.

[19] Lyall H. Powers, ed., *Henry James's Major Novels: Essays in Criticism* (East Lansing, 1973), p. xxxii.

[20] Tony Tanner, "Henry James's Subjective Adventurers: *The Sacred Fount*," in *Henry James's Major Novels*, p. 225.

Fiction as Interpretation

young woman who works in a postal-telegraph office in an elegant section of London. In the course of events or nonevents, she becomes particularly interested in one of her clients, Captain Everard; in fact, so great is her involvement in his love affair with Lady Aberdeen that the young woman delays her marriage to the dull Mr. Mudge so that she might be at her post in Captain Everard's hour of need. What makes the heroine of this tale an exemplary interpretant is that her interpretive activities bear solely on the written sign, on high society as inscribed in the messages that pass daily through her cage. Furthermore, the messages she deals with are by definition "coded" and incomplete: "*His* words were mere numbers, they told her nothing whatever; and after he had gone she was in possession of no name, of no address, of no meaning."[21] The heroine's hermeneutic hyperactivity is directly proportionate to the paucity of vital pieces of information: "missing the answers . . . she pressed the romance closer by reason of the very quantity of imagination it demanded" (ibid., pp. 184-85).

What is significant here is that interpretation is synonymous with imagination, it is a "creative" rather than critical activity; the young woman is not content merely to encode and decode, rather she delights in filling in the gaps, piecing together the fragments, in short, adding something of her own to the faulty, often trivial texts at hand. Her pleasure is not finding "the figure in the carpet," but weaving the whole cloth: "On the clearness therefore what she did retain stood sharply out; she snipped and caught it, turned it over and interwove it" (ibid., p. 190). In no other fiction of interpretation that we shall analyze is interpretation more closely linked to the production of the tale. The result of this unbridled imagination are "stories and meanings without end" (ibid., p. 189). Indeed, as practiced in *In the Cage*, interpretation is always in danger of giving way to overinterpretation, an inflation and

[21] James, *In the Cage and other tales* (New York: Norton, 1969), p. 182. All subsequent page references in the text are to this edition.

debasing of meaning: "Everything, so far as they chose to consider it so, might mean almost anything" (ibid., p. 205). So pervasive is this tendency that even the levelheaded shopkeeper, Mr. Mudge, is affected or infected by it: "Mr. Mudge himself—habitually inclined indeed to a scrutiny of all mysteries and to seeing, as he sometimes admitted, too much in things . . ." (ibid., pp. 228-29).

James was, of course, intensely aware of the problems inherent in excessive interpretation, both in the specific instance of *In the Cage* and in general. Thus, in his preface to *In the Cage*, he acknowledges: "My central spirit, in the anecdote, is, for verisimilitude, I grant, *too* ardent a focus of divination; but without this *excess* the phenomena detailed would have lacked their principle of cohesion."[22] But preternatural gifts of "divination" on the part of a character not only defy the laws of verisimilitude, they also lessen reader interest. Nothing, remarks James in the preface to *The Princess Casamassima*, would be duller than the "annals" of "the all knowing immortals" on Olympus: "Therefore it is that the wary reader for the most part warns the novelist against making his characters too *interpretative* of the muddle of fate, or in other words too divinely, too priggishly clever."[23] James's elaborate strategies for providing his interpretants with just the right dose of "bewilderment" to maintain reader interest are too well-known to be rehearsed here. In the case of the young heroine of *In the Cage*, James tempers the interpretive triumph she scores by having her discover in the end how much had eluded her as to the most essential facts of Captain Everard's affairs. After all her "theories and interpretations,"[24] she finds to her surprise and dismay that her knowledge of her hermeneutic object is mediated by a series of eminently unreliable narrators; there is no interpretation without mediation: "She might hear of him, now forever lost, only through Mrs. Jordan, who touched him through Mr.

[22] James, *The Art of the Novel* (New York: Scribner, 1962), p. 157; italics mine.
[23] Ibid., p. 64.
[24] James, *In the Cage*, p. 187.

Fiction as Interpretation

Drake, who reached him through Lady Bradeen" (ibid., p. 263).

PROUST, OR DOING IT
SWANN'S WAY

Any discussion of interpretation in *A la recherche du temps perdu* must begin with some mention of Gilles Deleuze's work, *Proust et les signes*, wherein he states flatly at the outset that his subject is "la Recherche comme interprétation."[25] What strikes me as a particularly fruitful insight on Deleuze's part is his insistence on "la violence du signe," the mechanism that sets the interpretive machine in motion: "Le grand thème du Temps retrouvé est celui-ci: la recherche de la vérité est l'aventure propre de l'involontaire. La pensée n'est rien sans quelque chose qui force à penser, qui fait violence à la pensée"; and elsewhere he remarks: "Le hasard des rencontres, la pression des contraintes sont les deux thèmes fondamentaux de Proust."[26] If Deleuze is justified in arguing that in Proust characters operate under an *interpretive constraint*, rather than being driven, as in James, by an *interpretive instinct*, then Proust's involuntary interpretants lie midway between James's typically nineteenth-century "subjective adventurers," with their "morbid" and "penetrating" imaginations, and Kafka's typically twentieth-century interpretants, with their singular interpretive deficiencies.

In order to test the validity and utility of Deleuze's thesis, let us consider the case of Swann in *Un Amour de Swann*. From the first Swann is presented to us as suffering from a mental condition inherited from his father; Swann is incapable of going to the bottom of things, especially unpleasant ones. When it occurs to him that Odette might be what is commonly referred to as a "kept woman," he suffers a characteristic seizure of this hereditary disease: "Il ne put approfondir cette idée, car un accès d'une paresse d'esprit qui était chez lui congénitale, intermittente et providentielle, vint

[25] Deleuze, *Proust et les signes* (Paris, 1971), p. 5.
[26] Ibid., pp. 187-88 and p. 23.

173

à ce moment éteindre toute lumière dans son intelligence, aussi brusquement que, plus tard, quand on eut installé partout l'éclairage, on put couper l'électricité dans une maison."[27]

Throughout the initial, euphoric stages of Swann's love affair with Odette, he continues to display his singular mental incapacity. Whereas James's heroine suffers from a pronounced *horror vacui*, Swann exhibits a remarkable *amor vacui*; whereas the young woman seeks to fill in the blanks, Swann cultivates them: "Car la tendresse de Swann continuait à garder le même caractère que lui avait imprimé dès le début à la fois l'ignorance où il était de l'emploi des journées d'Odette et la paresse cérébrale qui l'empêchait de suppléer à l'ignorance par l'imagination" (ibid., p. 283). The worldly and wealthy bourgeois is most sadly lacking in precisely the attribute the poor young woman possessed in abundance: the *supplement* of imagination.[28]

Swann's jealousy marks a decisive turning point in his amorous and mental activities. Driven by an *erotic constraint*, Swann becomes highly attentive to the smallest details in Odette's behavior; he goes from apathy to a veritable paranoia of jealousy, the paranoiac being, of course, the in-

---

[27] Proust, *A la recherche du temps perdu*, vol. 1 (Paris: Pléiade, 1963), 268. All subsequent page references in the text are to this edition.

[28] The interpretant's class, gender, and occupation are determining factors second in importance only to his place in literary history. Swann's "advantages" have jaded his interpretive appetite, while the postal clerk's deprivations have whet hers. If in James (and in Proust, too, viz. Charlus) male interpretants do often belong to Swann's class and age group, they operate out of some imperative affective constraint (though nothing so vulgar as jealousy—see, for example, Lambert Strether in *The Ambassadors*), or function as the author's persona which Swann, the narrator's foil, is most emphatically not. The case of female interpretants of this class is altogether different: they are always compelled by some sort of erotic constraint. As for the lower- and lower-middle-class characters, the male interpretants tend to be bureaucrats (Dostoyevsky), and the female, professional busybodies such as old maids and concierges (Balzac). The female bureaucrat, the young lady "in the cage," represents a super-interpretant, syncretizing as she does the "natural" interpretive attributes of her sex with the interpretive opportunities inherent in her position.

terpretant's psychotic double. Despite this stepped-up hermeneutic activity, however, Swann remains singularly inept at interpretation: he is not only the failed artist he has always been portrayed as being, but a failed critic as well. Swann's congenital laziness could be described in rhetorical terms, as an overreliance on synecdoche (cf. the narrator's predilection for metaphor): "Swann comme beaucoup de gens avait l'esprit paresseux et manquait d'invention. Il savait bien comme une vérité générale que la vie des êtres est pleine de contrastes, mais, pour chaque être en particulier, il imaginait toute la partie de sa vie qu'il ne connaissait pas comme identique à la partie qu'il connaissait. Il imaginait ce qu'on lui taisait à l'aide de ce qu'on lui disait" (ibid., p. 359).

Unable to imagine the difference between the known (visible) and the unknown (hidden), between the part and the whole, bound by an all-or-nothing rule, Swann oscillates between two equally extreme stances: either the refusal, or the compulsion, to interpret. When he receives a poison-pen letter, recounting Odette's lurid sexual past and proclivities, Swann cannot think who among his friends might have written such a letter: "il n'avait jamais eu aucun soupçon des actions inconnues des êtres, de celles qui sont sans liens visibles avec leurs propos" (ibid., p. 356). However, on further reflection, he decides that *all* of his friends are capable of authoring such a letter: "Mais alors, après n'avoir pu soupçonner personne, il lui fallut soupçonner tout le monde" (ibid., p. 357).

Finally, however much Swann errs in the direction of overinterpretation, reality always exceeds his interpretations. *Un Amour de Swann* is, in effect, divided into two equal parts, and *Swann II* functions largely as a reading of *Swann I*. A single example should suffice to illustrate the connection between structure and exegesis, the incidence of differed interpretation (*Nachträglichkeit*) on the ordering of narrative sequences. In the early part of Swann's affair (*Swann I*), he receives a letter from Odette, written on the stationery of a café, "la 'Maison Dorée.' " This letter, which reads in part, "Mon ami, ma main tremble si fort que je peux à peine écrire" (ibid., p. 225), is among Swann's most treasured possessions. Much later, in *Swann II*, when the romance is nearly over, Odette tells Swann that she was never at the Maison Dorée that day; not only were her sentiments insincere, but the very letterhead they were written under was a lie or lure (all that glitters . . .): "Ainsi, même dans les mois auxquels il n'avait jamais plus osé repenser parce qu'ils avaient été trop heureux, dans ces mois où elle l'avait aimé, elle lui mentait déjà! Aussi bien que ce moment . . . où elle lui avait dit sortir de la Maison Dorée, combien devait-il y en avoir eu d'autres, receleurs eux aussi d'un mensonge que Swann n'avait pas soupçonné" (ibid., p. 371). Proust's pairing of the man without suspicion and the woman who cannot but does tell lies only serves to hyperbolize the dilemma of the interpretant.

Paradoxically then, in what has long been considered the most reassuringly traditional section of *La recherche*, Proust has portrayed a strikingly modern character, one of the first in a long line of what I will call *reluctant interpretants*; as bizarre as this genealogy may seem, Swann is the distant ancestor of Meursault, Camus' stranger, whose story is also divided into two equal parts, Part II providing *the* or *an* interpretation of the events in Part I. Just as Swann's jealousy teaches him suspicion, obliges him to overcome his allergy to interpretation, Meursault's trial forces meaning on actions and observations that he had a particularly strong investment in regarding as meaningless. The obvious differences between Swann's and Meursault's reluctance—differences not only of degree, but also of outcome—can be accounted for, at least in part, by the intervening inscription of the Joseph K. of *The Trial*, that is the *failed interpretant*.

Kafka, or the Death of an Interpretant

In Kafka's fictional universe, the interpretant finds himself in a far graver situation than either James's young heroine or Proust's aging Lothario, for in Kafka, as Charles Bernheimer has phrased it, "the existential implication of a failed her-

Fiction as Interpretation

meneutic is death."[29] K.'s fatal interpretive failure is not, I hasten to point out, a result of any reluctance to interpret; on the contrary, once embarked on his trial, he makes a determined if not always successful effort to analyze the signs he perceives, the signals he receives. But, and this is what definitely sets K. apart from the interpretants discussed earlier, the prevailing rule in the world of the Court is the hermeneutic double bind: the absolute necessity to interpret goes hand in hand with the total impossibility to validate interpretation. All signs are irremediably ambiguous; whereas the signs Swann initially misses or misreads do eventually render their correct, that is hidden, meaning, K. is repeatedly confronted with signs suspended between two simultaneously plausible but contradictory meanings: "The Examining Magistrate sitting here beside me has just given one of you a secret sign. . . . I do not know whether the sign was meant to evoke applause or hissing, and now that I have divulged the matter prematurely I deliberately give up all hope of ever learning its real significance."[30]

That the inability of Kafka's interpretants to decode sign language should have given rise to feverish activity on the part of his many interpreters is not in the least surprising; it is at this juncture in literary history that the identification between interpretant and interpreter begins to produce diminishing narcissistic returns, and the interpreter feels compelled to work overtime lest he suffer the interpretant's sorry fate. What is surprising is that in their eagerness to rush into the semiotic breach, the interpreters have paid little heed to the veritable "allegory"[31] of interpretation that Kafka's texts constitute. Nowhere would this attention be better invested

[29] Bernheimer, "Symbolic Bond and Textual Play: The Structure of Kafka's *Castle*," in *The Kafka Debate*, ed. Angel Flores (Staten Island, N.Y., 1977), p. 367.

[30] Kafka, *The Trial*, p. 44. All subsequent page references in the text are to the Schocken edition.

[31] See Stanley Corngold, *The Commentators' Despair* (Port Washington, N.Y., 1973), pp. 31-38.

177

Naomi Schor

than in a reading of the penultimate chapter of *The Trial*, "In the Cathedral," where K. is assailed by a barrage of enigmatic signs: a foreign language (Italian), pictorial language (the altarpiece), gestural language (the verger), and finally the parabolic language of the Priest. To each semiology correspond specific modalities of hermeneutic distress and disaster: each sign system comes equipped with its own failure device.

In the instance of the "unintelligible Italian" (ibid., p. 201), K. does not meet the first interpretive challenge of the day—interpretation-as-translation—because of the gap between acquired linguistic "competence" and the native speaker's "performance." Despite his knowledge of Italian syntax and vocabulary, K. is unable to decode the Italian's speech: "He could understand him almost completely when he spoke slowly and quietly, but that happened very seldom, the words mostly came pouring out in a flood, and he made lively gestures with his head as if enjoying the rush of talk. Besides, when this happened, he invariably relapsed into a dialect which K. did not recognize as Italian but which the Manager could both speak and understand" (ibid., p. 200). The pointed contrast between K.'s confusion and the Manager's ease serves to underscore the fact that there is nothing intrinsically unintelligible about the Italian's discourse, it is not even ambiguous. And yet for K. it is totally opaque, obscured by a *series* of obstacles: "It became clear to K. that there was little chance of communicating with the Italian, for the man's French was difficult to follow and it was no use watching his lips for clues, since their movements were covered by the bushy mustache" (ibid.). What is reemphasized in this scene is K.'s characteristic lack of preparedness: he is always somehow taken by surprise, confounded by an unforeseen gap that appears between what he is ready to interpret and the signs he in fact receives.

The inefficacy of book learning is confirmed by K.'s second interpretive fiasco of the day, his misprision in the Cathedral. Despite his certified expertise in art history, K.'s appreciation of the altarpiece falls short of the mark:

Fiction as Interpretation

[I] The first thing K. perceived, partly by guess, was a huge armored knight on the outermost verge of the picture. [II] He was leaning on his sword, which was stuck into the bare ground, bare except for a stray blade of grass or two. [III] He seemed to be watching attentively some event unfolding itself before his eyes. [IV] It was surprising that he should stand so still without approaching nearer to it. [V] Perhaps he had been sent there to stand guard. [VI] K., who had not seen any pictures for a long time, studied this knight for a good while, although the greenish light of the oil-lamp made his eyes blink. [VII] When he played the torch over the rest of the altarpiece he discovered that it was a portrayal of Christ being laid in the tomb, conventional in style and a fairly recent painting [ibid., p. 205].

This passage provides us with a remarkable *mimesis* of interpretation as practiced by Kafka's interpretants, a process which progresses through the following stages:

1. The fascinated observation/description of the peripheral (I and II)

2. The (hypothetical) interpretation of the detail (III)

3. The metamorphosis of interpretation into fiction (introduction of elements of temporality and motivation) (IV and V)

4. The retroactive deflation of the entire sequence (stages 1, 2, and 3) (VI and VII)

But if this were all we saw in this passage we would, like K., be "beside the point"; what we have here is not just a *mimesis* of the interpretant's modus operandi, but a *mise en abyme*: we have K. looking at the Knight looking at something which we ultimately discover to be Christ being laid in the tomb. This breathtaking deepening of the visual field recalls the series of obstacles that prevent K. from communicating with the Italian and foreshadows the foliate structure of the parable.

From the overinterpretation of a relatively insignificant detail, K. goes on to the outright misinterpretation of a gesture, generally the least ambiguous of signs in Kafka's fiction: "The

179

Naomi Schor

old man kept pointing at something, but K. deliberately re-
frained from looking round to see what he was pointing at,
the gesture could have no other purpose than to shake K. off"
(ibid., p. 206). The gesture's "purpose" is, of course, exactly
the opposite of the one K. ascribes to it: it points K. in the
direction of the priest in his pulpit. The celebrated encounter
with the priest must then be seen in the context of this string
of interpretive fiascos, and this microcontextual[32] reading
cannot but produce results different from the macro- or ex-
tracontextual approaches that have traditionally predomi-
nated. The figure of the Priest manifests itself at this strategic
point in the text to instruct K., not so much in the ways of the
Law, as in those of exegesis. Viewed in this perspective, the
possible meaning(s) of the parable, "Before the Law," need
not worry us, for what matters is the Talmudic discussion
that follows it. The lesson borne in on K. is not the definitive
reading of the parable, the "correct" interpretation, but
something altogether different: the crucial fact that the parable is one with the commentators' interpretations, there is no
separating the gloss from the fiction. Even as the priest is
speaking, his performance is an interpretation: " 'So the
doorkeeper deceived the man,' said K. immediately, strongly
attracted by the story. 'Don't be too hasty,' said the priest,
'don't take over someone else's opinion without testing it. I
have told you the story in the very words of the scriptures.
There's no mention of deception in it.' 'But it's clear enough,'
said K., 'and your *first interpretation* of it was quite right' "
(ibid., p. 215; italics mine). The interpretant is deluded if he
thinks his access to the parable is direct and unmediated, if he
fancies himself the "first" interpreter; interpretation has always already begun: " 'So you think the man was not deceived?' 'Don't misunderstand me,' said the priest, 'I am only
showing you the various opinions concerning that point. You
must not pay too much attention to them. The scriptures are
unalterable and the comments often enough merely express
the commentators' despair' " (ibid., p. 217).

[32] See Michael Riffaterre, *Essais de stylistique structurale* (Paris, 1971), pp.
68-78.

180

Fiction as Interpretation

If we return, in conclusion, to James, we find that he was perhaps the first modern novelist to articulate the existence of what J. Hillis Miller has referred to as a "series of interpreters."[33] In the preface to *The Princess Casamassima*, James writes: "The teller of a story is primarily, none the less, the listener to it, the reader of it, too; and, having needed thus to make it out, distinctly, on the crabbed page of life, to disengage it from the rude human character and the more or less Gothic text in which it has been packed away, the very essence of his affair has been the *imputing* of intelligence."[34] We arrive thus at a three-tiered interpretive process: the "teller of a story" deciphers the "page of life," he then "imputes" his deciphering to interpretants, who in turn become the objects of interpreters. But even this vertiginous interpretive chain does not adequately represent the hermeneutic situation, for in fact the "teller of a story" has as little claim to priority as do either the interpretant or the interpreter; there is no sign on that "crabbed page of life" which is not already inscribed in the Great Chain of Interpretation. Here we come full circle and encounter Peirce when he writes: "The meaning of a representation can be nothing but a representation. In fact, it is nothing but the representation itself conceived as stripped of irrelevant clothing. But this clothing never can be completely stripped off; it is only changed for something more diaphanous. So there is an infinite regression here. Finally, the interpretant is nothing but another representation to which the torch of truth is handed along; and as representation, it has its interpretant again. Lo, another infinite series."[35]

Just as Sontag's attack against interpretation was, so to speak, a sign of her times, my concern with fiction-as-interpretation/interpretation-as-fiction is but an aspect of the preoccupation with infinitely receding origins that pervades structuralist and poststructuralist writings. As Edward Said has summarized this trend: "The problem as seen by all

[33] Miller, "The Interpretation of *Lord Jim*," in *The Interpretation of Narrative: Theory and Practice*, ed. Morton W. Bloomfield (Cambridge, Mass., 1970), p. 211.

[34] James, *The Art of the Novel*, p. 63.

[35] Peirce, *Collected Papers*, 1: 171.

structuralists—Lévi-Strauss, Barthes, Louis Althusser, and Emile Benvéniste among them—is that the authority of a privileged Origin that commands, guarantees, and perpetuates meaning has been removed."[36] To read literature in this gloomy (essentially Derridean) optic is not only to renounce any belief in the author's authority—a form of apostasy dating back to the origins of modern formalism—but to renounce any compensatory belief in the interpreter's omnipotence. In the end, what is perhaps most telling about Sontag's essay is her assimilation of interpretation to (masculine) forms of aggression and mastery: rape and imperialism. She is against interpretation as intellectual machismo. The commentators' despair is only the dysphoric corollary of what Sontag refers to as the interpreters' "arrogance," that is, their hubris. Reading Sontag with Peirce, with his metaphor of (impossible) unveiling, leads me to rephrase her conclusion —"In place of a hermeneutics we need an erotics of art"[37]—by calling instead for an *erotics of hermeneutics*, text-pleasure as striptease instead of rape. The recognition of the interpretant's role and situation should put an end to the interpreter's manic-depressive cycle and promote a "saner" mode or, better yet, mood: the commentator's humility, which is somehow bound up with a recognition of his (or her) femininity.

[36] Said, *Beginnings: Intention and Method* (New York, 1975), p. 315.

[37] Sontag, *Against Interpretation*, p. 23.

Pierre Maranda | The Dialectic
of Metaphor:
An Anthropological
Essay on Hermeneutics

In nonliterate societies, there are
no "texts." Yet anthropologists "read" those societies the
way their compatriots read books. And in our monographs
we write up peoples, events, cultures that have never felt the
need for an alphabet: we reduce to *linearity* (imposed by written descriptions) the nonlinear (because illiterate) societies
we describe. We phrase our accounts of the "others" so as to
make them understandable to other "selves"; we interpret
what we see and experience in so-called exotic societies in the
light of the ideologies that mold us, as we try to bear witness
to the diversity as well as to the permanent structures of
mankind.

In this respect, the anthropologist, like the poet, is a ped-
dler of "home movies." The former brings inklings of arcane
forms of mankind to those who cannot indulge in the exploration of strange areas; the latter brings inklings of arcane
forms of thought to those who cannot indulge in the exploration of strange ideas. But are not such endeavors basically
narcissistic? In the last analysis, the response will either be rejection ("That doesn't make sense, those people are crazy! /
That doesn't make sense, that writer is crazy!") or acceptance
("Marvelous! What a beautiful thing!"). We say that rejection
manifests a failure of the reader's accommodation to new parameters. But what is acceptance? Only when one has reduced a society or a piece of literature to congruency with
one's own prejudices and stereotypes does one have the feeling of proper understanding. Only when one has *made* sense
of a new stimulus does one have the impression of a richer

183

intelligence or life.[1] Could we not say that the tasks of the anthropologist and of the poet do not differ from those of the multinational hotel chains that enable the tourist to see the world without ever leaving the protective shell of reassuring appointments and menus even in the strangest and most frightening lands?

I approach my topic with my biases and limitations, those of a structural anthropologist. My limitations include a restricted knowledge of literary studies. Therefore, my propositions may very well be trivial for such "readers in my text" who are better read. In addition, some limitations are self-imposed. Though it is relevant to my study, I cannot here go into the theory of interpretation developed by quantitative social scientists, nor the apparently conflicting one of ethnomethodologists. Research done on pattern recognition in social psychology, in developmental physiology, and in computer science is equally relevant. Readers familiar with these fields will recognize ideas that I have borrowed for my approach, although I have not paused to acknowledge them explicitly.

My bias: I am in agreement with Lévi-Strauss that "les mythes se pensent dans les hommes." That is, we are thought out by the semantic structures that charter us. The traditions in which our lives are embedded "think themselves out," i.e., unfold and display their semantic resources through the people they traverse, and who perpetuate these traditions over time. In other words, the "myths," ideologies, or semantic charters of cultures and subcultures express themselves in their carriers whose thinking-processes, stereotypes, and attitudes they mold.[2]

Cultures—semantic systems—have an inertia and a momentum of their own. There are semantic domains whose inertia is high: kinship terminologies, the dogmas of authori-

---

[1] The literary reader of this essay is a test case: if not turned off already, the challenge will be to make sense, within his own framework, of the perspective outlined here.

[2] See P. Maranda, ed., *Mythology* (London, 1972), Introduction; Maranda, *French Kinship: Structure and History* (Paris, The Hague, 1974), chap. 5.

The Dialectic of Metaphor

tarian churches, the conception of sex roles. There are other domains where momentum will be high at given times in history: style, fashion, some areas of technology: "Inertia makes it possible for people to have a faith and for preachers to make sermons; makes it possible for friends to trust each other. Momentum makes it possible for people to cope with the unexpected and for poets and prophets to perform semantic engineering; makes it possible for people to fall in love."[3]

SEMANTIC CHARTERS AND ASSOCIATION PROBABILITIES

Semantic charters condition our thoughts and emotions. They are culture-specific networks that we internalize as we undergo the process of socialization. These mechanisms are at work both in category formation and in the establishment, consolidation, or rejection of relationships between categories:

> Within a semantic universe, some combinations of, i.e., relations between, elements are common, others are permissible but rare, others are poetic or archaic, and others are excluded.... We could say, inspired by Rousseau, that human communication is a social contract which rests on a body of subliminal laws, and that a culture's myths contain its semantic jurisprudence. Whether this can be reduced to an algebra depends on the power of the analyst. The rules are there at any rate, as evidenced by the fact that those unable or unwilling to abide and be conditioned by them are either confined in mental hospitals or marked off as foreigners.[4]

To make the above more explicit, let us take an example. It would be possible to rate the degree, and hence to build a

[3] See P. Maranda, "For a Theory of Modes of Communication," in I. Rossi, ed., *New Directions in Structuralism*, forthcoming.

[4] See P. Maranda, *Mythology*, pp. 15, 16.

Pierre Maranda

probabilistic model, of the following metaphors' acceptance in European-type cultures:[5]

Metaphors	Acceptability
Time is money	90-100%
Beauty is money	40%
Love is money	25%
Piss is money	1%

"Time is money" is easily translatable and, if properly translated, understandable and accepted in all cultures where time can belong to the category "commodity." The same statement would be grammatically valid in many Melanesian languages but would remain unintelligible, because time is not a commodity in those cultures. The relationship of equivalence established in that metaphor is a common saying—a proverb—in our culture; there are no doubts about its acceptability, which is widespread except among the members of what used to be called (appropriately) the *counter*culture.

"Beauty is money" is less usual. Many people would protest that it expresses a mercantile view. Despite the fact that art and aesthetics on the whole have a market value, despite the fact that a "beautiful" person can make a profitable marriage, etc., the statement would be felt as crude by the average educated member of our societies. This statement would be completely unintelligible to Melanesians, because their concept of "beauty" (like Plato's) is not dissociable from that of "goodness," and because both concepts are commonly expressed by a single term, e.g., *Lau*, "diana," which may be glossed as "perfection and purity stemming from order, transactional and/or cosmic." This concept has no relationship to "commodity."

"Love is money" would be accepted still more reluctantly than "beauty is money." Most members of our societies would reject it as an outrageous defilement or they would

[5] This can be tested in different populations according to such variables as age, sex, occupation, socioeconomic status, ethnic background, etc. The percentages given here are arbitrary.

186

The Dialectic of Metaphor

interpret it cynically. The reason may be in part that there is in our semantic charter, as evidenced in the New Testament, an association between the Devil and money, and between God and love, an association that the Weberian view on capitalism has not completely eroded. In contrast, Melanesians would agree with this equivalence: the love of ancestral spirits brings financial success to pious clan chiefs— Melanesians may be more Weberian than most of our compatriots.

The last metaphor, "piss is money," would reveal a "sick mind" or surrealist language among Melanesians as well as among ourselves. Such a statement is excluded from common speech not only on the grounds that it violates the rules of etiquette but also those of semantics. We thus reach a border of our system, similar to those on which humor plays. Such unacceptable statements show that we cannot speak or even think as freely as we would like to believe we can. There are limitations—external and internal—to our degrees of mental freedom.[6] And the same type of parameters constrain interpretation—rejection and acceptance.

To conclude this section, I wish to emphasize that semantic categories are culture-specific; that they consist of paradigmatic sets whose affinities for other sets (e.g., time and money) is finite and definable. "Affinities" are actually association coefficients that can be measured, be it in common speech or in poetic discourse. The set of these measurements constitutes a network of transition probabilities that enables the analyst to predict that once one is in the semantic state "time" or "love" or "piss," some expectations will materialize in the unfolding of a syntagm while others are very unlikely, and that the likelier the expectations, the readier the acceptance. Riddlers, poets, mythmakers, popular singers, advertising specialists, are the semantic engineers who can increase or decrease association probabilities, and thus control the semantic flow in the networks that provide the com-

[6] For an exploration of semantic censure mechanisms, see P. Maranda, "Cartographie sémantique et folklore," *Recherches sociographiques* 18 (1977), 247-70.

Pierre Maranda

munication infrastructure of a society.[7] They exploit cliché and metaphor structures so that unlikely (low-probability) connections will be activated, while at the same time they steer the audience's "train of thought" away from some other semantic connections.

INTERNALIZATION AND INERTIA
OF SEMANTIC CHARTERS

Formal schooling structures the rational-response mechanisms of the young. It conditions a society's emerging generations to perpetuate the society: it conditions youth to think according to accepted paradigms—historical, aesthetic, social, religious, etc. It thinks these out for them. The set of rational-response mechanisms acquired through schooling and other intellectual activities (reading, conversation, etc.) defines in youth what Lacan has called their *organisation intellectuelle* ("intellectual makeup"), which, it is hoped by the ruling classes, will become their emotional organization (*organisation passionnelle*) as well. Formal schooling is thus an important part of a society's survival mechanisms.[8]

The bulk of literature fulfills the same function. Literature has an audience because even though it enjoys a degree of freedom that enables it to be bolder and more exploratory than schooling, it remains essentially conservative in its endeavors: the alternatives proposed in the most outlandish novels, poems, and plays are innocuous to the established

---

[7] Successful semantic engineers are at least implicitly masters of what has become a field of its own, psychographics. This is a technique widely used in advertising to (1) map out potentially new markets, and (2) coin a product that will take those populations as a target. Specialists in the field define, on the basis of detailed surveys and analyses, the "psychograph" of the average target consumer. Politicians hire psychographers for help in designing their public images.

[8] A case among many: In a recent PTA meeting, a successful and well-known physician declared, "I am sending my children to school because I want them to become imbued with the same ideas and values that I was imbued with in my youth, so that we can communicate."

The Dialectic of Metaphor

order, i.e., against the pseudodemocratic hierarchical structure of our society.

Parallel and complementary to school and literature, folklore and popular art structure the "emotional" response mechanisms of our youth. In this respect, the long hours spent by teen-agers listening to their favorite records constitute an important conditioning process. Their developing egos are being molded and manipulated semantically in the privacy of their rooms, in the music sessions with others, in dances to their "Masters' Songs" (Leonard Cohen). This happens through exposure to the affective syntagms in which filmmakers, poets and, perhaps above all, popular singers combine and recombine their culture's anxiogenic paradigms. The result is a lexicon of loaded terms ("hot," "baby," etc.) and a syntax of affects ("Love Calls You by Your Name," "Across the Universe," etc.). Thus singers and other semantic engineers structure the "passions" of their target audiences by defining in egos an *organisation passionnelle* (Lacan's definition of ego), endowed as they are by their audiences with the trustworthy connivence of a spontaneously chosen means of personal exaltation.

However, whatever their petulance, no revolutionary art or counterculture can alter our deeply set semantic charter. It will take more than a new Bible and World Wars to modify drastically our thresholds of acceptance or rejection. We have developed such defense mechanisms (e.g., against unemployment, recession, and other menaces to our self-confidence) that we can quickly defuse and neutralize the very broad range of challenges that, a few decades ago, would have compelled us to revamp our thought structures. This shows that semantic and, consequently, social engineering is successful in our societies.

Our attitudes and value systems derive their inertia from a hierarchic relationship of domination of the natural and social environment (instead of, for example, a relationship of symbiosis). A case in point is our concept of property, which governs our behavior and thoughts with respect to people as well

Pierre Maranda

as to things.[9] We have indeed the legal right to kill someone who attempts to steal something we own. Property rights override another human being's right to live.

Will the impact of, say, Marxism or Buddhism eventually bring about a conversion from our complacency and arrogance to an acknowledgment of different priorities that even a Dostoyevsky or a Steinbeck have been incapable of instilling in us? We are hopelessly conditioned, it seems, by the myth (which "thinks itself out" in us) of our supremacy and of the mission that supremacy entails, which is to bestow generously on the rest of mankind the ultimate light we have been fortunate enough to receive from our privileged ancestry.

INTERPRETATION:
ACCEPTANCE AND REJECTION

According to the preceding views, to "interpret" is to accept what we recognize, while filtering out what is incompatible with our own semantic charter. Acceptance is an outgrowth of narcissism, which is itself a survival mechanism. For Freud, narcissism is the network structure that enables people to define and maintain their identities both rationally and emotionally and, consequently, to perpetuate themselves. Thus art, like love, like anthropology, is the exalting exploration of the ego's resources, as multiplied in mirrors that generate an image apparently apt to become a reality.

An audience is a constituency. It comes about through the human need of proving to oneself that one can cope, i.e., that one can reduce to a pattern the disquieting randomness of world and history. A singer, a filmmaker, a poet, any competent semantic engineer knows how to reassure his or her constituency by giving it renewed faith in its mental and emotional adequacy. For the text to work, however, for its author to have a constituency, it must be acceptable enough so that the reader may be open at least minimally to its flow. Once

[9] See L. Dumont, *Homo aequalis* (Paris, 1977).

The Dialectic of Metaphor

triggered, semantic momentum will carry the reader through a subnetwork of associations, either new or revisited. The result will be a consolidation of the ego's thought processes through what could be called a "semantic transfusion"—a sought-for or at least tolerated intrusion—that carries out, within the reader, the act of living more fully: the text is the light on my face that enables me to see myself in the one-way mirror I hold in front of it; the text allows me, Narcissus, to marvel at my mind, to believe in myself and, consequently, to have the impression that I live more competently. Rejection, on the other hand—or counteracceptance—is a negative move that is no less effective in semantic engineering than acceptance itself.

Almost fifty years ago, Jakobson described adequately the impact of both these primary forms of interpretation, acceptance and rejection:

The number of Czechoslovakian citizens who have read, for example, the poems of Nezval is not very great. To the extent that they have read and accepted them they will, without wishing to, joke with a friend, swear at an adversary, express their emotion, declare their love, and talk politics, somewhat differently. Even if they have read and rejected them, their daily language and rituals will not go unchanged. For a long time they will be haunted by an *idée fixe*: above all, don't be like this Nezval in any way. In every way possible they will shun his motifs, his images, his phraseology. Hostility towards Nezval's poems is, however, an entirely different psychological state from ignoring them. And his admirers and detractors will spread the motifs of this poetry and its intonations, its words and its relationships, more and more until they form the language and inner disposition of people who know Nezval only from the daily columns of *Politicka*.[10]

[10] R. Jakobson, "Qu'est-ce que la poésie?" in *Questions de poétique* (Paris, 1973), p. 125 [editors' translation].

Pierre Maranda

The challenge is always the same. How to defend oneself, individual or society, against what we call "entropy"; how to persist through time keeping uncertainty below a culture-specific threshold; how to preserve stability and quietness—i.e., predictability—despite growing disorder all around; how to keep the feeling that one's powers of ordering experience are adequate?[11] We can say of any "text" what I wrote elsewhere about myth: "The life of myths consists in reorganizing traditional components in the face of new circumstances or, correlatively, in reorganizing new, imported components in the light of tradition. More generally, the mythic process is a learning device in which the unintelligible—randomness—is reduced to intelligibility—a pattern: 'Myth may be more universal than history.' "[12]

We have long ago defined our defense mechanism; it is expressed in the postulate that culture is superior to nature.[13] This leads our peoples to overrate technology, to develop imperialist ideologies, and to favor hierarchical structures, i.e., to accept discourses on those lines and to reject counterdiscourses. Thus interpretation should rest on the study of what I have called elsewhere *l'infra-discours* ("sub-discourse").[14] But how do such defense mechanisms work? How does any dynamic force grow out of inertia, and how does it consolidate it in return? How do people recognize themselves in their historians, in their poets, in their prophets, in their critics?

---

[11] P. Maranda, *Mythology*, p. 8. Riddling is an exercise to tame anxiety in semantic practice and fulfills the same function as the poetic metaphor (see below, Eluard's line); see P. Maranda and E. Köngäs Maranda, eds., *Structural Analysis of Oral Tradition* (Philadelphia, 1971), Introduction.

[12] P. Maranda, *Mythology*, p. 8.

[13] This postulate is chartered in the Christian Bible and European philosophies: mankind dominates and exploits nature; in many other cultures, nature is superior to mankind and teaches people how to live in a rational symbiosis with their physical environments.

[14] P. Maranda, "Du drame au poème: L'infra-discours populaire dans la basse ville de Québec," *Etudes littéraires* 10 (1977), 525-44; Maranda, "The Popular Subdiscourse: Probabilistic Semantic Networks (Semantography)," *Current Anthropology* 19 (1978), 396-97.

The Dialectic of Metaphor

It is significant that so many societies take the myth of the serpent shedding its skin as a model of what immortality would have been like. For the model is true on the level of the corporate existence of the members of a society. A society—a corporation, in technical terms—is an entity that survives the death of its members. People, apparently superseding each other in a continuing replacement of old by young, are only the successive skins of the society that gave our ancestors, that gives us, and that will give our descendants an identity obtained through specific semantic charters.

Cultures are sets of binding categories and of taxonomic principles. While they give us a hold on the "outside" world, labels and rules inhibit alternate handlings of that same "world." Our semantic resources seem to be finite. Consequently, while we need them to stand conceptually on our own, we struggle to shed the categories that structure us and that imprison us from within. Whatever the number and types of gems we polish, we fail to bring them to transparency, and they fail to reflect faces other than our own.

Poets, like anthropologists, try to reach beyond such categories. Their exaltation persists as long as they remain unaware that the operations from which they derive the feeling of being "free" are the same as those that have structured them from the very beginning.[15] Some poets and some anthropologists realize the curvature of semantic universes (Mallarmé: "La chair est triste, hélas! et j'ai lu tous les livres."), and become painfully aware that the further back one pushes the borders, the closer one gravitates toward one's point of departure (T. S. Eliot: "In my beginning is my end"). But how could one think without categories; how could one step outside of oneself; how could one transcend one's semantic system and still *be*?

Let us now take a closer look at what it means to live and to think within a semantic system or charter. One of the first skills we need is to be able to reduce randomness to a pattern.

[15] On the nature of these operations, see E. Köngäs Maranda, "La Structure des énigmes," *L'Homme* 9 (1969), 5-48; Ricoeur reinvented the same view but more timidly: P. Ricoeur, *La Métaphore vive* (Paris, 1975), p. 32.

Pierre Maranda

This requires of us the capacity to juggle categories (i.e., to handle ambiguity). To do this, we need to perform certain dialectical operations, both verbal and conceptual. Though no culture could exist that would prescribe absolute univocality, we need to be familiar with its pertinent categories. Dialectical operations are performed in the poetic process as well as in the interpretation and writing of history, in political theory, even in theoretical physics. The following example, returning to metaphor, will illustrate the dialectics of a combinatorial power within a semantic charter.

La terre est bleue comme une orange
("The earth is blue like an orange").[16]

Eluard's metaphor seems to me a particularly interesting dialectical operation for two reasons: (1) It concatenates terms with well-established, commonplace connotations and denotations, and yet it is not commonplace; (2) it juggles taxonomies in a manner that disturbs the inertia of normal associations: "good" metaphors shake the mind out of the drowsiness of easily predictable associations. Here, in this metaphor, we have trivial categories whose coefficients of linear associations with other trivial categories are high; the shock value is the result of their unexpected (i.e., low-probability) and nonlinear association (see Figs. 1 and 2).[17]

CATEGORIES

We have here three explicit categories, "earth," "color," and "fruit," and one implicit category, a type of "sphere." These category labels could still be more general: namely, for the explicit ones, "planet," "spectrum," and "alimentation," and for the implicit one, "geometry"; but we need not dwell on

[16] This is the first line of a surrealist poem by Paul Eluard, which was published in the collection *L'Amour la poésie* (1929).

[17] The concluding paragraph of Ricoeur's book on metaphor hints at a similar view in a less formal and less technical way; *La Métaphore vive*, p. 399.

194

The Dialectic of Metaphor

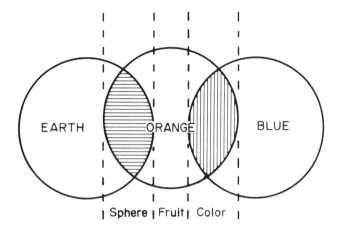

Fig. 1. Trivial linear syntagm: A ∧ B ∨ B ∧ C

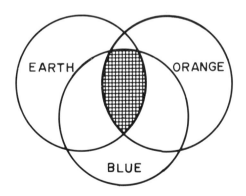

Fig. 2. Metaphoric non-linear syntagm: A ∧ B ∧ C

Pierre Maranda

this. The point is that these categories are constructions specific to our culture, and that this can be tested empirically by administering word-association tests.[18] With respect to the implicit category, it is posited on the basis of French elementary-school geography textbooks, in which children learn that the earth is not a perfect sphere but rather that it has the shape of an orange because it is slightly flat at the poles. Note that this semantic factor, taken into consideration in the analytic use of the *implicit* category "sphere," is perhaps exclusive to French culture: I do not know whether Anglo-Saxon, German, and other geography textbooks use the same metaphor; if not, the association sphere (earth = orange) would not readily come to the mind of readers from those cultures. Furthermore, since some recent French geography textbooks no longer use the metaphor, the sphere factor may lose its relevance over time because of this change in learning materials.

The first linear-type syntagm (Fig. 1) generates such simple metaphors as "the earth is an orange," while the second nonlinear type (Fig. 2) generates complex metaphors such as "the earth is a blue orange." Trivial linear syntagms can be expanded considerably: it is often possible to add a new element to the last one, until it reaches a lexicographic "dead-end" (in more precise terms, an "absorbing barrier") or loops back to one of the preceding elements in the chain (a "reflecting barrier"). For example: "The earth is an orange, an orange is a ball, a ball is a testicle, a testicle is an olive, an olive is a bug, a bug is a Volkswagen, a Volkswagen is a Rabbit, a rabbit is a bunny," etc. Metaphoric nonlinear syntagms probably cannot go beyond a limit of five elements—I do not know of any study of metaphoric depth that could investigate this point either theoretically or empirically. Theoretical approaches would have to deal with the *n*-dimensionality of nonlinear representations that could be encompassed by the human mind; empirical approaches would have to analyze

[18] The fact that other cultures may share them is irrelevant. Note, however, that in some Melanesian languages, "color" and "body" form one category.

The Dialectic of Metaphor

the actual dimensionality of the most complex metaphors ever produced—which would probably be poem-long.

Among the categories combined by Eluard, "earth" and "blue" seem unambiguous. "Earth" is a term coextensive with a category; "blue" is a term belonging to the higher-order category "color." "Orange," on the other hand, is ambiguous, since it can belong to two higher-order categories, "fruit" and "color." It would be easy to take the meaning given in dictionaries for these three terms and, with the help of word-association tests, to construct a probabilistic model of their respective sociosemantic profiles (according to variables such as status, degree of education, profession, age, sex, etc.). But all this is not necessary to realize that Eluard has juxtaposed these categories in such a way that they seem to be incongruous.[19] The "shocking" relationships established between the categories are dialectical in nature, and are the result of three basic mechanisms long ago recognized in symbolic anthropology.[20] First in terms of logical priority is *reduction*; second, *homology*; and third, *inversion*.

Operations on the Categories

The first operation reduces the earth and the orange to their shape, that of a sphere slightly flattened at the poles. The second operation establishes a homology between the two spheres: they are both members of the same class of spheres (flattened).[21] The third is inversion, and is dialectical in nature: at the same time that Eluard asserts the earth is like an

[19] I have used this metaphor repeatedly as an informal test, with colleagues, students, and several nonacademic people. The rejection rate is very high on the whole, except among respondents familiar with structuralism.

[20] H. Hubert and M. Mauss, "Esquisse d'une théorie générale de la magie," *Année Sociologique* 1902-1903, reprinted in M. Mauss, *Sociologie et anthropologie* (Paris, 1960), pp. 3-144.

[21] The advertising agency that designed the ticket envelope of Canadian Pacific Airlines (CPA) has exploited the same analogy and performed the same homology: oranges are used to represent the world and the major cities served by CPA. We should also take into account, however, that the flag of the Canadian airline is orange in color.

orange, he negates it. Everything happens as if the poet made the following assumptions (whether or not he did is irrelevant, since this is an exercise in interpretation, i.e., in constructing a model that can formulate the conditions for the internal consistency of the metaphor so that the surrealist challenge can be met, by showing it as amenable—reducible—to logical operations):

$$\text{shape (EARTH = ORANGE)}$$
$$\text{color (EARTH} \neq \text{ORANGE)}$$

The first assumption, with *shape* set as a factor, can be made on the basis of French intellectual paradigms (elementary-school textbooks here plugged into poetry). The second assumption may be that even if nobody knew what the color of the earth really is, it is certainly not orange.

Given these two assumptions, what will be the dialectical process that can express, through negation, the nonorangeness of the planet earth? Eluard used the strongest form of negation, that of inversion by complementarity. This implies two steps: first, a displacement (a permutation, in fact) of "color" from factor (or function) to *TERM*:[22]

$$\text{color (EARTH} \neq \text{ORANGE)} \rightarrow \text{earth (COLOR} \neq \text{ORANGE)}$$

This is a preliminary form of negation; it means, in prose, that "the earth's color is not orange." The next operation will transform the preceding one into a positive statement: what is the term which, within the domain of color, is all but orange? In other words, what is left, in the semantic universe of the color spectrum, that will be anything but "orange,"

[22] This is a complex permutation, described for the analysis of myth, by Lévi-Strauss in *Structural Anthropology* (New York, 1964), p. 228. It is akin to Lenin's definition of dialectics and especially to Mao Tse-tung's elaboration of the concept of contradiction (Mao Tse-tung, *On Contradiction* [Peking, 1923]). For an elaborate discussion, see E. Köngäs Maranda and P. Maranda, *Structural Models in Folklore and Transformational Essays*, 2nd ed. (Paris, The Hague, 1971), pp. 24-34.

The Dialectic of Metaphor

that will be the inverse of orange? It is the complementary color of orange, blue (Fig. 3).

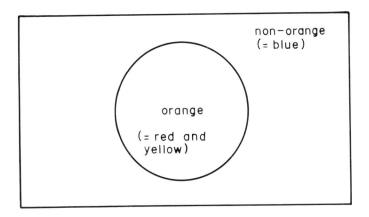

Fig. 3. orange=blue^{-1}

Therefore, earth (COLOR = ORANGE^{-1} = BLUE).

Four propositions can summarize this interpretation:

1. The domain of "shape" is kept constant and therefore is noncontrasting;[23]

2. the exploited contrast is between two colors: blue and, by association with the fruit from which the color's name comes, orange;

3. the colors "blue" and "orange" stand in a relationship of complementary colors in the spectrum as we define it; so that

4. the comparison "blue like an orange" is a negation of orangeness as a color but not as a shape.

And this is the core of the dialectical operation: to negate a criterial attribute through a positive statement while at the same time making a contradiction. Thus, the earth is an

---

[23] Eluard could have written *La terre est plate comme une orange* ("The earth is flat like an orange").

Pierre Maranda

orange with respect to shape similarity but not with respect to another major dimension of orange, namely color.

A similar type of dialectical operation occurs on the level of genders (this happens mechanically, because gender is a feature built into French; yet it is a component of the dialectics). The feminine article *une* in front of *orange* leads us to read the term as the noun that designates the fruit; in contrast, *orange* as a substantive designating color is masculine in French. Moreover, the adjective *bleue* emphasizes this contradiction: on the one hand, grammatically, it is in the feminine like *terre* and *orange* and, accordingly, increases the feminine momentum of the text and the reading of "orange" as fruit; however, at the same time, its semantic potential as a color term activates a reading of "orange" as color. The contradiction thus consists of a grammatical component (*une* orange = fruit; bleu*e*) and of a semantic one (*bleue* = complementary color of *orange*). Split-association probabilities seem to create a double-bind for the reader: while an association is reinforced grammatically (gender) it is negated semantically (lexically).

We are thus faced with a riddle structure: how can the earth be at the same time a fruit and so much not that fruit that its color is an inversion of that fruit's typical color? By being, like an orange, a flattened sphere; but the similarity stops there and the metaphor states it: the earth is an orange with respect to shape but so much not an orange as it is blue. On the other hand, it could be said that, rotten oranges being bluish, the metaphor could read: "The earth is a rotten orange." Even so, this interpretation would not draw on mechanisms of another nature than those suggested above. It would simply be less complex, since it would not imply a dialectical operation, but only reduction and homology.[24]

The "shock" value of the metaphor is due to the fact that

[24] The dynamic inversion was already inscribed in French, in the title of a novel by Yassu Gauclère, *L'Orange bleue*. I am grateful to Mrs. Monique Lévi-Strauss, who brought this to my attention. We should also keep in mind the triggering function of *bleue* as a color associative for *orange*. With respect to complementarity, the phenomenon that we call retinian projection is probably pertinent (seeing a blue spot when closing one's eyes after having stared at an orange source of direct or reflected light).

In comments on an earlier version of this paper, Inge Crosman suggested

200

The Dialectic of Metaphor

the reader does not expect orange after a statement of equivalence introduced by *comme*. Were it not for the further effectiveness of the metaphor, interpretation would cease right here, and we would conclude that this incongruity marks the passage to the surrealistic world or to some other paralogic universe. However, for someone who has learned geography in French elementary textbooks, intellectual stereotypes bring about second thoughts and compel one to agree ("Yes, the earth is like an orange"). For such a reader, interpretation must reach beyond resorbing the metaphor's incongruity by giving it the convenient label "surrealist"; he must deal with the dialectical relationship between *bleue* and *orange*. Inversion by complementarity will then become apparent, and Aristotle's principle of contradiction will be salvaged as per:

$$\text{ORANGE} = \text{TERRE} \neq \text{ORANGE}$$

That is, surrealism, after all, is amenable to logical interpretation. And on this, having fulfilled its task of reducing the apparently incongruous and unexpected to a familiar pattern, semantics can return to the drowsiness of an inertia reinforced by the evidence that, once more, the culture's interpreting powers have been proven adequate.[25] Eluard, like the Child Jesus as the Pantocrator, can hold the earth in his hand

---

the following counterinterpretation: "The world is as blue as an orange is (which is not blue at all)—hence the earth is not blue either." This train of thought can be followed, but I would structure it differently, viz.: the earth is blue like an orange; but an orange is not blue; therefore, the earth either is not blue or is not like an orange.

[Michael Riffaterre, taking up once more Eluard's startling poetic assertion, comes up with the following ingenious explanation: "Eluard's verse is positing an impossible simile: the earth is as blue as an orange is blue, which is to say not at all blue. This does not mean the reader is really expected to see earth and orange as comparable in their common lack. It is simply an expansion that fleshes out a simile structure with words not comparable—and this destroys the mimesis and triggers genuine literary behavior." (*Semiotics of Poetry* [Bloomington, 1978], pp. 62-63). Riffaterre concludes that poetic discourse is not mimetic, since the poem sets up its own semiotic system—ED.]

[25] W. Labov, "The Boundaries of Words and Their Meanings," in J. Bailey and R. W. Shuy, eds., *New Ways of Analyzing Variations in English* (Washington, D.C., 1973), p. 343.

Pierre Maranda

as a blue orange. He comprehends the world that comprises him. In his metaphor, the transgression of category borders resets the categorizing power of his culture's semantic system, from which, in the last analysis, come all the riddles he could invent.

DISCUSSION AND CONCLUSION

In order to maintain our confidence in our intellectual supremacy over the world, we must be able to reduce disorder to order, i.e., to categorize. But categorizing is not always successful. Some linguists have even suggested that the focus of research should shift from categories to category borders: "Many fields which study human behavior deal with categories that are not firmly enough established to allow the question, one category or two? . . . Instead of taking as problematical the existence of categories, we can turn to the nature of the boundaries between them. As linguistics then becomes a form of boundary theory rather than a category theory, we discover that not all linguistic material fits the categorical view: there is greater or lesser success in imposing categories upon the continuous substratum of reality."[26]

Anthropologists have long ago considered this problem of the categorizing activity. Over a century ago, Tylor, Morgan, and others reflected on the diverse manners in which human cultures structure their semantic systems and are structured by them. Since 1960, Lévi-Strauss and then Leach, Mary Douglas, and others have studied the structuring of the discrete lexical and semantic units of man's discourses.

The anthropological position sketched in these pages is based on a probabilistic view of cognitive diversity.[27] Accord-

[26] Labov, "The Boundaries of Words and Their Meanings," p. 343.

[27] Similar approaches have marked significant progress in recent linguistic theory, away from the transformational and generative approaches; see G. Sankoff, "Quantitative Analysis of Sharing and Variability in a Cognitive Model," *Ethnology* 10 (1971), 389-408; H. Cedergren and D. Sankoff, "Variable Rules: Performance as a Statistical Reflection of Competence," *Language* 50 (1974), 333-55.

The Dialectic of Metaphor

ing to it, we postulate semantic charters or collective representations, which people must share, beyond language, in order to understand each other when they talk. A contrast between the acceptability of Indo-European and Melanesian money metaphors has exemplified this theoretical position, and also the interpretation of earth as an orange for a generation of people who used French geography textbooks. Furthermore, culture-specific semantic charters are structured along stronger and weaker lines of affinity between concepts. Metaphor acceptance and rejection are semantic phenomena that can be tested and measured empirically.[28] The money metaphors were used to illustrate this point succinctly. Thus, one can specify the parameters of interpretation as well as the conditions of simulation models that enter into the interpretative process.

But simulation models do not explain: they emulate; they enable us to validate probabilistic models; yet we have to reach further if we want to understand interpretation.[29] The exercise in interpreting Eluard's metaphor made explicit the steps by which that surrealist statement could be amenable to traditional analysis. It took us back to the simple riddle structure, which is related to what we call the categorizing activity of the human mind, and to the function of ambiguity in semantic networks. However, whereas riddles take us along well-trod paths, metaphors, unless they are stereotypes, open up new roads in order to connect concepts that would otherwise stay unrelated. Both riddles and metaphors imply basic operations (reduction, homology, and inversion) that structure semantic syntagms—linear and nonlinear—in a given culture. The task of the analyst is to map out the syntax

[28] I have described elsewhere the computer programs I have designed to define the thresholds of metaphor acceptability, and to generate artificial metaphors whose degree of acceptance can be predicted, and I have tested them in two nonliterate societies; see P. Maranda, "Myth as a Cognitive Map," in P. Stone, ed., *Workshop on Content Analysis in the Sciences*, Centro Nazionale Universitario de Calcola Electtronico (Pisa, 1974), pp. 125-53.

[29] See P. Maranda, "Informatique, simulation et grammaires ethnologiques," *Informatique et sciences humaines* 28 (1976), 15-30.

Pierre Maranda

of those operations, which is specific to cultures and subcultures, and to inquire how it deals with new information.

Interpretation in this ethnosemantic perspective would, therefore, be a kind of survival mechanism—like narcissism —enabling the members of a society (1) to put to the test their thinking (= categorizing) power, and (2) to meet the challenge of the "new" by reducing it to the old. Is not interpretation—of the world by the artist, and of the work of art by its constituency—a conservative defense by which a society tries to perpetuate itself in the most economical way? And could we not say that gods seem to have created men in their image because men had first created the gods in theirs?

Jacques Leenhardt | # Toward a Sociology of Reading

> There are three kinds of readers: one who enjoys without judgment; a third who judges without enjoyment; and, in between, a reader who judges while enjoying and enjoys while judging.

> Goethe, Letter to
> J. F. Rochlitz, 6/13/1819

When raising the question of the reader's status in the text, we may have in mind two sets of problems. According to one approach, the reader is thought of as an end conceived by the writer, whose work, accordingly, may be read in reference to the idea we have of that reader. A certain number of studies have enriched the history of literary criticism in this way, showing that the expectations of a particular public aimed at by the writer were determinative down to the most secret strata of the text (Jauss's *Erwartungshorizont* for example).

In this perspective, one tends to oppose a real origin, the addressee, to a fictitious one, the writer, who is then considered as a mere purveyor of meanings and satisfactions whose specific character is created by others. Such, for example, is Friedrich Antal's approach in the field of the plastic arts.[1] Antal shows that the differences in styles between painters, at a time when the artists were under the immediate subordination of the patrons, may ultimately be reduced to the differences between the world views of the various groups that constituted the ruling class to whom the artists owed their commissions.

Lucien Goldmann's approach in *The Hidden God* is somewhat different.[2] Goldmann, who admits the notion of the

---

[1] Antal, *Florentine Painting and Its Social Background* (London, 1948).

[2] Goldmann, *The Hidden God: A Study of Tragic Vision in the "Pensées" of Pas-*

Jacques Leenhardt

"creator" 's autonomy in relation to the norms of the patrons, tries to prove that there is no duality between the writer and *his*[3] public; on the contrary (and provided the "public" be given its strictly limited definition), there is a relative homogeneity, a similarity in thought and, ultimately, a dynamic unity in the system of values. This unity Goldmann calls a "world-vision," which he defines as "the whole complex of ideas, aspirations and feelings which links together the members of a social group (a group which, in most cases, assumes the existence of a social class) and which opposes them to members of other social groups."[4] Therefore, writer and reader are included against the background of a common mental attitude in a limited period of time.

This approach offers the advantage of opening up the monad "creator," not to a field of contradictions where it would only annihilate itself in order to produce what will satisfy the "other," but to a collective field of praxis that is the basis of aesthetic communication and which makes possible the fullness of the "creative" venture, a venture that transcends the conceptual abilities of a single individual. Taking as an example Pascal and the various Jansenist groups during the first decades of the reign of Louis XIV, Goldmann not only gives us a brilliant demonstration of his method but provides us as well with a very fine analytic tool.

In order to be valid, however, this approach supposes a minimal social consensus. The writer and *his* reader may be equally considered as "creators"—insofar as the global structures of creation are concerned—as long as a minimal social homogeneity allows for a real intercommunication of ideas as well as for the inclusion of the writer in the community of his readers. We therefore should use Goldmann's hypothesis only when, and in the particular instances where, the social,

---

cal and the Tragedies of Racine, trans. from the French by Philip Thody (London, 1964; first published in French, 1955).

[3] The possessive case indicates here the limited social area in which the text is written and read. It excludes any distance, whether sociological or chronological, between author and readers.

[4] Goldmann, *The Hidden God*, p. 17.

Toward a Sociology of Reading

mental, and ideological distance between the agents of the literary phenomenon is small.

Over the past century, the development of specialization and the emergence of the professional writer as a member of a cultivated subclass that makes its living and justifies its existence through Culture (in exchange for the real, though dependent, privileges it enjoys) have completely modified the situation. We should not, therefore, go on using without modification a theoretical model that has proved heuristically useful in the study of past objects. Whatever the actual merits of Goldmann's hypotheses—hypotheses whose validity is necessarily a matter of conjecture—we are dealing nowadays with a reality quite different from the tacit understanding, the intimate dialogue, between people of the same community that may have existed in the seventeenth century.

As regards the problem of reading, an altogether new situation has been created with the formation of a new *reading public*, whose organic relationship to the producer has nearly completely disappeared. The codes of production of literary works have become alien to the spontaneous codes of readers. This gap between productive and receptive codes has recently been given a theoretical formulation, in order to designate as old-fashioned the procedures whereby meaning is communicated. Since all direct communication implies a homogeneity in the productive and receptive codes, certain contemporary critics have shown such communication to be the mere reproduction of the dominant ideology. They have argued that this homogeneity should be broken by means of the power of writing [*écriture*], through the creation of an infinite process of plays-upon-meanings in which any and every ideological stance would disappear. Having broken with meaning, the "modern" text would therefore be open to an active reading process, which would not simply be a mere *discovery* or an *unveiling* of meaning. "Modern" texts would therefore lead the reader to a new attitude because of their unstable configurations of meaning. In order to set up his theory of modernity, Jean Ricardou reformulates the dispute between the Ancients and the Moderns in the following

Jacques Leenhardt

terms: "Reading is not identical in the two instances: in the case of the ancient text [i.e., where meaning prevails—J. L.], reading is the *reproduction* of a meaning already present in the text; in the case of the modern text, it is a *production* of meaning resulting from a certain number of transformative operations."[5]

In actual fact, the difference stated here by Ricardou is only the reverse of what could be an extension of Goldmann's thesis. Ricardou, in taking for granted the existence of "reproductive" reading, assumes the reality of a homogeneity of codes, as if there were not necessarily, once meaning is at stake, a virtually infinite number of different, even contradictory, ways of seizing that very meaning; as if meaning, even that which is apparently the most simple and immediately conveyed, could be read as it was written; as if, furthermore, the writer always knew exactly what he was writing. This series of postulates implies—perhaps without meaning to, simply for the sake of opposing "modernity" to an outdated past—the illusions perpetuated by theorists of communication.[6] We should note, moreover, that this theory of modernity, even while excluding ordinary or vulgar reading, bestows on the critic and on learned criticism the status of a privileged intermediary. Some critics thus find their self-justification in their status as intermediaries between a writing that wanders in the labyrinths of its own devising, and a reader who is asked to play with the text but who, unprepared to do so properly, is more than ever dependent on the knowledge and the ingeniousness that characterize this generation of critics. The determination to transform the reader into a real "producer" contradicts, furthermore, the codes of reading forced upon this very reader by the educational system, which is not in the least ready to encourage plays-

[5] Ricardou, in "Lecture I: L'Espace du texte," Round Table published in *Esprit* 12 (1974), 777. Unless otherwise stated, all translations of quotations are by Brigitte Navelet.

[6] Cf. Harald Weinrich, "Für eine Literaturgeschichte des Lesers," in *Merkur* 31 (1977).

Toward a Sociology of Reading

upon-meaning and, even less, plays-upon-narrative elements.[7]

Such as we find it in Ricardou's theory, the refusal of any concern with meaning in textual practice—"meaning is what is best able to annihilate the text"[8]—leads necessarily, albeit unwillingly, to the exclusion of nonlearned reading. Among its very limited public, this kind of text will ultimately organize a permanent exchange of ingeniousness in which a given cultural heritage will always play a dominant role. The reader toward whom this literature is directed is thus an academician bristling with erudition.[9]

The call for a gratuitous literature, a literature that says nothing and will not communicate, closes every access to "saying" and reinforces the mandarinate of those who have the literary power and know-how to say nothing: "I have nothing to say, but I need a space to offer my refusal, and thus to write."[10] In believing that really modern literature must lay aside any concern with meaning, some critics and writers have in fact produced the theory of the total reification of consciousness. While they thought they were "democratizing" writing by liberating it of the necessity to communicate an exceptionally felt experience, these writers and critics have led, in spite of themselves, to the theoretical expression of the radical disappearance of any human consciousness. If literature were only a long verification of someone's inexistence, it would prove that Marcuse's worst fears in *One-Dimensional Man* have been realized.

We need not rehearse here the critique of the triumphant Cartesian consciousness—i.e., of the ego—that has been elaborated over the past century. But if the illusion of the *au-*

---

[7] Cf. Pierre Kuentz, "L'Envers du texte," in *Littérature*, no. 7 (October 1972), 3-26.

[8] Ricardou, "Lecture I," p. 942.

[9] Jacques Leenhardt, "L'Enjeu politique de l'écriture," in *Butor, Colloque de Cerisy* (Paris, 1974), p. 52 and pp. 170-84.

[10] Dimitrou Tsepeneag, in *Alain Robbe-Grillet, Colloque de Cerisy* (Paris, 1976), 2: 282.

tonomous subject has been eradicated, we cannot consider the swing to the extreme opposite as philosophical progress; it is merely a token of the very real crisis in philosophy which, as always, is also the crisis of social institutions. Although it is certain that in the current development of our social system there exists a tendency toward the effacement of the thetic consciousness, it would be false to believe, as some have done, that this evolution is already complete and that every kind of consciousness has disappeared. On the literary level (i.e., insofar as the concrete possibilities of writing are concerned), there may exist a kind of embarrassment that effectively prevents a writer from affirming his individuality on the blank page, precisely *because* he feels he has an individuality (be it personal or collective), when anonymity has become a necessity and the very condition of survival.

Whatever the outcome of this debate, the results of an experimental investigation I should like to describe here prove that the reading process actively involves the reader himself, and is not the area of a terrorist operation in which the text and its meaning are forced upon the reader. Even though it does communicate a meaning, the written text, when read, undergoes a very deep and complex process of appropriation. Reading is not only an act of docile consumption, and the meanings a text conveys do not repress the reader's activity to as large an extent as some have claimed. The appropriation of the text causes its original "truth" to break apart. To be sure, the sacred awe we feel in France toward *the* text—an awe cultivated by our educational system—creates an absolute respect for the text as such; but as soon as we move to the level of meaning, everything changes. If the text presupposes a fixed attitude on the part of the reader, it is impossible to say that this presupposition is fulfilled.

I would like now to describe a survey that shows how this theoretical debate, which has been going on in literary criticism for decades, might take a new direction when actual reading experiences are taken into account. As long as we attribute to the reader and his practice the preconceived ideas of "literary theories," it will be impossible to decide in favor

Toward a Sociology of Reading

of one or the other position. Empirical investigation should be a good means whereby to advance the debate.

My reflections on the function of the reader in the text stem from a study conducted by a group of researchers in Hungary and in France simultaneously (The Institute of Popular Culture in Budapest, under Peter Jozsa's direction; and the Group of Sociology of Literature, of the Ecole des Hautes Etudes en Sciences Sociales in Paris, under Jacques Leenhardt's direction). The complete results will be published in both countries and are beyond the scope of this paper. I shall confine myself, therefore, to what appear to be the most significant theoretical results of our investigations. The basis of the study was the reading of two novels,[11] one from each country, by five hundred readers from different social origins in both countries. Two surveys were established: the first concerned the reading habits and the particular interests of the participants with respect to daily newspapers, periodicals, and books; the second, which is the real innovation of our study, offered thirty-five open questions on each novel; these called for the readers' estimates and remarks concerning the most important facts, behaviors, and "literary effects" found in the novels.

A brief summary of the two novels will be useful here. *Les Choses*, by G. Perec, tells the story of a young married couple, both psychosociologists, torn between the ease of an undemanding though relatively well-paid job and the fascination they feel toward the "consumer goods" offered by the "affluent society," as these are displayed in fashionable magazines. They have to choose, but they cannot. They go and teach in Tunisia as a means of resolving their dilemma, but nothing in this experience appears to them as a real alternative. Eventually, they come back to France, laying aside a certain mode of "free" living characteristic of prolonged adolescence, to enter a normal and commonplace career in Bor-

[11] Georges Perec, *Les Choses: Une histoire des années soixante* (Paris, 1965). Endre Fejes, *Le Cimetière de rouille*, trans. from the Hungarian by Ladislas Gara and Ann-Marie de Backer (Paris, 1966) (first published in Hungarian, *Rozsdatemető* [Budapest, 1963]).

deaux; and, though they at last possess the *things* they wanted so much, everything seems tasteless to them.

The novel by E. Fejes consists of a series of very numerous brief scenes, in which the reader follows the story of a family who started as subproletarians and who lived through Hungary's recent history: the end of the fascist period during Horty's presidency, the Second World War, the creation of the Socialist Republic, the 1956 uprising, and so on to the sixties. One successively follows the parents' transfer from country to city, the difficulties of their life, which is nevertheless very warm, their various children, Janos and his three sisters, marriages and partings, the slow improvement of their circumstances against a nevertheless grim background. It is the story of a large family who remain united by necessity and by a real sense of solidarity, and who also split under various pressures, both internal (disputes) and external: changes in society and their consequences for individual lives.

We chose these two novels chiefly because they were intimately related to the history of the publics we wanted to investigate. The problem posed in *Les Choses* refers directly to the "consumer society" as it was beginning to be felt, and criticized, by the end of the sixties; the fresco presented by *Rozsdatemetö* plainly questions Hungary's social reality as it appeared during these same years. We thought we had, here, the double specificity whose effects we wanted to assess.

A brief description of the method, which was identical for both research institutes, will indicate the outlines a project whose target was to elaborate a methodology in the field of a sociology of reading—and, more generally, of a sociology of culture—as well as to elaborate a specific approach to the value systems and mental categories in France and Hungary.

I will now describe a few of our procedures based on the materials we recorded in answer to our second list of queries. Faced with the wide range of these materials—every interviewee was invited to comment at liberty, orally or in writing, on every one of the thirty-five questions on each novel—we considered it necessary to elaborate a method that would allow us to compare the answers obtained. We constituted,

Toward a Sociology of Reading

accordingly, a "typical-list of answers" for each of the seventy questions. Depending on the questions, the minimum number of items we could record varied, ten being an average; for a few questions we had to draw up two "typical-lists," which opened onto two different semantic spheres.

I will not deny that this kind of research, because it forces one to choose significant units, highly engages the researcher's own ideological commitments as well as his abilities. However, since these "typical-lists" were established after a long analysis of the raw material by two groups from different intellectual traditions, we hope that the distortions caused by our preconceptions have neutralized rather than reinforced each other! We called these typical-lists "standard lists of answers" (SLA) and, because they were easy to handle, we drew from them our statistical data.

One of our main concerns was, of course, to learn whether groups of readers belonging to different sociological categories would manifest uniform tendencies in the types of answers they gave.[12] To verify this hypothesis, we had the maxima and minima recorded for every standard answer, as well as the system of correlations between answers to the various questions (e.g., did an engineer who answered item 4 in SLA [Standard List of Answers] 12 tend to answer item 7 in SLA 17?). We tried to find these correlations on the basis of the sociodemographical data mentioned in note 12. As a result, we were able to describe tendencies whose origin could be ascribed to age, social mobility, schooling, and socioprofessional group membership. Unfortunately, it proved impossible to take account of the various possible combinations among the sociodemographical factors; we would have liked to have differentiated, for example, the system of an-

[12] Aside from nationality, our sociodemographical data were: age (not under 25); sex; social mobility in relation to the parents; schooling (level of education); and socioprofessional category—engineers, paraintellectuals (i.e., people who have had university training and do not work either in industrial production or the educational system), clerks, technicians, and small-tradesmen. This last category is irrelevant to the Hungarian sample.

Jacques Leenhardt

swers of a young *upwardly mobile* clerk from that of a young *downwardly mobile* one, and so on with other possible combinations. Given the great variety of answers we recorded in our SLA—and we felt that this variety was an absolute must—the achievement of such an exhaustive analysis would have required thousands of interviewees, which was beyond our scope.

I will therefore consider only a few results of our analysis of the maxima/minima lists and systems of correlations. Our three most important levels of pertinence are: the systems of reading, the structure of the reading of the socioprofessional groups, and the national reality.

What do we call a *system of reading*? We discovered that the reader's attitude toward the events, characters, or any sign of the author's intervention actually formed a system. Value judgments, reading attitudes, and expectations in the sphere of pleasure appeared to be organically interrelated to such an extent that we were able, for each national sample, to ascertain four large systems, four tendencies, that expressed the ideological specificity of the reader's relationship to the text.

Of course, this finding does not invalidate the hypothesis according to which the writer himself first forms an idea of what the public's expectations are, and then goes out to satisfy them. We could even imagine that a study such as ours might—for the greatest harm to literature—be used as a source of information to achieve a better conformity of the text with its public. But, while our study proves the existence of real systems of reading, it also proves that this reality tends to pluralize the notion of a public, and to undermine any simplistic notion of its unity. When speaking of *the* public, one frequently sees it as a whole; in actual fact, we only met *readers*, who form *publics* according to their sociodemographical characteristics. This particular notion of publics signifies consequently a grouping of ideological tendencies, evident in the approach to a literary text. *The* public, conceived as an undifferentiated whole in which multiple practices are combined, can no longer be considered as a valid notion where the process of reading is concerned.

Toward a Sociology of Reading

In our study, the determination of the systems of reading is based chiefly on a classification of the interviewees' systems of values; it is also possible to indicate, as I shall try to do here, the influence of the global systems of values on the specific system of aesthetic values and judgments.

We may begin with a general remark on the comparison between the materials collected in France on each of the novels. The examination of the lists of correlations shows that, when taking the questions in pairs, there are 240 correlations for *Les Choses*, while we find 400 for *Le Cimetière de rouille*. We might venture the hypothesis, then, that the French readers' reading of a foreign book is more coherent than their reading of a novel that stems from their own tradition. The system of correlations, and the richness of the semantic network it establishes, may in effect be considered an index of reading coherence. We shall see that this index of *coherence* must be compared to another index, quite similar as to the effects it designates, which we called an index of *stereotyping*. Actually, in France as well as in Hungary, reading the foreign book produces a more coherent reading from the ideological point of view. However, the list of correlations shows that in Hungary, reading the French novel produces a smaller number of correlations than reading the "national" one. Consequently, we are faced with two phenomena we might consider contradictory, given our methodological hypothesis that the degree of stereotyping can be deduced from the list of correlations. In actual fact, what we have are two distinct processes that lead to approximately the same end results.

A semantic analysis of the French materials shows that the fictive world of Fejes (the world of places, situations, but also the world of feelings and acts) appeared so different from what the French reader actually knows, so disconcerting one might say, that this reader tried to appropriate what he read by imposing on it rational schemes he already knew. By integrating the Hungarian reality shown in Fejes' book into the ready-made patterns of an analysis based on preconceptions, the French reader opposed the text with a violence that aimed at reducing its strangeness; by filtering the text through

Jacques Leenhardt

highly schematic patterns, this reader achieved a "logical-ized" resetting of the text. The attitude of this disconcerted reader thus results, paradoxically, in the production of cer-titude: the French reader pretends he knows precisely what is at stake in the novel, he poses as a know-it-all, and every written word, every situation, takes its place in his precon-ceived system of reading.

It is noteworthy that this reading process, described here on a semantic level, appears on the structural level as well. For example, since the Hungarian novel offers a fragmented narrative consisting of various scenes, each of which focuses on one of the numerous members of a large family—a clan-family one might say—the French reader, disturbed by this scattering, opted for a restructuration of the narrative around a central hero, thus building a narrative structure more famil-iar to him. Accordingly, if we find that the French reading is well organized, it is actually organized around a series of different stereotypes that attenuate the strangeness of the Hungarian text—which is called "Slavic," perhaps by a metonymy—and offer a substitute-knowledge allowing for the general organization and the systematic appropriation of the text.

The Hungarian reading of the French novel is quite differ-ent. It is as highly stereotyped as the French reading of the Hungarian novel, but in this instance the end result of the stereotyping is different. Far from leading to an organic coherence in the reading, it might be described as creating an agglomeration of stereotyped "kernels" unrelated to each other. There is accordingly no organizing principle in the reading of the foreign book, the latter being perceived only through isolated and autonomous approaches. It therefore appears that for the Hungarian reader, reading a foreign novel is unfavorable to a systematization of thought, while at the same time it increases stereotyping.

We may ascertain here, at the level of reading schemes, the impact of the main vectors which organize the two national readings. In France, we discover a search for coherent read-ing, an emphasis on the logic of the novel, and constant at-

Toward a Sociology of Reading

tempts at causal explanations; in the French reading, determinism is one of the essential principles. In Hungary, on the other hand, the French analytic approach is replaced by a judgmental code in which a hierarchy of values is predominant; good and evil are the criteria for a moralizing approach to the novel. It is the opposition between analytic and moralizing codes that accounts for the (respectively) globalizing and particularizing approaches we discovered in the two countries. In order to enact a logical-explanatory mode of perception, French readers need the dialectic of the whole and the part; in order to enact a moralizing reading, the Hungarian must apply a particularizing-individualizing approach in which the variants good and evil are relevant. Although these two modes of reading are not mutually exclusive from a logical point of view, it is significant that the empirical data show them to be mutually exclusive as far as a concrete reading experience is concerned.

I would like to consider now, on the basis of these global attitudes, the preferences declared by readers for various scenes in the novels. For *Rozsdatemetö*, question 26 asked the reader to declare which type of scene he preferred. These answers were gathered in an SLA which shows that the readers' selection is clearly related to their global system of interpretation. When comparing Hungarian and French answers, one realizes that the French mostly prefer scenes in which the picturesque primitiveness of the "clan-family" in Fejes' novel is apparent. These readers are thus attracted to the stereotype that forms the basis of their reading; they take pleasure in recognizing themselves by recognizing their own mental categories. By choosing, where the pleasure of reading is concerned, those scenes in which the clan-family is seen as coming closest to their preconceived ideas, French readers confirm their reading and justify their judgment, as well as enjoy themselves: an illuminating synergy in which the pleasure of redundancy is at its uppermost!

Since the system of reading is entirely different in Hungary, it is no surprise to discover that the selection of favorite scenes is also different. The effect of a moralizing reading can be seen there through the choice of dramatic scenes, which were preferred by twice as many readers in Hungary as in France. "Dramatization," which is opposed to the deterministic analysis that characterizes the French reading, allows the Hungarian reader to bring into play the essential principle of his code of perception: an individualizing judgment. By preferring dramatic situations in the novel, the Hungarian reader also brings his pleasure into conformity with his mode of perception, thereby giving himself the enjoyment of their consistency: he too delights in redundancy.

We thus find an identical movement from one end to the other in the continuum of our material. From the impact of the system of values, which forces the text to pattern itself according to the system, to the expression of the reader's pleasure, we find a single momentum that carries with it every level of the text.

Earlier, I insisted on the fact that we were led to differentiate numerous "publics" within our respondents; yet my discussion so far has been restricted to a few very general tendencies that can serve to characterize the French and Hungarian publics taken as a whole. I cannot advance much further in the description of our investigation in such a short space, but I would like, nevertheless, to characterize briefly the *systems of reading* I mentioned earlier. They are a kind of intermediate state between the national wholes, necessarily perceived at a very general level, and the socioprofessional groups we took as a minimal, though pertinent, social unit. In between, we find the sociodemographical parameters such as age, social mobility, and schooling, each with its own area of pertinence.

On the whole, we distinguished four systems of evaluation, which could be seen as corresponding to four autonomous systems of reading. Since our thesis, however, is precisely that the system of evaluation and the system of reading are but two faces of the same phenomenon, we adopted one single term, *system of reading*.

System I is constituted by all the answers which, in relation to the imaginary world of the novel, are almost totally undistantiated, that is to say, without any apologetic concerns. This system is accordingly characterized by a light optimism, a realistic sense of what is possible and what is not. Limits in the characters' range of action are taken into account, but the characters are never seen as the prisoners of an external network: they dispose of a certain freedom of action, which helps to maintain a classical definition of the individual subject.

In *Systems IIA* and *IIB*, we gathered answers manifesting two kinds of critical attitudes. The two systems were distinguished from each other according to the values in reference to which the criticism was formulated.

System IIA consists in a critical attitude based on the claim for certain values which function as an *ideal*. This ideal is defined, depending on the individuals and on the book in question, as "culture," "liberty," "consciousness," or "community"—in short, every fundamental vector of action in our Western societies.

System IIB, which is often more passionate in its expression, consists of the answers based on *ethical* criteria. Whether the character is accused of weak or irresponsible behavior, or of an irresolute or nonenergetic kind of action, the criticism is based on the idea of a necessary dynamism of the person, where work and progress are all-important. Seriousness and moral strength are, quite literally, the rule in this *System IIB*.

System III is characterized not so much by *values* as by the mode of reading itself, which we called a synthesizing or "sociologizing" mode of reading. Its chief characteristic is a constant attempt to situate actions and judgments within a sociological or historical framework, in other words, to refer individual responsibility to its global determinants. Social causality is always invoked here to mediate the responsibility of the individual.

Unfortunately, lack of space prevents me from discussing the correlations we found between these systems and our sociodemographical data. We may note, however, that if the systems of reading are indeed relatively structured ideologi-

Jacques Leenhardt

cal frameworks, one must go beyond the analysis of these frameworks themselves, toward an analysis of the mental *habitus* developing within different categories, defined in particular on the basis of types of schooling and group membership. We can then achieve a more and more refined analysis, which can show how the levels of structuration, and consequently of meaning, are articulated in the reading process.

The hierarchical and totalizing representation suggested by our systems of reading must not hide the fact that we encountered processes contrary to it. Let us take a specific example, which will elucidate this new kind of phenomenon.

In the Hungarian reading of *Les Choses*, we can ascertain that the "ideal" of social and professional integration, of a search for a good salary and a fixed and sure job, is in accordance with the Hungarian readers' opinion *at the level of values*. This can be proven by a few quotations from Hungarian answers: "I believe they will eventually live a normal, very calm life; this is also my ideal," and "It is normal, one always hopes for the best circumstances." Despite this irrefutable evidence, however, when Hungarian readers were specifically asked: "Does the life that Jérôme and Sylvie prepare for themselves in Bordeaux correspond to your ideal?" they answered no in 45 percent of the cases.

To explain this divergence, we had two hypotheses. Either the abruptness of the question led to an answer in conformity with the official system of values dominant in Hungarian society, which condemns the characters' frenzy for consumption; or Perec's own critical attitude[13] momentarily *displaced* the Hungarian readers' personal system of values, as evidenced in their previous spontaneous replies. In either case, the readers, despite their own tendency to adopt the system that Perec criticizes, have obeyed a law that is not totally internalized by them: the law of social control, or the law of the book.

Whatever the explanation, the phenomenon we discovered

[13] This is obvious for the French reader and, I think, for every reader who adopts a somewhat *cautious* attitude.

Toward a Sociology of Reading

here shows that the reader's own system of values can be questioned, one might say short-circuited, during the reading process. We called this phenomenon a *short-circuit effect.*

Through this example, which is an extreme case, I wanted to show that reading cannot be described only as an effect of mental structures. As a matter of fact, the first intuition of our investigation was to prove—against others—the determining influence of mental structures in the reading process. As such, our investigation sought to contest those theories which underestimate the importance of mental structures. However, it turns out that the process of aesthetic impact cannot be adequately described by this fundamental approach alone. What we have called the short-circuit effect proves, for example, that the mental structures of the receiver do not totally coincide with the field of possibilities opened up by a work of art or of literature. The gap thus brought into evidence is not—as some would have it—what characterizes works of art as such; the extent of this gap varies, and depends not only on the works of art themselves (and on their complexity in particular), but also on the historically changing characteristics of the mental space in which they occur. I am thus by no means suggesting a return to a definition of literature—of "literarity"—as whatever is "left over," inaccessible to understanding; on the contrary, if we notice a gap between mental structures and the field of possibilities opened up by a work of art, we must analyze the conditions that make a complete superposition of the two impossible, rather than seek to ontologize the gap itself. These conditions are in fact a parameter in the historical process of meaning.

What, then, does the short-circuit effect demonstrate? It points to an absence of superposition, to something that is incommensurable though analyzable. Through it, a deficiency in the totalizing system (i.e., the system of mental structures) is made manifest. The phenomenon brings to light a weak point of the system, for it counteracts (short-circuits) the system's "perfect" functioning. It is thus the "normal," principal system mediating the reading process that is short-circuited in the aesthetic relationship. As a result, the text has a direct

Jacques Leenhardt

and immediate impact on the reader, an impact over which we may say he has no control.

We should note that these short-circuit effects do not belong in any of the categories analyzed above. For example, such answers do not have any structural link with the rest of the materials (which is ascertained by the fact that we cannot establish any correlations). Does this mean that such answers, which are imposed, as it were, on the other answers we recorded, are completely foreign to those who give them? Of course not. They are, in fact, all the more interesting in that they indicate the points of rupture, or the "chinks," in a structured system. The dysfunctioning that they reveal suggests, I believe, the possibilities for change within these very systems. These points of rupture are in fact probably one of the means whereby structures of perception can be renewed, reelaborated. It goes without saying that the plurality of layers of literary meaning, when this plurality exists, tends to multiply the odds for such a process. The need for putting mental structures into question is in such cases even more apparent.

Through the above example, I have tried to show how a more rigorous analysis on the aesthetic level can deal with the phenomenon of rupture. Almost every theory of modernity, from Shklovsky to Jauss or Kristeva, is based on the idea that modern art is characterized by a rupture with given codes, that literarity is a break with automatism. According to these theories, the value of all true literature is that it departs from the established codes. My purpose is neither to confirm nor to deny this assumption; having worked with two novels whose "modernity" is not at all apparent, the specific conclusions I was able to draw from them are not generalizable to more self-consciously modern texts in which the "referential" plays only a minor part. Above all, I think we must be careful not to attribute a general value to any kind of functioning. As Shklovsky put it: "a work may be (1) prosaic for its author and perceived as poetic, (2) poetic for its author and perceived as prosaic."[14] A literary effect, in other words, varies

[14] Victor Chklovski, *Sur la théorie de la prose* (Lausanne, 1973), p. 11.

according to time and place. M. Riffaterre is right when he emphasizes that "to speak of the truth or untruth of a text is largely irrelevant; we can only explain it by evaluating its adequacy to the verbal system, by inquiring whether it obeys the code conventions or transgresses them."[15] But we should not stop the analysis here. Adequacy or inadequacy to the verbal system is only one aspect of the reading process. To limit the analysis to the narrow field of the verbal code is to overlook the fact that every approach to this code is itself imbued with ideological tendencies. We never find on the one hand a text as text, and on the other the relationships between text and author, and between text and reality. This creation of autonomous fields, which allows for the specificity of stylistics—as it is conceived by Riffaterre[16]—is a delusion that leads to a misrepresentation of the totalizing character of the reading process.

The study I have described helps to specify a few aspects of this totalizing character. By establishing the reality of national patterns of literary perception, our research points to the predominant unifying cultural schemes whose efficiency is felt even in the most general attitudes of readers toward the text. These patterns are brought into play according to the place of the individual in the systems of hierarchization and of the division of labor in society. It is therefore not surprising to discover the importance of particular types of schooling, both as regards the use of language (and consequently the activity of reading), and as regards familiarity with a certain literary tradition, which always comes into play in the reading process. All these factors have their place in a sociology of knowledge, and in a sociology of the transformations that the structures of knowledge undergo once they are put into practice.

Let me be more specific. The sociology of knowledge must not be a mere rewriting of the illusions of the theory of communication; it must take into account the specific hierarchiza-

---

[15] Michael Riffaterre, "L'Explication des faits littéraires," in Serge Doubrovsky and Tzvetan Todorov, eds., L'Enseignement de la littérature (Paris, 1971), p. 335.
[16] See "L'Explication des faits littéraires."

tion of the processes of meaning, at every point of social reality. Such an approach would not overlook the fact that cultural objects are produced and received according to schemes elaborated by collective rather than by individual entities, and that accordingly the "code" in no way transcends the text but, on the contrary, is produced by the "message" at the moment when the latter manifests itself in social reality. Abstract notions such as "code" and "message," as well as "addresser" and "addressee," are no longer meaningful when applied to literature or any other cultural object, because it is the process of meaning alone, the process of the emergence of meaning, which in every instance gives the cultural object its specific characteristics.

Lastly, our research helps to specify how the unexpected or innovatory can enter into the structural schemata. The short-circuit effect indicates that there is a "hole" in the checkerwork of meaning, a hole whose importance must be stressed because it is through it that the text may perturb the preestablished reading scheme and thus destabilize the mental structures of reception. I have tried to demonstrate that this short-circuit effect is produced whenever a conflict of meanings cannot be resolved. Actually, this system of dysfunctioning arises from a failure in the regulating system, which normally tends to master innovation in order to transform it into what is already known, i.e., into a reiterative reality. It is through the study of such symptoms that we arrive at a description of the processes whereby mental structures are constantly renewed and placed into question. In these processes, the perception of aesthetic works—and consequently their social function—plays an important, if not privileged, role.

Translated from the French
by Brigitte Navelet
and Susan R. Suleiman

Gerald Prince | # Notes on the Text as Reader

Reading is an activity that presupposes a text (a set of visually presented linguistic symbols from which meaning can be extracted), a reader (an agent capable of extracting meaning from that text), and an interaction between the text and the reader such that the latter is able to answer correctly at least some questions about the meaning of the former. A text like

(1) "The two suites on the second floor were taken, one by an old gentleman named Poiret; the other by a man of forty, who wore a black wig, dyed his whiskers, said he was in business, and called himself Monsieur Vautrin."[1]

for instance, allows only one correct answer to

(2) How old was Monsieur Vautrin?

and a text like

(3) "The one who was leaning on the chair, that is, the noisy one, the laughing one, was a beautiful girl of nineteen or twenty."[2]

allows only one correct answer to

(4) Was the one leaning on the chair an ugly girl?

---

[1] Honoré de Balzac, *Le Père Goriot* (Paris, 1960), pp. 14-15. Subsequent page references are given in the text. All translations from the French are by Gerald Prince.

[2] Alexandre Dumas, *Le Vicomte de Bragelonne* (Lausanne, 1963), 1: 29.

Gerald Prince

Should anyone reading texts (1) and (3) answer questions (2) and (4) with

(5) Monsieur Vautrin was seventy-one.

and

(6) Yes, she was an ugly girl.

respectively, we would most probably not conclude that he was reading (1) and (3) in a highly idiosyncratic manner but, rather, that he was misreading them or not reading them at all. Thus, it is clear that, to a certain extent, the text acts as a guide to and constraint on the activity of reading.

It is also clear, however, that many if not all texts allow for more than one possible answer to some of the (relevant) questions that may be asked about them. A text may be constituted in great part by words and sentences having several semantic possibilities, only a few of which it specifies; it may lead to a large number of inferences that are neither mutually exclusive nor mutually dependent; it may allow for different kinds of connections to be made among its constituent parts; it may be summarizable in several ways; it may lend itself to several symbolic interpretations; and so on and so forth. If we asked what *Le Noeud de vipères* was about, for example,

(7) It is about a conversion.
(8) It is about a man in search of an audience.

and

(9) It is about a man who mistakes appearance for being.

would constitute acceptable answers; and if we asked what connotations the name Bonnelly had in *En attendant Godot*,

(10) Bonnelly suggests "bon et lie."

226

Notes on the Text as Reader

and

(11) Bonnelly suggests "bon Eli."

would both be quite valid. In other words, many if not all texts lend themselves to being read in several ways, which are more or less different from one another, though they may have various points in common.

If the activity of reading (and its results) depends on the text being read, it also depends on the reader. In order to read a given text—and, more specifically, a given narrative text—it is obvious that we must know the language of that text, the linguistic meaning of the words and sentences constituting it, the linguistic code in terms of which it manifests itself. I could not read (1) or (3) if I did not understand (some) English and I could not read *A la recherche du temps perdu* if I did not understand (a lot of) French. Reading a narrative text, however, asking relevant questions about it, and answering them in a correct or valid fashion, implies much more than knowing a language. The code of such a text—the set of norms, rules, and constraints according to which it is decipherable, understandable, readable—is far from being monolithic; it conjoins, combines and orders several (sub-)codes, only one of which is linguistic in nature. Consider, for instance,

(12) He shook his head from left to right several times.

In order to answer a question like

(13) What did he mean by shaking his head thus?

I must know the meaning of the action recounted. Now, according to some cultural codes, such an action implies negation or disapproval, and according to some others, it implies affirmation or approval. My comprehension depends, therefore, on the cultural code that I understand to be framing the narrative, the code in terms of which the actions, events, and situations related by a set of sentences mean something in a

Gerald Prince

certain cultural context. Furthermore, as I read a (relatively long) narrative, I am capable of summarizing it thanks to what Roland Barthes identified as the proairetic code or code of actions: I know which constituent parts of the narrative may be disregarded in a summary and which may not, and I know how to group the activities or events recounted into larger activities or events.[3] Given

> (14) It was five o'clock and the sun was shining brightly. After staring at him for a long while, John punched Jim; then Jim kicked John, then they threw bottles at each other, then they calmed down and went out to have a drink and became friends once again.

I know how to summarize it as

> (15) There was a fight between John and Jim followed by a reconciliation between them.

Moreover, as I read a narrative, I can also consider it according to what Barthes called a code of enigmas or hermeneutic code: I organize it in such a way that some of its constituent parts function as mysteries and others as solutions to these mysteries, or partial solutions, or mere clues. For instance, in

> (16) It was seven o'clock. The young man was standing on a dark and filthy corner of 42nd Street. At five past seven, it started to rain very hard. The young man did not move. He was a spy and he had to meet the head of the CIA on that corner at ten past seven.

the second sentence leads to certain questions by pointing to the existence of certain mysterious states of things (Who is this young man? What is he doing on that dark and filthy corner?); the fourth sentence functions in a similar way (Why

[3] On the question of narrative (sub-)codes, see Roland Barthes, *S/Z* (Paris, 1970), pp. 23-28, and his "Analyse textuelle d'un conte d'Edgar Poe," in *Sémiotique narrative et textuelle*, Claude Chabrol, ed. (Paris, 1973).

Notes on the Text as Reader

does he not move even though it is raining very hard?); and the last sentence represents an answer to the questions raised, a solution to the mysteries. Finally, as I read a narrative, I am able to perceive that some of its constituent parts can function in terms of a symbolic code (they are what they are and also something greater, more general and/or more fundamental which they stand for): given the appropriate context, the account of a trip from France to Algeria may represent that of a spiritual quest (*L'Immoraliste*), the description of a garden may evoke paradise (*Candide*), and references to snow may function as references to the Holy Ghost (*La Chute*). In short, the activity of reading depends, to some extent, on the way the reader uses various codes he is armed with to decipher and interpret the text being read.[4]

Of course, a given reader may be very tired or not at all, very young or very old, in a good mood or in a bad one; he may have a very good or a very deficient memory, a very great or very limited capacity for decentration, a considerable or moderate attention span; he may be a more or less experienced reader; he may be reading the text for the first, second, or tenth time; he may find the sentences and situations presented more or less familiar; he may want to read for fun or out of a sense of duty; he may show particular interest in the language, the plot, the characters, or the symbolism; he may hold one set of beliefs or another; and so on. In other words, his physiological, psychological, and sociological conditioning, his predispositions, feelings, and needs may vary greatly and so may his reading: his knowledge, his interests, and his aims determine to a certain extent the conventions, assumptions, and presuppositions he takes to underlie the text, the kinds of connections he is particularly interested in making, the questions he chooses to ask, and the answers he brings to them.

The variety of interpretations to which a narrative text

[4] My enumeration of the various (sub-)codes constituting the narrative code is clearly not complete. For example, as I read, I may resort to a code of characters in order to organize the narrative around heroes, false heroes, villains, helpers, and so on.

Gerald Prince

lends itself and the variety of reader responses to that text result in an indefinitely large number of possible readings. Many a narrative text presents, in part, one of these possible readings. It performs some of the reading operations that a given reader may perform. It specifically answers questions pertaining to the nature, the meaning, the role, the appropriateness of its constituent parts.[5] It functions as a text reading itself by commenting explicitly and directly on these constituent parts taken as units in one of the above-mentioned codes.[6]

A narrative often contains passages which provide a metalinguistic commentary on some of the words and phrases of which it is made up. It may, for instance, define an exotic vocable, a technical locution, or a slangy expression. Thus, in *Eugénie Grandet*, the narrator writes: "In Anjou, the *frippe*, a colloquial word, designates what goes with bread, from butter spread on toast—the commonest kind—to peach preserve, the most distinguished of all the *frippes*";[7] and in *Le Père Goriot*, terms belonging to the jargon of thieves are explained at length: "*Sorbonne* and *tronche* are two energetic words of the thieves' vocabulary, invented because these gentry were the first to feel the need of considering the human head from two standpoints. *Sorbonne* is the head of the living man, his intellect and wisdom. *Tronche* is a word of contempt, expressing the worthlessness of the head after it is cut off" (p. 32). In other terms, the text functions as if it were answering directly such questions as

[5] Sometimes it even asks those questions. In Proust's *A la recherche du temps perdu*, for example, an exquisite pleasure invades Marcel's senses when he tastes a *petite madeleine* soaked in tea, and several questions are raised in relation to this extraordinary event: "Whence could it have come to me, this all-powerful joy? . . . Whence did it come? What did it signify? How could I seize upon and define it?" ([Paris, 1954], 1: 45).

[6] Cf. my "Remarques sur les signes métanarratifs," *Degrés*, nos. 11-12 (1977). Textual interest in reading is also manifested by the numerous fictional characters portrayed as readers and by the more or less detailed descriptions of narratees that many narratives provide. On narratees, see my "Introduction à l'étude du narrataire," *Poétique*, no. 14 (1973), 178-96.

[7] Balzac, *Eugénie Grandet* (Paris, 1961), p. 76.

230

Notes on the Text as Reader

(17) What does the word *frippe* designate?

or

(18) What is the meaning of *Sorbonne* and *tronche*?

Sometimes, as in *The Sun Also Rises*, it is a foreign term that is translated into the main language of the text: "I had taken six seats for all the fights. Three of them were barreras, the first row at the ring-side, and three were sobrepuertas, seats with wooden backs, half-way up the amphitheatre."[8] Sometimes it is the meaning of an abbreviation that the text makes clear. In *Invisible Man*, for example, the narrator writes: "If you made an appointment with one of them, you couldn't bring them any slow c.p. (colored people's) time."[9] A narrative may also comment on the appropriateness of a given word: "with the first glimpse of the building, a sense of insufferable gloom pervaded my spirit. I say insufferable; for the feeling was unrelieved by any of that half-pleasurable, because poetic, sentiment, with which the mind usually receives even the sternest natural images of the desolate or terrible."[10] It may specify the connotations carried by a perfectly ordinary term: "The observers, those people who insist on knowing where you buy your candelabras, or who ask what your rent is when your apartment seems nice to them . . ."[11] Or again, it may indicate what a certain pronoun refers to: "I would remember that if he ('he' meant any of the important gentlemen) should begin a topic of conversation . . . I would smile and agree" (*Invisible Man*, p. 120). Finally, it is often the case that a text defines the various proper names appearing in it.

[8] Ernest Hemingway, *The Sun Also Rises*, in *The Hemingway Reader* (New York, 1953), p. 217. Subsequent page references are given in the text.

[9] Ralph Ellison, *Invisible Man* (New York: Vintage paperback, 1972), p. 125. Subsequent page references are given in the text.

[10] Poe, "The Fall of the House of Usher," in *The Works of Edgar Allan Poe* (New York, 1904), 6: 83.

[11] Balzac, "Sarrasine," in *La Comédie Humaine* (Paris, 1950), 6: 88. Subsequent page references are given in the text.

Gerald Prince

Indeed, this kind of definition abounds even in narratives that are reluctant to provide explanations. Thus, within a few pages of "Un Coeur simple," we find: "Robelin, the farmer of Geffosses . . . Liébard, the farmer of Toucques . . . the Marquis de Gremanville, one of her uncles . . . Guyot, a poor devil employed at the town hall . . ."[12]

If the narrative text often acts as if it were processing linguistic data, it also acts frequently like a reader organizing his reading in terms of nonlinguistic codes and answering questions pertaining to the cultural, proairetic, hermeneutic, or symbolic meaning and function of the various events and situations that it recounts. Consider the following, for instance:

(19) He had a cabin of his own, which meant that he had reached adulthood.

(20) He was wearing a yellow jacket, which meant that he was a nobleman.

In neither case does the text answer any question about the linguistic nature or significance of any of the words and sentences constituting it. In both cases, however, the text indicates explicitly the meaning of the state of things presented in terms of a sociocultural code; in other words, it specifically answers such questions as

(21) He had a cabin of his own. What did it mean (according to the relevant sociocultural code)?

and

(22) He was wearing a yellow jacket. What did it mean (according to the relevant sociocultural code)?

Given any group of events or situations that it recounts, the text can thus comment directly on its functioning as a unit in

[12] Gustave Flaubert, *Trois Contes* (Paris, 1969), pp. 12, 13, and 14.

232

Notes on the Text as Reader

a given set of cultural rules and constraints. The text can also define the position of that unit in terms of a proairetic code, indicating whether or not it constitutes an integral part of the plot, showing that it belongs to one plot sequence or another, or pointing out how it can be summarized: think of chapter and section titles, for instance, which indicate at least one of the meanings of a set of events in a narrative; or again, think of the various demonstrative+noun groups that refer to a series of sentences or paragraphs while summarizing them for us, as in

(23) John punched Jim, then Jim kicked John, then they threw bottles at each other. This fight lasted a few seconds only.

or

(24) "Jussac was, as was then said, a fine blade, and had had much practice; nevertheless, it required all his skill to defend himself against an adversary, who, active and energetic, departed every instant from received rules, attacking him on all sides at once, and yet parrying like a man who had the greatest respect for his own epidermis. This contest at length exhausted Jussac's patience."[13]

Furthermore, the narrative text can specify the hermeneutic dimension of one of its constituent parts, deciding that it functions as an enigma, as a clue to the solution of that enigma, as a red herring, and so on. Consider the following narrative passages:

(25) Joan was more and more tamed under John's yoke.
(26) Joan was more and more tamed under John's yoke. This was a mystery.

[13] Quotation from Alexandre Dumas, *Les Trois Mousquetaires* (Lausanne, 1962), 1: 106. Note that, frequently, demonstrative+noun groups indicate the illocutionary force of a set of utterances ("This promise . . . ," "This threat . . . ," "This request . . .").

233

Gerald Prince

The reader of (25) may or may not view Joan's behavior as mysterious and may or may not, therefore, search for explanations of the mystery in the rest of the narrative. In (26), on the other hand, the text interprets Joan's behavior as unequivocally constituting a mystery; it reads what is recounted in (25) according to a hermeneutic code. Finally, a narrative text may, of course, offer a symbolic reading of any of its constituent parts: in "Sarrasine," for example, after the detailed description of a hideous old man accompanied by a ravishing young woman, we find the narrator exclaiming: "Ah! it was death and life indeed!" (p. 82).[14] In short, many a narrative text is partly constituted by the result of various reading operations it performs on itself.

Note that the passages in a narrative which I am taking to function as a reader reading and which may be called "reading interludes" are explicitly predicated on other passages considered as units in a narrative (sub-) code and provide direct answers to such questions as

(27) What does passage x mean in the (linguistic, proairetic, hermeneutic . . .) code according to which the narrative can be read?

or

(28) How does passage x function in the (linguistic, proairetic, hermeneutic . . .) code according to which the narrative can be read?

Reading interludes thus differ from the many passages in a narrative that implicitly and indirectly refer to and comment on the meaning or function of other passages. Consider, for instance, the following: "She . . . took a telegram out of the leather wallet. . . . 'Por ustedes?' I looked at it. The address was 'Barnes, Burguete.' 'Yes, it's for us' " (*The Sun Also Rises*,

[14] Note that a text may also perform reading operations in terms of a code of characters, a rhetorical code, a thematic code, and so forth. Thus, a narrative may refer to a character as "our hero" or "our protagonist."

234

p. 217). *Yes, it's for us* is obviously an answer to *Por ustedes?* and it can be concluded, therefore, that the latter expression means something like *Is it for you?*. But *Yes, it's for us* is not predicated on *Por ustedes?* and it does not directly answer a question such as "What does *Por ustedes?* mean in the linguistic code used?"

Note also that reading interludes constitute a distinctive type of what is often designated as commentary. Compare, for example, (19), (20), or (24) with such other types of commentary as we find in

(29) "Like all narrow-minded people, Madame Vauquer never looked beyond the limits of the events around her, nor troubled herself about their hidden causes" (*Le Père Goriot*, p. 211).

(30) "We have just said that, on the day when the Egyptian and the archdeacon died, Quasimodo was not to be found in Notre-Dame."[15]

and

(31) "It is the idea of duration—of earthly immortality—that gives such a mysterious interest to our own portraits. Walter and Elinor were not insensible to that feeling, and hastened to the painter's room."[16]

No part of (29), (30), or (31) is explicitly predicated on a passage considered as a unit in a narrative (sub-)code and no part directly answers such questions as (27) or (28).

Finally, note that if the text reads a given passage in a certain way, it does not necessarily mean that another reader would read that passage in exactly the same way. Thus, given

(32) They were eating gumbo (a famous spaghetti dish from Sweden).

[15] Victor Hugo, *Notre-Dame de Paris* (Paris, 1975), p. 498.
[16] Nathaniel Hawthorne, "The Prophetic Pictures," in *The Complete Short Stories of Nathaniel Hawthorne* (New York, 1959), pp. 93-94.

Gerald Prince

I may not interpret "gumbo" as the text does and I may view (32) as a joke. Similarly, the text may consider a passage from a proairetic standpoint whereas another reader may also consider it from a hermeneutic one; or else, it may explicitly propose only one of several possible symbolic readings; or again, it may summarize a series of events in only one of many acceptable ways. After all, readers differ and a text frequently lends itself to various readings.

The reading interludes scattered in a text have a variety of functions, which are not necessarily unique to them. They may, for example, help impart a certain rhythm to the narrative by regularly slowing down the pace at which events and situations are introduced: it is clear that they do not so much provide new information as they constitute an interpretation of old information. Furthermore, they may serve as a characterization device since they are not always ostensibly introduced by a narrator but may be initiated by a character, in the course of a dialogue, for instance, or in a letter to another character. It is obvious, for example, that a character who defines a technical term or foreign expression, or who explains the position of a series of events in terms of a hermeneutic code, or who indicates the symbolic dimension of a given situation differs from characters who never perform similar actions. Reading interludes also help define the narrator and his relationship with the narratee. To begin with, the number, the kind, and the complexity of reading operations performed by a narrator contribute to his characterization as pedantic or unassuming, humble or condescending, cunning or straightforward, and so on. Moreover, they help delineate the way he views the audience he is addressing and specify whether he respects it, is well disposed toward it, or considers himself to be infinitely superior; whether he feels it needs having certain locutions explained—even very ordinary ones—and certain symbolic possibilities made clear; whether he thinks it longs for periodic summaries of what has been presented and periodic reminders of what enigmas are to be solved and what clues may allow for their solution. Finally, the distribution of reading interludes may indicate a change

Notes on the Text as Reader

in the narrator's attitude vis-à-vis his narratee: if he stops making metalinguistic statements after having multiplied them, for instance, it may be because he has come to realize that his narratee is perfectly able to do without them.

Reading interludes, however, are perhaps most interesting as an index of the stance taken by the narrative with regard to its own communicability and readability, as an indication of how it ostensibly wants to be read and a cue to the kind of program it considers most useful for its decoding, and as a factor determining to some extent the response of any reader other than itself.

The very presence of these interludes in a text underlines the fact that portions of that text at least are readable in certain more or less straightforward ways (you can read this passage according to a proairetic code and you can read this other passage according to a hermeneutic code; this third passage is not difficult to interpret, provided you know the linguistic code well; as for that one, it is simple too, when interpreted along symbolic lines). Their appearance is equivalent to that of a (fragmentary) text in the text, constituting a language that is *other* in the language of the text and instituting (some of) the intertextual coordinates of a communicative situation. Since they function as decipherments of various passages and, as such, can act as partial substitutes for them, they serve to specify the assumptions made by the text as reader, the presuppositions of that text, and the decoding contracts endorsed by it. In other words, they clarify the premises of textual communicability (if you read me in terms of the hermeneutic code, you will see how everything falls into place; if you interpret me in terms of a symbolic code, you will understand that I am saying much more than I seem to; I will summarize for you this sequence of events and that one, but you will have to summarize the others).

More particularly, reading interludes tend to emphasize certain aspects of the identity of a given text. The kinds of passages subject to metacommentary and shown to be sharable and the kinds of reading codes that most often come into play are always revealing as to the avowed import of the text.

Gerald Prince

Reading interludes indicate the kind of text that a text (super-ficially) views itself to be. They point out what the text is more than willing to admit, what it (apparently) considers important to understand, and how it would like to be read. A narrative specifying hermeneutic functions that are obvious is, of course, different from a narrative not specifying them. Similarly, a narrative favoring proairetic readings is different from one showing particular interest in symbolic readings. Indeed, certain classes of narratives, certain genres or sub-genres, are so characterized by their extensive use of one kind of reading commentary that a text can identify itself as a member of a given class by resorting frequently to the type of reading favored by that class. The case of the classical detec-tive story is exemplary. The latter may be defined as a story in which metahermeneutic commentary is particularly promi-nent: some of its constituent parts assert that there are certain mysteries to be solved, others explicitly formulate these mys-teries (Who is it? What is it? How is it that?), and others still are expressly designated as constituting a solution, contribut-ing to it, or representing an obstacle to it. In the works of Agatha Christie, Dorothy Sayers, or John Dickson Carr, for example, the narrator often establishes (partial) lists of the various enigmas that the detective must solve as well as lists of the various clues that will help him succeed. As for the pro-tagonist's genius, it consists in formulating enigmas which no one else thought of formulating and in finding answers to them: whereas his colleagues try to understand how a corpse has been concealed or how a gun has been stolen, Hercule Poirot asks himself why a silk scarf has not disappeared and he succeeds in finding a solution that leads him to *the* solu-tion. The detective story constitutes an exacerbation of the metahermeneutic dimension and, on one level at least, any text giving particular importance to decoding in terms of a hermeneutic code presents itself as a detective story.

By clarifying the premises on which a given text stands, by proposing a partial definition of its nature, by attributing a certain function, meaning, or importance to one passage or another, textual instances of decoding cannot but affect decisively any given reader's reading and response. On the one hand, they may help him by presenting him with a set of directions to follow and a set of constraints to respect and by doing part of his work for him. As I tried to show earlier, reading a narrative implies organizing it and interpreting it in terms of several more or less complex (sub-) codes. The reader frequently has to determine the connotations of a given passage, the symbolic dimensions of a given event, the hermeneutic function of a given situation, and so on. Reading interludes provide him with certain specific sets of connotations; they make *some* symbolic dimensions explicit; they define the hermeneutic status of *some* situations. In short, they may allow for rest periods, as it were, and may facilitate understanding. On the other hand, instead of acting as an aid to reading, they may, at times, represent an obstacle to it. Performed by an ignorant or ill-intentioned narrator, the readings put forth may really be misreadings; even though they are given as quite satisfactory, they are inadequate and set the reader on the wrong track. Saying that an event constitutes the solution to a mystery when it actually does not or saying that a situation functions as an enigma when it ultimately is not enigmatic at all is equivalent to deceiving the reader. Sometimes also, reading interludes may contradict one another, imply conflicting assumptions, lead to opposite conclusions; they thus add to a reader's difficulties in his attempt to process textual data. Finally, they may present a definition of the text that is at best superficial or off-base; they may, for example, emphasize its proairetic dimension where a symbolic decoding would prove most fruitful and interesting. In this case, rather than performing as readers, they perform as counterreaders.

Of course, whether they are intended as allies or enemies for the reader, whether they actually propose acceptable decodings or unacceptable ones, whether they identify the main thrust of a text or not, their ultimate effect depends on the nature of the reader whom they are guiding and constraining and thus varies from one reader to another. After all, some readers are more difficult to deceive than others; some are

Gerald Prince

very much in need of metalinguistic commentary and others are not; some may find that they always agree with the readings put forward by the text while others may find that they always disagree with them; some may like to be guided while others may resent it. Experienced readers of detective stories, for example, will not necessarily accept at face value the hermeneutic views initially advanced by such stories; and the reader of *La Chartreuse de Parme* will react differently to Stendhal's novel depending on whether he knows Italian or not: the numerous translations of Italian phrases provided by the text may tire him, amuse him, or reassure him. In short, reading interludes determine in part the distance between a particular text and a particular reader and play an important but ever-changing role in the way that text is received each time it is read.

Peter J. Rabinowitz | "What's Hecuba to Us?" The Audience's Experience of Literary Borrowing

CLASSIFICATION

In choosing the title "Phorion" ("Stolen Goods") for his hallucinatory fantasy on a Bach prelude, Lukas Foss wittily summed up not only a swelling subgenre of contemporary music, but a major trend in literature and film as well. We live in an age of artistic recycling: Alain Robbe-Grillet's *Les Gommes* borrows from *Oedipus;* Tom Stoppard's *Rosencrantz and Guildenstern Are Dead* incorporates passages from *Hamlet,* while his *Travesties* takes Joyce's *Ulysses* (itself built on Homer) and Wilde's *The Importance of Being Earnest* as basic material. Peter Maxwell Davies, Hugh Hartwell, George Rochberg, and Karlheinz Stockhausen have in their diverse ways "recomposed" earlier music.

Of course, artists have always felt free to loot earlier sources. Yet no two ages do the same thing in quite the same way; consequently, the terminology developed for such practices in older works of art inadequately describes contemporary procedures. The terms parody, burlesque, mock-heroic, spoof, and travesty, for instance, are ambiguous not only because they have all been variously defined; moreover, what definitions there are often depend on agreed-upon distinctions between high and low style, serious and trifling subjects—distinctions hard to apply to moderns like John Barth and Luciano Berio. Herman Meyer's "borrowing" and "quotation"[1]—or words like *citation* and *allusion*—avoid these

---

[1] Meyer, *The Poetics of Quotation in the European Novel*, trans. Theodore and Yetta Ziolkowski (Princeton, 1968), pp. 6-8.

241

Peter J. Rabinowitz

difficulties by distinguishing techniques according to how accurate or explicit the copying is. But they don't discriminate among the ways the models are used, and thus tell us little about the effects they produce.[2] As for the more recent and increasingly popular term *intertextuality*[3]: it includes literary borrowing, but it also covers other linguistic phenomena, such as the "polyphonic novel,"[4] which use no literary borrowing as such. Thus, the term is needlessly broad for the field we are addressing here.[5]

As a result, we have no precise terms for many of our modern works. What exactly *has* Robbe-Grillet done to *Oedipus*? The critics are vague: *Les Gommes* is "a sort of parody of the Oedipus story"[6]; it is "patterned . . . upon the Oedipus myth"[7]; it "recreates the Oedipus theme."[8] Since a similar vagueness haunts the descriptions of Stoppard's modern *Hamlet*, the radically different procedures of these two authors end up in a pile with those of the other moderns who reuse old works: Barth, Bogdanovich, Bond, Brooks, Butor . . .

Such a lumping, except insofar as it suggests a broad trend, is of limited use; in order to analyze and judge the art of these borrowers, we need to discriminate more sharply. Exactly *how* we do this, of course, depends on the questions we want

---

[2] See Jean Weisgerber, "The Use of Quotations in Recent Literature," *Comparative Literature* 22, no. 1 (1970), 36-45.

[3] See Julia Kristeva's definition in *Semeiotike: Recherches pour une sémanalyse* (Paris, 1969), p. 255.

[4] Mikhail Bakhtin, *Problems of Dostoyevsky's Poetics*, trans. R. W. Rostel (Ann Arbor, 1973), especially chap. 1.

[5] A good selection of essays on intertextuality can be found in *Poétique*, no. 27 (1976); see also Michael Riffaterre, "The Poetic Functions of Intertextual Humor," *Romanic Review* 65 (1974), 278-93; and Susan Suleiman, "Reading Robbe-Grillet: Sadism and Text in *Projet pour une révolution à New York*," *Romanic Review* 68 (1977), 43-62.

[6] Laurent Le Sage, *The French New Novel: An Introduction and a Sampler* (University Park, Pa., 1962), p. 120.

[7] Vivian Mercier, *The New Novel from Queneau to Pinget* (New York, 1971), p. 30.

[8] Kathleen O'Flaherty, *The Novel in France 1945-1965: A General Survey* (Cork, 1973), p. 111.

Audience's Experience of Literary Borrowing

to ask: a sociologist studying nostalgia, for instance, might classify works according to the date of the originals, in order to learn what historical periods have the greatest current appeal. In the present essay, I shall be inquiring into the ways an artist's technical procedures contribute to the work's effects: specifically, the way that the new work uses the audience's knowledge of the original.

This approach leads beyond the relationship between original and copy to an examination of how the two works interact with the audience; and this in turn demands a definition of "audience." Of course, we have the *actual audience*: the flesh-and-blood readers or viewers. Study of the actual audience is properly the province of sociological or psychological criticism and—valuable as it is—falls outside the scope of this essay.[9] Instead, I propose to focus on two implied audiences that can be discussed without questionnaires and surveys.

The multiplicity of audiences arises because all representational art is "imitation" in that it pretends to be something it is not. A piece of stone, for instance, is presented as David. As a result, the aesthetic experience exists on two levels at once. We can treat the work neither as what it is nor as what it appears to be; we must be simultaneously aware of both aspects. A viewer is hardly responding adequately to *Hamlet* if he leaps on stage to warn the prince that the fencing match is rigged. Neither, however, should he refuse to mourn Ophelia because he knows that she is really backstage studying her lines for *Barefoot in the Park*. The proper response treats *Hamlet* as both "true" and "untrue" at once.

This duality generates our two implied audiences. First, authors can never know their actual readers; but they cannot make artistic decisions without prior assumptions (conscious or unconscious) about their audience's beliefs, knowledge, and familiarity with conventions. In *The Possessed*, for example, Dostoyevsky has assumed that his readers will recognize his citations of Pushkin and his caricature of Turgenev in the figure of Karmazinov. How could he make such assumptions

[9] One of the few critics to work with actual readers is Norman Holland, *5 Readers Reading* (New Haven, 1975).

243

Peter J. Rabinowitz

without knowing his actual readers? The best he could do was, as authors have always done, design his book for a hypothetical audience, which I call the *authorial audience*. Since the structure of any work is designed with the authorial audience in mind, we must—as we read—come to share its characteristics if we are to understand the text.

Since fiction is generally an imitation of some nonfictional form (usually history), the narrator (implicit or explicit) is generally an imitation of an author. He too writes for an audience—an imitation audience that I call the *narrative audience*. Anton Lavrentevich, the narrator of *The Possessed*, is an imitation historian. As such, he writes for an audience which not only knows (as does the authorial audience) that the serfs were freed in 1861, but which also believes that Stavrogin and Kirilov "really" existed. To read *The Possessed*, we must not only join Dostoyevsky's authorial audience (which treats the text as *what it is*—a novel), but must at the same time pretend to be members of Anton Lavrentevich's narrative audience (which treats the text as if it were really what it *pretends to be*—a history). Unconsciously, this is what all competent readers do when approaching the text.[10]

Drama, of course, does not have a narrator in the way that narrative fiction does (although *Travesties* and Anouilh's *Antigone* come close). But even though the dynamics are slightly different (drama imitates the fictional event itself, while a narrative imitates an account of it), there is the same triple role for an audience watching a performance too. In *The Possessed* we are simultaneously our real selves, the hypothetical readers called for by Dostoyevsky, and the imaginary

[10] For a fuller discussion of actual, authorial, and narrative audiences—plus a fourth, not germane to this essay—see my "Truth in Fiction: A Reexamination of Audiences," *Critical Inquiry* 4 (1977), 121-41. For different perspectives on multiple audiences, see also Walker Gibson, "Authors, Speakers, Readers, and Mock-Readers," *College English* 11 (1950), 265-69; Wayne Booth, *The Rhetoric of Fiction* (Chicago, 1961), pp. 137-44 and *passim;* Wayne Booth, *A Rhetoric of Irony* (Chicago, 1974), p. 126 and *passim;* Gerald Prince, "Introduction à l'étude du narrataire," *Poétique*, no. 14 (1973), 178-96; and Walter J. Ong, S.J., "The Writer's Audience Is Always a Fiction," *PMLA* 90 (1975), 9-21.

readers who believe that Anton Lavrentevich's world is real. So too in viewing Sophocles' *Antigone* we must not only be our real selves, but must also try to become those hypothetical viewers addressed by the playwright (temporarily sharing their beliefs about burial), while we simultaneously pretend to react to the characters as real people. For simplicity, I shall use the term *narrative audience* for drama as well as fiction.

The narrative audience, then, takes the work before it as real. Normally, joining the narrative audience simply requires taking on minimal beliefs beyond those we already hold—for example, that a city called Zenith really exists. Occasionally, a work's demands are greater: the narrative audience of "Goldilocks" believes in talking bears. But to whatever extent the narrative audience possesses "knowledge" of nonexistent facts, or believes in nonexistent things, these facts and beliefs must be provided to the reader. We will always assume that the narrative audience is much like the authorial audience, with its beliefs, prejudices, hopes, fears, and expectations, and its knowledge of society and literature—unless there is evidence (textual or historical) to the contrary. Thus, joining the narrative audience does not require us to accept everything the narrator tells us, any more than reading history requires accepting the historian's word; there are unreliable narrators, just as there are unreliable historians.[11]

All novels and plays have both an authorial and a narrative level; but in a given work, one or the other may predominate, with consequent effects on the way we relate to the text. *War and Peace* creates such a strong illusion on the narrative level that its readers may almost forget that it is art. On the other hand, reminders of our role as authorial audience will generally intrude on the illusion of reality, and limit our involvement in the world of the work before us. Barth's "Lost in the Funhouse" refers so frequently to the storyteller's difficulties in writing that we may almost forget about the narra-

[11] See Booth, *Rhetoric of Fiction*, pp. 158-59 and *passim*. In our terms, an unreliable narrator is one who lies, conceals information, or misjudges with respect to the standards of his narrative audience, not the real world.

Peter J. Rabinowitz

tive level. An author, of course, may strike a balance any-where between these extremes, or may shift that balance to create special effects.

Once we understand the distinction between authorial and narrative audiences, we can return to the terminology for literary borrowing. Specifically, if we ask what the two audi-ences of a new work know about the work from which it bor-rows, we can distinguish seven categories of literary recy-cling.

1. First, does the authorial audience know that there is a previous work being incorporated? If not, and if discovery of the source will diminish the effect, we have plagiarism. Lau-tréamont's *Chants de Maldoror* filches some descriptions from Dr. Chenu's *Encyclopédie d'histoire naturelle;*[12] once we know the truth, Lautréamont's imagery loses its punch. Similarly, Emerson, Lake, and Palmer's rock piece "The Barbarian" pales when we know its unattributed source, Bartók's "Al-legro Barbaro."

2. Coincidentally, Bartók's piece may be in turn a homage to Alkan. But if so, then Bartók's work is of a second type: the authorial audience's knowledge of the original is irrelevant, since it produces much the same impact regardless of whether we have ever heard of Alkan. In literature, this type of borrowing is found in *The Threepenny Opera.* Brecht knew that few of his viewers would be familiar with *The Beggar's Opera,* so he didn't assume such knowledge when he made his artistic choices. But since the political message and the brilliant songs provide *Threepenny's* real impact, disclosure of Brecht's burglary doesn't interfere with our pleasure. I call this procedure *adaptation.*

3. Most works in which we are interested depend on the authorial audience's knowledge that there is a previous

[12] Maurice Viroux, "Lautréamont et le Dr. Chenu," *Mercure de France* 316, no. 1,072 (December 1952), 632-42. Lautréamont's plagiarism doesn't quite fall within the confines of this essay, since Chenu's encyclopedia isn't *art;* but the evidence is indisputable. A more ambiguous case can be found in Robbe-Grillet's apparent use of Bely's *St. Petersburg* in *Les Gommes* (see note 14).

Audience's Experience of Literary Borrowing

source. This does not always mean, however, that the authorial audience has actually experienced the original work. There is a class of works which can be called *retellings*, which present the authorial audience with a new version of a work it knows exists but has never read. Retellings include simplified versions for children (Lamb's Shakespeare, Classic Comics) and Masterplots for graduate students; translations (especially of poetry) might be seen as a special subclass.

4. Assuming that the authorial audience is actually familiar with the source, we can turn to the relation between the narrative audience and the original work. First, does the narrative audience know the model? In certain cases, which I call *parodies*, the authorial audience knows the original, while the narrative audience does not. Since the pleasure of parody consists in comparing the original with the copy (comparing Karmazinov's "Merci" in *The Possessed* with Turgenev's originals), and since only the authorial audience knows those originals (for the authorial audience, Karmazinov "is" Turgenev, but for the narrative audience he is simply Karmazinov), parody as I have defined it tends to emphasize the authorial level. This in turn diminishes our involvement on the narrative level. Thus, it is no accident that Dostoyevsky's parodies play such a small role in his novels. He may have begun *Notes from Underground* as a parody of Chernyshevsky, but—whether consciously or not—he saw that it reduced the novel's power of illusion, and kept it at a minimum.

5. In other works, both the authorial and the narrative audiences know the text being assimilated. Here we can distinguish between those where the narrative audience considers the original as fiction, and those where it treats it as nonfiction. In the former, even within the world of the work being read, the original is a work of art. Thus, *Play It Again, Sam* refers to *Casablanca*; but even for the narrative audience, *Casablanca* is a movie, not reality. Such a procedure can aptly be called *criticism*, not only because it frequently involves an interpretation of the original work, but also because, by paying attention to how the characters approach the original, we can often discover how we in turn should treat the work in

247

Peter J. Rabinowitz

front of us. For instance, characters may use previous works to define or explain themselves, as Turgenev's "Hamlet of the Shchigrovo District" uses Shakespeare to explain his melancholy. In so doing, they map out a course by which *we* might use the works *we* are reading. Nabokov's heroes, in contrast, often discuss previous works from the perspective of art-for-art's sake—a clue that Nabokov does not want us to read as Turgenev does. And when Rheingold, in *Ghost at Noon*, gives a psychological reading of *The Odyssey*, he is suggesting yet a third approach, one that Moravia wants us to apply to *his* novel. The same techniques, of course, can be used ironically as well. Emma Bovary's relation to romantic fiction is a warning, not a model.

6. In contrast to criticisms are works in which the narrative audience treats the original work as nonfictional.[13] The narrative audience of Barth's "Menelaiad" does not think of *The Odyssey* as an art work (as the narrative audience of Moravia's novel does), but rather believes that the actions in Homer are real and historical. Here we can ask a further question: When the narrative audience believes that the previous work is nonfiction, does it believe it to be true or false? In real life, after all, some works are both nonfictional and false (Richard Nixon's *Six Crises*, for instance). So too, within a work of art, a narrative audience can treat a prior work as dishonest history, yet still not as art. The narrative audience of *Shamela* does not consider *Pamela* fiction, although it does consider it untrue, with its "many notorious Falsehoods and Misrepresentations" being "exposed and refuted" by the text at hand. Such works might be called *revisions*.

7. Finally, we have works I call *expansions*, where the narra-

---

[13] There is a similar distinction in music. Some compositions simply build upon others, as Liszt's *Réminiscences de Don Juan* develops themes from *Don Giovanni*. But other pieces imitate a particular *performance* of other works: the second movement of Ives's *Fourth Symphony* doesn't simply quote old tunes—it imitates less-than-perfect performers playing them. (To confuse matters, it also has a literary source, Hawthorne's "Celestial Railroad"—a case of stolen goods in its own right.) For a more complete discussion of different types of musical borrowing, see my "Fictional Music: Toward a Theory of Listening," *Bucknell Review*, forthcoming.

tive audience believes the original to be true. In "The Celestial Railroad," the narrative audience is familiar with *Pilgrim's Progress* as history, not art, and believes it. Hawthorne takes that familiarity for granted and works on it without upsetting that belief. Completions and sequels—Thackeray's *Rebecca and Rowena*—are variants of this technique.

INTERPRETATION

Fortunately, literature is too complex to be neatly pigeonholed. A work may treat several quoted sources differently (*The Possessed* is a parody with respect to Turgenev, but a criticism with respect to Pushkin) or may even shift its stance with respect to a single source. I said above, for instance, that *Rebecca and Rowena* is an expansion, and it is—primarily. There are moments, though, when Thackeray suggests that Scott did not quite tell the truth, and his novel veers off into revision; and at other points, Thackeray speaks of *Ivanhoe* as a novel, and we find ourselves reading a criticism.

More interesting, however, are works whose classification is either difficult or ambiguous, for this leads to problems of interpretation. Any reading, after all, involves a decision about what authorial and narrative audiences to join; and if a text uses stolen goods, this requires placing it, consciously or unconsciously, in one or more of our categories. If two readers do this differently, they will experience, and consequently interpret, that text differently. But unless the distinction between the audiences is understood consciously, the source of their divergence may remain obscure.

Let me demonstrate, by turning to Robbe-Grillet's *Les Gommes*, how my model can help in interpretation. The story concerns Wallas, an agent dispatched to find the assassin of a certain Dupont, who is the apparent victim of terrorists. Unfortunately, Wallas does not know that Dupont's assassination has been botched, and that he is still alive; and in the climax, the agent shoots Dupont, mistaking him for the killer.

Woven through this plot is the story of Oedipus. The detective turns out to be the murderer; the man he kills, his father;

Peter J. Rabinowitz

a woman he desires, his father's ex-wife. All this occurs in a web of Oedipal imagery: floating garbage (suggesting the plague?) takes the shape of a Sphinx; a drunk keeps trying to ask the Sphinx's riddle; Wallas passes pictures of Thebes and of events from Oedipus' life; at the end of the novel, his feet are swollen.

While all critics now agree that the Oedipus references are there,[14] the meaning of these parallels has been a source of confusion. Is Robbe-Grillet making a statement about "fate"—either metaphysical or psychological? Laurent Le Sage sounds a forceful *no*: "These references to the classic tale, strewn along the narrative like detective-story hints, create the awesome atmosphere of a fate tragedy without, however, carrying any of the moral or metaphysical implication of ancient myths. Robbe-Grillet uses the Oedipus story merely as a pattern—it would be absurd to deduce from it the author's concept of destiny, etc."[15] This analysis conforms to

[14] They have failed, however, to notice yet another text beneath *Les Gommes*: Bely's *St. Petersburg*. The novels are each divided into prologue, epilogue, and chapters—each divided into subchapters, which are, in turn, divided into short sections ranging from a few lines to a few pages. Both shift point of view from character to character and place to place as the novel moves from one section to the next. Both concern terrorist assassinations, and in both the central event is a patricide (although Bely's protagonist doesn't quite succeed). Robbe-Grillet's novel takes exactly twenty-four hours, and while Bely's lasts longer, it centers on the twenty-four hours of a ticking bomb; both discuss how this twenty-four hour period resolves into nothing. A subsidiary character in both novels is an unstable subordinate member of the terrorist gang, whom we watch go slowly mad: we see the world through his eyes as it dissolves before him. Both novels employ the same motifs: a geometric city with long boulevards and waterways; a crucial bridge; a cubic paperweight; a sphinx; a hero who, by the end of the novel, is limping.

[15] Le Sage, *The French New Novel*, p. 121. See also Valerie Minogue, "The Workings of Fiction in 'Les Gommes,' " *Modern Language Review* 62, no. 3 (1967), 430-42; and David I. Grossvogel, *Limits of the Novel: Evolutions of a Form from Chaucer to Robbe-Grillet* (Ithaca, 1968), pp. 283-91. Grossvogel, whose conception of a dual reader is similar to my distinction between authorial and narrative audiences, says of the Oedipal imagery, "This part of the world does not belong to Wallas; it is the author's, and a parafictional sign to the reader" (p. 285)—in our terms, it exists on the authorial level.

Audience's Experience of Literary Borrowing

what has become the orthodox view of the "nouveau roman," which postulates that these novels are self-referential, primarily about themselves and their creation.[16]

But other critics see a closer link to the "real world." Bruce Morrissette, for instance, contends that the references to Oedipus provide "une image . . . profonde de la condition humaine" and a key to understanding Wallas' psychological condition.[17] Who is right? The issue remains unresolved at least partly because the critics haven't clearly articulated their disagreement; they haven't understood its roots, and have hence been unable to figure out how to approach the text to settle it.

This argument is of special interest to Robbe-Grillet's readers, but it is of wider concern, too, as an instance of the broader question of how we interpret patterns found in any literary work—are they "form" or are they "fate"? Artists who consciously use the art/life and author/god metaphors frequently remind us of a parallel between the way that form organizes artistic experience and the way that our lives are organized by "fate" (using the term broadly to include any predetermined ordering of the universe: divine, psychological, physical, socioeconomic). And since imitative art always at least implies an art/life metaphor, we constantly face the question of whether the harmony found in a work is a quality of the art or of the world it imitates.

It will be easier to understand *Les Gommes* if we turn to this

[16] See, for instance, John Sturrock, *The New French Novel: Claude Simon, Michel Butor, Alain Robbe-Grillet* (London, 1969) and Jean Ricardou's discussion of "euphorie du récit" and "contestation du récit" in *Le Nouveau Roman* (Paris, 1973), pp. 27-31. Robbe-Grillet's own views, not always consistent, can be found in *Pour un nouveau roman* (Paris, 1963). For an incisive reply to some of the tenets of this orthodox criticism, see Suleiman, "Reading Robbe-Grillet."

[17] Morrissette, *Les Romans de Robbe-Grillet* (Paris, 1963), pp. 54 and 37-75. Leon Roudiez, agreeing that the Oedipus imagery has philosophical import, argues that Robbe-Grillet is *negating* the myth, since the references are "false leads that have absolutely no bearing on the plot of the novel." ("The Embattled Myths," in Frederick Will, ed., *Hereditas: Seven Essays on the Modern Experience of the Classical* [Austin, Tex., 1964], p. 84.) It is hard to agree: the references actually determine the plot.

more general question first. How do we know how to interpret a given pattern? If it is perceived by the authorial but not
the narrative audience, then it will be interpreted as "form,"
since the authorial audience sees what is before it as art, and
any pattern it alone sees must be a quality of the work as art.
For instance, the limitation on the number of actors in Aeschylus is a formal principle that helps explain why certain
things happen as they do; but it operates solely on the authorial level, so its implications are purely artistic, not metaphysical.

But if a pattern is also perceived by the narrative audience,
it may have broader implications, for the narrative audience
considers the fiction as real, and may view the pattern as a
reflection of the actual shape of the world. For the narrative
audience, the success of Horatio Alger's heroes is not an aesthetic device, but rather the justice of a world where virtue is
rewarded.

It is not always simple, however, to determine whether a
pattern is perceived by the narrative audience. In Anouilh's
Antigone, for instance, the Chorus tells us in advance what
will happen, stressing its inevitability. But who is this "us"?
Some readers assume it to include the narrative audience,
and consequently interpret *Antigone* as a statement about inevitability in the world outside the play.[18] But the Chorus
also reminds us that this is a tragedy and that those on stage
are actors, which suggests that his statements are addressed
only to the authorial audience. Thus, one can justifiably
argue that the Chorus is speaking about the inevitability in
certain works of art (form) rather than the inevitability inherent in the world (fate).[19] And if the inevitability does not intrude on the narrative level, it is possible to see Antigone not
as the victim of a preordained fate, but rather as what

[18] See, for instance, Carolyn Asp, R.S.C.J., "Two Views of Tragedy," *Barat
Review* 5 (1970), 42-49; Jean Firges, "Tragédie et drame: Une théorie du
théâtre de Jean Anouilh," *Neueren Sprachen* 70 (1971), 215-21.

[19] Peter Nazareth has even taken the Chorus's statements ironically, interpreting the play as an attack on tragedy: "Anouilh's *Antigone*: An Interpretation," *English Studies in Africa* 6 (1963), 51-69.

Audience's Experience of Literary Borrowing

Thomas Bishop calls an "existential heroine" who "chooses freely in a given situation and defines herself through her acts."[20] Much of the disagreement about the play's meaning stems from this ambiguity.

But even if a pattern is unambiguously recognized by the narrative audience, it need not follow that the work is making a statement about fate. In the first place, the narrative audience will not interpret all patterns it sees as some order preexisting in its world. The narrative audience may well decide that a pattern in a novel or play arises from the imagination of the narrator rather than from reality, just as we may attribute some order found in a history to the historian rather than to the events themselves. In Michel Butor's *L'Emploi du temps*, for instance, Jacques Revel ties his story to the Theseus-Ariadne tale. The narrative audience understands his allusions (the work is a criticism), but it is not convinced that his life really reenacts the myth—only that he wishes it would. This kind of shaping is neither fate nor form in our sense—we might call it "narrative form" since it is order imposed by the narrator on the narrative level.

Alternatively, the narrative audience may believe that a pattern exists in the world, but may still not consider it fate because it does not reflect a preexisting order. Dostoyevsky's Myshkin mirrors Christ, but that is because he has freely chosen this path. The parallels, while recognized and accepted by the narrative audience, do not suggest determinism.

Even if the narrative audience decides that a pattern is inherent and preexisting in its world, the authorial audience (which must ultimately interpret the work) may view it differently. The narrative audience of *Candide* believes that the world is ruled by coincidence, but the authorial audience does not interpret the coincidences as a serious metaphysical statement.

To decide if a given pattern should be considered a serious representation of the operation of fate, then, we need to ask four questions. Does the narrative audience recognize the

[20] Bishop, "Anouilh's *Antigone* in 1970," *American Society Legion of Honor Magazine* 41 (1970), 44-45.

253

pattern? Does the narrative audience see it as a true reflection of reality, rather than a product of the narrator's false presentation of reality? Does the narrative audience believe that the pattern is preexisting? Is the fatalistic argument made so that the authorial audience will give it credence? These four questions suggest the most productive route by which we might appeal to the text for a resolution of the conflict between Le Sage's assertion that the Oedipus story in *Les Gommes* is "merely a pattern" and Morrissette's counterclaim that it is a profound image of the human condition.

First, I would argue that the narrative audience *does* recognize the Oedipal pattern, and that *Les Gommes* is a criticism rather than a parody. Were it otherwise, the narrative audience would have to be unfamiliar with Sophocles' play; but Robbe-Grillet has not created a fictional universe which calls forth such a narrative audience. After all, we assume a narrative audience very much like the authorial audience, unless the work has made it clear that we should not (as the opening sentence of Kafka's *Metamorphosis* forces us to suspend our belief in the laws of nature). And nothing in the novel suggests, implicitly or explicitly, that we are to pretend to be the sort of person who, when coming across the words *Sphinx*, *oracle*, *Corinth*, *Thebes*, and *riddle*, wouldn't be able to put it all together. Indeed, the opening words of the novel are a slightly altered epigraph from *Oedipus*, explicitly attributed to Sophocles—surely a clue that as narrative audience we are supposed to know the play (as play, not as reality).

The narrative audience, then, sees the parallels between Wallas and Oedipus. But does it see them as existing in nature, or as narrative form arbitrarily imposed by the narrator? Were the novel written from a single point of view the problem might be difficult. *Les Gommes*, however, uses multiple points of view. Bits and pieces of the pattern are seen by different characters, whose experiences confirm each other. Nor can the pattern be willfully imposed by these characters, for in contrast to Jacques Revel (who imposes the Theseus legend on the world of *L'Emploi du temps*), none of them is aware of it or its significance. For the narrative audience,

Audience's Experience of Literary Borrowing

then, the Oedipal images must be somehow *in the world*. They may reside in the objects and events themselves, or they may reside in the perceptions of those events—but if so, they result from the nature of perception in general, not from the particular perceptions of a particular narrator. Either way, the Oedipal structure is characteristic of the world that is imitated, and does not reside solely in the text.

Nor can we doubt that the order in *Les Gommes* is preexisting. While we may not become aware of the Oedipal pattern until finishing the book, the grievous accident has nonetheless been foreshadowed from the first. If Wallas can kill his father through an apparently outrageous series of coincidences, and if signs in his world turn out, in retrospect, to have predicted this catastrophe, how can the narrative audience escape the conclusion that his tragedy was predetermined?[21]

But how seriously are we meant to take this vision as authorial audience? This is the toughest question, for it relies less on formal analysis than on intuitive literary judgment. But there are three compelling arguments for interpreting *Les Gommes* as a statement about fate even on the authorial level.

First, were this a work that presented itself as "about art," the authorial audience might reasonably dismiss its fatalistic overtones as metaphors about form. But while *Les Gommes* is self-consciously arty, flaunting its technical virtuosity, it does not discuss itself *as art* in the same way, say, that Barth's "Lost in the Funhouse" does. We are never directly urged to give the fatalistic statements a formal reading, as Le Sage does.

Second, we have Robbe-Grillet's rhetoric. Had he wished us to discount the fatalistic implications, he might well have

---

[21] Contrast this with the presentation of the Oedipal images in *St. Petersburg*. Since we know from the beginning that the story concerns a son who wishes to kill his father, the Oedipal imagery comes as a consequence of this central fact and foretells nothing. While an Oedipal pattern seen dimly in the life of an ordinary man who turns out later to kill his father appears to be a sign of fate, Oedipal references in a story overtly concerned with patricide strike us as simply an after-the-fact comparison.

Peter J. Rabinowitz

made them more obvious, since modern readers thrive on irony and suspect the obvious, and since any apparent fatalistic pattern—like O'Neill's in *Mourning Becomes Electra*—seems absurd as soon as we look at "life" and see that such simple repetitions do not occur. Instead, however, Robbe-Grillet has gone to some length to bury his clues (deeply enough so that most of the early readers and critics missed them[22]), which encourages us to take them seriously. This is partly because we tend to believe in the validity of our own discoveries (since we like to congratulate ourselves on our cleverness, and since the activity of the search involves our egos in its outcome). Furthermore, if the pattern is hidden in the novel, we can always believe that the reason we do not see it in reality is simply that we have not looked deeply enough.

Finally, Robbe-Grillet has chosen one of the myths that we are most disposed to accept fatalistically. *Oedipus* may be a fiction (even for the narrative audience), but it is one of the "truest" fictions in our culture. We can laugh at Henry Carr in *Travesties*, because it is manifestly absurd that the universe is modeled on an Oscar Wilde play. But *Oedipus*, especially in the post-Freudian era, has a special claim to validity; we have a natural propensity, even before opening the book, to believe that the world might in fact be patterned this way. Robbe-Grillet, by choosing *this* myth, urges the authorial audience to accept the fatalistic implications of his novel.

The total meaning of *Les Gommes* may still elude us. We may not know exactly what kind of fate the novel posits (psychological, divine), nor whether it would prevail with equal force over a man more self-aware than Wallas. But by examining the roles of the various audiences with respect to Robbe-Grillet's stolen goods, we have been able to make at least the first interpretive step: the Oedipus story in *Les Gommes* does have metaphysical dimensions.

EVALUATION

The concepts of authorial and narrative audience are of value not only in classifying and interpreting, but also in

[22] See Morrissette, *Les Romans de Robbe-Grillet*, p. 53.

Audience's Experience of Literary Borrowing

evaluating—in judging an author's means with respect to the effects he has chosen to create. To show the directions such an evaluation might take, I propose to look at Stoppard's use of *Hamlet* in *Rosencrantz and Guildenstern Are Dead*.

Stoppard starts with a thesis like that enunciated by the Doctor in Barth's *End of the Road*: "Everyone is necessarily the hero of his own life story. *Hamlet* could be told from Polonius's point of view and called *The Tragedy of Polonius, Lord Chamberlain of Denmark*. He didn't think he was a minor character in anything."[23] But Stoppard goes a step further. While we are the central characters in our own lives, we simultaneously play minor roles in larger stories that baffle and confuse us: there is a larger pattern behind our lives, but we lack the vision to see it.

Besides presenting this intellectual thesis, Stoppard also wants to create a particular emotional effect—to make us share his characters' anguish while we transcend their intellectual limitations. This demands a double vision. On the one hand, it is necessary to infect us with his characters' bewilderment—bewilderment that recalls Beckett's *Waiting for Godot*.[24] But at the same time, Stoppard must show that in the larger context, these apparently absurd lives—unlike those of Vladimir and Estragon—make a grim sense. Such an effect requires that his audience recognize and comprehend the larger order, although his protagonists do not.

Herein lies the dilemma. To the extent that Stoppard presents his larger story, he will upstage his main characters and dilute the force of their perplexity; but to the extent that he emphasizes their confusion he runs the risk of losing the sense of the greater order. How can he do both at once?

Since this double vision is a form of traditional "dramatic irony," it is not surprising that Stoppard has turned to a traditional device: since the days of the Greeks, playwrights

[23] John Barth, *End of the Road* (New York, 1960), p. 71 (chap. 6).

[24] The Beckett influence is discussed by almost all Stoppard critics. See, for instance, Jill Levenson, "Views from a Revolving Door: Tom Stoppard's Canon to Date," *Queen's Quarterly* 79 (1971), 431-42. Levenson also touches upon Stoppard's debt to Barth, although she sees this primarily in the "mythotherapy" of playacting (p. 437).

Peter J. Rabinowitz

have retold familiar tales to permit their spectators knowledge denied to their characters. But traditional devices can seldom be inserted unaltered into modern plays; what served Sophocles well has a limitation that threatens Stoppard's enterprise.

The problem emerges as soon as we ask *which* of our audiences knows the old story. Drama, unlike fiction, takes place in the present tense; except in a few instances ("narrated" dramas like *Travesties*; plays with flashbacks), the narrative audience in a theater is seeing the events as they are occurring.[25] Thus, in *Oedipus*, the authorial audience already knows that Oedipus is the killer he seeks; but the narrative audience is caught in the suspense of events seen for the first time. (*Oedipus*, in its handling of old sources, is a parody in our sense.) Much of the special power of the tragedy—the combination of fear for and knowledge of the future—comes from the resulting tension between the audiences.

But the author must handle this tension carefully. To the extent that we become conscious of the split, we will remember that we are watching art, not reality. Consequently, involvement on the narrative level—and the play's power to evoke sympathy for the characters—will be reduced. Such detachment may have its aesthetic uses; but it will not serve Stoppard's needs in *this* play.[26]

Why doesn't the authorial/narrative split diminish our con-

[25] There is thus a major difference between plays which tell old stories using the original names and settings, and plays which alter the names or use contemporary settings. The narrative audience of *Mourning Becomes Electra* can have knowledge of the *Oresteia*, since O'Neill's events take place after those of Aeschylus; but the narrative audience of Sartre's *Les Mouches* can have no previous knowledge of the Electra story, since it is watching it occur for the first time. In fiction, of course, the situation is different: the narrative audience reads of the events after they have taken place.

[26] For a different interpretation, see Normand Berlin, who argues that Stoppard's play is primarily about art, and that we watch it from a fundamentally "critical" perspective, without "direct involvement." While he astutely points to certain elements that remove us from the action, he fails to account for the techniques which counteract that distance. Berlin, "*Rosencrantz and Guildenstern Are Dead*: Theater of Criticism," *Modern Drama* 16 (1973), 269-77.

Audience's Experience of Literary Borrowing

cern for Oedipus? Remember that what reduces involvement on the narrative level is not so much the gap between the audiences as our awareness of it; even though the narrative audience of *Metamorphosis* is quite far from the authorial audience, Kafka can create concern for Gregor by seducing us into forgetting this distance. Likewise, when watching a Greek play, we are less aware of the distance than we generally are with modern texts using literary borrowing. This is because we don't demand that traditional artists be "original" or technically ingenious; but we *do* expect modern art to be. When we go to Sophocles' version of an old story, we simply watch it, without concentrating on how it compares with our prior experience of the story. However, when we go to a modern rendering of a familiar tale, we are immediately alerted. We *expect* the story to be ingeniously altered, and we compare it carefully with the original, duly noting the virtuosity of the larceny; and our awareness of the virtuosity will be at the authorial level, unless the technique can be passed off as the narrator's (common in fiction, but rare in drama). Each difference that we see, consciously sought out and relished, further increases our awareness of the split between the audiences.

Stoppard's problem, then, is to find a way to present the old story without driving a wedge between the narrative and authorial audiences. He succeeds through careful handling of his source. First of all, while Stoppard's authorial audience, thanks to its prior experience of *Hamlet*, knows facts which the narrative audience does not, at no point does the narrative audience's experience seriously *contradict* that authorial knowledge. In this, Stoppard differs from most other contemporary parodists. Ionesco's *Macbett*, for instance, brutally twists the familiar story. Characters whom the authorial audience remembers as virtuous in Shakespeare's play appear as villains before the narrative audience, while Ionesco's contemporary slang jars with memories of Shakespeare's poetry. There is a good reason for this. Shakespeare ends with hope for a better future; Ionesco's assertion that things only get worse is sharpened by the contrast. But since we are asked to

Peter J. Rabinowitz

contrast what we see as narrative audience with what we remember from Shakespeare as authorial audience, the irony exists between the two levels. And to make this irony as strong as possible, Ionesco stresses our consciousness of the authorial level. This underscores the thesis but makes it unlikely that we will care about the characters.

Such detachment may suit Ionesco's needs in *Macbett*, but it will not do for Stoppard, so he has to handle his source differently. Stoppard's play may fill out *Hamlet*, but it never directly contradicts it.[27] Whenever we are watching an event that Shakespeare has portrayed—whenever anyone but the twin protagonists or the players are on stage—Stoppard reverts to unadulterated Shakespeare. Hamlet, Claudius, Gertrude, Polonius: all speak their lines as in the original.[28] The only exception to this rigid technique is the presence of Hamlet on the boat in Stoppard's Act III—a scene never enacted in Shakespeare. Hamlet doesn't speak in this scene, however, and his actions correspond to those described in Shakespeare.

True, there are some minor inconsistencies between the texts: Tom Stoppard's Rosencrantz and Guildenstern, for instance, witness parts of scenes they did not witness in *Hamlet*; Ophelia's "O, what a noble mind is here o'erthrown" is inaudible.[29] But only a viewer who knew Shakespeare intimately—a teacher or critic or actor—would notice the discrepancies. Most persons reasonably familiar with the original text (and this is clearly the authorial audience for Stop-

[27] Levenson asserts that Stoppard's play is "a reduction to absurdity of everything noble and weighty in *Hamlet*" ("Views," p. 436). She bases her argument on Stoppard's "rewriting" of Shakespeare, but fails to account for the accuracy of his quotations—surely one of the most striking aspects of the play.

[28] In "Burlesque Hamlet," Mark Twain tried something similar. He too kept the original text, adding a character and interpolating his lines. But whereas Stoppard's techniques emerge as a solution to a concrete dramatic problem, Twain seems to have been amused by the technique per se. While clever, it couldn't be sustained; Twain never finished it.

[29] Stoppard, *Rosencrantz and Guildenstern Are Dead* (New York, 1968), p. 78.

Audience's Experience of Literary Borrowing

pard's play[30]) would agree that while Stoppard plugs the holes in Shakespeare, he leaves *Hamlet* intact. The contrast between the experience of the narrative audience and the memories of the authorial audience is more muted than in Ionesco's play, and we are consequently less discouraged from becoming involved on the narrative level.

But Stoppard has done more than minimize our awareness of the authorial/narrative gap; he has actually used the necessary remnants of this awareness as a plot element. For while the play begins as parody, the narrative and authorial audiences move together as the play progresses—consequently the play turns into an expansion. This happens in two ways. First, the narrative audience comes to "know" the *Hamlet* that the authorial audience already knows, since it sees large portions of that play in the same form that the authorial audience knows it. Thus, as the play continues, the narrative audience comes to share the authorial audience's knowledge of the past. But in addition, Stoppard has the Players act out the coming demise of Rosencrantz and Guildenstern. Thus, the authorial audience's knowledge of the future comes to be shared by the narrative audience as well. Appropriately, this double closing of the gap parallels the changing mood of the play. The first act, where the distance between the audiences is greatest and most obvious, is also the most comic—and detachment is appropriate to comedy. As the play becomes more despairing, the gap narrows; and at the point where our concern for the characters should be greatest (Act III), the split between the narrative and authorial audiences—and our awareness of it—is at a minimum. Indeed, the play at this point hardly depends on Shakespeare; the larger story in which Rosencrantz and Guildenstern are trapped has already been told insofar as it influences them, and Stoppard, having

[30] The play had its first professional production at the Old Vic by the National Theater Company and, as John Russell Taylor points out, Stoppard was thus assured of an audience familiar with the "root material," although less so with the traditions of the theater of the absurd. Taylor, *The Second Wave: British Drama for the Seventies* (New York, 1971), p. 101.

Peter J. Rabinowitz

moved us ever closer to his heroes, wisely avoids pointing up the authorial level by refraining from quoting *Hamlet* at all. Only at the very end—when he wishes to remind us that the death of our heroes is but one strand in a larger fabric—does he return to Shakespeare's text.

There is a great deal more in the play that demonstrates Stoppard's regard for the balance between authorial and narrative audience. We might just mention his treatment of the theater/life metaphor, since it contrasts so tellingly with that of Anouilh in *Antigone*. Anouilh's Chorus delivers this metaphor directly to the audience in the theater, leaving it unclear whether we are to respond as narrative or authorial audience. Stoppard, however, has the Player direct his theorizing about theater to Rosencrantz and Guildenstern themselves. Thus, however the authorial audience ultimately takes it,[31] the metaphor exists on the narrative level—within the play as reality—and doesn't remove us from the play as Anouilh's intrusions do.

There are, of course, many questions of quality that my analysis does not address. It can't help us decide whether the wit in this play is really clever, or simply warmed-over Beckett; it can't help us decide whether Stoppard's vision of the human condition is philosophically valid; it can't tell us whether the play helped Stoppard in his psychological development. But it does help us appreciate Stoppard's technique of literary borrowing, one that maintains greater involvement with the characters than do the techniques of Ionesco or Anouilh. Whatever we ultimately decide about *Antigone* or *Macbett*, we can at least agree that Stoppard's techniques are the most appropriate for *his* play.

The use of stolen goods in literature, film, and music continues, and constantly poses new critical questions. Some are fairly concrete. How has Stoppard managed, in *Travesties*, to write a Broadway hit despite the fairly esoteric knowledge

[31] See Berlin, "*Rosencrantz and Guildenstern*," and William Babula, "The Play-Life Metaphor in Shakespeare and Stoppard," *Modern Drama* 15 (1972), 279-81.

Audience's Experience of Literary Borrowing

demanded by his references? Edward Bond's *Lear* makes sense without the references to Shakespeare, which appear to undercut his radical socialism by encouraging elitism; what does he gain through borrowing that makes the sacrifice worthwhile? Other questions are more abstract. What connection is there between the use of quotation and the aggressive antinaturalism in the works of Barth, Borges, and Nabokov? What sorts of effects are produced when a literary artist borrows from a nonverbal medium—as Anthony Burgess has done in *Napoleon Symphony* (based on Beethoven's *Eroica*)?

Literary borrowing is a rich field that has hardly been mined by critics. And while there are many productive approaches, the scheme for classification, interpretation, and evaluation set forth here should help begin the digging.

Cathleen M. Bauschatz | Montaigne's Conception of Reading in the Context of Renaissance Poetics and Modern Criticism

In "De l'expérience," Montaigne describes the process of verbal communication with an intriguing parallel from tennis: the listener (or person receiving the ball) must be as actively involved as the speaker (or person serving) if the message (or ball) is to be transmitted, and more importantly, to be returned:

> La parole est moitié à celuy qui parle; moitié à celuy qui l'escoute. Cettuy-cy se doibt preparer à la recevoir selon le branle qu'elle prend. Comme entre ceux qui jouent à la paume, celuy qui soustient se desmarche et s'apreste selon qu'il voit remuer celuy qui luy jette le coup et selon la forme du coup.[1]

> Speech belongs half to the speaker, half to the listener. The latter must prepare to receive it according to the motion it takes. As among tennis players, the receiver moves and makes ready according to the motion of the striker and the nature of the stroke.[2]

Although this description purports to concern speaking and

[1] Michel de Montaigne, *Oeuvres Complètes*, ed. Albert Thibaudet & Maurice Rat (Bruges, 1962), III. 13. 1066, *b* (references are to book, chapter, and page; the letters *a*, *b*, and *c* will be used in this study to represent the editions of 1580, 1588, and 1595, as is standard in Montaigne scholarship).

[2] *The Complete Essays of Montaigne*, trans. Donald M. Frame (Stanford, 1965), III. 13. 834, *b*.

Montaigne's Conception of Reading

listening, it could also describe Montaigne's view of reading. For the visual element of reading is suggested with "selon qu'il voit," and "la forme du coup." Montaigne makes the comparison between reading and tennis explicit in "Des livres," when he declares that "Les Historiens sont ma droitte bale . . ." (II. 10. 396, a) ("The historians come right to my forehand . . ." [II. 10. 303, a]). The reception of verbal communication, whether visual or oral, seems to require as much participation on the part of reader or listener as it does on that of writer or speaker.

This belief in the equal involvement of writer and reader (or speaker and listener) seems surprisingly modern. Roland Barthes' conception of the modern text as *scriptible* ("writerly"), in which the reader is "non plus un consommateur, mais un producteur du texte"[3] ("no longer a consumer, but a producer of the text"[4]), is not very different in some respects from Montaigne's description of reader and writer on opposite sides of the tennis net. Contemporary critics who emphasize the experience of the reader in literature[5] rather than defining the text or imagining the thoughts of the writer as he writes come close to Montaigne's parallel with the reception of a serve in tennis. Although Montaigne reserves more consideration than they for the intentions of the writer, "celuy qui luy jette le coup," he does clearly recognize that words cease to be the property of the speaker or writer once they leave his mouth or pen.

The belief in the active role of reader or listener, demonstrated in Montaigne's analogy with tennis, is not typical of earlier literary theorists, whether classical, medieval, or Renaissance. Platonic ideas on reading, from Plato himself to Augustine and to the Italian and French academies of the fif-

[3] Roland Barthes, *S/Z: Essais* (Paris, 1970), p. 10.

[4] Roland Barthes, *S/Z: An Essay*, trans. Richard Miller (New York, 1974), p. 4.

[5] See for example Norman Holland, *The Dynamics of Literary Response* (New York, 1968); and *5 Readers Reading* (New Haven, 1975). See also Stanley E. Fish, *Self-Consuming Artifacts: The Experience of Seventeenth-Century Literature* (Berkeley and Los Angeles, 1972); and Wolfgang Iser, *The Implied Reader: Patterns of Communication in Prose Fiction from Bunyan to Beckett* (Baltimore, 1974).

teenth and sixteenth centuries,[6] stress if anything the reader's passivity. He is "transformed" by the "effects" of poetry, whether he will or no. The Judeo-Christian tradition, with its emphasis on the primacy of the Word,[7] similarly places the reader or listener in a relatively subordinate position, while the text itself reaches out and converts or otherwise touches and changes him.

The terminology and imagery of classical rhetoric, used by writers of poetics as well as theology to describe the way in which a poet or orator moves his audience, carries with it a strong feeling for the relative power of the speaker and weakness of the listener. When Renaissance humanists and men of letters began to reread Cicero and Quintilian, they seem to have accepted this belief, and to have transferred it to their own descriptions of listening and reading. Du Bellay's *Deffence et illustration de la langue francoyse* (1549) is a good example of this phenomenon. Not only does he urge the aspirant poet-reader to copy the techniques of the classical masters in French, but also to try to move the listener as Horace or Virgil might have done. The following description presents the poet as a sort of Orpheus figure, manipulating the listener through language:

> . . . saiches, Lecteur, que celuy sera veritablement le poëte que je cherche en nostre Langue, qui me fera indigner, apayser, ejouyr, douloir, aymer, hayr, admirer, etonner, bref, qui tiendra la bride de mes affections, me tournant ça & là à son plaisir.[8]

> . . . know, Reader, that he will truly be the poet whom I seek in our Language, who will make me indignant, calm me, delight me, hurt me, make me love, hate, admire; as-

[6] See Frances Yates, *The French Academies of the Sixteenth Century* (London, 1947; reprinted Nendeln/Liechtenstein, 1973).

[7] See Walter J. Ong, S.J., *The Presence of the Word: Some Prolegomena for Cultural and Religious History* (New Haven, 1967).

[8] Joachim Du Bellay, *La Deffence et illustration de la langue francoyse*, ed. Henri Chamard (Paris, 1966), ii. 11. 179.

tonish me: in brief, who will hold the bridle of my emotions, turning me here and there at his pleasure.[9]

The way in which this magical transformation is to be effected, and the reader's role in it, however, are not usually examined any more closely by Renaissance theorists than they were by classical aestheticians. Norman Holland has commented in *5 Readers Reading* on this nonanalysis of the role of the reader throughout the rhetorical tradition:

> This tradition—assuming a uniform response on the part of readers and audiences that the critic somehow knows and understands—goes back to Aristotle's concept of catharsis, and his notions about people's apparently fixed responses to details of wording. Or this tradition might even have originated in Plato's assertion that poetry debilitates. Although the Greeks observed the phenomena that they ascribed to audiences better than later theorists, the tradition flourished after them, reaching a peak with the rules of the lesser neoclassical critics. (p. 5)

Montaigne's *Essais* (1572-1592), unlike earlier and even most contemporary writings, do examine whether and how a book can make a transformation in a reader. In the first two books of the *Essais*, as reader himself, Montaigne confronts the problem of whether the ancient models of virtue he has studied can really influence his own actions. It is illuminating to examine these discussions for what they tell us about Montaigne's view of the reading process. If he accepts the Platonic view of reading, he will assume that reading about good actions causes the reader inevitably to act well. But it is immediately obvious that Montaigne does not feel admiration necessarily makes imitation possible: he may admire "le jeune Caton," but doesn't feel capable of equaling him:

[9] My translation. To my knowledge, there is no published translation of the *Deffence*.

Ma foiblesse n'altere aucunement les opinions que je dois avoir de la force et vigueur de ceux qui le meritent. . . . Rampant au limon de la terre, je ne laisse pas de remerquer, jusques dans les nües, la hauteur inimitable d'aucunes ames heroïques. (I. 37. 225, *a*)

My weakness in no way alters my necessarily high regard for the strength and vigor of those who deserve it. . . . Crawling in the slime of the earth, I do not fail to observe, even in the clouds, the inevitable loftiness of certain heroic souls. (I. 37. 169, *a*)

This passage explains very clearly Montaigne's belief that perception and action are two distinct realms, and that one does not necessarily lead to the other, unless personal inclination and an effort of will are involved as well.

In "De la praesumption," this belief is more clearly applied to reading and writing literature. The fact that Montaigne admires "les productions de ces riches et grandes ames du temps passé," does not cause him to be able to write as well as they do. He distinguishes reading or critical appreciation from the action of writing:

J'ay tousjours une idée en l'ame . . . qui me presente . . . une meilleure forme que celle que j'ay mis en besongne, mais je ne la puis saisir et exploiter. . . . Ce que j'argumante par là, que les productions de ces riches et grandes ames du temps passé sont bien loing au delà de l'extreme estendue de mon imagination et souhaict. . . . Je juge leur beauté, je la voy, si non jusques au bout, au moins si avant qu'il m'est impossible d'y aspirer. (II. 17. 620, *a*)

I have always an idea in my mind . . . which offers me . . . a better form than the one I have employed, but I cannot grasp it and exploit it. . . . From that I conclude that the productions of those great rich minds of the past are very far beyond the utmost stretch of my imagination and de-

Montaigne's Conception of Reading

sire. . . . I judge their beauty; I see it, if not to the utmost, at least enough so that I cannot aspire to it myself. (II. 17. 482, *a*)

While Du Bellay urges: "Ly donques & rely premierement (ò Poëte futur), fueillete de main nocturne & journelle les exemplaires Grecz & Latins . . ." (II. 4. 107) ("Read then and reread first of all [oh future Poet], leaf night and day through Greek and Latin texts . . ."), Montaigne does not feel that reading teaches one how to write. It cannot achieve a Protean transformation overnight—"ainsi qu'un Prothée vous transform [ant] en diverses sortes . . . lysant ces aucteurs . . ." (I. 5. 37) ("as a Proteus transforming you in various ways . . . by reading these authors . . .")—as Du Bellay felt was possible.

An area where Du Bellay and Montaigne are quite similar, however, is in their treatment of the classical digestive metaphor for reading. Both feel that the reader must actively assimilate the works of antiquity, to make them relevant to his own needs. Du Bellay urges the French writer to "devour" Latin poets as the Romans had "digested" the Greeks (I. 7. 42), by "Immitant les meilleurs aucteurs Grecz, se transformant en eux, les devorant & apres les avoir bien digerez, les convertissant en sang & nouriture." ("Imitating the best Greek authors, transforming themselves into them, devouring them and, after having well digested them, converting them into blood and nourishment.") Montaigne also uses the image of digestion, in a passage strongly reprimanding those readers who do not "appropriate" the ideas they take from others:

Nous prenons en garde les opinions et le sçavoir d'autruy, et puis c'est tout. Il les faut faire nostres. Nous semblons proprement celuy qui, ayant besoing de feu, en iroit querir chez son voisin, et, y en ayant trouvé un beau et grand, s'arresteroit là à se chauffer, sans plus se souvenir d'en rapporter chez soy. Que nous sert-il d'avoir la panse pleine de viande, si elle ne se digere? si elle

269

Cathleen M. Bauschatz

ne se trans-forme en nous? si elle ne nous augmente et fortifie? ("Du pedantisme," i. 25. 136, *a*)

We take the opinions and the knowledge of others into our keeping, and that is all. We must make them our own. We are just like a man who, needing fire, should go and fetch some at his neighbor's house, and, having found a fine big fire there, should stop there and warm himself, forgetting to carry any back home. What good does it do us to have our belly full of meat if it is not digested, if it is not transformed into us, if it does not make us bigger and stronger? (i. 25. 101, *a*)

The images of digestion and transformation are similar to those found in Du Bellay, but the insistence on active choice and involvement on the part of the reader is even stronger in Montaigne. In particular, the analogy with the person who forgets to bring fire (perhaps representing inspiration) home with him seems important to me. By remaining at his neighbor's in front of the fire, he is indeed feeling its "effects," and is in fact "transformed" to the extent that he feels warmer. But Montaigne clearly realizes that unless he takes the practical step of making this inspiration his own—of separating it from its original source—it will have only a very temporary effect on him. He will remain in a subordinate position with respect to the neighbor or source of the fire of inspiration: that is, as a reader, to the authority of a writer. One could say that Montaigne has chosen a "reader-centered" rather than an "author-centered" or "text-centered" definition of reading here.

He realizes that reading is only a first step in the learning process. A well-known passage in "De l'institution des enfans" compares the judgment resulting from reading to the honey produced by bees:

Les abeilles pillotent deçà delà les fleurs, mais elles en font après le miel, qui est tout leur, ce n'est plus thin ni marjolaine: ainsi les pieces empruntées d'autruy, il les

Montaigne's Conception of Reading

transformera et confondera, pour en faire un ouvrage tout sien, à sçavoir son jugement. Son institution, son travail et estude ne vise qu'à le former. (I. 26. 150-51, *a*)

The bees plunder the flowers here and there, but afterward they make of them honey, which is all theirs; it is no longer thyme or marjoram. Even so with the pieces borrowed from others; he will transform and blend them to make a work that is all his own, to wit, his judgment. His education, work and study aim only at forming this. (I. 26. 111, *a*)

Not only does Montaigne here enlarge the role of judgment from a secondary tool in the reading process (as it was for Du Bellay)[10] to its ultimate goal, but he also questions the premise basic to most earlier discussions of the place of reading in imitation: the belief that the new thing created is of the same nature as the original source. Montaigne's originality is to point out that the new "ouvrage" ("le miel") is of a different nature from the "pieces empruntées" ("thin ni marjolaine"). The student reads and then learns indirectly, by transforming and blending what he reads and by making it his own, rather than directly by copying it. Unlike earlier writers who used the image of bees making honey to describe reading and learning, Montaigne focuses on the process as well as on the result.[11]

Once Montaigne grasps the idea that reading is only a first

[10] Of the poet reading in order to learn how to imitate he says, "Avant toutes choses, fault qu'il ait ce jugement de cognoitre ses forces" (II. 3. 107) ("Before everything, he must have the judgment to know his own power").

[11] The *topos* of bees and honey, coming from the *Ion*, Horace and Seneca, is also found in the *Courtier*: "And even as in green meadows the bee flits about among the grasses robbing the flowers, so our Courtier must steal this grace from those who seem to him to have it, taking from each the part that seems most worthy of praise" (Baldesar Castiglione, *The Book of the Courtier*, trans. Charles S. Singleton [Garden City, N.Y., 1959], pp. 42-43). Castiglione's description of the process of imitation is much more superficial than Montaigne's, and does not take into account the intermediate process necessary for absorption of the qualities admired.

271

Cathleen M. Bauschatz

step in the learning process (thus showing what it is not), he is freer to examine the reading process itself for what it is. As we leaf through the late chapters of the first two books of the *Essais*, we increasingly have the feeling that all Montaigne wants reading to provide is enjoyment. For example, in "Des livres" he says: "Je ne cherche aux livres qu'à m'y donner du plaisir par un honneste amusement" (ii. 10. 388, *a*) ("I seek in books only to give myself pleasure by honest amusement" [ii. 10. 297, *a*]). He moves further and further from his earlier struggle with the view that reading should supply instruction or moral improvement.

In Book Three of the *Essais*, Montaigne explores the question of the effect of text on reader from the viewpoints of writer as well as reader.[12] Some of the most original ideas on reading to be found in the *Essais* come in the discussions of the book and the way in which Montaigne expects we will approach it, particularly in Book Three, but also in the "Au lecteur," and in later additions to many of the earlier essays. In these passages the essayist moves beyond the images of the rhetorical tradition, which shaped his discussions of reading in the first two books.

One might expect the "Au lecteur" to describe the role that Montaigne assumes his reader will play in the book.[13]

[12] As far as I am aware, these two aspects of Montaigne's view of reading have not been treated as one in recent Montaigne criticism. Trinquet and Sayce have talked in detail, respectively, about Montaigne's early reading and about his expressed attitudes toward the books he knew and liked best (Roger Trinquet, *La Jeunesse de Montaigne: Ses origines familiales, son enfance et ses études* [Paris, 1972]; and R. A. Sayce, *The Essays of Montaigne: A Critical Exploration* [Evanston, Ill., 1972], especially Chap. 3, "Imitation and Originality: Montaigne and Books"). Pouilloux and McGowan have discussed the problem of how a modern reader can approach the *Essais*, and the techniques of persuasion with which Montaigne attempted to influence the reader (Jean-Yves Pouilloux, *Lire les "Essais" de Montaigne* [Paris, 1970]; and Margaret McGowan, *Montaigne's Deceits: The Art of Persuasion in the "Essais"* [Philadelphia, 1974]). But none of these critics has attempted to describe how Montaigne viewed the reading process itself, although McGowan comes the closest to this in her discussions of the participation of the reader expected by Montaigne.

[13] In modern terms, it should create what Father Ong has called the "fic-

Montaigne's Conception of Reading

Strangely enough, this preface seems rather to deny that Montaigne expects anything particular of the reader, as it also denies that the book has any special value for the reader. Although he begins with the famous statement: "C'est icy un livre de bonne foy, lecteur" ("Au lecteur," p. 9) ("This book was written in good faith, reader" ["To the Reader," p. 2]), what he means is that the book sincerely makes no claim to serve the reader: "Je n'y ay eu nulle consideration de ton service, ny de ma gloire" ("I have had no thought of serving either you or my own glory"). The seemingly hostile attitude toward the reader found in the "Au lecteur," however, can be seen in a much more positive light when compared with some of Montaigne's statements about reading itself.

The "Au lecteur" explains that the *Essais* are only destined to give his "parens et amis" some knowledge of him "en ma façon simple, naturelle et ordinaire" ("in my simple, natural, ordinary fashion"), after his death. This, of course, is just the kind of book Montaigne himself liked to read, as it treats "ce qui part du dedans" ("what comes from within") rather than "ce qui arrive au dehors" ("what happens without").[14] He ends the preface with a warning about the uselessness of the book: "Ainsi, lecteur, je suis moy-mesmes la matière de mon

---

tionalized reader" ("The Writer's Audience Is Always a Fiction," *PMLA* 90 [1975], 9-21), or what Gérard Genette refers to as the *narrataire*. In his *Figures III* (Paris, 1972), Genette defines the "narrataire" thus: "Comme le narrateur, le narrataire est un des éléments de la situation narrative, et il se place nécessairement au même niveau diégétique; c'est-à-dire qu'il ne se confond pas plus à priori avec le lecteur (même virtuel) que le narrateur ne se confond nécessairement avec l'auteur" (p. 265) ("Like the narrator, the narratee is one of the elements of the narrative situation, and he occurs necessarily at the same diegetic level; that is to say that he isn't identical, a priori, to the reader [even virtual] any more than the narrator is identical to the author" [my translation].)

[14] II. 10. 396, *a*: "Or ceux qui escrivent les vies, d'autant qu'ils s'amusent plus aux conseils qu'aux evenemens, plus à ce qui part du dedans qu'à ce qui arrive au dehors, ceux là me sont plus propres" ("Now those who write biographies, since they spend more time on plans than on events, more on what comes from within than on what happens without, are the most suited to me" [II. 10. 303, *a*]).

livre: ce n'est pas raison que tu employes ton loisir en un sub-ject si frivole et si vain" ("Thus, reader, I am myself the mat-ter of my book: you would be unreasonable to spend your lei-sure on so frivolous and vain a subject"). But this disclaimer only reinforces the impression we have already gained from Montaigne's statements about reading: he does not expect any directly utilitarian results from books unless the reader himself is prepared to initiate the process of transformation. On the other hand, if he only spends his "loisir" at it, what is wrong with "un subject si frivole et si vain"?

The "Au lecteur" is a rhetorical display of positive and negative attitudes toward the *Essais*, involving the reader and the "fictionalized reader" in a peculiar conversation with the book, author, and narrator. It eliminates what we should not expect from the *Essais*, but it does not really prescribe what we should see in them. Ultimately the reader is free to do as he likes with the book, and Montaigne's nervousness in the preface indicates an awareness of that fact. He continues to undermine the traditional conception of didacticism, with the weak role it assigns to the reader. And thus he leaves open the possibility of a stronger function for the reader, which we will see develop in some statements in the third book.

In the chapters written after the "Au lecteur," Montaigne repeats frequently that although the *Essais* study himself, he cannot pose as a didactic model: "Les autres forment l'homme, je le recite" (iii. 2. 782, *b*) ("Others form man; I tell of him" [iii. 2. 610, *b*]), and "Je n'enseigne poinct, je raconte" (p. 784, *b*) ("I do not teach, I tell" [p. 612, *b*]). However, since we already know that he does not believe in the automatic applicability of a model anyway, this does not necessarily mean that there is nothing of value in the self-definition it-self. It simply means that he does not want to, or believe he can, impel the reader to imitate him. Montaigne is still re-defining the concept of didacticism here, from the point of view of reader rather than writer. For he often does take a prescriptive stance in talking about moral problems. This stance is usually aimed at defining a problem, however, rather than at forcing his solution down the reader's throat.

Montaigne's Conception of Reading

As we saw in studying the "Au lecteur," the reader is free to accept these prescriptions or not, as he chooses.

The relationship between reader and writer is now presented as one of friendship, rather than pupil-teacher or disciple-master, which Du Bellay felt it to be. The following description of reading in "De trois commerces" implies a very personal rapport with books from the point of view of Montaigne the reader:

> Pour me distraire d'une imagination importune, il n'est que de recourir aux livres: ils me destournent facilement à eux et me la desrobent. Et si, ne se mutinent point pour voir que je ne les recherche qu'au deffaut de ces autres commoditez, plus reelles, vives et naturelles; ils me reçoivent tousjours de mesme visage. (III. 3. 805, b)

> To be diverted from a troublesome idea, I need only have recourse to books: they easily turn my thoughts to themselves and steal away the others. And yet they do not rebel at seeing that I seek them out only for want of those other pleasures, that are more real, lively and natural; they always receive me with the same expression. (III. 3. 628, b)

Once again, however, we are also given a strong depiction of the freedom that Montaigne associates with reading. As books "me reçoivent tousjours de mesme visage," the reader can bring any number of moods to them. In that respect, reading is preferable to friendship, because personal obligations do not hamper interactions with books. The book serves the reader rather than prescribing to him.

In subsequent chapters of Book Three, Montaigne seems to enjoy playing (as he did in "Du repentir") with the ways in which his book does not enforce a model on the reader, and yet offers some sort of lesson. Reading proposes a set of choices more complex than the simple attempt to imitate the writer. "De l'art de conferer" begins with the humorous idea that the description of himself will show the reader what to avoid:

Cathleen M. Bauschatz

Mes erreurs sont tantost naturelles et incorrigibles: mais, ce que les honnestes hommes profitent au public en se faisant imiter, je le profiteray à l'avanture à me faire eviter. (III. 8. 899, *b*)

My errors are by now natural and incorrigible; but the good that worthy men do the public by making themselves imitable, I shall perhaps do by making myself evitable. (III. 8. 703, *b*)

Obviously the action to be learned differs from the model presented, in this case. The reader is free to reject the example presented, but may still profit as a result of familiarity with it.

A paradox like this one raises again (as in the discussions of imitation) the question of the perceived relationship between thought and action in the *Essais*. Montaigne's constant emphasis on the faculty of judgment (as in the bee-honey metaphor) is part of his attempt to close the gap between the two for the reader. In the later parts of Book Three, Montaigne begins to resolve this dilemma with respect to literature, from his own point of view as writer, but with obvious implications for the reading process as well. Because he talks about himself in the *Essais*, the discrepancy there between "action" and "discours" (which Sidney tried to resolve with the concept of "speaking picture"[15]), is not seen as a real problem:

Au pis aller, cette difforme liberté de se presenter à deux endroicts, et les actions d'une façon, les discours de l'autre, soit loisible à ceux qui disent les choses: mais elle ne le peut estre à ceux qui se disent eux mesme, comme je fay: il faut que j'aille de la plume comme des pieds. (III. 9. 969, *b*)

---

[15] "Now doth the peerless poet perform both: for whatsoever the philosopher saith should be done, he giveth a perfect picture of it in someone by whom he presupposeth it was done, so as he coupleth the general notion with the particular example" (Sir Philip Sidney, *An Apology for Poetry*, ed. Forrest G. Robinson [New York, 1970], p. 27).

Montaigne's Conception of Reading

At worst, this deformed liberty to present ourselves in two aspects, the actions in one fashion and the speeches in another, may be permissible for those who tell of things; but it cannot be so for those who tell of themselves, as I do; I must go the same way with my pen as with my feet. (III. 9. 758, b)

Here we begin to see Montaigne's most original contribution to the definition of a book—in particular his own. Portrait and man are identical (from a narrative point of view), and thus subject and object, thinker and thought, appear the same ("ceux qui se disent eux mesme"). "Plume" and "pieds" can be playfully substituted one for the other, as all are functions of the multivalent narrative "je." The imagined lack of distinction between author and book also implies a simplification of the reading process: the reader cannot ask questions like What does the author really mean? before such a book, because the text defines the author. In addition, the book cannot be any more didactic than the life it describes.

The idea of the equivalence between "plume" and "pieds" is later expanded with the notion of consubstantiality of book and man. This concept is developed in a late addition to "Du démentir," and has profound implications for understanding Montaigne's late view of the reading and writing processes:

Je n'ay pas plus faict mon livre que mon livre m'a faict, livre consubstantiel à son autheur, d'une occupation propre, membre de ma vie; non d'une occupation et fin tierce et estrangere comme tous autres livres. (II. 18. 648, c)

I have no more made my book than my book has made me—a book consubstantial with its author, concerned with my own self, an integral part of my life; not concerned with some third-hand, extraneous purpose, like all other books. (II. 18. 505, c)

Montaigne's conception of "consubstantiality" appears sev-

277

eral times in the *Essais*. Two examples from the third book are
the following:

> Icy, nous allons conformément et tout d'un trein, mon
> livre et moy. Ailleurs, on peut recommander et accuser
> l'ouvrage à part de l'ouvrier; icy non: qui touche l'un
> touche l'autre. (III. 2. 783, *b*)

> In this case we go hand in hand and at the same pace, my
> book and I. In other cases one may commend or blame
> the work apart from the workman; not so here; he who
> touches the one, touches the other. (III. 2. 611-12, *b*)

> Je prens si grand plaisir d'estre jugé et cogneu, qu'il
> m'est comme indifferent en quelle des deux formes je le
> soys. (III. 8. 902, *c*)

> I take such great pleasure in being judged and known
> that it is virtually indifferent to me in which of the two
> forms I am so. (III. 8. 705, *c*)

Consubstantiality implies that reading the *Essais* is equivalent to getting to know Montaigne, and offers something as
intimate—as real—as other forms of acquaintance or experience. The concept shows a belief seen very frequently in the
Essais: the idea that reading is like experience. "Du pedantisme" informed us that reading broadens awareness as does
observation (I. 25. 133, *a*); "Des livres" pointed out that Montaigne reads history primarily to learn about "l'homme en
general" (II. 10. 396, *c*); and "Sur des vers de Virgile" even
finds that reading is more vivid than experience:

> Mais de ce que je m'y entends, les forces et valeur de ce
> Dieu se trouvent plus vives et plus animées en la pein-
> ture de la poësie qu'en leur propre essence,
> *Et versus digitos habet.*
>
> JUVENAL

> Elle represente je ne sçay quel air plus amoureux que
> l'amour mesme. Venus n'est pas si belle toute nue, et

Montaigne's Conception of Reading

vive, et haletante, comme elle est icy chez Virgile. (III. 5. 826, *b*)

But from what I understand of it, the powers and worth of this god are more alive and animated in the painting of poetry than in their own reality,

And verses have their fingers to excite.

JUVENAL

Poetry reproduces an indefinable mood that is more amorous than love itself. Venus is not so beautiful all naked, alive, and panting, as she is here in Virgil. (III. 5. 645, *b*)

One could see these statements as simple examples of the distorted perceptions of the "pedante": lacking a capacity for active experience, Montaigne takes reading to be *real*.[16] On the other hand, it is also possible to see in these random observations the formulation of a perceptual definition of the reading process, similar to some of those current in the reading research of psychologists, linguists, and educators,[17] as well as literary critics. Before developing the implications of this parallel, however, it will be instructive to examine

[16] Wayne Booth is one reader who does not accept the idea that the Montaigne of the book is the real Montaigne: "The Montaigne of the book is by no stretch of the imagination the real Montaigne, pouring himself onto the page without regard for 'aesthetic distance' " (*The Rhetoric of Fiction* [Chicago, 1961], p. 228).

[17] An interesting book in this respect is David H. Russell, *The Dynamics of Reading*, ed. Robert B. Ruddell (Waltham, Mass., 1970). In it, Russell gives many examples of the described experience of reading by writers, statesmen, etc., and comments that all testify to the profound effect which reading, like other forms of experience, had on them throughout their lives. He admits that the empirical evidence is scanty, however, because psycholinguistic reading research has principally concentrated on eye movements, etc., while social psychologists have mainly studied the psychological effects of mass media on listeners (Chap. 1). A combination of these various approaches would help us to understand better what reading *is*, as well as what people *think* it is. These questions are outside the scope of strictly critical approaches to reading, but we should nonetheless be aware of their existence in formulating theories of literary response.

Cathleen M. Bauschatz

another possible interpretation of the equivalence between self and book.

This equivalence is stated at numerous points in the late *Essais*, implying not only the obvious truth that the book is like the man, but also the opposite and more complex idea that the self is like a book, or that experience is like reading, in that one can constantly study it and learn from it. This is a quite original use of the metaphor of the Book of Nature,[18] whose changing status has been discussed by McLuhan,[19] and which Montaigne earlier used indirectly in "De l'institution des enfans," as well as in the "Apologie de Raimond Sebond."

In the earlier chapter, we learned that "tout ce qui se presente à nos yeux sert de livre suffisant: la malice d'un page, la sottise d'un valet, un propos de table, ce sont autant de nouvelles matieres" (I. 26. 151-52, *a*) (". . . everything that comes to our eyes is book enough: a page's prank, a servant's blunder, a remark at table, are so many new materials" [I. 26. 112, *a*]). The same view was repeated several pages later:

> Ce grand monde, que les uns multiplient encore comme especes soubs un genre, c'est le miroüer où il nous faut regarder pour nous connoistre de bon biais. Somme, je veux que ce soit le livre de mon escholier. (I. 26. 157, *a*)
>
> This great world, which some multiply further as being only a species under one genus, is the mirror in which

[18] Curtius describes the use of the metaphor of the book of nature, from the Latin Middle Ages through the Renaissance, in his chapter "The Book as Symbol" (*European Literature and the Latin Middle Ages*, trans. Willard R. Trask [London, 1953]). The first use of the image of the book of the self which he mentions, however (p. 322), is in Descartes, who obviously borrowed the concept from Montaigne.

[19] Marshall McLuhan describes the changing use of the metaphor of the Book of Nature when he says, "The medieval Book of Nature was for *contemplatio* like the Bible. The Renaissance Book of Nature was for *applicatio* and use like movable types" (McLuhan, *The Gutenberg Galaxy: The Making of Typographic Man* [Toronto, 1962], p. 185). This transformation has definite implications as well for the change in attitude toward books in general, illustrated by Montaigne's more active approach to reading.

280

Montaigne's Conception of Reading

we must look at ourselves to recognize ourselves from the proper angle. In short, I want it to be the book of my student. (I. 26. 116, a)

Later, in defending Sebond and his "Liber Creaturarum," Montaigne saw the variety and extraordinary phenomena in nature as indirect proof of man's presumption and inanity. In a somewhat related way, in the chapters written after the "Apologie," he uses the book of the self ("ma métaphisique, ma phisique")[20] as a source for the study of human nature at its best and worst (for "chaque homme porte la forme entiere de l'humaine condition" [III. 2. 782, b] ["Each man bears the entire form of man's estate" (III. 2. 611, b)]).

This second interpretation of the concept of consubstantiality—that the man is like a book—is more radical than the first (that the book is like the man), although it has received considerably less critical commentary. It ultimately tells us something about the relationship between word and thing for Montaigne, as the equivalence between "plume" and "pieds" did. They are of the same nature, but it is the word which defines that nature and thus here seems primary.

One of Montaigne's clearest differences from Du Bellay and other earlier Renaissance theorists is in the order of priority with which he views language and the world, as well as in the more modest definitions he adopts for both. Du Bellay and Sidney, for example, retained the strong belief that language is subordinate, and often false, in its attempts to represent the higher reality that poets can perceive.

Montaigne's originality lies in the fact that he accepts the limitations of language ("De la vanité des paroles"), but uses them as a model for perceiving the limitations to human na-

[20] "Je m'estudie plus qu'autre subject. C'est ma metaphisique, c'est ma phisique" (III. 13. 1050, b). See also the continuation of this comparison on the next page: "J'aymerois mieux m'entendre bien en moy qu'en (c) Ciceron. (b) De l'experience que j'ay de moy, je trouve assez dequoy me faire sage, si j'estoy bon escholier." ("I study myself more than any other subject. That is my metaphysics, that is my physics." and, "I would rather be an authority on myself than on (c) Cicero. (b) In the experience I have of myself I find enough to make me wise, if I were a good scholar" (III. 13. 821-22, b].)

281

ture ("De la vanité"). In the process, he manages to turn this acceptance into something much more positive, as Du Bellay and other Pléiade poets were not able to do. While Du Bellay seems never to have recovered from his disillusionment with Rome and the inspired view of literature that it stood for, Montaigne appears almost relieved not to have to live with giants like Cato the Younger or Virgil. And as literature ceases to have a superhuman dimension, the role of the reader is stronger and more creative.

The equality between reader and writer that Montaigne's smaller-scale definition of literature and life permits brings us back to the parallel between tennis and verbal communication with which we began: "La parole est moitié à celuy qui parle, moitié à celuy qui l'escoute." The primacy of language, which we saw suggested in the second interpretation of the concept of consubstantiality of book and man, is alluded to here, and begins to explain in part Montaigne's seeming modernity to the twentieth-century reader. "La parole" at times appears more important than either writer or reader, although it is completely dependent on both of them, arising out of a dialectical relationship between them.

Montaigne again takes a step beyond earlier sixteenth-century theorists in thus describing the relationship between reader and writer. Although many earlier writers (for example Rabelais) perceived the author's relationship to the reader to be one of rivalry or even hostility[21]—typical of the competitive aspect of the tennis game—Montaigne views that interaction as a more creative or productive one, when he sees the possibility of the reader's applying the techniques of self-study to himself. Montaigne believes that the ultimate goal in his relationship with the reader is communication—keeping the ball moving—not accumulation of points on either side.

Montaigne implies that a "reading" of the self could take place in the person who has read the *Essais*. For example:

Si les autres se regardoient attentivement, comme je fay,

[21] See Ong on the polemical role of the Word, typical of the oral and rhetorical traditions. He feels that typography gradually puts an end to the use of language to express hostility (*Presence*, chap. 5).

Montaigne's Conception of Reading

ils se trouveroient, comme je fay, pleins d'inanité et de fadaise. (III. 9. 979, *b*)

If others examined themselves attentively, as I do, they would find themselves, as I do, full of inanity and nonsense. (III. 9. 766, *b*)

This sentence suggests that we examine our own shortcomings, in an almost sermonly fashion. But it also contains the positive message that the reader is just as capable of self-scrutiny as the essayist. Whether or not the reader of the *Essais* writes (and reads) his own self-portrait, in responding to the *Essais* he will create a verbal image of himself equivalent to "writing" (or reading) a new book of the self. The "je" of the *Essais* blends imperceptibly with the "je" of the reader.

Montaigne frequently draws an analogy between introspection and reading (as in the statements that he studies himself like a book) to clarify the nature of the project of self-study. But this analogy can also be used to shed light on his conception of language and particularly of the reading process. In this respect he anticipates theories of reading extending far beyond the sixteenth century. Rousseau, for example, in the *Confessions*, dates self-awareness from the time that he began to read:

> . . . je ne sais comment j'appris à lire: je ne me souviens que de mes premières lectures et de leur effet sur moi: c'est le temps d'où je date sans interruption la conscience de moi-même.[22]

> I do not know how I learnt to read. I only remember my first books and their effect upon me; it is from my earliest reading that I date the unbroken consciousness of my own existence.[23]

---

[22] J. J. Rousseau, *Oeuvres Complètes*, vol. 1, *Les Confessions & Autres Textes Autobiographiques*, ed. Bernard Gagnebin and Marcel Raymond (Bruges, 1964), Livre Premier, p. 8.

[23] *The Confessions of Jean-Jacques Rousseau*, trans. J. M. Cohen (London, 1970), book 1, p. 19.

Cathleen M. Bauschatz

Georges Poulet has also described the close relationship between reading and introspection, which is something Montaigne seemed to be groping for in his parallels between self-study and reading:

> . . . reading implies something resembling the apperception I have of myself, the action by which I grasp straightway what I think as being thought by a subject (who, in this case, is not I).[24]

Poulet appears to be saying that through reading one objectifies one's concept of the self. This is a rather Proustian process, as Genette has pointed out: "En réalité, chaque lecteur est, quand il lit, le propre lecteur de soi-même." ("In reality, each reader is, when he reads, his own reader."[25])

In suggesting that the reader engage in introspection as the *Essais* have, Montaigne comes close to the modern view of reader as creator described by Barthes and others.[26] To return to *S/Z*, Barthes explains in its introduction his concept of the

[24] Georges Poulet, "Phenomenology of Reading," *New Literary History* 1 (1969), 53-68, 57.

[25] Genette quotes Proust here (*Figures III*, p. 267, my translation). See also in this respect Iser's statement that the reader discovers himself at the same time that he discovers the meaning of a text: "the reader is forced to discover the hitherto unconscious expectations that underlie all his perceptions, and also the whole process of consistency-building as a prerequisite for understanding. In this way he may then be given the chance of discovering himself, both in and through his constant involvement in 'home-made' illusions and fictions" (*Implied Reader*, p. xiv).

Paul Ricoeur has also commented on the close relationship between reading and introspection, a process he refers to as "Appropriation": "By appropriation I mean several things. I mean first that the interpretation of a text ends up in the self-interpretation of a subject, who henceforth understands himself better. This completion of text-understanding in self-understanding characterizes the sort of reflective philosophy which I call concrete reflection" (Ricoeur, "What Is a Text? Explanation and Interpretation," in David M. Rasmussen, *Mythic-Symbolic Language and Philosophical Anthropology: A Constructive Interpretation of the Thought of Paul Ricoeur* [The Hague, 1971], pp. 135-50, 145).

[26] See for example Norman Holland's thought-provoking article, "Unity Identity Text Self," *PMLA* 90 (1975), 813-22.

Montaigne's Conception of Reading

"writerly" text, "le scriptible," which does not alienate writer and reader from each other:

> Pourquoi le scriptible est-il notre valeur? Parce que l'enjeu du travail littéraire (de la littérature comme travail) c'est de faire du lecteur, non plus un consommateur, mais un producteur du texte. Notre littérature est marquée par le divorce impitoyable que l'institution littéraire maintient entre le fabricant et l'usager du texte, son propriétaire et son client, son auteur et son lecteur . . . il ne lui reste plus en partage que la pauvre liberté de recevoir ou de rejeter le texte. (p. 10)

> Why is the writerly our value? Because the goal of literary work (of literature as work) is to make the reader no longer a consumer, but a producer of the text. Our literature is characterized by the pitiless divorce which the literary institution maintains between the producer of the text and its user, between its owner and its customer, between its author and its reader. . . . He is left with no more than the poor freedom either to accept or reject the text. (p. 4)

The cooperation between reader and writer projected by Barthes here is similar to the productive interaction through introspection and imagination which Montaigne occasionally outlines.

Barthes has developed the connection between reading and imagination in numerous places. In *Le plaisir du texte* he talks about the relationship between reading and creative musing, something that would have been very understandable to Montaigne:

> . . . il [le texte] produit en moi le meilleur plaisir s'il parvient à se faire écouter indirectement; si, le lisant, je suis entrainé à souvent lever la tête, à entendre autre chose.[27]

> . . . it produces, in me, the best pleasure if it manages to

[27] Roland Barthes, *Le Plaisir du texte* (Paris, 1973), p. 41.

make itself heard indirectly; if, reading it, I am led to look up often, to listen to something else.[28]

He later defines the activity of reading as a sensual "lire-rêver":

> . . . nous sommes engagés dans une pratique homogène (glissante, euphorique, voluptueuse, unitaire, jubila-toire), et cette pratique nous comble: *lire-rêver.* (p. 61)

> . . . we are engaged in a homogeneous (sliding, euphoric, voluptuous, unitary, jubilant) practice, and this practice overwhelms us: *dream-reading.* (p. 37)

Here the reader is obviously as actively involved as the writer in creating a new text, a product of personal associations called up by the original text. The element of pleasure in reading is surprisingly close to what we saw Montaigne condone in "Des livres." It is evident that the pleasure of reading is related to the strong sense of self which both writers feel reading helps to develop.

I have mentioned Roland Barthes in particular here, because his tantalizing position midway between the linguistic or textual and the reader-oriented critical approaches seems particularly close to Montaigne's. There are many affinities between the two writers, including Barthes' evolution from an interest in the role of language in reading (*S/Z*), to a preoccupation with the "pleasure" of reading (*Le Plaisir du texte*), to a study of the process of introspection that accompanies it (*Roland Barthes*). The personal nature of the *Essais*, which distinguishes them from "impersonal" books like most others, is similar to Barthes' definition of his *Roland Barthes*:

> Quoiqu'il soit fait apparemment d'une suite d'"'idées," ce livre n'est pas le livre de ses idées: il est le livre du Moi, le livre de mes résistances à mes propres idées.[29]

---

[28] Barthes, *The Pleasure of the Text*, trans. Richard Miller (New York, 1975), p. 24.

[29] *"Roland Barthes"* par *Roland Barthes* (Paris, 1975), p. 123.

Montaigne's Conception of Reading

Although it apparently is made up of a series of "ideas,"
this book is not the book of *its* ideas: it is the book of Myself, the book of my resistance to my own ideas.[30]

This parallel brings us back to a consideration of Montaigne's
concept of consubstantiality.

In analyzing the equivalence between "livre" and "autheur" in the *Essais*, one must retain at once the idea that the
book is like the man, and that reading is thus another form of
experience; as well as the reverse—that experience is controlled by language—in this case that living is like reading, or
that the self is like a book. Although Montaigne occasionally
hints at the primacy of language in shaping our concept of reality and especially of the self, he does not believe only this.
His gentlemanly, nonscholarly point of view, and his continuing emphasis on the moral benefits to be derived from
reading, maintain paradoxically the belief that language and
literature are subordinate to the men who read and write
them. Montaigne certainly would have recognized the artificiality of a completely linguistically constructed self, as he
saw the falseness of any distraction from basic humanity: "Et
au plus eslevé throne du monde, si ne sommes assis que sus
nostre cul" (III. 13. 1096, *c*) ("And on the loftiest throne in the
world we are still sitting only on our own rump" [III. 13. 857,
c]).

In examining the problem of language in Montaigne,
Michel Foucault has commented on one of the most famous
sentences in the *Essais*:

Il y a plus affaire à interpreter les interpretations qu'à interpreter les choses, et plus de livres sur les livres que sur
autre subject: nous ne faisons que nous entregloser. (III.
13. 1045, *b*)

It is more of a job to interpret the interpretations than to
interpret the things, and there are more books about
books than about any other subject: we do nothing but
write glosses about each other. (III. 13. 818, *b*)

[30] My translation. The published translation of *Roland Barthes* was not
available to me at the time that I wrote this.

287

Cathleen M. Bauschatz

He feels that Montaigne is simply describing here the role which language occupied in the sixteenth century:

> Ce n'est point là le constat de faillite d'une culture ensevelie sous ses propres monuments: mais la définition du rapport inévitable que le langage du XVIe siècle entretenait avec lui-même.[31]

> These words are not a statement of the bankruptcy of a culture buried beneath its own monuments; they are a definition of the inevitable relation that language maintained with itself in the sixteenth century.[32]

I agree with Foucault's assertion that Montaigne is aware of the problem of the relation between word and thing, and of the need to define which is primary (as we have seen above). But I do not support his interpretation of Montaigne's point of view on this problem. The sentence refers to the kind of bookishness usually associated in the *Essais* with scholasticism and humanism. As we have seen throughout this study, Montaigne usually criticizes the kind of reading associated with these movements, for not offering the reader an active enough role. Therefore, I would support the interpretation of this sentence one finds in more traditional Montaigne scholarship: that it is a criticism of the alienation of books from life he feels to have been common in the Middle Ages and earlier Renaissance. In that respect Montaigne anticipates the world-view described by Foucault as belonging to the seventeenth century: the loss of faith in the automatic "resemblance" between word and thing, and the need to recreate that link by an active effort on the part of writer or reader. Ultimately the question of which is primary—language or experience, book or self—is less important for Montaigne than the need to create a balance between them. The reading process is a prime example of a way to maintain this balance.

[31] Michel Foucault, *Les Mots et les choses* (Paris, 1966), p. 55.
[32] Michel Foucault, *The Order of Things: An Archaeology of the Human Sciences* (translation of *Les Mots et les choses*) (New York, 1970), p. 40.

Montaigne's Conception of Reading

Of the two predominant approaches in modern criticism, Montaigne is probably closer to the active, reader-oriented view of literature as a form of experience than to the more passive, text-centered conception of the role of the reader, although as we have seen, the essayist is well aware of the importance of language in self-definition and in reading. The emphasis by "reader response" critics on reading as a form of experience retains analogies with all the senses and with their psychological repercussions as Montaigne does. While Norman Holland and Stanley Fish both take as an assumption the notion that reading is like experience, some critics have gone into more detail in trying to describe how this is true. For example, Wolfgang Iser devotes a chapter of the *Implied Reader* to the reprinted article, "The Reading Process: A Phenomenological Approach." In comparing the experience of reading with ordinary experience he observes that "the way in which this [reading] experience comes about through a process of continual modification is closely akin to the way in which we gather experience in life" (p. 281). We do not perceive the text as a whole, but assimilate it through time as we are affected by it. In Montaigne's terms, "Je ne peints pas l'estre. Je peints le passage" (III. 2. 782, *b*) ("I do not portray being: I portray passing" [III. 2. 611, *b*]). This conception of the writing of the *Essais* necessitates an equally phenomenological view of the reading process.

Which modern critical approach Montaigne would have preferred is, of course, idle speculation. What does emerge, however, is that an oscillation between a belief in the text or author as dominant in the reading process and a view of the reader himself as creator of it is present in the *Essais*, and is itself a constant in the history of criticism. The fact that Renaissance writers phrase their beliefs about reading in the terminology of classical rhetoric should not obscure the fact that they were talking about some of the same questions being discussed today. Criticism and poetics are not only complementary, as Genette has observed,[33] they are fundamen-

---

[33] "La critique, elle, est et restera une approche fondamentale, et l'on peut présager que l'avenir des études littéraires est essentiellement dans l'échange

Cathleen M. Bauschatz

tally similar in their attempts to record and explain readers' reactions to literature.

It might be argued that a basic difference between Montaigne's approach to reading and that of contemporary criticism is to be found in the moral orientation of the former and relative ethical freedom of the latter. Certainly Renaissance men of letters never question the existence of a didactic element in literature or criticism. Even Montaigne, who seems to offer a large degree of latitude in interpreting his book, ultimately tells the "lecteur" to study himself as the *Essais* do. Introspection emerges from the *Essais* less as a right than as a duty. The receiver of a serve in tennis could choose to let the ball go by, but once he agrees to play the game he really has to try to return it.

But Montaigne does modify the simple conception of didacticism as he received it from classical, medieval, and earlier Renaissance sources. As we have seen, his loss of faith in the ability of a text to single-handedly transform a reader as he reads also leads to skepticism about the lasting effects of the text without a personal effort at application and change.

On the other hand, is there really no prescriptive element in subjective criticism? I feel that there is: in concentrating on the experience of the reader in literature, we are creating or even endorsing the experience of reading as a valuable form of activity. In that respect we are no less didactic than Sidney or Montaigne, who were also concerned with retrieving reading from a position of isolation from action.

The act of reading involves the reader in a contract to assimilate what he reads in some way. We are obligated to feel something when we read: "le plaisir du texte" is offered to the "littérateur" who is sensitive to esthetic experience, and the "dynamics of literary response" can operate only in the

---

et le va-et-vient nécessaire entre critique et poétique—dans la conscience et l'exercice de leur *complémentarité*" (*Figures III*, p. 11) ("Criticism itself is and will remain a fundamental approach, and one can predict that the future of literary studies is essentially in the exchange and the necessary back-and-forth movement between criticism and poetics—in the consciousness and the exercise of their *complementarity*" [my translation]).

290

Montaigne's Conception of Reading

reader who does respond. The recent emphasis on the reader's freedom also entails a consideration of his responsibility for authenticity in performing and reporting the perceptual action we now conceive reading to be.

The value currently placed on response itself involves a redefinition of the dynamics of didacticism, from the point of view of reader rather than writer. This redefinition was indirectly initiated with the rhetoric of self-study in the *Essais*. Like many contemporary critics, Montaigne felt that the only "lesson" which could come from reading was an increased sense of self-awareness. Although this message is particularly appropriate from a book of self-study, it can contribute to an understanding of the nature of the reading process itself, and indicates a direction in which reading research might profitably move.

Nicolas Poussin, *The Arcadian Shepherds* (Musée du Louvre, Paris; photo Giraudon)

Louis Marin | Toward A Theory
of Reading in the
Visual Arts: Poussin's
The Arcadian Shepherds

This paper is an attempt at read-
ing a single painting—Poussin's *The Arcadian Shepherds*
(Louvre)[1]—but such a tentative reading cannot be truly accomplished without being aware of the operations involved
in the contemplative process, their implications on theoretical
and practical levels, and the hypotheses which guide that
process. My essay can thus be considered as an approach to a
partial history of reading in the field of visual art. To put my
undertaking in more general terms, I wish to test some notions and procedures elaborated in contemporary semiotic
and semantic theories by using a specific painting as an experimental device, a paradigm or model to validate, refine, or
question those notions and procedures when they are displaced into a domain for which they were not primarily constructed. Although the study of Poussin's painting (one of his
best-known and most often discussed works) aims at constructing a theory of reading and determining the notion of
reader in painting, the final result of the enterprise will also be
a description of that painting as such, in its irreducible
singularity—our aim being to discover the system that underlies the pictorial text, making it coherent and noncomparable
to other pictorial texts, as well as to locate the viewer-reader

[1] *The Arcadian Shepherds.* 85 x 121 cms. Musée du Louvre, Paris (734). See
A. Blunt, *The Paintings of Nicolas Poussin, a Critical Catalogue* (London, 1966),
pp. 80-81, for the discussions about the date of the painting. A. Blunt's conclusion is the period after 1655. See also the exhaustive bibliography of the
painting until 1966, as well as the catalogue of the 1960 Exhibition in Paris, p.
127, no. 99.

in a position that is also a specific one, I mean one appropriate only to this painting. It seems to me that all studies of pictorial and literary texts are exposed to such a tension between the pole of theoretical and methodological generalization and that of unique and individual description, an opposition I might rephrase as that between *the structure of messages* in painting in general and *the system of a pictorial text* in particular. The concrete reading-viewing of a painting and the practical position of its reader-viewer thus have a twofold nature, a bidimensional constitution: on the one hand, *competence*, whose structure is constructed from the messages produced by codes and received by the viewer in the process of reading that particular painting as an example among many others or as a cluster of visual "quotations" of several pictorial and extrapictorial codes; on the other hand, *performance*, whose system depends on that painting as a unique object of contemplation, which organizes it as an individual reading and is appropriate only for it in a unique situation of reception. The main problem such an approach encounters is the connection between these two dimensions, the determination of a level of analysis—and consequently a set of notions and relationships—intermediate between competence and performance, structure and system, messages and text, codes and individual reading-viewing. In a certain sense, the analyses that follow are attempts to construct such a level and to determine such relationships and notions.

Methodological Problems

My main reason for choosing Poussin's painting as a model to deal with the questions I have just raised is that it combines in a single ensemble two semiotic systems: language—more specifically, writing—and painting. *The Arcadian Shepherds*—to call the work by its commonly accepted title—contains, visibly and legibly represented, the following words carved on a tomb: "Et in Arcadia ego . . ." The words inscribed on the tomb are a part of the pictorial representation—a represented epitaph—and constitute the central focus of the story that the

Poussin's *The Arcadian Shepherds*

painter gives his viewer-reader to contemplate and to narrate.

Before coming to a more precise analysis of the painting, I must state the paradigms of my own reading, consequently my working hypotheses and basic presuppositions. My starting point will be the distinction made by E. Benveniste between discourse (*discours*) and narrative (*récit*).[2] I shall transfer this distinction from textual to iconic propositions, putting aside for practical reasons any doubts about the epistemological validity of that transference; considering, in other words, the spontaneous discourse *about* (representational) painting, the statements made by the reader in front of the painting: "It is a tree, it is a man, it is a tomb," as the immediate discourse *of* the painting itself. I can thus rewrite Benveniste's formulation in this way: a historical painting is a set of iconic narrative propositions which displays in its own language the narration of an event. By the latter term I refer to the domain of what Panofsky calls *motives* as well as that of what he calls *stories*. A motive implies a practical recognition of gestures, things, persons; a story implies literary knowledge. Although stories are carried by motives, both imply readings that are different but nonetheless integrated by practical experience and literary knowledge. The events of the story that the narrative proposition undertakes to tell are iconically located at the conjunction of motives and themes.[3]

The first preiconographical and iconographical references of the painting to the "story" imply a second reference to the very operation of narrating, whatever the medium used by this operation may be. But—this is the fundamental thesis of Benveniste—in the case of narrative as opposed to discourse, the specific modality of its enunciation is to erase or conceal the signs of the narrator in the narrative propositions. So the basic characteristic of the narrative enunciation is the exclusion of all "autobiographical" forms like "I," "you," "here,"

[2] E. Benveniste, *Problèmes de linguistique générale*, vol. 1 (Paris, 1966), 237-50.

[3] E. Panofsky, *Studies in Iconology: Humanistic Themes in the Art of the Renaissance* (New York, 1962), pp. 3-31.

"there," "now," as well as of the present tense. On the contrary, it uses a well-defined past tense, the preterite, and the third person "he," "she," "they."

When this specific narrative apparatus of enunciation is translated to the historical painting, we have to ask questions that are not very easy to answer: What are the levels and the modalities of enunciation in this kind of painting? What is its narrative agency? How could a painting narrate a story since, at least apparently, there is no verb, no temporal marker, no adverb or pronoun in painting as in language?

ICONIC STRUCTURES OF TIME

I shall try to answer these questions methodically by analyzing the iconic propositional content of the painting, since it is at this level that the references to the narrator are inscribed or not, and by first asking another question: What is the relationship between the time of the story and the time of the narrative? Is there actually a narrative time in a historical painting? This last question is relevant, since a painting is a piece of space totally and immediately exhibited to the viewer's eye: this may be an insuperable semiotic constraint of painting in general.

A painting is "read" by the viewer's eye, that is, its space is successively traversed by the viewer's gaze. However, in contrast to a written text, the eye's routes are much freer, and whatever may be the constraints of composition, distribution of values and colors, they do not exert their powers in a strictly determined way. So the question remains: If the story exists in time, how does the iconic proposition become a narrative proposition within the space of representation which is the "substance" of the representational painting?

In order to answer this question, we must define a few terms characterizing the space of a representational painting: first, the space of the painting as such, the representational *screen*, or the painting as a window open to the world and/or as a representational mirror; second, the representation of space on that screen, the illusory depth created by specific

Poussin's *The Arcadian Shepherds*

means on the surface of the canvas or the representational *stage*; third, belonging to the stage, the loci where the various narrative propositions are situated, propositions which basically consist in the representation of human actions corresponding to the successive events of the story. The distinction between screen, stage and loci is useful insofar as it permits a structural organization framing in a complex way the narrative proposition. The reading of a painting would then consist in projecting the time of the story onto the stage (the representation of space) and in putting into order with respect to "before and after" the loci of the stage: that is, the hierarchical structure of the time of reading. However, we have to understand that the very time of the referential story regulates the order of the loci and finally imposes a reading order on the viewer.

Now the "classical" painting is characterized by the unity of its stage: there is only a single represented space in the space of representation, although the stage may be differentiated into, for instance, a foreground, a middle ground and a background. These planes are the loci of the stage where the narrative propositions or sequences may be located. Now, what happened to this clear-cut organization when the painter wanted to depict a narrative in which the same actors had to perform successively different actions according to the referential story? Painters attempted to elaborate various compromises, but theoretically just one possibility was left to them: to displace the temporal diachronic sequences of the narrative into a synchronic, atemporal order or into a structural organization of space based upon the rational connection of the parts in the whole. As LeBrun explained to the members of the French Academy in his lecture on Poussin's *Manna*, "the historical painter has only to represent one moment where simultaneous actions take place."[4] The historical painting is a painting whose "tense" is present, whose time is the present moment when it is seen, and the only possible way of making the story understood by the

[4] Félibien, *Entretiens sur les Vies et les ouvrages des plus excellents Peintres anciens et modernes* (London, 1705), 4: 111.

viewer, or "read" by him, is to distribute, all around this central represented moment, various circumstances that are logically connected to it by implication or presupposition. This is the reason why historical painting is considered as the most difficult and also the most prestigious genre of painting, because in the present presence of the pictorial representation, it has to express diachrony, temporal relationships, yet can do so only through the network of a whole that generates its parts logically or achronically by its own signifying economy. The time of the story, its succeeding parts related to the succession of events, is neutralized in the intelligible space of a model that represents only the logical relationships of elements subordinated to a center. This is the paradox of the classical painting of history. The representational process cannot "presentify" time except in terms of a model in all senses of the term: original, paradigm, absolute presence, pure rationality. The paradox consists precisely in the fact that time is definitely not a model. It cannot be a logical or metaphysical paradigm. It always admits a "before" and an "after," a "not yet" and an "already gone." It is this "truth" that classical painting dismisses and points out at the same time through its own process of representation. Far from being a remote application of the "classical *episteme*" in the domain of the arts, historical painting, because it necessarily presents in a spatial medium a model of time-intelligibility, is its ultimate paradigm.

Nevertheless, in front of the painting, the viewer tells a story to himself, he reads the painting, he understands the narrative messages. This means that he converts the iconic representational model into language, and more precisely into a story, thanks to the mimetic power, the fascinating likeness of the objects represented by the painting he looks at. On the one hand, a moment of representation is offered to our eyes as the center or the core of the intelligible structure of the whole. On the other hand, the reader narrativizes the model in a story which gives him logos, presence in a temporal form. Between these two poles characterizing historical painting and its reading, a "chiasmus" is operating: the

Poussin's *The Arcadian Shepherds*

model is built on its perfect structural intelligibility in order to allow a story to be told: reading-enunciation. But such a reading, such an enunciation, has to be dismissed from the painting itself in order to posit the moment of representation in its objective and universal truth. In other words, the subject of enunciation-representation has to be at one and the same time present and absent. When he is absent, events are manifestations of being itself, pure and universal essences; when he is present, they exist in their actual temporal succession. The painting is at one and the same time an instantaneous moment of evidence in the Cartesian sense—when an eternal truth is presented—and an ontological proof in the same Cartesian sense when, from that essence, existence is analytically unfolded.

The instantaneous eclipse of the subject of enunciation can be rephrased in less metaphysical terms as the subject's negation (in the Freudian sense). He is at the same time articulated in and excluded from the painting: in Benveniste's terms, "In order for there to be narrative (*récit*), or story, it is necessary and sufficient that the author remain faithful to his enterprise as historian and banish all that is foreign to the narrative of events (discourse, personal reflections, comparisons)."[5] The completion of this operation requires that the narrator be banished from the text as the subject of enunciation (discourse) or as the term of an enunciating reference, reflection, comparison. "The events are set down as they occurred, as they gradually appear on the horizon of the story. Nobody is speaking here. The events seem to tell themselves."[6]

Representational Models

It is not surprising to ascertain that such a narrative notion of language in general was, in the perspective of the classical *episteme*, the fundamental level, the basic truth upon which the various modalities of language—and more generally, the whole system of representation—were founded. I shall now

[5] Benveniste, *Problèmes*, p. 241.
[6] Ibid.

Louis Marin

deal briefly with this general principle of representation in the very process of its constitution, using the Port-Royal *Grammar* and *Logic* as my main references. I shall distinguish, as the Port-Royal grammarians and logicians did—and we find that distinction in Benveniste as well—the level of signs from the level of discourse, or in contemporary terms the semiotic level from the semantic one.[7]

A principle we may call the principle of representation relates language and thought to each other: Mind is the mirror of things and it will not be the first time we find the mirror playing such a metaphorical and theoretical role in the classical *episteme*; ideas are things themselves within the mind, ideas represent things in the mind and for it. Language is the mirror of mind: signs—and especially verbal signs, words—are things that represent ideas. Signs represent representations of signs. To give an idea, a sign is to give the mind an idea whose object represents what constitutes the idea.

The principle of representation has a correlated principle which concerns the very structure of a sign or a signifying system. In a sign, there are two "subrelations": a relation between ideas and signs, and between signs and things. But a sign allows a process of substitution to take place between its object and the idea of the signified object, a substitution that operates, in the case of language, from the thing to the sign: the idea of the signified object is substituted for the sign. Because of their arbitrariness, words are transparent to the primary relation of representation: they are necessary only to permit communication between minds and within the mind itself.

On the contrary, because of their mimetic nature, pictorial signs make the substitution operate from the sign to the thing: the pictorial sign (whatever it may be) is substituted for the thing or the idea of the signified object. This is precisely what seventeenth-century art critics and theorists called the pictorial deception: the fact that painting deceives the eye

[7] See *Grammaire générale et raisonnée* (Paris, 1660), and *Logique de Port-Royal* (Paris, 1685; Lille, 1964), pp. 119ff. See also E. Benveniste, *Problèmes de linguistique générale*, vol. 2 (Paris, 1974), 63-66.

300

Poussin's *The Arcadian Shepherds*

constitutes its greatest aesthetic value. When Pascal questions the validity of painting and, perhaps, artistic values in general, he contests them precisely for that reason, taking for granted such a substitutive operation: "How vain is painting which attracts admiration by the resemblance of things the originals of which we do not admire."[8]

An idea or a representation possesses, then, a double nature: it is a modification of mind and it is a representation of a thing; it has, in Cartesian terms, a formal reality and an objective one (that does not mean for Descartes that it has an objective validity). This "model" of representation can be developed by dividing the sign into two subrelations which permit us to take into account two varieties of signs, the verbal or oral signs and the written signs. The latter represent sounds, which in their turn represent, by combination, ideas. It is remarkable that pictorial signs are also divided into two parts, design and color. We may observe that this theoretical distinction, which has had an extraordinary importance since the Renaissance and certainly before, has remained in effect up to our own time (see for example the discussion about line and color in Pollock's work). Design, logicians and art theorists as well as painters have observed, is an essential component of the pictorial sign, but its most remarkable feature is that it remains invisible in a painting. It is the structure, metaphorically the "soul" of the sign; it constitutes the painting's intelligible, rational part. On the contrary, color is its visible component, its "flesh and body." Color could not exist without design, like modes without a substance underlying them and giving them an ontological and axiological support. True experts in painting know how to recognize the formal qualities of design beneath the visible brightness of colors. It is interesting to observe that in such a model, there is an implicit valorization of sounds and voice compared to writing and an explicit but reverse valorization of design compared to colors, for the very reason that both sounds and design are almost immaterial. Line, the basic constituent of design, has

[8] B. Pascal, *Pensées*, ed. L. Lafuma, 2nd ed. (Paris, 1952), no. 77.

only a "modal" reality as a limit of a body, Descartes observed. Generally speaking, that means that in a painting, the material elements of representation, and precisely the traces left by the painter's work—by his transformative activity in the painting—have to be erased and concealed by what the painting represents, by its "objective reality."

Now, at the level of discourse or the semantic plane in Benveniste's sense, the minimal unit is the sentence, and the heart of the sentence is the verb. We observe, in the famous analysis of the verb by the Port-Royal logicians, the same operations that consist in positing and erasing the subject of enunciation: "The verb is a word whose principal use is to express affirmation, that is to say, to denote that a discourse wherein the verb is employed is a discourse of a man who not only conceives things (that is, representations, ideas) but who judges and affirms of them."[9] Developing this definition, Port-Royal logicians show: (1) that every verb can be reduced to the verb "to be"—Peter vivit: Peter est vivens; (2) that all uses of the verb "to be" can be reduced to the present tense: that means that every sentence can be reformulated in this way: Peter vixit: Ego affirmo: Peter est vivens (in the past); (3) that all uses of the verb "to be" can be reduced to the third-person singular. This last "reduction" compared to the two preceding ones is extremely important, because according to Benveniste's article on pronouns, the third person signifies in fact a nonperson (what he calls the co-relation of personality I-you versus he-she).[10] Thus the result of the seventeenth-century grammarians' analysis of the verb—the central term of a sentence, the minimal unit of discourse—is a kind of general statement like "it is" connected to various determinations. By the first reduction, the copulative function of every verb becomes self evident: the copula "is" links two representations to each other. By the second reduction (to the present tense), the copulative function is related to a subject, an "ego affirmo" who utters the connection between two rep-

[9] *Logique de Port-Royal*, p. 138.
[10] Benveniste, *Problèmes*, 1: 255-56.

Poussin's *The Arcadian Shepherds*

resentations as *his*, as one of his "manners" of thinking, a mode of *his* thought. By the third reduction to the third person, the subject of enunciation marked in the utterance by "I," "ego" disappears, and for this reason the representations connected to each other in the sentence by the verb "is" can ontologically appear as the things themselves that they represent, ordered in a rational and universal discourse, the discourse of reality itself. However, at the same time, by reducing verbs to the indicative mood and present tense, the sentence is related to a subject, a mind—or rather, since judgment is in Descartes' terms an act of will, the sentence is related to a power (or a desire) which, by making an assertion, appropriates things, reality as *his* things, *his* reality. The pervading notion of language as representation is thus founded on the three interrelated functions of the verb "to be": copulative—it connects representations to each other; existential—these connections are those existing between things represented; and alethic—the resulting discourse has a truth value. But we have to understand the two processes that produce such a notion: first, the position of a subject of discourse; but thanks to the first two reductions of verbs, such a subject is not located in time and space with all their determinations, but acts as a universal and abstract mind whose function is only to judge of things and to affirm them. And yet, by the very same gesture, this subject is erased: nobody is speaking; it is reality itself that speaks. At the same time, we understand better the significance of Descartes' profound conception of the "ego affirmo" as will: of course, the Cartesian subject of enunciation is a "theoretical" subject, but he is also a will, a desire. This means that he is a power of theory or a desire of representation. So, into the mirror model a quality of power is introduced that calls into question the very structure of the model, and in a certain sense my whole critical undertaking will consist in disentangling desire from theory, force from science. If we may define power as desire bound by and caught in representation, my critical attempt would be to explore representational systems as apparatuses of power.

Louis Marin

To put it in slightly different terms, the representational system, through its use in the discourse, is made equivalent to things themselves; we may understand this process as one by which a subject inscribes himself as the center of the world and transforms himself into things by transforming things into *his* representations. Such a subject has the right to possess things legitimately because he has substituted for things his signs, which represent them adequately—that is, in such a way that reality is exactly equivalent to his discourse.

Now to come back to historical painting, which we have already defined as the paradigmatic model of the "classical *episteme*," we can understand, after the analyses of the representational models built by the Port-Royal logicians, why in that *episteme* the fundamental mode of enunciation is the historical one, in which, to quote Benveniste, "Nobody is speaking. Events seem to narrate themselves from the horizon of the past." And we can understand why, for that *episteme*, the autobiographical mode—that is, one in which discourse exhibits the markers referring to the subject who produces utterances—is only a kind of perverted or secondary form of enunciation. It may be of interest to note here that these statements are in agreement with Kuroda's conclusions in his essay "On the Foundations of Narrative Theory,"[11] but from a completely different viewpoint, mine being more historical, his purely theoretical.

THE READING PROCESS:
Deixis AND REPRESENTATION

The first problem we are able to raise about historical painting in general is one that we may articulate as the "negation-structure" of enunciation in pictorial representations.[12] The

[11] S. Y. Kuroda, "Réflexions sur les fondements de la théorie de la narration," in *Langue, discours, société: Pour E. Benveniste*, eds. J. Kristeva, J. C. Milner, and N. Ruwet (Paris, 1975), pp. 260-92.

[12] Cf. S. Freud, "Negation" [*Die Verneinung*, 1925], in *Standard Edition of the Complete Psychological Works*, ed. and trans. James Strachey et al., 24 vols. (London, 1953-74), 19: 236f.

Poussin's *The Arcadian Shepherds*

problem is of the utmost importance, for it defines, by its very terms, the viewer-reader's position in front of the painting, the process of reading or the reception of the visual message emitted by the painter.

A possible approach to the problem resulting from the transference of the linguistic model of communication to painting is the study of the deictic structure of painting. Every linguistic utterance occurs in a determined spatio-temporal situation. It is produced by a person, the speaker (or sender) and addressed to another person (the hearer) who receives it. The *deixis* of an utterance is constituted by the orientational traits of language, traits related to the time and the situation where the utterance takes place. In language, these traits are personal pronouns, whose meaning is defined by reference to the deictic coordinates of the typical situation where the utterance is emitted, as well as adverbs of time and place. Moreover, we must notice that the typical situation of emission is egocentric, every linguistic exchange implying automatically the shift of the center of the deictic system when emission passes from one interlocutor to the other. Finally, we may add that the deictic system expands to include demonstrative pronouns, verb tenses, and ultimately frames the whole linguistic process. This should hardly be surprising, since a situation of communication implies that the linguistic system is actualized in a specific place and time, a place and a time that deictics refer to and whose structure is inscribed in the utterance.

Now, if the characteristic of the "historical" enunciative modality is that events narrate themselves in the story as if nobody were speaking, this means that the whole deictic network has to be erased in the narrative message. Is it possible to point out in Poussin's *Arcadian Shepherds*, say in its narrative content, the "negation" of iconic deictics? Does such a question make sense in the iconic domain? My hypothesis is the following: except for the very existence of the painting and the fact that we are looking at it, nothing in the iconic message marks its situation of emission and reception; that is to say, no figure is looking at us as viewers, nobody ad-

305

dresses us as a representative of the sender of the message. As viewers-readers we just catch the figures performing their narrative functions. Apparently they do not need us in order to narrate themselves. We are only the distant spectators of a story, separated from it by a "spectacular" distance that is the insuperable distance of the painter-narrator from the story he narrates. A comparison with portrait painting may illuminate the point. It has been observed that a full-face portrait functions like the "I-You" relation which characterizes the discursive enunciation, but with an interesting difference that I shall only mention here: the sitter of the portrait appears only to be the *represented* enunciative "ego," who nonetheless defines the viewer's position as a "Tu" he addresses. The sitter portrayed in the painting is the representative of enunciation in the utterance, its inscription on the canvas screen, as if the sitter here and now were speaking by looking at the viewer: "Looking at me, you look at me looking at you. Here and now, from the painting locus, I posit you as the viewer of the painting." In a word, the typical situation of reception is equivalent to the typical situation of emission, through the "representation-representative" who plays the role of a shifting operator of the center of the deictic system.

What is remarkable is that we find in Alberti's *Della Pittura* a clear articulation of the problem we have just raised, in the figure he called the "commentator." Sometimes, Alberti explains, it would make a historical painting more emotionally effective to introduce in the "istoria" a character who, by his gestures and emotional expression, points out the important part of the story to the viewer at whom he looks, and thus establishes a link between the scene represented and the viewer.[13] The fact that in Poussin's painting nobody is looking at us allows us to state, according to our hypothesis, that the represented scene operates in its propositional content the "negation" of all marks of emission and reception of the narrative message.

[13] L. B. Alberti, *Della Pittura*, trans. J. R. Spencer (New Haven, 1956), p. 78.

Poussin's *The Arcadian Shepherds*

The Reading Process: The Syntax of Visibility and Its Self-Representation

I would like to go a little further and rephrase in a more formal way, on a syntactic level one might say, the problem of iconic *deixis* (its system, properly speaking) as it works in classical representation. What corresponds here to the equivalence between painter and viewer that we find in the particular example of the full-face portrait? As in the case of the historical locus for the shifting operator in Alberti's "commentator," the equivalence between painter and viewer, eye and vision (to use Lacan's terms)[14] was structurally established, within the representational system historically determined as the optico-geometrical network of the Renaissance, by a kind of experimental device built by Brunelleschi; this device, an optical box whose description is given by Brunelleschi's biographer Manetti, may be used in our analysis as a paradigmatic model pointing out the elements of the problem we have just raised. Brunelleschi pictured the church of San Giovanni and its surroundings directly in front of him on a small panel about half a *braccio* square.

He assumed that it had to be seen from a single point which is fixed in reference to the height and the width of the picture, and that it had to be seen from the right distance. Seen from any other point, the effect of the perspective would be destroyed. Thus, to prevent the spectator from falling into error in choosing his viewpoint, Filippo (Brunelleschi) made a hole in the picture at that point in the view of the church of San Giovanni which is directly opposite to the eye of the spectator who might be standing in the central portal of S. Maria dei Fiori in order to paint the scene. This hole was as small as a lentil on the painted side, and on the back of the panel it

[14] J. Lacan, *Le Séminaire (livre XI) Les quatre concepts fondamentaux de la psychanalyse* (Paris, 1973), pp. 65-109.

Louis Marin

opened out in a conical form to the size of a ducat or a little more, like the crown of a woman's straw hat. Filippo had the beholder put his eye against the reverse side where the hole was large and while he shaded his eye with his one hand, with the other he was told to hold a flat mirror on the far side in such a way that the painting was reflected in it. The distance from the mirror to the hand near the eye had to be in a given proportion to the distance between the point where Filippo stood in painting his picture and the church of San Giovanni. When one looked at it thus, the perspective of the piazza and the fixing of that point of vision made the scene absolutely real.[15]

Brunelleschi's optical box established the equivalence between the eye of the spectator and the vision of the painter—the reception point and the emission point—through the identification of the viewpoint and the vanishing point actually operating in the panel, and its reflection in the mirror the spectator holds in front of it. In other words, the mirror in which the viewer's eye looks at the reflection of the scene represented on the panel acts as if to endow the painting itself with vision: the painting looks at the viewer-painter like an eye. Brunelleschi's device provides a model or an experimental metaphor of the theory itself. I emphasize the fact that it is only a metaphor: it refers to a specific representational structure among others equally possible. The viewer is posited in the system as a spectator; he is immobilized, caught in the apparatus as a peeping Tom. It is as if what the viewer looked at through the small hole in the panel was the painting's vision, the mirror being the operator of that "as if." But this function does not appear as such in Brunelleschi's device, since what the spectator looks at is a scene represented on the panel. He forgets the very fact that he is looking at a picture, he is fascinated by his own "scopic" desire (or drive).

[15] A. Manetti, *Vita di Ser Brunelleschi*, quoted in *A Documentary History of Art*, vol. 1, *The Middle Ages and the Renaissance*, ed. E. Gilmore Holt (New York, 1957), 170-73.

Poussin's *The Arcadian Shepherds*

We may provisionally conclude that the apparatus of iconic representation constituted by the perspective network is a formal apparatus that integrates the propositional represented contents, the "discourse" of the painting, according to a theoretically reversible process which constitutes the space represented by the painting. In a less abstract way, we may theoretically consider that in the vanishing point, in its hole, the things represented gradually disappear (reception-process) or that from the viewpoint they gradually appear to be distributed in the represented space (emission-process). And the reversibility which constitutes that space theoretically neutralizes the temporal and successive scanning of the painting by the viewer's eye in a kind of permanent present of representation.

Before coming back once more to Poussin's *Arcadian Shepherds*, I would like to emphasize the paradigm of the specular image in the pictorial representational model since the Renaissance. In this paradigm the painting, a window opened onto the world, functions—in its theoretical and even technical constitution—as a mirror duplicating the world. The actual referent of the picture is present on the canvas as an absence, that is to say as its image, its reflection, its shadow, scientifically built in its perceptual reality (an assumption whose universality can be questioned, as Panofsky has shown in his essay on perspective as a symbolic form).[16] More generally speaking, these are the contradictory axioms of the representational system: (1) the representation screen is a transparent window through which the spectator, Man, contemplates the scene represented on the canvas as if he saw the real scene in the world; (2) but at the same time, that screen—actually a surface and a material support—is also a reflecting device on which the real objects are pictured.

In other words, the canvas as a support and as a surface does not exist. For the first time in painting, Man encounters the real world. But the canvas as a support and as a surface does exist to operate the duplication of reality: the canvas as

[16] E. Panofsky, "Die Perspektive als 'Symbolische Form,' " *Vortrage der Bibliothek Warburg* (Leipzig / Berlin, 1924-25), pp. 258-330.

Louis Marin

such is simultaneously posited and neutralized; it has to be technically and ideologically assumed transparent. Invisible and at the same time a necessary condition of visibility, reflecting transparence theoretically defines the representational screen. We find here, in the iconic field, the *same* process we encountered in the Port-Royal reductive analysis of judgment.

A READING OF *The Arcadian Shepherds*

The Three Levels of Analysis

Now we can come back to Poussin's painting, equipped with the models we have just built on various levels of generality, to observe that the relationships which do not appear on the plane of representation—I mean those we analyzed between the painter, the viewer-reader, and the representational screen—are precisely the "subject" or the *"istoria"* told by the painting: Three figures, one on the left, the two others on the right, are "exchanging" gestures and gazes, an exchange that concerns a fourth figure, a man who is kneeling in front of a tomb. Such a dialogue is entirely iconic, since its manifestations (gestures, gazes) are visible either directly (gestures) or indirectly (gazes that are recognizable through the positions of heads and the orientation of eyes). Three figures exchange a message whose referent is what the fourth figure is doing. We may observe, in particular, that the shepherd on the extreme left has nothing in common with the two figures on the right except the fact that he is looking at his kneeling companion. Iconically, he emits the kneeling man as a visual object while the shepherd on the right points to that same man and the woman beside him "receives" that object by looking at him. At the same time, by his gaze directed at her, the shepherd on the right obviously asks her a question concerning the kneeling man he is pointing to.

We may sum up the scene represented according to the various functions of a communicational exchange as defined

Poussin's *The Arcadian Shepherds*

by Jakobson: emission—message—reception—reference—code.[17] The shepherd on the left visually emits a message, which the woman on the right receives, while the man on the right refers to the kneeling shepherd, and by his interrogative gaze toward the "shepherdess," designates the code: What does it mean? What is he doing?—the kneeling man being the message whose "code" or meaning is in question. We may represent schematically the iconic dialogue in this way (straight arrows are gestures, dotted arrows, gazes):

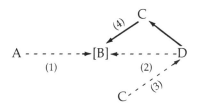

A = shepherd on left
B = kneeling shepherd
C = shepherd on right
D = shepherdess

A few remarks about this analysis, which transposes the Jakobsonian model of communication to the painting not as an explanatory sketch, but as the very subject matter of the story the painting tells us: First, in a sense, the painting is the pictorial representation of that model. Second, the painter and/or the beholder occupy the metaiconic/linguistic position of the linguist who constructs a model about a communication process. Third, the scheme is oriented from A to D for pictorial reasons (the balance and composition of the painting) and nonpictorial ones, following precisely the reading orientation of a written text in our culture, which implies a starting point on the left, an observation that is particularly relevant to our painting since a legible text is carved on the tomb. Four, when D is looking at B, we may interpret her

[17] R. Jakobson, "Linguistics and Poetics," in T. Sebeok, ed., *Style in Language* (Cambridge, Mass., 1960), p. 353.

gaze simultaneously as a way of closing the model and as an enigmatic answer in the dialogue that the figures are involved in. Five, a single figure—C—condenses two functions: C is overdetermined.

The third level of our analysis concerns the "message." What is in question on this level is B, the kneeling figure: That shepherd is looking at a written line, pointing at it with his forefinger, reading it or rather trying to read or to decipher it. Moreover he is visually saying the written sentence since the three first words, "Et in Arcadia," are inscribed just out of his open mouth in a modern version of the medieval phylactery. So B sees, points at, reads, says a written message whose signification he attempts to grasp. In other words, the figure B clusters all the semantic functions we already recognized represented by the other figures, but now related to the text at the very center of the painting, a text about which we as readers-beholders of the painting may ask, exactly like the kneeling shepherd, Who has written it? What is its meaning? What is the name of "ego"?

Unfortunately we cannot enter any further into the painting: our vision is stopped by the wall of the tomb. The only thing we can say is this: somebody has carved its opaque and continuous surface, has written a few words on the stone, somebody whose name is *ego*.

Now if we relate the three levels of our analysis to each other, we ascertain two missing terms at the extreme poles of the descriptive sketch: on the first level, the fact that nothing indicates the painter and/or the viewer; on the third one, the fact that nothing in the inscription gives the name of its writer. Two missing terms that, once related to each other, reveal a relationship between the painter-viewer and the writer, the indication of the viewpoint of the whole painting and the name, the signifier of the vanishing point at its center.

However, at the same time, the question concerning a missing term at the "origin" of the painting and another one at its end allows us to acknowledge another function of the

Poussin's *The Arcadian Shepherds*

kneeling figure B: for, exactly like us who behold, read, "speak" the painting, the shepherd beholds, reads, "speaks" the written text on the tomb.

The Syntax of Legibility: Displacement

What is in question in this painting is finally what is in question in all paintings: What does it mean "to represent"? How is such a representational process articulated in and by its product, a painting that is a surface and a material support, geometrically defined, limited, and framed, in which the depth of another world is made visible? Here it would be useful to recall the results of our previous analyses:

1. The distinction between semiotics and semantics.
2. The distinction between discourse and story (narrative).
3. The transference of the first distinction to iconic representations:
   a. the legitimate perspective as a metaphor of the formal apparatus of enunciation;
   b. the contradictory postulates regarding (the mimetic representation displayed by) the representational screen as a transparent window open onto the world *and* as a mirror reflecting it.

Now my working hypothesis concerning the transference of the distinction between discourse and story to historical or narrative iconic representation is the following: The denial (in the Freudian sense) of the representational apparatus consists in the displacement of the vanishing point to the central movement of the story represented, and in the "lateralization" of the depth dimension from the level of *enunciation* (representation) to the level of what is *enounced* (the story represented).

I would like to emphasize this last point in our example: The whole critical literature devoted to *The Arcadian Shepherds* has underscored the contrast between an earlier version called the Chatsworth version[18] and the Louvre version. The

[18] *The Arcadian Shepherds.* 101 x 82 cms. The Chatsworth Settlement,

Louis Marin

change consists precisely in the lateralization of the depth structure of representation by situating the figures represented, the *istoria*, in a frieze parallel to the representational screen. The change has always been interpreted historically as a move from a baroque organization to a classical one.[19]

But it seems important to analyze the operations implied by such a move. They consist in: (1) displacing the vanishing point from the deep visible structure of perspective (i.e., the horizon of the represented space) to the central point of the legible foreground of the story represented (i.e., a lateral structure); (2) operating a ninety-degree rotation of the network of optical rays (whose poles are the viewpoint and the vanishing point) in order to locate them in a plane parallel to the representational screen, a plane which is scanned by the frieze disposition of the figures in two symmetrical groups where the equivalence of the viewpoint and the vanishing point appears simply reversed.

The viewpoint of the formal representational network becomes the starting point and the final point of the represented story, and the vanishing point becomes the central event, the moment of representation that is the focus of the story.

As J. Klein observed in his 1937 article,[20] the starting point of the story, the fact that A is looking at B, is reflected symmetrically by D looking at B and this is the end of the story, while the vanishing point is displaced to the central part of the scene, the two hands, the two forefingers pointing out

---

Chatsworth, Derbyshire, before 1631. Cf. A. Blunt, *Paintings of Nicolas Poussin*, p. 80, no. 119.

[19] See E. Panofsky, "*Et in Arcadia ego*: Poussin and the Elegiac Tradition," in *Meaning in the Visual Arts* (Garden City, N.Y., 1955). See also W. Weisbach, "*Et in Arcadia ego*: Ein Beitrag zur Interpretation antiker Vorstellungen in der Kunst des 17. Jahrhunderts," *Die Antike* 6 (1930); J. Klein, "An Analysis of Poussin's *Et in Arcadia ego*," *Art Bulletin* 19 (1937), 314ff.; A. Blunt, "Poussin's 'Et in Arcadia ego,' " *Art Bulletin* 20 (1938), 96ff.; W. Weisbach, "Et in Arcadia ego," *Gazette des Beaux-Arts* 2 (1938), 287ff.; M. Alpatov, "Poussin's 'Tancred and Erminia' in the Hermitage: An Interpretation," *Art Bulletin* 25 (1943), 134.

[20] J. Klein, "An Analysis," pp. 315-16.

Poussin's *The Arcadian Shepherds*

the locus of the event, the reading of an inscription—and even more precisely, the place of a cleft in the wall of the tomb and the place of a letter in the epitaph.

What is at stake in the "transformation" is to make representation escape its own process of constitution, which it nevertheless requires; to posit representation in its "objective" autonomy and independence, which it gets only from a subject who constitutes it in constituting himself through it.

But the story set on the stage by Poussin in this painting— the "event"—is not a historical event. The event here is the story of enunciation, or of representation. What is represented is the very process of representation. It is the enunciative *Aufhebung*, the negation-position of discourse, its self-referentiality, which is set on the stage by Poussin, who reverses the reference to the world into a reference to the subject-*ego*.

Spatial Structures and Iconographical Inferences

The three next stages of my analysis will be the following: (1) the spatial structure of the painting constituted by the disposition of the figures, the iconographical inferences concerning these figures and at the same time the hypotheses about the significance of the space that the location of the figures displays; (2) the semantic problem posed by the inscription and the implications of that problem concerning the painting itself; (3) the question of the central locus of the picture: text and icon, and its implications concerning the representational negation.

We may forget for the moment the figures in the foreground to describe the stage and the setting of the story: a wild and rustic landscape, an Arcadia according to Polybius' *Historiae*,[21] a desert—as people called it in the seventeenth century—quite similar to landscapes we find in some of

[21] Polybius, *Histories*, iv. 20. On the relation between Arcadia and death, see Pausanias, *Graeciae Descriptio*, vol. 8, chap. 36, and the analyses of Rochholz, "Ohne Schatten, Ohne Seele, der Mythus von Körperschatten und vom Schattengeist," *Germania* 5 (1860), reprinted in *Deutscher Glaube und Brauch* 1 (1867), 59-130.

Louis Marin

Poussin's other paintings: *The Israelites Gathering Manna*, for example, whose "desert" had been discussed in the Royal Academy.[22] That wild nature is displayed in an amphitheater setting, a curved space enclosing the tomb, whose bulky and heavy volume neutralizes all transitions between the foreground and the background, a technique which Poussin masters in his "ideal" landscapes. Such an opposition between the landscape setting and the tomb is here a radical one, since compared with the tomb in the Chatsworth version, the tomb in the Louvre *Arcadian Shepherds* is located in a plane almost parallel to the plane of the screen.

However, the fact that the tomb is presented in a slightly oblique position creates a dynamic stage-space on which the scene is represented, and at the same time emphasizes the two still and static figures standing at the front corners of the tomb. The woman on the right and the shepherd on the left in a sense play the role of the corner statues of the tomb, living statues such as one finds often in Poussin's paintings, but monumental and static enough to possess a particular significance in the narrative groups they belong to. The fact that the tomb is obliquely located on the representational stage places the man behind and the woman in front and gives them the function of the virtues found traditionally in the funerary art of the sixteenth and seventeenth centuries, which protect the deceased and exalt his attributes.[23]

It may be useful to explore such a reading hypothesis for a moment. With these two figures, as we have already seen, the narrative begins and ends by coming back to its central sequence through their two gazes. With them the narrative action finds its beginning and its end in two attitudes of rest and stillness, which nevertheless underlie the central moment of the story. But considered as Tomb-Virtues, these two figures somehow go beyond the mere narrative level: as symbolic figures or allegories, they illustrate in some way what Poussin meant by *delectatio*, the very end of painting. As

[22] Félibien, *Entretiens*, p. 98.

[23] See E. Panofsky, *Tomb Sculpture: Its Changing Aspects from Ancient Egypt to Bernini* (New York, 1964).

Poussin's *The Arcadian Shepherds*

A. Blunt has pointed out: "Diletto or delectatio had a very specific sense for the art critics at the end of the sixteenth century, for whom allegory was the essential part of poetry. For them, the genuine delectatio was produced by the intellectual beauty of allegory."[24] However, in *The Arcadian Shepherds*, Poussin integrates allegories into the story in so very subtle and almost indiscernable a way that as readers of the painting we cannot give demonstrative evidence of the significance of the figures, but only what we imagine or dream about them. For example, if we compare the attitude and the appearance of the shepherd on the right with the Apollo in *The Inspiration of the Epic Poet*, we may think of him as a symbolic figure of history, the prose epics, with the difference that in the *Inspiration* the poet is going to write under Apollo's dictation, while in *The Arcadian Shepherds* the man he beholds only attempts to read something that is already written. On the right side, the "shepherdess" (the interlocutor of the shepherd whom she taps gently with her hand but whose silent question she seems to ignore; the woman who contemplates the kneeling man with a peaceful aloofness) makes the beholder-reader dream of a figure of Mnemosyne who remembers an enigmatic meaning, the meaning of the epitaph by an ineffable anamnesis. Her monumental stature, her presentation in profile, the position of her left arm and hand on her hip, her statuelike eye without vision, all these traits evoke a Cartesian admiration, the originary passion for knowledge without any bodily effects, the memory of an originary loss. Is not the sense of the question silently asked by her companion: "What is the name of the written *ego* in the inscription that the reader tries to decipher?" And the sense of her answer: "You, reader, are condemned to decipher, and nevertheless, you will not know anything. You remember only one thing: that you have always already forgotten everything." A silent dialogue without any anxiety: decipherment, the fate of an endless interpretation, is in its very indecidabil-

[24] A. Blunt, ed., *Nicolas Poussin: Lettres et Propos sur l'Art* (Paris, 1964), pp. 162-64, n. 18.

Louis Marin

ity the way in which living people neutralize the anxiety of an originary loss and liberate themselves from death.

We may now come back to the narrative and to its two loci occupied by the two "active" figures of the two opposed groups on the left and on the right (Figures B and C), two figures symmetrically distributed in complementarity, reversed in relation to a central axis, the first one spelling out the inscription through his gaze and gesture, the other pointing out the tomb and/or his companion and questioning the "shepherdess" Memory, his memory. Subtle differences make this symmetry more sophisticated: the counterpoint of a dominant movement spreads out from the left to the right, that is, in the reading orientation of the painting and of the inscription, an orientation emphasized by the gaze of the shepherd toward the woman. That movement is combined with another compositional line, a zigzag diagonal which is broken in the middle of the painting at the very center of the architectural "chiasmus" that the two groups of figures exhibit: a focus point that is the geometrical center of the whole painting, just between the right and the left hands of B and C. Superimposed upon this complex compositional articulation, the shepherds' staffs trace a vigorous network of straight lines. And if A. Blunt can read the Heraclitean bow and lyre (objects which are represented in the painting as Apollo's and Cupid's attributes) in the composition of Poussin's last work, *Apollo and Daphne*,[25] why should I not read in *The Arcadian Shepherds* an enigmatic ideogram, or better still a monogram, M, as the first letter of *Mors* inscribed by the very organization of the painting as well as by what it represents, a tomb and an epitaph?

A last remark about the distribution of the figures: through the way in which B and C are joined to A and D, the corner statues of the tomb, they may be viewed as their figurative emanations but with a reversion that allows, in spite of the shallowness of the stage, for the opening of a spatial and semantic depth. The Apollo-like figure on the left produces

[25] A. Blunt, *Nicolas Poussin*, Bollingen Series 35: 7 (New York, 1967), 348-50.

Poussin's *The Arcadian Shepherds*

the shepherd who reads the inscription, while on the right the man who asks what is its meaning and *ego*'s name, turns to the Memory figure, who seems to know the answer. Such a reading, which springs out of the formal and compositional organization of the representation, may be substantiated by a piece of iconographical evidence: the roughly squared rock, a plastic metonymy of the tomb upon which the right group is connected, appears, from Raphael to Ripa, as one of the attributes of Clio, the Muse of History, a sign of her correct remembrance of past events;[26] hence that movement from the back to the front which is reversed at the very place of the inscription. From history to its decipherment and from the question about meaning to Memory, the space of the representation is unfolded through the represented figures by a twist in the center area, while at the same time the narrative sequence is articulated—or more exactly, the discourse by which the story is articulated is allowed to take place.

"Et in Arcadia ego": A Semantic Problem

Once more our reading is led to that central locus, a syncope or break between the two groups of figures, a locus and a moment of the narrative transformation which is filled up by the inscription "Et in Arcadia ego." We have now come to its grammatical and semantic analysis, which was the subject of Panofsky's remarkable study. How are we to translate the inscription: "Even in Arcady, I am" or "I too was born or lived in Arcady"? In the first case, it is Death itself that writes the inscription on the tomb; in the second, it is a dead shepherd who has written his epitaph. Panofsky builds his essay on a cross-argumentation: If we choose the first translation, we do not take into account the elegiac meditation that gives the Louvre version (as compared to the Chatsworth one) its specific atmosphere. With the second translation, we are faithful to the nostalgic mood of the painting but we make a

[26] See, for instance, an engraving after Raphael by Marcantonio Raimondi: *Clio and Urania,* and E. Wind's commentary in *Pagan Mysteries in the Renaissance* (London, 1958), p. 127; or the painting by Le Sueur: "Clio Euterpes and Thalia."

Louis Marin

grammatical mistake, since "the adverbial *et* invariably refers to the noun or the pronoun directly following it and this means that it belongs, in our case, not to *ego* but to *Arcadia*."[27] The way in which Panofsky poses the problem is perfectly consistent with his philosophy of art history as a constant displacement of motives and themes, forms and legends, vision and iconography—connections and displacements that point out the iconological level of cultural symbols. For some years, a very fruitful controversy has taken place between Panofsky, Weisback, Blunt, and Klein, a discussion that was initiated, as Panofsky observed, in the seventeenth century with the diverging interpretations of Bellori and Félibien.[28]

However, the question of the translation and meaning of "Et in Arcadia ego" does not seem to me correctly raised by Panofsky in his apparently rigorous philological analysis: "The phrase *Et in Arcadia ego* is one of those elliptical sentences like *Summum jus, summa injuria, E pluribus unum, Nequid Mimis*, or *Sic Semper tyrannis*, in which the verb has to be supplied by the reader. This unexpressed verb must therefore be unequivocally suggested by the words given, and this means that it can never be a preterit. . . . it is also possible though fairly unusual to suggest a future as in Neptune's famous *quos ego* ("These I shall deal with"); but it is not possible to suggest a past tense."[29] It seems to me that the key question lies in the difference between a phrase like *Summum jus, summa injuria* and Neptune's *quos ego*. Do we have a nominal sentence (*Summum jus . . .*) or an *oratio imperfecta*, an incomplete sentence? If it is a nominal sentence, then, according to Benveniste's study,[30] its basic characteristics would be the following: (1) it is a sentence that cannot be reduced to a complete sentence whose verb "to be" would be absent; (2) it is a nontemporal, nonpersonal, nonmodal sentence, since it bears upon terms that are reduced to their basic semantic con-

[27] *Meaning in the Visual Arts*, p. 306.
[28] See note 19 above, as well as G. Bellori, *Le Vite dei pittori, scultori et architetti moderni* (Rome, 1672), pp. 447ff.; and Félibien, *Entretiens*, p. 71.
[29] *Meaning in the Visual Arts*, p. 306.
[30] *Problèmes* 1: 151ff.

Poussin's *The Arcadian Shepherds*

tent; (3) such a sentence cannot relate the time of an event to the time of discourse about the event, since it asserts a quality appropriate to the subject of the utterance without any relationships to the speaker (the subject of enunciation); (4) the inventory of its uses in Greek and Latin texts shows that it is always employed to state permanent truths, and it assumes an absolute and nontemporal relation expressed as an authoritative proof in direct speech. What seems to me to make difficult the interpretation of *Et in Arcadia ego* as a nominal sentence is the presence of *ego* in the phrase, *ego* which designates the speaker. In *ego*, a present is here and now implied and not a nontemporal present of a general assertion: "I (who speak here and now to you) lived in Arcadia." The past is referred to as past, but in relation to the present moment when I articulate the sentence.

So I am inclined to interpret the sentence as an incomplete one, *oratio imperfecta*, some parts of which have been erased. It lacks its verb, but also the proper name corresponding to *ego*. We may compare it, for instance, with one of the iconographical referents of the painting, Virgil's *Fifth Eclogue*, in which we find this epitaph of the shepherd Daphnis:

Daphnis ego in silvis hinc usque ad sidera notus
Formosi pecoris custos, formosior ipse.

"Daphnis ego in silvis . . . notus (sum)": *ego* is twice determined by the proper name, Daphnis, and by a verb in a past tense "notus sum." And we know that the identifying presence of the proper name is a permanent feature of funerary poetry.[31]

These last observations do not, however, solve all the questions raised by a statement written in the past tense and including an "enunciative" *I* and a proper name. In memoirs or autobiographical narratives, the *written I* is at one and the same time "I" and "he-she," "I—as he (or she)," I as another whose identity is nevertheless assumed by the writer beyond

[31] Cf. E. Galletier, *Etude sur la poésie funéraire romaine* (Paris, 1922); and John Sparrow, *Visible Words* (Cambridge, 1969).

321

the temporal gap marked by the past tense. In this case, "I" possesses, through writing, the status of a permanently divided *ego*, but one whose scission is constantly reinscribed and neutralized by the writing process. With an epitaph, the paradox of the writing "I" and the written "I" is insuperable, since the writer inscribes here and now—that is, *after* his death—his ego as a dead man.

My hypothesis would be to leave the inscription to its indiscernible meaning, an indeterminability which may be the sense of Poussin's painting: I mean a self-reflexive writing of history. The fact that *ego*'s name has disappeared makes *ego* a kind of "floating signifier" waiting for its fulfillment by our reading. The absence of a conjugated verbal form locates the sentence between present and past, identity and alterity, at their limits which are the very limits of representation. In other words, a certain representation of death refers to the process of representation as death, which writing (and painting as a writing process) tames and neutralizes among the living people who read and contemplate it.

The obliteration of the name and the verb in the inscription points out the operation enacted by the representational-narrative process and represents it as the concealment of the "enunciative" structure itself, thanks to which the past, death, loss, can come back here and now by our reading—but come back as representation, set up on its stage, the object of a serene contemplation exorcising all anxiety.

Text and Icon: The Representational "Negation" Represented

It seems to me that Poussin's *Arcadian Shepherds* bears some traces of the functioning of the historiographical process. But I do not offer this next stage of my reading as a conclusive explanation; it will be only a step further into the indeterminable area which is ultimately the contemplative reading of a painting—that area between proving and dreaming, vision and fantasy, analysis and projection, that Poussin calls delectation.

I would like to come back to the central space between the two groups of figures, and precisely to the part of the paint-

Poussin's *The Arcadian Shepherds*

ing imperatively pointed out by the two shepherds' forefingers. The index finger of the shepherd on the left is located on the letter *r* of the word *Arcadia*, that is the central letter of the inscription and also the central point of the painting resulting from the displacement of the vanishing point from the horizon of the representational stage to the wall of the tomb. That *r* is the initial of the name of Cardinal Rospigliosi, who invented the phrase "Et in Arcadia ego" and commissioned the painting we have been studying. This letter *r*, a pure signifier which takes the place of the vanishing point and viewpoint on the tomb, the place of death, is a kind of "hypogrammatic" signature of a name, that of the author of the motto and of the painting as well. It is the signifier of the name of the Father of the painting in the place of the painter-beholder: Rospigliosi, who commissioned two other paintings by Poussin whose allegories might signify the symbols that *The Arcadian Shepherds* reveal: *Time Saving Truth from Envy and Discord*, and *A Dance of the Ages of Life to the Music of Time*.[32]

The other shepherd's forefinger is located on a vertical cleft in the tomb wall, a crack situated straight up the break which divides the stage ground and isolates the "shepherdess" on the right. That cleft splits the inscription, the legible syntagm written in the painting. Moreover, while it runs *between* the two words of the first line, *in* and *Arcadia*, it *divides e/go*. That "pun," right in the center of the painting, indicates what is at stake in it: a gap between two gestures, between the initial of the name of the Father (of the motto and the painting) and the splitting of the writing-painting Ego, the *ego* of the representation of Death in Arcadia; a scission of the absent name of the painter, who nevertheless has made the painting and who signifies that he too is in Arcadia, but as one absent from that blissful place which is nothing else than the painting itself.

A last word: We observe that the light of the sunset projects

[32] See Bellori, *Le Vite dei pittori*, pp. 447ff., and Panofsky, *Meaning in the Visual Arts*, p. 305, n. 29. See A. Blunt, *Paintings of Nicolas Poussin*, p. 81, no. 123 for *Time Saving Truth from Envy and Discord*, original lost; in the Palazzo Rospigliosi till about 1800.

the shadow of the shepherd who attempts to decipher the inscription onto the tomb wall, as an unexpected version of the Platonic myth of the cave: his shadow, his vanishing double, his image, is inscribed in that other painting within the painting which is the opaque wall of the tomb. So, the tomb is somehow the painting, a surface reflecting only shadows, reflections, appearances where the actual happiness, Arcady, is lost and found again but only as its double, or rather as its representation. If the shadow of the shepherd's arm and hand points out the letter *r* of the Father's name, it traces too on the wall of the tomb, not an arm and a hand, but a scythe, the attribute of Saturn, who reigns over the Arcadian Golden Age, the attribute of Cronos too, the castrating God and Chronos, Time, who makes everything pass away; the scythe which we also find as an allegorical sign in the two other paintings commissioned by Rospigliosi and which would be in *The Arcadian Shepherds* a kind of "hypogrammatic icon."

Demonstration or fantasy, I leave my reading indeterminate: self-conscious intentions of Poussin, who modestly said: "Je n'ai rien négligé," or enigmatic operations of the painting always in excess of its reading. This may be the "Golden Bough" Poussin alludes to,[33] Virgil's Golden Bough that opens the gates of horn and ivory through which the actual shadows and dreamed recollections come to light: my reading of *The Arcadian Shepherds* has no other justification than my "delectation" in a painting of Poussin, who was said by Bernini to be a great myth maker.[34]

Et in Arcadia ego could be read as a message sent by Poussin in order to signify that from the representation of death—that is, the writing of history—to representation *as* death and as delight, history in the history painting is our contemporary myth.

[33] N. Poussin, *Correspondance*, ed. Jouanny, de Nobele, Archives de la Société de l'Art français (Paris, 1968), p. 463.

[34] P. Fréart de Chantelou, "Voyage du cavalier Bernin en France," in *Actes du colloque international Poussin* (Paris, 1960), 2: 127.

| *Michel Beaujour* | Exemplary Pornography: Barrès, Loyola, and the Novel |

We are "infantilized" by all "higher" forms. Man, tortured by his mask, fabricates secretly, for his own usage, a sort of "subculture": a world made out of the refuse of a higher world of culture, a domain of trash, immature myths, inadmissible passions . . . a secondary domain of compensation. That is where a shameful poetry is born, a certain compromising beauty.

Witold Gombrowicz
Preface, *Pornografia*

In order to avoid the kind of frivolity that holds ethical concerns to be irrelevant in a discussion of the reader in (of) texts, it may be wise to revisit briefly the Russian critical tradition. This tradition has entertained with high seriousness the notion—somewhat disreputable in the West—that literature, and particularly fiction, must be held accountable, since it encodes messages which affect not only the subjective world view of readers, but their attitudes and actions. Novels are presumed capable of endangering (or reinforcing) the structure of society and the legal order.[1] Rufus Mathewson's analysis of Russian radical poetics and its Soviet progeny[2] pinpoints a persistent bias of the rhetorically skewed poetics:

[1] This view is shared by rhetorical critics, such as Wayne C. Booth, but they water it down to meaninglessness in trying to exculpate "great" novels.

[2] Rufus W. Mathewson, Jr., in *The Positive Hero in Russian Literature* (New York, 1958), p. 118, describes the Russian radicals' intent "to control the

Michel Beaujour

Radical criticism displayed a parental concern for the immediate effect of a literary work upon the reader's conduct and morale. In this setting art becomes discourse not between equals but between teacher and students, or for that matter, between fathers and children. Turgenev's remark that Chernyshevsky's dissertation set forth a view of art for "immature" people is very shrewd, for these matters are the proper concern of juvenile literature.[3]

While experienced readers may wish literature to be a liberal intercourse between mature people who have resolved their "Oedipal" conflicts and achieved a *modus vivendi* with law and order, the conception of literature as a teacher and/or corrupter of minors (including women) has been—and may still be—prevalent. This attitude is particularly suspicious of the novel, and fiction in general. Roland Barthes' provocative remarks: "Can literature be for us anything but a childhood memory?" and "Literature is what is taught, period. It is a school subject"[4] are less paradoxical than incomplete: for literature also is that which teaches outside the classroom, and for a long time its domain was virtually divided between classics, and the rest: the classics taught (or were made to teach) what is proper, while the rest taught what is improper, particularly to women and idlers. Much of that rest was made up of romances and novels. Thanks to Georges May's excellent

---

reader's response by drawing the conclusions within the work of art, and by showing the action they hoped he would take." This account of Russian radical poetics broadly coincides with Susan Suleiman's definition of the *roman à thèse*: "A narrative told by the narrator who addresses directly the reader, telling him how to interpret the narrative and commanding him, in the end, to perform a series of actions imitating those of the protagonist of the narrative" [author's translation]. "Pour une poétique du roman à thèse: l'exemple de Nizan," *Critique* 330 (1974), 1001.

[3] Mathewson, *The Positive Hero*, pp. 117-18.

[4] Barthes, "Réflexions sur un manuel," in Doubrovsky and Todorov, eds., *L'Enseignement de la littérature* (Paris, 1971), p. 170. Barthes is, of course, suggesting here that texts written for, and enjoyed by, adults ought to be called by a name other than *littérature*. That is another set of problems.

Barrès, Loyola, and the Novel

account of the controversy, we know the many arguments formulated for and, overwhelmingly, against the novel in mid-eighteenth-century France. One ingenious—or naive —argument against its outright ban was that the novel could be a painless complement (or ersatz) to rhetorical training: "The main merit of novels being that they are usually well written, it follows that their readers gain a certain ease of expression, either in correspondence or in conversation, which cannot fail to make them worthier of note in society." Still, the writer of these words, Mme de Benouville, is careful to stress that the novel is beneficial only to those readers with a firm soul and a trained mind who have reached a reasonable age and are imbued with solid principles. The novel ("ingenious twaddle," in her words) can therefore benefit only those readers who do not normally indulge in novel reading.[5] It may well be that the situation has changed only insofar as the criteria for inclusion among the classics have been relaxed, and all sorts of books, including novels, are now used to teach what is proper. Moreover, all literary modes of address and encoded-reader responses to them have been so modified, if not perverted, by academic mediation that a study of the reader in (of) texts may have become a purely academic question. But let us pretend that literature still functions as it did in more innocent, more threatened, times.

Turgenev (who knew something of these matters) perceived that Chernyshevsky's esthetics considered the father-to-children or teacher-to-pupil mode of allocution the most efficient one, because it infantilized the audience. Turgenev apparently assumed that other allocutory vectors were possible: the father-to-father vector, for instance, which would imply some sort of antichildren complicity; or the child-to-children (woman-to-woman) vector which, suggesting as it does an antifathers or antihusbands conspiracy, might be more modern; and finally there might be child-to-fathers, woman-to-men addresses, implying a plea, or a recrimina-

[5] See May, *Le Dilemme du roman au XVIIIe siècle* (Paris, 1962), p. 70.

327

Michel Beaujour

tion. It is clear that the addresser enjoys authority over his addressee only within the Chernyshevskyan scheme. The above are all simple, and probably oversimplified, models. More complex and interesting are the intermediate modes, in which the distance (or proximity) between addresser and addressee is merely attenuated or made ambiguous. Such modes of address would encode some degree of resistance to paternal law. One variant of this oblique mode might be called Gombrowiczian, another Barrèsian. Texts generated along these vectors can indeed be called *juvenile*, if we load the word with other connotations than those conveyed by *juvenile literature*, and closer perhaps to those of *juvenilia*. The addresser of these texts enjoys limited authority since he does not stand *in loco parentis*, nor does he purport to win children over to paternal law. Yet these oblique modes may adumbrate a new law, or appeal to a law different from that of the fathers.

Thus, the Gombrowiczian model sees adult man split between two sets of incompatible laws:

> Man, as we know, aims at the absolute. At fulfillment. At truth, at God, at total maturity. . . . To seize everything, to realize himself entirely—this is his imperative.
>
> Now, in *Pornografia* it seems to me that another of man's aims appears, a more secret one; undoubtedly, one which is in some ways illegal: his need for the unfinished . . . for imperfection . . . for inferiority . . . for youth.[6]

The guilty choice of immaturity and imperfection ties Gombrowicz to a modern tradition which, in French literature, runs at least from Baudelaire to Bataille, Genet, and beyond. In this scheme, despite his awareness of "higher" forms and their demands, a reluctant grown-up incites his lower, law-breaking self to address whatever is immature in other grown-ups, through a "shameful poetry" derived from a

[6] Witold Gombrowicz, Preface to *Pornografia*, trans. Alastair Hamilton (New York, 1967), p. 5.

"domain of trash, immature myths, inadmissible passions."[7]
In the Gombrowiczian model, guilt upholds the higher law.
The title of Gombrowicz's novel indicates that such texts are
not revolutionary, for they invite the reader to guilty in-
dulgence rather than to the overthrow of mature paternal im-
peratives. Pornography is not a thesis, nor even an antithesis;
if the *roman à thèse* always implies the possibility of a dialectical progress, the *roman pornographique* is, in Bataille's terminology, heterological. Yet it may express (at once manifest
and defuse) a protest by the politically, socially impotent.

Hence, the following hypothesis: there is at least one category of novels which serves for its reader the same function
as does *possession* in those societies where the body/mind separation is less rigid than in the West. Such novels incite fantasy rather than coded hysterical behavior: reading them is an
attenuated form of protest against fathers, husbands, and social rules that discriminate against women as well as against
other social and age groups. Novel reading is a mild disas-
sociative state, in which the reader is possessed by alien
spirits. Novels are diabolical, or at least one of the devil's favorite vehicles into the hearts of the weak and immature, but
fantasizing is, in the eyes of authority, preferable to acting
out. Yet, sterner religious and political thinkers condemn fantasy and the novel as strenuously as they do active sin: they
are well aware that sinning in thought may be useful to the
peace of home and school, but it is nonetheless serious sinning and potentially disruptive.[8]

The Gombrowiczian stance, then, postulates a more harmonious, less rigorous order than the one imposed by mature
norms when they triumph over all forms of immaturity. In
short, Gombrowiczian pornography is homologous to most
modern poetics that have claimed to redress the imbalance
inherent in modern, technical societies. The only major practical differences arise from ideological and historic con-

[7] Ibid., p. 8.
[8] For a survey of fantasy's apotheosis in modern times, and traditional
theological condemnation thereof, see Elemire Zolla, *Storia del Fantasticare*
(Milan, 1964).

Michel Beaujour

straints: poetry may be allowed to vegetate in its ghetto, or it may be suppressed and driven underground.

Barrès' model, in *Un homme libre*, is more subtle, for it plays the periphery against the center, and the norm against its transgression. Instead of a dualistic anthropological model, in which two hierarchical levels oppose their conflicting laws, we find three poles in Barrès: the mature norm, the immature desire, and a distant mediator, or archaic norm. The novel invites its reader to take advantage of a situation where an archaic deity can be invoked, in devious fashion, against the new secular norm (itself ironically termed alien or *barbarian*). The ritual of possession by the displaced deity is turned into that of self-possession. The old God is used against the new ones, but not reinstated to his former central, normative position. He remains as a source of negativity for the secular positive hero, and for the reader.

The hero of this ironical first-person narrative[9] is a very young man of independent means and exquisite sensibility. Wearied of the soulless vulgarity of the world and its pragmatic philosophies—but quite alien to Christian charity and self-denial—he retires with a like-minded friend to a big house in a dull part of France that happens to be the province of their ancestry. The two lead a scrupulously self-indulgent, monastic life, devoting much of their time to spiritual exercises and meditation upon the lives and works of various romantic figures. These meditations, which adapt to strictly egotistic ends the methods of Christian spirituality, are reported in detail. There are also meditations upon the quite unremarkable landmarks of Lorraine, which provide a bridge to the virtues of the hero's forebears. After a few months of this excitingly dull way of life, the hero travels to Venice, where he finds at last the objective correlative for his self, as

[9] *Un homme libre*, published in 1889 when Barrès was twenty-seven years old, is the second volume of the trilogy, *Le Culte du moi*. The trilogy, and *Un homme libre* in particular, made Barrès famous, earning him the title of "prince de la jeunesse." A few years later, the publication of *Les Déracinés* (1897), which inaugurated a new trilogy, *Le Roman de l'énergie nationale*, signaled Barrès' "conversion" from individualism to right-wing nationalism.

Barrès, Loyola, and the Novel

the dying city makes him realize that the self extends well beyond the empirical, and even the ancestral, into an ancient unconscious. He is but an avatar of past selves. Strengthened by this timeless self-awareness, and freed from the limits of mere ego, the hero, now a Free Man, goes back into the world, which he scornfully challenges. This narrative will serve as a model for other young men to follow.

The oblique scheme devised by Barrès, and outlined in his dedication of *Un homme libre* to schoolboys (*collégiens*), may be seen as a hybrid combining some features of Gombrowiczian pornography, and some of the *roman à thèse*: "I write for children, and very young men. Were I to please grown-ups, I should be very proud, but there really is no need for them to read me. They have undertaken by themselves the experiments I am about to record, they have systematized their lives, or else they were not born to hearken to me. In either case, reading this would be superfluous."[10] The status of the addresser is unclear. On the one hand, he refers to adults in childish language ("grown-ups"), thus embracing the immaturity of his alleged audience; on the other, he addresses adults (ostensibly excluded from that audience) over the head of his immature audience: he knows all about experiments leading to mature systematization. The addresser, like his language, straddles childhood and adulthood.

But Barrès' dedication does not simply define an audience (a certain category of youths). It also defines the book as a guide to be followed in the course of a transgressive *rite de passage*. The verbal gesture warding off adults while paying lip service to their wisdom raises the specter of law, of a limit perhaps to be transgressed, but it does not clarify the position that the addresser assigns to himself. There is neither a call to revolt nor a defense of the status quo.

Un homme libre presents itself as a *method* to be followed by sensitive schoolboys who, while wishing to avoid despair and the condition of barbarians, seek to achieve peace and happiness: "This *method*, I have explained and justified it, I

[10] Barrès, dédicace d' *Un homme libre*, *Le Culte du moi* (Paris, 1964), p. 139. [Author's translation.] Further citations are given in the text.

Michel Beaujour

believe, in the fiction the reader is about to read. I should have wished to gather it into a symbol, to emphasize it in twenty-five very erudite, very obscure and somewhat severe pages; but my only care being the service of those schoolboys I cherish, I restrained myself to the most juvenile form imaginable: a diary" (p. 141). This last paragraph of the dedication, a commentary on the generic and stylistic choices that produced the fiction in question, is exactly homologous to the first. The opposition between a virtual adult form (nonfictional, concise, erudite, severe) and the deliberate realization of a childish one emphasizes that the addresser, while not being himself a child, can make himself childlike. No such alternative is open to his intended readers, the juvenile diary writers. The addresser chooses the form rhetorically best suited to his audience. However, this is not a *true* diary, but a *trope* for a conceptual, philosophical essay.[11] This is also an invitation to read the novel "philosophically," at least "symbolically" or allegorically: there is more to it than meets the eye. The symbol or dense treatise is a *higher* form than the *conceit* of the diary; yet the *lower* form has been deliberately chosen as more likely to provide its young reader with an immediately useful model.

Thus Barrès exemplifies the deliberate choice of literary juvenility, through which the addresser of the text is enabled to dodge the alternative: *in loco parentis* or *in loco pueri*? Although obviously rhetorical and "manipulative," the mode of address is made to appear horizontal rather than vertical, allowing a maieutic mediation to operate between the reader and his inchoate desire.

The scheme, however, seems even more obvious when we try to construct, as Susan Suleiman did in her analysis of Nizan's *romans à thèse*, the Greimasian model of *Adjuvants* and *Opposants*:[12] the paternal slot, although ostensibly a mild and

---

[11] Sartre's decision to turn his "factum sur la contingence" into a fictional diary (first written with the allegorical—or emblematic—title of *Melancholia*, then with the "realistic" title of *La Nausée*) is analogous. We know it did not fail to attract schoolboys.

[12] For the Greimasian model of actants, see A.-J. Greimas, *Sémantique*

Barrès, Loyola, and the Novel

easily placated *Opposant* here, can also be filled by an ideological superego (the cult of ancestors, for instance, or that of a *genius loci*), and thus become a *Destinateur*, the very role performed in Nizan's *romans à thèse* by Communist orthodoxy—a role that could be performed by any authority with a claim to legitimacy. Barrès, as it turns out, aims to undermine the law of the fathers by appealing to that of worthier ancestors, the once and future Law.

We have achieved a preliminary fix on addresser and text: both embody a deliberate (but neither innocent nor "authentic") choice of juvenility. There remains the question of the addressee and actual audience. Although not an isolated case, Barrès' dedication is unusually specific as to the target of the book: schoolboys, adolescents. Grown-ups are not to bother. Not a word about girls, women: we understand they also are to keep out. An exceptionally narrow audience, and much less flexible than, for instance, Stendhal's "happy few": anyone may fancy himself/herself among the elect (who, indeed, would feel left out by Stendhal's gentlemanly flattery?), but one either *is* a schoolboy or not. Is this choice of a male juvenile audience to be taken seriously, however? In short, does *Un homme libre* tend to "fictionalize" its readers, despite its verbal gesture toward a real, sociologically and historically determined audience?

It is striking, and perhaps not altogether coincidental, that the formidable, controversial, and paradoxical assertion "The writer's audience is always a fiction"[13] should have been made by the man most responsible for our understanding of the process of infantilization undergone by classical literatures (and poetics) in the rhetorically oriented classroom. Of course, if one shares his ontological assumptions, one hardly

---

structurale (Paris, 1966), pp. 172-92; for Suleiman's analysis, see "Pour une poétique du roman à thèse," pp. 1004-7 and 1012-16.

[13] Walter J. Ong, S.J. "The Writer's Audience Is Always a Fiction," *PMLA* 90 (1975), 9-21. I suspect that in this essay, Ong does not use the word *fiction* in its literary, but in its *legal* sense: e.g., "certain fictions which writers of learned articles and books generally observe and which have to do with reader status" (p. 19).

Michel Beaujour

needs a demonstration or empirical evidence to accept Ong's statement, which is as "true" as any ideologically overdetermined tautology. If only Presence of the Word is "real," then even the Gospel's and Saint Paul's audiences are fictions. But this begs the question: aren't subjects involved in communication—verbal, written, or otherwise—always "fictions"? there remains only a question of degree, of differences that are best studied in the context of cultural semiology, to which Ong has also contributed important studies (on bilingualism, oral residue in written texts, classroom procedures, and the significance of Method in the Renaissance).

Whether readers of *Un homme libre* must learn "to conform themselves to the projections" of the addresser and "fictionalize" their response is both a trivial and an incomplete question; a trivial one because it applies to all cultural texts that are perceived as such, and an incomplete one because it leaves out the cultural determinants of both "conformity" and "fictionalization."

On the other hand, Barrès' choice of the juvenile diary form is meaningful, for this is not a classical genre; Barrès' book could not, therefore, be confused, by an audience of schoolboys for whom classical (both ancient and French) literature had been infantilized and turned into a pedagogical tool, with those texts that were used for classroom imitation and indoctrination. *Un homme libre* was to be read as a nonschool book, as an antitextbook, an antidote to classroom ideology: not only as a *novel*, which in itself would have been a slightly sinful allurement, but as a secret shared among young people, and ipso facto, a transgression.

The fictional diary hardly conforms to the expectations raised by our preliminary description: it deals very scantily with sex, religious doubts, vague yearnings. But it does purport to provide its reader with a *Method*, and this Method is derived from unexpected sources: mainly the *Imitation of Jesus-Christ* and Loyola's *Spiritual Exercises*. The reader is invited to model himself on the (unnamed) diarist who has devised and applied through action, exercises, and meditation a method for the cultivation of the Self. This method is an

Barrès, Loyola, and the Novel

adaptation to secular and self-centered purposes of the most efficient procedures devised by Renaissance Christianity to help believers shape themselves (with God's grace) on the pattern of the Savior.

Whatever contradictions we may anticipate in this curious undertaking, a formal one is immediately apparent: how can a *diary* also be a *method*? We easily understand that the diary, presenting an *example*, is one possible form of exemplary fiction; all diaries, for that matter, are both exemplary and cautionary. But one expects a method to be presented in a didactic, impersonal, expository fashion, rather than through personal narrative. Yet, Descartes himself resorted to the exemplary rather than the didactic mode of exposition:

> My present design, then, is not to teach the method which each ought to follow for the correct conduct of his Reason, but solely to describe the way in which I have endeavored to conduct my own . . . as this Tract is put forth merely as a history, or, if you will, as a tale in which, amid some examples worthy of imitation, there will be found, perhaps, as many more which it were advisable not to follow, I hope it will prove useful to some without being hurtful to any, and that my openness will find some favor with all.[14]

Descartes' *captatio benevolentiae* relies on the same pedagogic assumptions, the same low profile, as Barrès' "dedication." The best way to convey a method is not to teach it but to narrate one's own experience, in the hope that others will see its worth and follow in the same path, while avoiding the leader's errors. This is an initiatory pedagogy, rather than a preceptive one. It addresses a solitary reader, unlike textbooks which posit a classroom situation.

In this passage Descartes blurs the old Aristotelian distinction between *history* (true, but not necessarily *vraisemblable*) and *tale* (or fiction: *vraisemblable* but not necessarily true); and

[14] René Descartes, *Discourse on Method*, part I (London, 1912), trans. John Veitch.

he insists on the notions of *example* and *imitation*: "I set down my own experience in such a way that it may become an example worthy—on the whole—of imitation."[15] One is led to the conclusion that the *Discourse on Method* is a modern, secular, "first-person" variant of the Christian *Imitatio*, while Descartes' *Meditations on First Philosophy* ought to be seen as an adaptation to philosophical enquiry of models developed for the purpose of religious meditation. In either case, the story of Christ and his Passion is displaced by the narration of an individual's quest for universally valid secular certainties. Yet this quest retains certain features of its religious model. In the process of transcoding—even though no sacrilege is intended by Descartes—the Christian quest appears as *one* possible variant of a structure, and it therefore loses its absolute referential status as a norm. The door is open to a generalized relativism, in which any *ego* will be able to place himself squarely (or obliquely) in the position previously reserved for Christ: the seeker and the sought are in a sense one, although divided between several conflicting instances. Furthermore, the meaning of "imitation" is turned around. In the Christian model, the reader is expected to imitate Christ, not the author of the text, or to meditate on His life, not on that of the writer, while the secular model enjoins its reader to imitate the addresser of the text and to meditate on his individual thoughts. For the Renaissance, of course, with its ability to separate the domain of Faith and that of Reason, and for Descartes particularly, who believed his method to be universal rather than idiosyncratic, the opposition is purely functional. One could imitate both Christ and Descartes, or rather seek salvation as well as rational certainties. For Descartes, there is nothing personal, self-centered, autobiographical, about his rhetorical choice of the exemplum as a persuasive exposition of universal procedure. Yet, as Philippe Lejeune has so justly noted,

[15] Susan Suleiman, "Pour une poétique du roman à thèse," and "Le récit exemplaire," *Poétique*, no. 32 (1977), proposes the hypothesis that the *roman à thèse* is an extension of the traditional, rhetorical exemplum. The *Discourse on Method* would therefore be a *roman à thèse*. I would suggest that the *roman à thèse* is an orthodox variant of the exemplary novel.

following Valéry, the *Discourse on Method* "may be the model for autobiography because of the simple and powerful fashion in which the narrative explains how an intellectual personality builds itself up against the surrounding world, but also because of the peculiar position the *Discourse* holds in Descartes' work, functioning not as a theoretical treatise, but as a personal balance-sheet."[16] Descartes' exemplum becomes, therefore, polysemous: we can read it as an example of the positive intellectual hero, as a universal model for the conduct of reason, or as a fateful departure from Christian Imitation.

The personal exemplum is a very slippery device. Barrès made explicit in *Un homme libre* some repressed implications of his chosen model, as he trampled on the French classical tenet "le moi est haïssable." One of these implications is that the personal, secular exemplum is still felt (within Christian culture) to be a perverted variant of the *Imitatio Christi*. The addresser-narrator is perceived (though faintly or virtually) as a *figura*—positive or negative—of Christ, because there is no mode of self-exemplification that is not derived, perhaps across several mediations, from the discourses originally devised, in a Christian cultural context, to bring the believer into greater conformity with his Savior and to shed, in the process, his own sinful peculiarities. Paradoxically, then, the personal exemplum remains orthopedic even when it purports to present a model of egoism: the subject of the exemplum seeks greater conformity with his presumed entelechy and destiny; at the same time, the addresser enjoins the addressee to undertake the same quest of ego, to shed in the process all that is not his own glorious idiosyncrasy. Descartes' *Discourse* again appears to be an unwitting archetype for this type of discourse. Approaching such texts as the *Discourse* or *Un homme libre* with a purely contemplative or esthetic bias would be grossly to misread their rhetorical, persuasive, exemplary intention.

Barrès, of course, reveals his intention through his choice

---

[16] Lejeune, *L'Autobiographie en France* (Paris, 1971), p. 59.

of predominant intertexts: the *Imitatio*, and above all Loyola's *Spiritual Exercises*. The latter is a peculiar text indeed, which the narrator-hero of *Un homme libre* describes as follows: "An arid book, but an infinitely fecund one, its machinery always was, for me, the most suggestive sort of reading; the book of a dilettante, and a fanatic. It dilates my skepticism, and my contempt; it strips down all that is held respectable, while ministering to my desire for enthusiasm; it could make me a free man, the absolute master of myself."[17] This is a deliberate misreading. Yet, malicious enemies of the Jesuits might praise Barrès' perspicacity. The exact nature of the *Exercises* is a peripheral issue, however; the central one is that the nameless narrator of Barrès' novel presents himself to the reader in the guise of a reader, underscoring the power of a book to make him *free* and a *master of himself*, thereby implying that the addressee can, in his turn, derive the same benefit from *this* text. But the implicit equation "you stand to gain from this book as I did from the *Exercises*" obscures an important difference, hinted at in the application of the word *machinery* to Loyola's book. The *Exercises* are quite a different sort of *method* from either Descartes' or Barrès': Loyola, far from narrating a personal exemplum, sets out to teach a practice, step by step, and in a progressive order. The *Exercises* do not attempt to persuade or delight the casual reader, who is *not* addressed. Loyola's manual constructs two distinct categories of addressees: those who *give*, and those who *receive* the exercises. Neither category is expected to read the manual for pleasure, or for immediate spiritual profit. The manual merely spells out rules on how to conduct and practice spiritual exercises. The exercises themselves, as they are carried out, are no more to be found in Loyola's manual than are any other kind of actual practice between the covers of a *how-to* book. Such handbooks, implicitly or otherwise, distinguish between the moment of reading and the moment of actual practice. We need not expatiate on this distinction: everyone has used a cookbook or a guidebook. Such books

[17] Barrès, *Le Culte du moi*, pp. 156-57.

Barrès, Loyola, and the Novel

may, of course, also be read in a contemplative frame (they give aesthetic satisfaction in inverse ratio to their effectiveness or timeliness as manuals), and thus become a "suggestive sort of reading." That is tantamount to saying that given a favorable "set," or "frame," and context, any text can be perceived as "poetic"; in Barrès' context, the incongruity of a textbook becoming "the most suggestive sort of reading" is emphasized by oxymorons: arid-fecund; machinery-suggestiveness; dilettante-fanatic, which may well be euphemistic realizations of an erotic cliché, with overtones of perversity. The text suggests that Loyola's "machinery" (*mécanique*) can be made to function as pornography. Thus the very absence of actual descriptions, meditations, exhortations in the text of the *Spiritual Exercises* incites the reader's imagination to wander off, provided that having given up any Christomorphic intention he strives, rather, toward polymorphous perversion. "Absolute master of myself," indeed! Barrès' hubristic intimation of enthusiasm and sovereignty lies a short step away from Bataille's views on eroticism and the sacred.

Of Loyola's method, Barrès retained only a transgressive dimension: the breaking down of what is held respectable by wordly people generates excess (dilates skepticism and pride), thus fostering a *desire for enthusiasm*, i.e., possession. It may be worth noting that at least within the French context, modern revolts against a degradation of Cartesian method into rationalism, specialization, and positivism resort to Loyola's method for an alternative: from Barrès to Bataille, in each case a redefinition of the reader is at stake, since the Cartesian method calls for acquiescence to what is reasonable, clear, and distinct, while the antimethod exalts all that cannot be encompassed by common sense, all that is scandalous, discontinuous, relegated to the periphery of the Cartesian clearing. Transpositions of Loyola's method are made possible by the very generality of its theoretical and pedagogical tenets. Loyola generalized the principle, implicit in previous manuals of meditation, that spiritual progress can be achieved (with the grace of God) through a controlled use of the senses, contemplating and imagining and interpreting the places and scenes of Christ's life and Passion, as well as Hell and Heaven. But Loyola, by merely referring to "the history" rather than retelling it himself and interpreting it—by giving practical advice on how the meditant is to proceed, on his own, in order to reorient his life and make his own choices with the guidance of an instructor—constructed a "grammar" rather than a "surface." The *Exercises* are like a grammar which (depending on the history, exempla, places, images, selected for meditation—that is, first of all, for imaginative recreation) might produce a variety of discourses that, in their written forms, would range from fictional, initiatory itineraries to the self-conscious construction of self (*ego-moi*), as is the case with Barrès.

Paradoxically, in the orthodox context of Christian exercises a great deal of latitude is left to both the meditant and his guide. A passage from the preliminary "annotations" will exemplify both the allocutory situation obtaining in the *Exercises*, and the demand it places on the addressees:

> . . . the person who gives to another a method and order of meditating and contemplating ought faithfully to narrate the history for such contemplation or meditation, merely running through the chief heads of it with a summary statement; because the person who contemplates, by taking the true foundation of the history, by reflecting and reasoning for himself, and by finding something that makes the history a little plainer and that brings it more home to him—be it by his own reasoning or inasmuch as his understanding is enlightened by divine grace—derives greater spiritual relish and profit than if the giver of the Exercises had discoursed at great length and dilated upon the meaning of the history: for it is not abundance of knowledge that fills and satisfies the soul, but the inward sense and taste of things.[18]

[18] *The Spiritual Exercises of St. Ignatius Loyola*, trans. Joseph Rickaby, S.J. (London, 1915), annotation 2.

Barrès, Loyola, and the Novel

We can measure the distance separating this call to effort—or "work," as modern psychotherapists are wont to say—from Descartes' narration of personal practice and Barrès' combination of narration and description of the "inward sense and taste of things." The crucial differences, of course, lie in the nature of the history being meditated upon, and in the presumed intentions of both writer and actual reader. Just as Loyola assumes that the Christian desires salvation and therefore wants to apply the lesson of Christ's life and Passion to his own life, Descartes assumes that man, endowed with reason, wants to reason properly in order to achieve universally valid certainties. In neither case is the purpose achieved through mere reading and understanding of the "method." It must be put into practice. In one case, however, the exemplum, being sacred lore, has intrinsic transcendental value, while in the other the exemplum is merely a pedagogical device.

In Barrès' case, the exemplum entitled *A Free Man* implies that the reader desires freedom (while the general title of the trilogy, *The Cult of the Self*, implies that the reader also wishes to find and cultivate his ego). But the Barrèsian method combines two incompatible features of the Loyolan and Cartesian methods: if the exemplum is a personal, individualized narrative, referring to specific places (Lorraine, Venice) and events, the reader may hesitate: is the story told for its own sake, for its intrinsic value, or is it a pedagogical device? Does it invite the reader to undertake his own quest for freedom and self, using the Jesuit method adapted to his own places, experiences, intercessors (e.g., should he meditate on the lives of intercessors other than Benjamin Constant, Sainte-Beuve, [Baudelaire], and if so, which? What would be the result if he chose X, Y, or Z?) or should the reader take the hero of *Un homme libre* for his model, imitating his contingent conditions and features? This question, of course, is not resolved in the novel.

In other words, although *Un homme libre* calls itself a *method*, it is (only) a *fiction*. The practical consequences are obvious: the Loyolan and Cartesian methods have been put

Michel Beaujour

into general practice, they are true canonical *arts*, while the Barrèsian "method" is not a workable machine or a working model: it is a fiction of a method, or a fiction about method. It modelizes the fantasies of an ego-trip.

Un homme libre is a fiction that records (or feigns to record, in a form approximating the diary) a very idiosyncratic mis-use or malpractice of Loyola's method. Were it not for the text's open avowal, one can assume that few readers besides Jesuits—and the Jesuit-trained—would have noticed this filiation/transgression. References to the *Exercises* and other devotional works might be perceived in context as neo-Christian "decadence," or as a deliberate bypassing of the tradition of the French *moralistes*. Barrès' young *lycéens* were quick to spot this ouster. In the *fin de siècle* context, recourse to religious authority in a scandalous and antiauthoritarian novel was perceived as a subversive act among the upper class. But in the final analysis, *Un homme libre*, as a transfor-mation of Christomorphic practice into ego building, brought into the open the secret *telos* of the modern novel: "self-realization" was to replace self-sacrifice and the imitation of Jesus Christ. This purpose had been camouflaged and fic-tional egotists had often been struck at the last minute by providential retribution, but, as we know, religious cen-sors—and their worthy heirs, the Russian radical and Soviet critics—knew that any hero who is not in some sense Chris-tomorphic cannot be a positive hero: for there is only one true purpose and one proper way of achieving it, while error, opinion, betrayals, heresies, and individuals are beguilingly multifarious.[19] The modern novel is predicated not only on the recognition but on the positive valorization of individual difference and variety of desires. If, as René Girard has so el-egantly shown, within the novel's universe desire is prompt-ed, mediated, and shaped by the Other's desire (whence the

[19] Andre Sinyavsky, "On Socialist Realism," *Dissent* 7 (1960), 39-66. "Still less can there be [substantial differences of opinion] among honest Soviet people, and least of all among positive heroes who think only of spreading their virtues all over the world and of re-educating the few remaining dissi-dents into unanimity."

notion of "triangulated desire"), it is true that fictions mediate and shape desire for their readers; and in the modern period in particular, they foster the desire to be *unique*: the reader wants to be as unique as this or that fictional hero. The epigraph to Girard's book, taken from Max Scheler, sums it all up rather succinctly: "Man either has a God or an idol."[20] But One God, especially an incarnate God with His own history, demands imitation: only an Antichrist—like Zarathustra—would demand of his disciples that they not imitate him.

The novel, unless it presents a Christomorphic (or positive) hero, does not demand imitation as such; rather, it lures the reader into desiring for himself (herself) distinctive features, a unique personality, incomparable fantasies. There can be as many perfections as there are individuals. Or to put it another way: perfection is approached through cultivation of the self in its difference, and through struggle against its enemies.

This romantic lie is more powerful than the novel's truthfulness about triangulated desire: the endurance and multiplication of the novel testify to the durability of illusion in both writer and reader; for they would have given up the writing and reading of fiction if they did not believe the fictional text to be the locus where authentic desires are revealed. Then again, from Girard's Christian perspective, this can be turned inside out: "Modern man, in the eyes of the novelist, does not suffer from refusing to achieve a full and complete awareness of his autonomy, he suffers because this awareness, real or illusory, is unbearable to him. The need for transcendence seeks satisfaction in the here and now, and leads the hero into all sorts of follies" (p. 164). This ontological conception of a "transcendence deflected toward the human" is a remarkably useful key to understanding the evolution of the modern novel in its historical context. It illuminates the transformation of Loyola's method for the im-

---

[20] René Girard, *Mensonge romantique et vérité romanesque* (Paris, 1961), in English, *Deceit, Desire and the Novel*, trans. J. Freccero (Baltimore, 1965). (Subsequent page references to this translation are given in the text.)

Michel Beaujour

itation of Christ into Barrès' method for the cultivation of the Self. It explains, in particular, why Barrès' method cannot bring satisfaction to his hero, who ends up seeking, beyond the self and the here and now, a transcendence in ancestry, nation, culture: the commonplaces into which, after having found himself—and found himself wanting—he can lay down the burden of self.

In an ontological sense (rather than in the subordinate, specialized, ethical sense), the novel has been the modern rival of the *Imitatio*, and of Christian meditation in general. The desire to be Christlike (with all that is implied in the *like*) is deflected toward the desire to be like someone else, which is indistinguishable from the stated desire to be *oneself*. The novel has prompted as well as frustrated this desire. Of course, on a different level the novel is also a *method*: it provides educational models, and it fulfills a rhetorical function insofar as it presents exempla of social, ethical, political conduct. When the Dadaists held a mock trial for Barrès, it was because they knew that his wartime patriotic hysteria was the ultimate betrayal of the revolt they had learned to rationalize through his early novels, which contained an inherent defeatist message, and an overt encouragement to idleness, to rejection of bourgeois virtues.

The novel, especially that of the personal-exemplary variety, has thrived as Christianity lost its hold over the reading classes. Its centrifugal, libidinous, antipaternal, and transgressive essence was felt so sharply in the post-Tridentine period that the Roman church deliberately attempted to harness the libidinal images and fantasies it could not suppress: Salesian and Jesuit spiritual advisors put Christian meditation and exercises into novelistic form for the use of their giddy and hedonistic clientele. This, of course, was but a repetition of an earlier attempt to *moralize* the erotic allegory of the *Roman de la Rose*. The Christian novel, from the *Quête du Graal* to *Pilgrim's Progress*, is of necessity allegorical, and so is the socialist-realist novel and the *roman à thèse* in general. This implies that an authority in the text—echoing outside

Barrès, Loyola, and the Novel

authority—interprets the meaning of all that gives libidinal satisfaction in the text.

The "good" or righteous novel will therefore indulge in a lot of intratextual transcoding in order to eliminate ambiguity and therefore delimit the range of interpretation allowed to the reader. On the other hand, transcoding in the "bad" or transgressive novel is centrifugal and in the direction of increased ambiguity or polysemy. We have a clear case of this in *Un homme libre*, where Loyola's precise terminology: ("composition of place," "colloquy") and the elements of Christian progress are transcoded into the nebulous code of a quest for Self. When this type of novel "draws conclusions within the work of art," it is usually to disguise, *in extremis*, the centrifugal exemplum into a cautionary tale, in order to circumvent repression. Since conclusions, interpretations, are, like the moral of a fable, on the side of the law (or at least of some law, which may be waiting in the wings for its opportunity to become legal), even the radical *roman à thèse* (that of Nizan, for instance) is a stalking horse for the law of the father and for social dictatorship.

But, as Gombrowicz noted, there is also the illegal desire, the desire for the inconclusive, "for imperfection . . . for inferiority . . . for youth." This is a desire the novel can, and normally does, provoke and nurture. Paul Bourget, who was the father of the *roman à thèse*, saw clearly why *Un homme libre* is not really "*à thèse*": "This masterpiece of irony which only lacks a conclusion."[21] To be sure, Barrès published a series of explanations, prefaces, appendices to new editions of *Un homme libre*, when after his "conversion" to nationalism and traditionalism his earlier position became awkward; but he never confessed to having changed his mind. Nor did he modify or suppress his early novels. Barrès was one of the happy few who can eat their cake and have it, and play both ends against the middle.

Appropriately, the only part of Wayne C. Booth's *The*

---

[21] Quoted by Barrès in his 1904 "Preface" to *Un homme libre*, p. 492.

Michel Beaujour

Rhetoric of Fiction which seems to have any specific pertinence to a discussion of the exemplary novel and its readers is the one entitled "Morality of Narration," in which he analyzes at some length, and from the point of view of a "naive reader," Céline's *Journey to the End of Night*. The book is judged, in the end, immoral (incidentally, Trotsky and Nizan reviewed this novel with greater understanding but reached analogous conclusions), because it is a dishonest picture, and "not a realized picture at all."[22] Indeed, *Journey . . .* is an *immature* book: its real readers are the young, and, in the sense suggested by Gombrowicz, it appeals to a secret, illegal desire in its readers, a desire for a lack of realization in the picture, for absence of method and resolution. It is an exemplary novel in the sense not only that Bardamu's journey can be perceived as a perversely exemplary, allegorical progress, but mostly because it does what most novels do when *properly* read: it excites and confuses. Booth himself provides, in that context, an instance of exemplary (if somewhat single-minded) novel reading:

> An intelligent friend of mine has admitted to using the works of [Aldous] Huxley throughout his adolescence as a steady source of pornography. . . . Most of us, especially if we read widely when young without guidance from more experienced readers, can recall misreadings of this kind. They can range all the way from sadistic pleasure in scenes intended to rouse horror or revulsion to the acceptance of intellectual positions that the author intended to satirize.[23]

And Booth adds this remarkable, if qualified, denial: "Such misreadings prove little, perhaps, except that they are misreadings." Really! How could such a prevalent perversion, such a general phenomenon, "prove little, perhaps"? Does it not prove, on the contrary, that many novels are indeed pornographic, as all "experienced readers," serious parents,

[22] Booth, *The Rhetoric of Fiction* (Chicago, 1961), p. 383.
[23] Ibid., p. 309.

346

Barrès, Loyola, and the Novel

ecclesiastics, and commissars, but not modern professors of literature, have always known? Misreadings, indeed! The libidinous little reader will have his hands bound until his head is expurgated by an experienced exorcist. Of course, one can also read certain novels maturely, without missing serious issues and with both hands on the table. But is it worth it, unless this happens to be one's way of making a living? Unless the teacher enjoys a rather orthopedic turn of mind? A miracle, too, that our friend did not lose his intelligence to excessive misreadings!

Any discussion of "the reader" is futile which fails to account for, or at least to deal openly with, the fact that (on the whole) novels are just as pernicious—and exemplary—as comic books, TV, movies; that they serve *essentially* (or have served, given differences in "permissiveness" and technical development) the same function as "girlie" magazines, but that they are infinitely more subversive: because they modulate and diversify desire beyond sex and violence, as they challenge obliquely all forms of "realization" and "conclusion" imposed by the law of the father, the law of the family, the law of production, the law of the Barbarians—Barbarians, whom Barrès identified as "the not-I, all that can harm or resist the Self,"[24] a self which he equated with the unconscious and with desire.

In the chapter to which we have referred, Booth mentions—without embracing his extreme views—Edmund Fuller, who, in his *Man in Modern Fiction* (New York, 1958), accused "modern writers of abandoning the 'Judeo-Christian tradition' " and of forgetting that man "inhabits an orderly universe," that "his fundamental laws are commands of his Creator," and that he is "individual, responsible, guilty, redeemable."[25] Now, here is a consistent if somewhat limited critic; for he has put his finger on the only interesting question: Why are (modern) novels disorderly, transgressive, and dirty? All calls for morality in the novel and for the morality of

[24] *Examen*, p. 472.
[25] Booth, *The Rhetoric of Fiction*, p. 379, n. 2. The whole note is a striking example of the fudging inherent in repressive liberalism.

347

technique are transparent denials of this waywardness. Located somewhere between Loyola's *Exercises* and our young friend's "misreadings," the novel proposes only mediated desires, confusions, wishful thinking, bad faith, and lies. Why do young readers, minor readers, female readers, know this better than those experienced readers who struggle amidst the contradictions of repressive liberalism? Although in practice the novel can be made to convey the Christian or Communist messages of self-oblivion, deferred gratification, desire for the law, its deeper appeal always lies in the depiction of sin, error, disorder, in all that is transgressive, excessive. *Muckraking* is indeed a good term for the ambiguous novel: no matter who handles the rake, and to what law-abiding purpose, he exploits the allurements of *muck*, and muck sticks to the rake.

To pursue this line of thought would lead into considerations about purity and defilement, structure and dirt, pollution and the sacred, transgression-violence-expulsion.[26] Suffice it to say that in our culture, novels are dirty and powerful because they are, at least on one level, a mimesis of dirt and share in its powers. The reader partakes of this pollution, he becomes part of the disorder as he rolls in the muck. He is possessed by it. The personal examplary novel, like *Un homme libre*, is more forthright than the *roman à thèse*, which is always manipulative, a paternal surrogate. For once the example of the One has been removed, there is no limit (except those imposed by censorship, if it exists) to the proliferation of examples and their "viciousness." Then, as Harry Levin put it, "the great responsibility for discrimination rests with the reader."[27] But it is difficult to see how "discrimination between artistic imagination and autistic fantasy" will drive the pornographers out of business, unless the critic and

[26] The reader will have recognized references to the thought of such religious anthropologists as Mary Douglas, *Purity and Danger* (London, 1966) and René Girard, *La Violence et le sacré* (Paris, 1972), and, of course, to Georges Bataille.

[27] Levin, "The Unbanning of the Novel," in *Refractions* (New York, 1966), p. 307.

the teacher succeed in replacing the censor. There is no good reason to believe that, in the novel at least, "artistic imagination" is not a sublimation of "autistic fantasy." Readers of novels, if "mature," seek both levels, for we are "infantilized" by all "higher" forms as Gombrowicz said in his preface to *Pornografia*. But if readers are immature (and readers of novels are by definition immature, at least so long as they are possessed by the fiction), then they will seek to deconstruct the artistic structure in order to reach the vicarious autistic fantasy that has always been the lure of the novel. Or else they may heed another powerful injunction of fiction, and start writing their own personal exemplary novels.

Norman N. Holland

Re-Covering "The Purloined Letter": Reading as a Personal Transaction

Begin with the text, they say. For me, one central fact about the text is that I am reading this story in Pocketbook No. 39, the copy of Poe I had as a boy—one of the first paperbacks in America. "Kind to your Pocket and your Pocketbook." Hardly a distinguished edition, yet I find myself agreeing with what the man I call Marcel says in the library of the Guermantes: "If I had been tempted to be a book collector, as the Prince de Guermantes was, I would have been one of a very peculiar sort. . . . The first edition of a work would have been more precious to me than the others, but I would have understood by that the edition in which I read it for the first time."[1]

The Great Tales and Poems of Edgar Allan Poe. Complete and Unabridged. Bound in Perma-Gloss—and the book is indeed in perfectly respectable shape for a paperback published in 1940. I was thirteen years old then. I am fifty-two now, and I have learned, alas, that I am not bound in Perma-Gloss.

The book, then, as what? As a part of me from then that is not broken or worn down. Literature endures, while we change. Yet as we change we change it, so that this "Purloined Letter" both is and is not the same "Purloined Letter" I first read almost forty years ago.

"Purloined," that lovely, artificial word, so typically Poe-etic; it comes from *porloignée*—Norman French or, if you like, Norm's French. When I studied French in school, my favorite

[1] Marcel Proust, *Remembrance of Things Past*, trans. C. K. Scott Moncrieff and Frederick A. Blossom, 7 vols. in 2 (New York, 1932), 2: 1007.

350

Re-Covering "The Purloined Letter"

province was, inevitably, Normandy. I feel protective toward
that word *purloined*. It is not to be confused (as Lacan, for
example, does[2]) with words meaning "alongside." This is
truly *porloignée*, from *loin*, "far," hence, "to put far away." As
the Minister D—— does. As Dupin himself does.

"Purloined" means the letter was taken from one place to
another, in that shifting of signifiers which first attracted Lacan. Indeed, the whole story proceeds by the moving of papers from one place to another: the two letters, the check for
50,000 francs, the third letter containing the two lines of
poetry. A story around the placing of letters. If one found the
letter in concealment, then one would know, *That* is the letter. In the open, that *cannot* be the letter. A study in contexts.
Things are in their place and therefore not noticeable, or they
are out of their place and to be discovered by the bureaucratic
methods of the Prefect of Police. Or so Poe would have us believe.

Yet the Prefect's techniques of search, as he enumerates
them, are marvelous: the long needles, the microscopes, the
grids that account for every tiny bit of space. "The fiftieth part
of a line could not escape us," he says. Nevertheless, I cannot
believe, as Dupin does, that the Prefect's methods are fool-
proof. Somewhere, inside the wainscoting, painted under a
picture, rolled into a window groove, somewhere in a building as large and intricate as a French *hôtel particulier*, a person
as clever as D—— could hide a single letter so that no police
officer, no matter how painstaking, could discover it.

Therefore, I do not really believe the basic premise of Poe's
story. I believe there is a mechanical solution to the Minister's
problem of concealing the letter that would make Dupin's
oh-so-clever strategy useless. In the same way, I disbelieve
that, in the Prefect's incredibly expensive and time-

---

[2] "Le Séminaire sur 'La Lettre volée' " (1955), *Ecrits*, Collections "Points"
(Paris, 1966), 1: 19-75; "Seminar on 'The Purloined Letter,' " trans. Jeffrey
Mehlman, *French Freud: Structural Studies in Psychoanalysis*, *Yale French
Studies*, no. 48 (1972), 38-72. Lacan misreports the *Oxford English Dictionary*
on p. 39 in the French and p. 59 in the English.

consuming searches, someone would not have examined the letter in the card case. One's secrets are always found out by the sheer bigness and brute force of governmental power.

Yet I dare not say so. Poe bullies me by suggesting that only inferior minds would resort to physical concealment. A trick has been worked—not just on the Prefect and the Minister—but on me.

Yet my very doubts turn me again to the special sense of space I get in this story: secret, small places, hidden drawers, gimlet holes, microscopic dust on the chair rungs, the little card case. Yet we move by analogy, outward from these tiny concealing spaces to the *troisième arrondissement*, to the schoolyard, to the royal apartments, to an intrigue between Dupin and D—— in (where else?) Vienna.

The central movement of the story is to turn the letter inside out, to turn the hidden, important inner space outward so that it seems trivial. The Prefect turns the physical surroundings of the Hôtel D—— inside out, but that is of no use. Dupin, however, turns the mind inside out. He can bring out into the open one's very thoughts. He moves by analogy, deduction or, as he says, by simile and metaphor, which will actually strengthen an argument as well as merely embellish. The poet thinks this way, rather than the mathematician, he says. But also, I would add, the psychoanalyst.

Dupin turns our narrator's mind inside out when he reveals his inner reverie on the shortness of the actor Chantilly in "The Murders in the Rue Morgue." He turns the mind of D—— inside out by analogizing to his chain of reasoning and realizing the letter must be in plain sight. He turns the letter itself inside out, not by probing into all the secret places the Prefect's needles had probed, but by having a lunatic shout in the street outside.

Dupin turns minds inside out by playing with inside and outside. He quotes the advice of a clever schoolboy who won all the marbles at even and odd: " 'When I wish to find out how wise, or how stupid, or how good, or how wicked is any one, or what are his thoughts at the moment, I fashion the

Re-Covering "The Purloined Letter"

expression of my face as accurately as possible in accordance with the expression of his, and then wait to see what thoughts or sentiments arise in my mind or heart, as if to match or correspond with the expression.' " The outer face turns the inner mind inside out, just as Dupin's substitution of a facsimile for the purloined letter duplicates the Minister's original theft by substituting a trivial letter for the crucial one right out in plain sight.[3] So the story's outside calls forth my inside, and I must bring my doubts outside and take the story inside.

My doubts must be hidden in this story about hiding, which is also about not hiding. Like those lines to conceal the names and dates. 18—. "The Prefect of the Parisian police, G——." "The Minister D——." Does Poe really think he can conceal police chiefs and cabinet ministers by little lines? "The fiftieth part of a line could not escape us." That which is most obviously hidden is most easily discovered—is that not the moral of the story?

That which is most obvious, by contrast, is most hidden. The minor peccadillo covers the greater—the letter in the little feminine hand conceals the greater sin of the greater woman. She is the Queen, some critics say—Lacan does, for example—but the story does not. "A personage of most exalted station" who comes alone to the royal *boudoir*, as, indeed, does the Minister D——. A royal mistress perhaps? A sister? A cousin? We shall never learn her name or her secret. "Questions remain," remarks Harry Levin, "which M. Dupin is much too discreet to raise: what was written in that letter? by whom to whom? and how did its temporary disappear-

---

[3] Lacan attributes the similarity in thefts to the repetition compulsion (which, if used to explain all likenesses, explains none). Daniel Hoffman traces it to the exact identification of Dupin with his foe D——. *Poe Poe Poe Poe Poe Poe Poe* (Garden City, N.Y., 1973), pp. 121-22 and 131-33. Hoffman's splendidly personal study builds on an associative method like my own. One of the virtues of this kind of "open" criticism is that it permits the cumulation of different readings by different personalities into a larger view of the work. I have gained from Hoffman's associations.

353

ance affect the writer and the recipient?"[4] We shall not learn in this story, where brains defer to beauty.

I read this story when I was thirteen and I also had something to hide, something that is perfectly known to anyone who knows anything at all about thirteen-year-old boys. Most obvious, yet most carefully concealed. In the Prefect's phrase, "This is an affair demanding the greatest secrecy, and . . . I should most probably lose the position I now hold were it known that I confided it to any one." Yes, indeed, one must keep up one's position, regardless of what others know about you. Thus, the villainous D—— "is, perhaps, the most really energetic human being now alive—but that is only when nobody sees him." Can a thirteen-year-old boy find something of himself in D——?

Hiding. My scarcely containable pleasure at knowing what others do not know. As a boy playing hide-and-seek, I could barely control my impulse to burst out of my hiding place to shout, Here I am, to reveal my magic secret. Here Dupin tells. I—Kilroy—was here. I took the letter, and I left the MS behind. I got away with *it*, the precious, ambiguous object both male and female, both big and black and small and red, both concealed and unconcealed, that I will tell you no more about. Now I know all their secrets of royal sex and power.

When I talk that way, I must sound like the early "Freudism" of Marie Bonaparte. Everything is open. Let it all hang out. "The Purloined Letter," she says, expresses "regret for the missing maternal penis." The letter hangs over the fireplace just as a female penis (if it existed) would hang over "the cloaca" here represented by the symbol of fireplace or chimney. Not even the clitoris is omitted—it is the little brass knob from which the card rack hangs. The struggle between Dupin and the Minister D—— is an Oedipal struggle between father and son, but of a very archaic kind, a struggle to seize not the mother in her entirety but only her penis, only a part therefore. A Bone-a-part, I suppose.

She then can link the wicked D—— to figures in Poe's life

[4] Harry Levin, *The Power of Blackness: Hawthorne, Poe, Melville* (New York, 1967), pp. 141-42.

Re-Covering "The Purloined Letter"

and, of course, to Poe himself, so that the tortured author is here equating himself with the hated but admired father by the same talent he discusses abstractly in the story, identification. Dupin receives the check for 50,000 francs and restores the woman her symbolic letter or missing penis. "Thus, once more," says Bonaparte, "we meet the equation gold = penis. The mother gives her son gold in exchange for the penis he restores."[5]

Strange as all this sounds, some of it carries over into Lacan's reading—as Jacques Derrida points out.[6] Like most readings from first-phase or symbolic Freudianism,[7] it costs nothing. It cost me something to admit to you that I masturbated, even thirty-nine years ago and at an age when all boys do. It costs nothing to say a little brass knob stands for the clitoris. It is all "out there," quite external and inhuman, quite, therefore, foreign to the spirit of psychoanalysis as a *science de l'homme*, quite like Dupin's abstract intellect or perhaps Lacan's or Derrida's.

Bonaparte comes closer to a human truth when she talks about Dupin as a young man struggling for a woman against an older man, against three of them in fact. The Prefect G—— is a watcher who, ratlike, ferrets out secrets from tiny hiding places. Clumsy and pompous, he conceals the royal group in a cloud of unknowing. "The disclosure of the document to a third person who shall be nameless would bring in question the honour of a personage of most exalted station." By contrast, the Minister D—— easily learns of sexual, familiar secrets and uses them to hold a woman in thrall. A third father is scarcely mentioned, the royal personage who does not know and cannot aid the royal woman, the perhaps cuckolded, and certainly helpless, monarch.

---

[5] Marie Bonaparte, *The Life and Works of Edgar Allan Poe: A Psycho-Analytic Interpretation*, trans. John Rodker (London, 1949), pp. 383-84.

[6] "Le facteur de la vérité," *Poétique*, no. 21 (1975), 96-147; "The Purveyor of Truth," trans. Willis Domingo et al., *Graphesis: Perspectives in Literature and Philosophy, Yale French Studies*, no. 52 (1975), pp. 31-113. See pp. 115-17 (French) or 66-71 (English).

[7] See my "Literary Interpretation and Three Phases of Psychoanalysis," *Critical Inquiry* 3 (1976), 221-33.

Norman N. Holland

I feel the presence of various fathers, a cuckolded one, a helpless, impotent one, a clever, dangerous one, and not just the characters of the story—other fathers whom I must outwit are Lacan and Derrida. Is it not natural that I feel like a son? Dupin speaks for me when he says, "I act as a partisan of the lady concerned."

Dupin reminds me even more, though, of Prometheus, whose name means "forethought" and who stole a sacred object, black and red like this royal letter, a fragment of glowing charcoal hidden in a giant fennel stalk. No vulture for this Prometheus, however. He gives the enfolded red and black back to the gods and is given 50,000 francs for his forethought. This Dupin-Prometheus thus restores the connection between the gods and men, between the miraculous and the natural, between man and woman. When I was thirteen I used to do magic tricks for my parents' patient guests: the cut rope restored, the missing ace recovered, the marked penny found inside a little red bag inside a matchbox inside a bigger red box all bound up with rubber bands. And always *I* was the one who knew the secret, not these adults.

So many magic tricks depend on disappearance or loss recovered in a novel and astounding way. They form an image of human development. In infancy, we give up union with a nurturing other to gain individuality. We give up the freedom of chaos to find autonomy. We give up a mother's supporting hand to stand on our own feet. We lose in order to gain. We lose the card or cut the rope or see the handkerchief disappear to gain new wisdom about human possibilities. The royal lady loses the letter but, thanks to the magician Dupin, gains new power over the villainous D——. As he points out, "She has now him in [her power]—since, being unaware that the letter is not in his possession, he will proceed with his exactions as if it was. Thus will he inevitably commit himself at once to his political destruction."

Dupin and I are Prometheus, Magicians, Rescuers of royal ladies. I also, like Dupin, am a decipherer of texts.[8] When he

[8] Joseph J. Moldenhauer, "Murder as a Fine Art: Basic Connections Between Poe's Aesthetics, Psychology, and Moral Vision," *PMLA* 83 (1968),

Re-Covering "The Purloined Letter"

visits D——, he already knows where to look and what to look for, for he has solved the Prefect's long narration of the theft, the letter, the hiding, and the rest. Similarly, he solved the cases of the Rue Morgue and of Marie Rogêt by interpreting newspaper accounts. I work the same way with his stories, or try to.

Dupin exists in a world of texts, but he himself is not a text to be read. Behind the green spectacles, he sees but is not seen. The story gives no information about the physical appearance of Dupin. He and his friend are only half there.

This is a story of two bachelors enjoying "the twofold luxury of meditation and meerschaum," in the quiet digs *"au troisième, No. 33."* Twos and threes. Female twos and male threes in an old symbolism. Odd numbers. I remember the Prefect's "fashion of calling everything 'odd' that was beyond his comprehension."

By contrast, Dupin and Narrator enjoy the intellectual pleasures: "I was mentally discussing certain topics which had formed matter for conversation between us at an earlier period of the evening . . . the affair of the Rue Morgue, and the mystery attending the murder of Marie Rogêt." The story is a talking among men and a conflict between two men, a regression to being boys, really. "These characters are a boy's dream of men," says Daniel Hoffman, "because they interact only one-dimensionally, that being in the dimension of the intellect" (*Poe* . . . , p. 117). They have a boys' relationship like Huck and Tom on the island, sitting and smoking and talking about intellectual issues, or like my roommate and myself in graduate school. Even the adversary is part of this company. Dupin visits him intellectually, through "a topic which I knew well had never failed to interest and excite him."

True, it is only one dimension, yet how vital a dimension it is for me. I share the ambition Poe reveals in Dupin's disquisition on mathematics, the feeling that his own intellect has powers not granted to lesser beings. How intelligent I

284-97, 291, points out that Dupin does what literary critics do: he analyzes texts.

357

Norman N. Holland

thought myself when I was reading this story at thirteen; and I am not entirely over that vanity yet, as you can see by my choosing to write about a story that two major French thinkers have analyzed. They are all to be outwitted, all these fathers like the Prefect or the Minister, or, for that matter, Lacan or Derrida. As the easygoing narrator observes, "You have a quarrel on hand . . . with some of the algebraists of Paris." Yes, I do. I am confronting them as Dupin confronts the mysterious D——, through an intellectual "discussion . . . upon a topic which I knew well had never failed to interest and excite him."

We interpreters are all like the boy who won the whole school's marbles playing "even and odd" (that mystery again of the odd male and the even female). The aim is to bring hidden information out, and we pride ourselves on our cleverness at being able to do that. Others might be stronger, more capable, more likable—but we are smart. We can bring the secret out and make it public, like odd or even fingers brought out from behind one's back.

The intellectual brilliance will hide all those doubts one has of oneself at thirteen (or at fifty-two). Behind green spectacles the thinker will see but not be seen. Madness is outside, a cry in the street. Inside, all is rational, masterful. Atreus, Thyestes, those terrible struggles between the generations will be enfolded in the sleek Alexandrines of Crébillon—only another puzzle. This becomes a story about converting sex, murder, cannibalism, or adultery into an intellectual game.[9] The pure-loined letter.

Inevitably, then, it is also a story about the inadequacy of pure intellect to cover human limitations. The key relation (for me) is that between Dupin and his friend the narrator—the relater (my pun intended). He does not know as much as Dupin and he knows he does not know, but it is all all right. He is secure. He trusts and is trusted. He relates. Holmes and

---

[9] Allan Tate speaks of Poe's "intellect moving in isolation from both love and the moral will, whereby it declares itself independent of the human situation in the quest of essential knowledge." "The Angelic Imagination," *The Man of Letters in the Modern World* (New York, 1955), p. 115.

358

Watson pair off more or less the same way, as do Nero Wolfe and Archie Goodwin or Lord Peter Wimsey and Bunter: the cool detective and his kindly sidekick. They embody two kinds of relations to the world, the knower and the one who relates to the world more as ordinary people do. He acts. He trusts and believes, often without guile, the way Watson is so conventional.

By contrast the knower needs to see under and through and behind. Behind the green spectacles he knows the guilty secret, but he does not have the empathy that encourages Maigret's criminals to write him even after he has packed them off to prison. This kind of detective is only a knower, only an adversary.

For me, as for Dupin, knowing is safer. Basic trust is for the Watsons of this world who do not need to know everything. The Dupins, the Holmeses, and the Hollands need to see through everything. We need to know even the contents of our friends' heads, to say nothing of the blackmail schemes of the powerful political fathers and the weaknesses of policemen. Then, sitting over meditation and meerschaums, we can feel secure—because we know.

I love this story, as I love the Holmes stories, because I can be both the Dupin one admires and the relater who loves and is loved of Dupin. I find something of the same satisfaction in teaching, for I hover between teaching "it" and teaching "someone." As a relater, I am the benevolent instructor who wears his authority lightly and tries to be loved by his students. As Dupin, I know and you do not and I am going to show you what I know that you do not, but then you will know and we will be friends again and relate the ways relaters (not Dupins) do. As after a game of hide-and-seek.

Here, Dupin is a teacher to his friend the narrator, but to the mysterious D——, he is an adversary. Men of mind fighting with mind. As Dupin points out, the adversaries here are both poets, so that the core of the story is a contest between two poets which is decided by the quotation of two lines of poetry. Would not Robert Graves see here a battle between two bards for the possession of the magic letter and the protection of the White Goddess? Might not even Northrop Frye see here a flyting? Dunbar and Kennedy alliterating each other into hell itself, or even further in the dark backward and abysm of time, Beowulf and sour-mouthed Unferth, a pair of bearskinned savages hurling sarcasm and litotes and knucklebones at each other across a haunch of beef. How essentially Poe-etic to mask that primitive, magical contest with the elegance and decadence of his two Paris intellectuals and their embroidery of literary and philosophical allusion. Poe's art is artifice—another kind of hiding, the covering of the opposite.

"But," as D. H. Lawrence says, "Poe is rather a scientist than an artist."[10] Poe responds to the world through this very tendency to embellishment. He thinks of reality as a solid core under a surface of ornament, and when he writes, he creates artifice in order to break it down. Inside out again. For him, the essence of criticism, politics, mathematics, or philosophy becomes a kind of detection, bringing the correct solution out from under the covering text.

Still deeper within that detection I sense Poe's radically romantic belief that there is in fact a solution to be found. He holds a deep faith that there is some sort of thereness at the core of things, even if it be the beating of a murdered heart beneath the floorboards or the first feeble movements in the hollow coffin in the cellar of the House of Usher. That there be *something* there, something one can identify oneself with, is preferable, no matter how horrible that something, to absence. "When the self is broken," says Lawrence of Poe, "and the mystery of the recognition of *otherness* fails, then the longing for identification with the beloved becomes a lust."[11] In Poe, it is a desperate hunger, something that goes beyond even the need to know: Poe—my Poe—is the child who must know by mind alone the Other he should have held in his mouth or heart. "To try to *know* any living being is to try to

[10] "Edgar Allan Poe" in *Studies in Classic American Literature* (1923; rpt. New York, 1964), p. 65.
[11] Ibid., p. 76.

Re-Covering "The Purloined Letter"

suck the life out of that being," says Lawrence, more psychoanalytic than he knows.[12]

It is through this theme, the contrast between knowing and trusting, between Dupin and his relater, that I can articulate for myself those two shadowy figures lurking through my associations, Lacan and Derrida.

Lacan points to similarities in the two thefts of the fateful letter, its theft by the Minister from the Queen, then its theft by Dupin from the Minister. He finds in this mirroring pattern an instance of the repetition compulsion (or, as he calls it, "automatism"), hence of the "insistence" of the signifier, which is itself "symbol only of an absence."

Thus, in his analysis of the Poe story, as in his other writings, Lacan's theme is absence. I suppose it is the psychoanalysis in me, but I hear in that very preoccupation a longing for presence. Derrida calls it "this rush to truth" (p. 57), "la précipitation vers la vérité" (p. 11). Lacan seeks, as does Dupin himself, the hermeneutical decoding of the text, but for Lacan it is psychoanalysis—Lacanian psychoanalysis—that occupies the place of Dupin, the detective, the magician, the critic, the analyst. "The purloined letter," he tells us, as Poe himself might, is "like an immense female body," and it is Lacan/Dupin who will undress and possess that body—a conclusion completely Poe-etic.

As Jacques Derrida points out in his brilliant and relentlessly skeptical critique of Lacan's seminar on "The Purloined Letter," Lacan's conclusion springs from a variety of tacit assumptions. He assumes, for example, that the signifier has a proper, preordained trajectory; that a letter cannot be subdivided into parts; that one can ignore the story's formal, narrative-within-a-narrative structure; that femaleness is defined by castration, and so on. If the story's theme, for Lacan, is fusion with a body of knowledge, for Derrida it is another major theme I glean from Poe, trust (or, for Derrida, distrust). In a world of deconstructions, the greatest intellectual sin is

---

[12] Ibid., p. 70.

Norman N. Holland

to try to take a fixed position. Derrida, I think, writes out of a need not to believe, a need to *dis*trust. Yet, as with Lacan, I feel the absence is itself a presence. Disbelief is itself a belief in disbelief. Derrida turns his shiftings and doublings and changes of perspective into a credo and a method to be as automatically applied by his disciples as ever the once-New criticism was or as Lacan's shuffling of signifiers is.

Such disbelief I would expect to mask a disappointed need to believe. It shows, I feel, in Derrida's distinctive ambiguity, as for example, in the opening sentences of his brilliant critique of Lacan's seminar: "La psychanalyse, à supposer, se trouve. Quand on croit la trouver, c'est elle, à supposer, qui se trouve." Derrida provides abstractions—texts usually, but here, "la psychanalyse"—as the subjects for verbs that need physical or animate subjects—here, *se trouver*. For me, the effect is to make concrete and abstract hover between presence and absence, activity and inactivity, animate and inanimate. *À supposer.* I sense, in short, Derrida's own version of Poe's quest and Lacan's for a living and dead—someone.

And what of me? The phrase that first comes to mind is: *I want to place myself* in relation to this story and Derrida and Lacan, and even as I say those words, I realize I am re-creating still another motif for "The Purloined Letter": articulating states of mind by physical places and changes of mind by movements from place to place or inside out as in so many of Poe's stories of hiding and burial. Here, I move from the boyish intellections of Dupin and his roommate, out to an active struggle over the possession of a text (and a woman), back again to the quiet, now-prosperous, bachelor apartment. In the same way I now want to retreat from my small skirmish with Lacan and Derrida to larger theoretical concerns.

What have I been doing in a theoretical sense? What kind of a reading is this? I call it *transactive criticism.* [13] By that I mean a

[13] See, for example, my essays: "*Hamlet*—My Greatest Creation," *Journal of the American Academy of Psychoanalysis* 3 (1975), 419-27; "Transactive Criticism: Re-Creation Through Identity," *Criticism* 18 (1976), 334-52; (with Leona

criticism in which the critic works explicitly from his transaction of the text. Of course, no critic can do anything else, and in that sense, all criticism is at least de facto transactive. It becomes de jure transactive when the critic explicitly builds on his relationship to the text.

When he does so, he aligns himself with what I believe are the true dynamics of the reading transaction. Yes, behind my casual, even reckless associations, there is a model of reading. It begins, like Dupin, with the obvious: the text is the same, but everyone responds to it differently. How do we account for the differences?

Many theorists assume there is some kind of normal response with individual variations. The normal response is the one caused by the text, when it is read in a particular way, variously called the hermeneutic circle (by German critics), or the quest for organic unity (by formalist or "New" critics), or simply the formulation of a centering theme around which all the separate details of the work become relevant. When we read that way, we look at each part to anticipate the whole and then we use our sense of the whole to place each part in a context.

Now let me pose a contrast to that kind of reading, in which one folds the text tightly in on a centering theme. Instead of taking the text as a fixed entity, let us think of it as a process involving a text and a person. Let us open up the text by assuming the person brings to it something extrinsic. It could be information from literary history, biography, or an archaic ritual like the flyting between primitive bards. It could even be some quite personal fact like my reading this story in

---

F. Sherman) "Gothic Possibilities," *New Literary History* 8 (1977), 279-94; "Transactive Teaching: Cordelia's Death," *College English* 39 (1977), 276-85; "Literature as Transaction," in *What Is Literature?*, ed. Paul Hernadi (Bloomington, 1978), pp. 206-18. Other examples would be Murray M. Schwartz, "Critic, Define Thyself," in *Psychoanalysis and the Question of the Text*, ed. Geoffrey Hartman (Baltimore, 1978), pp. 1-17, or David P. Willbern, "Freud and the Inter-Penetration of Dreams," *Diacritics* 9, no. 1 (1979), 98-110.

Pocketbook No. 39 or my finding it at a time in my life when I had something sexual to hide.

It seems to me not only possible but likely that whenever we read, we are associating such extratextual, extraliterary facts to the supposedly fixed text. Now rather than strip those associations away, what will happen if we accept these things outside the text and try to understand the combination of text and personal association? That is what I have been trying to do with you in this essay. That is the first step in transactive criticism. It is also the question that I am posing to Lacan and Derrida. Is not a transactive criticism truer to the human dynamics of literary response than the linguistic glides of a Lacan or the deconstructions of a Derrida? Is it not better to have a literary and especially a psychoanalytic criticism that is grounded in the body and the family?

The question leads to theories of reading. One model assumes that there is a normal response to a text, which the text itself causes, and that the differences in people's responses are idiosyncracies which there is little point in trying to account for. This theory, which I call "text-active," has one basic trouble. It simply does not fit what we know of human perception: namely, that perception is a constructive act in which we impose schemata from our minds on the data of our senses. If it were true that texts in themselves caused responses, reading would be an anomalous procedure, quite different from our other acts of interpreting the world around us.

Consider for a moment what used to be called optical illusions. Equal vertical lines with oppositely pointing arrowheads at their ends appear to be unequal. A flight of stairs seems to flip from right-side up to upside down. A drawing alternately shifts from a vase in silhouette to two human profiles.

Psychologists no longer think of these as "illusions" because they serve instead to demonstrate a fundamental truth about human perception. We see more with our brains than with our eyes. There is no way that two vertical lines of equal length can make you think they are unequal. There is no way

Re-Covering "The Purloined Letter"

a still picture of a flight of steps or of a vase can flip your perception of it first one way, then another. You are doing this to yourself. You are demonstrating again something already demonstrated over seven decades of psychological research—that perception is a constructive act. When we see those vertical lines, we bring something to bear on them; call it a schema, specifically our schema for recognizing rectangular shapes in perspective. What we perceive is the interaction between the lines, the text, if you will, and the schema. We end up with something more than just what is "there."

To take that extra something into account, we need a more sophisticated theory of response than the first, text-active theory. We need a theory in which a text and its literent (reader, viewer, or hearer) act together to cause the response—call it a biactive theory. I think of *Rezeptionsäs-thetik*,[14] for example, as biactive, or speech-act theory,[15] or Fish's "affective stylistics"[16] or Riffaterre's collection of selected readers into a "super-reader."[17] In all these theories, the text sets limits, then the literent projects into the text within those limits. You can see this kind of distinction in Hirsch's differentiation between "meaning" and "signifi-

[14] See, for example, Wolfgang Iser, *The Implied Reader: Patterns of Communication in Prose Fiction from Bunyan to Beckett* (Baltimore, 1974), or Hans Robert Jauss, "Literary History as a Challenge to Literary Theory," *New Literary History* 2 (1970), 7-37. The movement is summarized by Rien T. Segers, "Readers, Text and Author; Some Implications of *Rezeptionsästhetik*," *Yearbook of Comparative and General Literature* 24 (1975), 15-23.

[15] See Richard Ohmann, "Literature as Act," *Approaches to Poetics*, ed. Seymour Chatman (New York, 1973), pp. 81-107.

[16] Stanley Fish stated this approach in "Literature in the Reader: Affective Stylistics," *New Literary History* 2 (1970), 123-62, but has much modified it since then. See "Interpreting 'Interpreting the Variorum,' " *Critical Inquiry* 3 (1976), 191-96, which concludes that all interpretive methods are fictions.

[17] See Michael Riffaterre, "Describing Poetic Structures: Two Approaches to Baudelaire's *Les Chats*," *Yale French Studies*, nos. 36-37 (1966), 200-242. Riffaterre, in subsequent work, has become more semiotic and hence more of a text-active theorist. See, for example, his analysis of Blake's "The Sick Rose," "The Self-Sufficient Text," *Diacritics* 3, no. 3 (1973), 39-45. At the Modern Language Association Meeting, December 27, 1976, he stated, "It is . . . essential that we underscore how tight is the control, how narrow are the limits imposed by the text upon the reader's reactions to it."

Norman N. Holland

cance"[18] or in Iser's notion of determinacy and indeterminacy. The novel may speak of a woman, but it is we who
endow her with a broad forehead, an aggressive stride, or
whatever. The biactivity shows most clearly, perhaps, in
Stanley Fish's stop-motion method of reading (which surely
came from watching too much football on television). First we
read two lines of Lancelot Andrewes during which the text
acts on us. Then we stop and project into the text. Then we
read two more words. Then we project—and so on until
touchdown.

A biactive theory marks a big step forward over the simple
text-active theory. It acknowledges that literents do find more
in texts than just what is "there." Further, it admits a more
than purely linguistic response. People bring social and historical ideas to bear as well as mere linguistic competence.

Nevertheless, the biactive theory seems to me to have two
difficulties. First, it is really two theories, a new theory of
reader activity plus the old text-active theory in which the
text does something to the reader. The biactive theory builds
on the false text-active theory; it thus guarantees it can never
be more than half right.

Further, the biactive theory divides responses into two
stages, as in Fish's stop-motion reading of sentences. But
when I test it against the optical illusions, a two-stage theory
does not fit. I do not first see the lines and then decide that I
will interpret them as though they were perspectives of
rectangles. I do it all in one continuous transaction. I never
see the lines without a schema for seeing them.

If so, texts cannot simply cause or even limit response in
any direct way independent of our schemata, intellectual,
moral, or aesthetic, for reading literature. In fact, if you actually collect people's free responses to texts, they simply do
not show a uniform core (from the text) and individual variations (from the people). The responses have practically nothing in common. One has to conclude, I think, that any uni-
formity we achieve in the classroom comes not from the text

[18] See E. D. Hirsch, Jr., *The Aims of Interpretation* (Chicago, 1976), chap. 1.

Re-Covering "The Purloined Letter"

but from our own skill and authority as teachers, that is, from agreed-upon (or insisted-upon) methods of teaching.

Therefore, I move on from a biactive theory to a transactive theory in which the literent builds the response, and the text simply changes the consequences of what the literent brings to it. The literent creates meaning and feeling in one continuous and indivisible transaction. One cannot separate, as in the biactive theories, one part coming from the text and another part coming from the literent. In a transactive model, I am engaged in a feedback loop no part of which is independent of the other parts. The schemata, conventions, and codes I bring to bear may be literary, biological, cultural, or the results of economic class, but it is I who bring them to bear with my unique identity. It is I who start the loop and I who sustain it. It is I who ask questions of the text in my personal idiom and I who hear and interpret the answers. It is I who mingle the covering of the purloined letter and the Perma-Gloss of my Pocketbook No. 39.

In short, a transactive theory of response has two advantages over either a text-active theory or a biactive theory. First, it fits what the psychologists tell us about the way we perceive meaning in other contexts besides literature— actively, constructively, if you will, creatively. It does not therefore require literature to be an aberration. Second, a transactive theory will account both for the originality and variety of our responses and for our circumscribing them by conventions. In fact, it will do more. By means of psychoanalytic concepts like identity or fantasy or defense, we can connect literary transactions to personality. Precisely because literary experience is so personal, we can understand it through a technique like free association by which psychoanalysts articulate experience in other contexts. With a transactive theory of response, you can relate the rich variety of literary experience to the rich variety of human beings themselves.

You can, but will you? Is it possible for me to make such highly personal associations as my magic tricks when I was

Norman N. Holland

thirteen years old meaningful to you? Can we add them to the text in such a way as to enrich our shared understanding of the story? I think we can, if we go a step beyond the associating I did in the first part of this transacting of "The Purloined Letter."

I can give you my feelings and associations and let you pass them through the story for yourself to see if they enrich your experience. For example, I remember this story in one specific paperback I read when I was thirteen years old. Obviously, you cannot do that, but you can take my association through "The Purloined Letter" by reading the story as a contrast between such tight, spatially defined texts as my paperback or the letter that Dupin physically removes and the indefinite texts of all the different narrations, the Prefect's story, Dupin's story, the Narrator's story (which extends outwards to include two other Dupin stories) and, I would say, extends even to the Perma-Gloss binding of my thirty-nine-year-old copy. Can you get a richer experience of this story by thinking of it as a prototype of all stories—both physically defined but conceptually and emotionally infinite—open to a million different transactions of it?

Another example: the word *purloin* cues me to think of this as a story about moving from place to place, a study in the way context changes text and text changes context, so that D——'s open card case becomes a hiding place because of what is inside it, while the most secret and enclosed places in his house are not hiding places at all. The concealed becomes the open and the open becomes the concealed, a sentence that lets me bring to the story a variety of psychological themes: displacement, abreaction, transference, or repression. I can respond to this story as a study in the way we use spatial metaphors for states of mind.

I can also feel in it the exuberance of human development. Like magic tricks, we give up something, the lost card, the cut rope, in order to get something even more precious, the knowledge which is power. Is that a feeling you can take through the story?

For me, this is a story about hiding, especially the hiding of

Re-Covering "The Purloined Letter"

sexual secrets and how painful and costly it is to let another know that kind of secret, how cheap and easy it is to publish other kinds of secrets. I can feel in this story the detective's, the magician's, the critic's, the psychoanalyst's glee, at being able to turn the Perma-Gloss inside out, and at the same time how shameful it can be for the one whose secret is revealed. Like Mario in *Mario and the Magician*.

I sense a similar contrast between the purely intellectual, safe, powerful kind of knowing practiced by magicians like Dupin and the relating exemplified by the narrator. Intellect is a celibate state of mind to be contrasted with the personal and heterosexual secrets neither Dupin nor the story ever reveals. At that intellectual level, where I am still a graduate student, I can find in this story a flyting: one poet throws lines of poetry at another to win the magic letter and the exalted woman, muse, white goddess, or even the wronged mother. I can read a primitive barbaric magic into the elegant, artistic battle of wits between Dupin and D——, or, for that matter, between Lacan and Derrida (with Holland challenging the winner).[19]

That is a purely intellectual kind of knowledge, though, and my associations suggest a more emotional theme: a story about the difference between trusting the world and needing to know it—to know all of it, the under, the behind, the backward, the inside—a theme to which literary critics are surely no strangers. Ordinarily, we try to bring out what my students sometimes call "hidden meanings," although I, at least, used to protest they are "right out there," like the royal letter, to be seen by anyone who knows how to look for them.

The transactive critic tries to bring into the critical arena

---

[19] After this essay was written, another knight errant entered the lists: Barbara Johnson wittily and winningly pitted Lacan's and Derrida's essays against each other. Unlike my transactive and psychoanalytic skirmish, however, her "theoretical 'frame of reference' is precisely, to a very large extent, the writings of Lacan and Derrida." It is, of course, no less transactive for that. "The Frame of Reference: Poe, Lacan, Derrida," *Literature and Psychoanalysis: The Question of Reading: Otherwise*, ed. Shoshana Felman, *Yale French Studies*, nos. 55-56 (1977), 457-505; *Psychoanalysis and the Question of the Text*, ed. Hartman, pp. 149-71.

Norman N. Holland

another kind of obviousness. He wants to use the obvious truth that we each read differently. More orthodox critics sometimes try to hide or get rid of that embarrassing fact by using differences in response as an occasion for eliminating difference. I suggest a movement in the opposite direction. Instead of subtracting readings so as to narrow them down or cancel some, as Lacan and Derrida do, let us use human differences to add response to response, to multiply possibilities, and to enrich the whole experience.[20] That way, we can re-cover the letter purloined by such abstract, intellectual readings as Lacan's or Derrida's. We can restore stories to their rightful owners—you and me and all of you and me, our emotional as well as our intellectual selves—by recovering reading as a personal transaction.

[20] This new method of reading (deliberately opening a poem outward to include the extratextual) is spelled out in greater detail and with more examples in a collective paper by the seminar English 692, "Poem Opening: An Invitation to Transactive Criticism," *College English* 40 (1978), 2-16. "Poem opening," using the criticism, even the rejected criticism, of others, occurs in my "How Do Dr. Johnson's Remarks on Cordelia's Death Add to My Own Response?" in *Psychoanalysis and the Question of the Text*, ed. Geoffrey Hartman (Baltimore, 1978), pp. 18-44.

Vicki Mistacco | The Theory and Practice of Reading Nouveaux Romans: Robbe-Grillet's *Topologie d'une cité fantôme*

A critic interested in how we read nouveaux romans might very well be allergic to terms like *convention*, *naturalization*, and *literary competence*. Being institutional, conventions rest upon a foundation that smacks uncomfortably of the "dominant ideology" so often decried by Ricardou and his disciples. Naturalization involves constructing "communicative circuits"[1] into which we can fit a literary text; the nouveau roman officially rejects the idea of literature as communication.[2] And although the reader's intertext has been invoked as an important factor in processing a given text,[3] the model of literary competence has been challenged by that of performance, presumably less constrained by the institutional practices implicit in the notion of competence.[4]

That literary competence and conventions of reading are at work, even in the nouveau roman, is nevertheless obvious. Culler and Heath have shown how the radical otherness of nouveaux romans may be reduced by reading them as illus-

[1] Jonathan Culler, *Structuralist Poetics* (Ithaca, 1975), p. 134.

[2] See Françoise van Rossum-Guyon's summation of the 1971 proceedings at Cerisy in *Nouveau roman: Hier, aujourd'hui*, vol. 1 (Paris, 1972), esp. 405. (*Nouveau roman: Hier, aujourd'hui* will henceforth be abbreviated *NRHA*.)

[3] Claudette Oriol-Boyer, *"Dans le labyrinthe* et le discours social: Propositions pour une lecture," in Jean Ricardou, ed., *Robbe-Grillet: Colloque de Cerisy*, vol. 2 (Paris, 1976), 383-84 and discussion, 405.

[4] François Jost, "Les Téléstructures dans l'oeuvre d'Alain Robbe-Grillet," in *Robbe-Grillet: Colloque de Cerisy*, 2: 238.

Vicki Mistacco

trations and enactments of the practice of writing.[5] To this even Ricardou would give his assent. That certain approaches to these works have become institutionalized is also reflected in the remarkable homogeneity which, despite surface differences, characterizes the nearly nine-hundred-page transcript of the 1975 Colloque de Cerisy on Robbe-Grillet. Four years earlier, in the same setting, Robbe-Grillet proudly pointed to sales statistics to show that the nouveau roman had succeeded in inventing its own audience, comprised of more than just a handful of literary intellectuals.[6] Clearly, that audience has evolved expectations from its reading, expectations whose tenacity has elevated them to the status of conventions. After almost a quarter of a century of nouveaux romans, it is therefore legitimate to ask what "new" conventions they presuppose instead of those they seek both theoretically and pragmatically to displace, and to what extent these conventions strain existing theories of ideal (Culler) and implied (Booth, Iser) readers as well as correlative theories of the narratee (Prince, Genette).

Without ignoring its specificity, I shall present *Topologie d'une cité fantôme*[7] as an exemplary novel that reinforces a series of conventions which, although characteristic of Robbe-Grillet, are also operative in the antirepresentational fiction of other nouveaux romanciers. The practice of reading *Topologie* is offered as a framework for reassessing current reader theory.

The conventions at work in the novel may be highlighted by reference to mathematical topology. Topology is, in fact, a recurrent metaphor in theoretical discussions of the "production" of both reader and writer of contemporary texts, and it is surely with a good deal of critical self-consciousness that Robbe-Grillet borrows the term for his title and organizes the

[5] Culler, *Structuralist Poetics*, pp. 151-52; Stephen Heath, *The Nouveau Roman: A Study in the Practice of Writing* (Philadelphia, 1972), passim.

[6] *NRHA*, 1: 143-44.

[7] All page references to Alain Robbe-Grillet, *Topologie d'une cité fantôme* (Paris, 1976) will be given in the text. The translations are my own.

novel's space accordingly.[8] His most obvious critical reference, Bruce Morrissette,[9] uses topology to elucidate by analogy structural relationships and configurations, particularly in Robbe-Grillet's later novels, involving complex modes of containment through interior duplication. While these structural relationships certainly affect the reader's path(s) through the text, it is in the writing of others, not immediately concerned with Robbe-Grillet, that we find topology more directly linked with the operations of reading.

In a theoretical leap that is symptomatic of the difficulties one encounters in trying to locate the reader and define the conventions of reading in novels like *Topologie*, Roland Barthes, in the space of four years, moves from a typically structuralist attitude concerning the reader's inscription in the text (the analysis of "narrative communication" entails "describing the code by which the narrator and reader are signified throughout the narrative itself")[10] to one whereby reading implies neither narrative communication as such nor codes of narration: "Reading . . . is not a parasitical gesture, a complementary response to a form of writing (*écriture*) that we adorn with all the prestige of creation and anteriority. It is work . . . and the method of this work is topological: I am not hidden in the text, I am merely unlocatable: my task is to move, to relay systems whose prospect stops neither at the

[8] Topology is that branch of geometry which studies the qualitative properties and relative positions of geometric entities, independent of their form and size. Topological properties are therefore those which remain the same despite distortion, stretching or twisting. Primarily interested in connectedness and continuity, topology studies not only spatial continuity as we may experience it in life (Möbius strips) but also other, physically impossible types of continuity (for example, the Klein bottle, a one-sided surface that passes through itself without making a hole). Topology concerns itself more with the logic of its results within the rules and limits it has set than with their "truth" or applicability to the world.

[9] "Robbe-Grillet N⁰ 1, 2 . . . X," in *NRHA*, 2: 119-33; "Topology and the French *Nouveau Roman*," *Boundary 2*, vol. 1 (1972), 45-57.

[10] "Introduction à l'analyse structurale des récits," in Barthes et al., *Poétique du récit* (Paris, 1977), p. 38. (originally published in *Communications* 8 [1966].)

text nor at 'myself.' "[11] Kristeva similarly stresses the dynamism of production, pointing up in that context the usefulness of the topological model for dealing with the nonrepresentable in both science and literature.[12] In a more Derridean perspective, topology has been seen as a means of occulting the originating metaphor and, by Derrida himself, as a characteristic resulting from the signifier's lack of ultimate unity and finality.[13] For Deleuze, topological surfaces are the locus of meaning, the place where preindividual nomadic singularities appear as nonorientable topological events, and where two series of signs become mutually, but nonhierarchically, resonant.[14] In this theoretical climate, it is no wonder that analysis of reading becomes such an elusive task. The reader has lost the very traits which are prerequisite to his apprehension by the precise tools that critics like Booth, Culler, Iser, Fish, Prince, Genette, Todorov, and others have given us: identity and the capacity to be represented. And because the text itself has been stripped of origin and finality, reading, that is, the reader's movement through the text, tends to lack both direction and definition. If, for strong ideological reasons, authors and readers have forfeited their authority over the text, the critic, too, seems to have been reduced to nonauthoritarian and less than authoritative metaphors. What follows is an attempt to walk a critical tightrope, to respect the metaphor of topology while formulating the conventions of a "new" kind of reading.

[11] Roland Barthes, *S/Z* (Paris, 1970), p. 17. Culler observes that "the absence of any code relating to narration (the reader's ability to collect items which help to characterize a narrator and to place the text in a kind of communicative circuit) is a major flaw in Barthes's analysis" (p. 203). Indeed a flaw, it is nevertheless a logical consequence of Barthes's emphasis on production, movement, topology and on reading as "metonymical sliding" (*S/Z*, p. 99), and it suggests why texts with a similar emphasis render identification of the reader and his activity problematic at best.

[12] Julia Kristeva, *Séméiotikè* (Paris, 1969), pp. 39-40. The nonrepresentable exists in tension with the representable, but escapes formalization by representational models.

[13] Joseph Duhamel, *NRHA*, 2: 153-54; Jacques Derrida, "The Purveyor of Truth," *Yale French Studies*, no. 52 (1975), 65-66.

[14] Gilles Deleuze, *Logique du sens* (Paris, 1969), pp. 124-27.

TOPOLOGICAL SPACE

From the outset of *Topologie d'une cité fantôme* the text is equated with a topological space[15] in which narrator, implied author (*scriptor*, as he is now called in France to reflect his diminished authority), and reader move about freely, unconstrained by the laws that preside over real space and its traditional fictional counterpart. Despite its generic attribution, the text therefore begins by violating the long-standing contract that a novel will produce a world corresponding to habitual models of intelligibility (Culler, *Structuralist Poetics*, pp. 189-90). Topology allows Robbe-Grillet to carry out his "ludic" intentions,[16] creating a space whose referential aspects are deconstructed by means of nonreferential "distortion" according to arbitrary rules. The interaction of ludism and the spatial metaphor governing the elaboration of the text is suggested by the opening narrator: the blood of the first in a series of violated virgins forms a pool on the ancient black-and-white chessboard pattern of a marble floor (p. 13). De-realized by its characteristic ludic setting, the crime is further distanced from reality when the death-dealing "broad-bladed knife" (p. 11) becomes the instrument for textual inscription of another, topologically homologous, imaginary space: "gravant dans le schiste avec la pointe du couteau à large lame, j'écris maintenant le mot CONSTRUCTION, peinture en trompe-l'oeil, construction imaginaire par laquelle je nomme les ruines d'une future divinité" (p. 13) ("engraving the schist with the point of the broad-bladed knife, I now write the word CONSTRUCTION, *trompe l'oeil* painting, imaginary construction by which I name the ruins of a future divinity"). This process of naming focuses attention on the literal

[15] The novel is in fact organized into five "spaces," four of which are subdivided into sections roughly approximating chapters. These spaces are framed by an "Incipit" and a "Coda."

[16] "Ludism" may be simply defined as the open play of signification, as the free and productive interaction of forms, of signifiers and signifieds, without regard for an original or an ultimate meaning. In literature, ludism signifies textual play; the text is viewed as a game affording both author and reader the possibility of producing endless meanings and relationships.

Vicki Mistacco

transformation of a constant set of generators and carries the reader along from realistic construction to realistic construction, each one abolishing its predecessor, while the temporal dimension is similarly sabotaged. The "Incipit" thus establishes a tension between the literal and the referential aspects of the text and posits mobile structures, setting up the novel's own conventions of reading.

As rectangles are remade into topologically homeomorphic circles and ellipses, and groups of five are replaced by groups of three, the condition of readability in a Robbe-Grilletian text becomes clear: a tension due to oppositions, to "irreconcilable polarities among novelistic elements (*éléments romanesques*) and a form of writing (*écriture*) which was not meant for the novelistic," a "break between the novelistic itself and the narration which operates on it."[17] Thus, although the substitution of curved for angular forms is realistically announced in the "generative cell" (p. 24) when the narrator suddenly "remembers" that the wooden chairs are really classic garden chairs made of iron and full of curves, sinuous lines, and spirals, it is the nonnarrative functioning of writing that brings about the conjoined metamorphoses of fives to threes and angles to curves when the generative cell is transposed on stage:

> un tableau vivant constitué par deux filles entièrement nues sert de sujet à la jeune photographe . . . qui opère en face d'elles avec un gros appareil de forme archaïque: une boîte noire ovoïde, munie d'un oeil rond à diaphragme apparent et d'un cordon à poire actionnant le déclencheur, dressé sur un support de bois verni à trois minces pieds coulissants. Vêtue avec élégance d'une sorte de complet d'homme en toile blanche . . . l'artiste se penche en avant pour apercevoir dans le viseur la gracieuse image de bain dont elle vient de régler méticuleusement la mise en scène: deux adolescentes debout l'une près de l'autre, la plus grande faisant couler

[17] Vicki Mistacco, "Interview with Alain Robbe-Grillet," *Diacritics* 6, no. 3 (1976), 35, 36. Hereafter referred to as "Interview."

Reading Nouveaux Romans

sur l'épaule de sa compagne le contenu d'un pot à eau
ventru . . . comme on utilisait autrefois pour la toilette;
une cuvette assortie repose à leurs pieds sur le sol . . .
ainsi qu' un porte-savon tout en courbes glissantes . . . A
l'opposé, c'est-à-dire en arrière et sur la droite, un grand
miroir ovale . . . renvoie vers l'opératrice l'image bien
cadrée des fesses arrondies de la baigneuse. (Emphasis
mine) (pp. 64-65)

a tableau vivant made up of two entirely naked girls
serves as subject for the young photographer . . . who is
working opposite them with a large apparatus of archaic
form: an ovoid black box, outfitted with a round eye and
its visible diaphragm and with a pear-shaped shutter release bulb, set up on a lacquered wood support with
three slim extendable legs. Elegantly attired in a kind of
white linen man's suit . . . the artist leans forward to see
in the viewer the gracious image of bathers she has just
meticulously arranged: two adolescent girls standing
close together, the taller one pouring onto the shoulder
of her companion the contents of a pot-bellied water jug
. . . like those used in the past for one's toilet; a matching
basin rests at their feet on the floor . . . along with a soap
dish full of slippery curves . . . Opposite, that is, in back
and to the right, a large oval mirror . . . reflects back to
the camera operator the well-framed image of the
bather's round buttocks.

On the level of the signifier, an obvious proliferation of
phonetic and lettristic *o*'s reinforces the omnipresent rounded
forms as signifieds. But it is the intersection of the *oi* in "trois"
and "ovoïde" that explains, at this point in the novel, a simultaneous profusion of threes[18] and curves and the liquidation
of the previous generators. Literal permutations supersede
referential logic. And it is for similarly nonreferential reasons,

[18] Of course, the triangles and the three groups of women in the generative cell provide long-range preparation for the shift to three. But once the
oi's combine in this way, not only do curves, circles, and ellipses dominate,
but threes become obsessive: see especially pp. 65, 68, 69, 71, 71-72, 73.

377

Vicki Mistacco

as the novel draws to a close and the liquidation of *all* geometric generators is begun, that both curved and angular forms are eroded. Through such procedures, the diegetic matrix, variations on the theme of the raped virgin, is at once preserved and deterritorialized or neutralized.[19]

The textual and referential holes that punctuate the novel on virtually every page facilitate topological operations and, in so doing, sustain the ambiguous status of the diegetic material. In fact, the entire narrative which returns us, typically, to the void, "l'interminable couloir vide, immuablement net et propre" (p. 201) ("the interminable empty corridor, immutably clear and clean"), can be said to have literally and figuratively emerged from a hole, its opening sentence left incomplete, followed by suspension points, then by a series of negations that the text will, of course, materialize:

> Avant de m'endormir, la ville, de nouveau
> . . .
> Mais il n'y a plus rien, ni cri, ni roulement, ni rumeur lointaine . . . (p.9)
>
> Before I fall asleep, the city, once again
> . . .
> But there is nothing left, neither a cry, nor rumbling, nor distant noise . . .

As ironic origin of the phantom city, the hole stresses the antimimetic functioning of the novel. With neither a preexisting world nor preordained meanings, the text is offered solely as the terrain for an arbitrary game of construction. Empty spaces, absence, gaping holes, undifferentiated landscapes, are as obsessive as the mobile configurations of the generative material to which they repeatedly give rise. With similar irony, the "absent, imaginary, goddess of necessity" (p. 44),

---

[19] For an analysis of deterritorialization in *Projet pour une révolution à New York*, see Sylvère Lotringer, "Le Texte en fuite," in Ricardou, ed., *Robbe-Grillet: Colloque de Cerisy*, vol. 1 (Paris, 1976), 223-30; neutralization is discussed by Renato Barilli in "Neutralisation et différence," ibid., pp. 391-407.

Reading Nouveaux Romans

a parodic rendition of the ubiquitous omniscient author, commands the inscription of generative objects. This kind of creation out of the void is designed precisely to undermine referential notions of origin and subjectivity and to contest any authoritative perspective on the narrative—be it that of the implied author or merely of a narrator—that the reader may seek to construct. For the narrator also "has fallen into the hole, and in *Topologie*, he reappears on the other side. He comes out into another space, but he has lost all the features of a character" ("Interview," p. 37). Unsettling all forms of representation, the text provokes a series of topological *glissements*, a shifting identity for the narrator and consequently for the narratee, and an incessant sliding from textual space to textual space.

Like Möbius strips and Klein bottles, the space in this novel is nonorientable. Emblematic of the free play of signs, elements of one space can be propelled into another by means of a hole in the space represented:[20] a window, a door, a crack in a wall, a keyhole, the absent fourth wall of a theatrical stage. A cry from outside heard in the generative cell thus permits a transition through the window to the outer landscape where, a few pages later, five women tourists contemplate the same window *"from* which the cry of terror seemed to come a moment earlier" (p. 31, emphasis mine). Here, as in Klein bottles, it is impossible to distinguish what is outside from what is within a given space and therefore to organize the text as a coherent representation of reality.

Instead, in a chapter whose title, "Landscape with Cry," recalls the earlier proliferation of nonoriented cries, a reading based on the idea that any point in space, that is to say, any sequence or element of a sequence, may organize countless

[20] B. Morrissette was the first to describe this phenomenon in earlier Robbe-Grillet novels (*Dans le labyrinthe*, *Projet pour une révolution à New York*). See "Robbe-Grillet N° 1, 2 . . . X" and "Topology and the French *Nouveau Roman*." Without necessarily depending on holes to effect transitions, other nouveaux romans, most notably Claude Simon's *Triptyque* (Paris, 1973), exhibit a similar nonorientability permitting the free exploration of signifier and signified.

connections is supported by three developments on the word *réseau*, the second of which constitutes a virtual *mise en abyme* of the activity of both writer and reader in the text:

> les rails en acier poli . . . forment un réseau serré de lignes blafardes qui courent d'est en ouest à des distances variables l'une de l'autre, se réunissant par endroit, se séparant un peu plus loin, finissant par communiquer toutes entre elles, ici ou là, par un jeu compliqué d'aiguillages. (pp. 168-69)

> rails of polished steel . . . form a tight network of pale lines running from east to west at variable distances from each other, joining in spots, separating a bit further on, all ending up by communicating with each other, here or there, by a complicated play of switches.

What the reader of this type of antirepresentational fiction has been made to expect is not the security of linear development but the possibility of topological sliding in all directions, linking textual units in a variety of configurations to which only she or he can set limits. Typically post-modern in this respect, *Topologie* formalizes a convention of reading based on open, plural, fluid structures inviting the renewable and alterable performance of the reader.

This implies that we must go beyond the "conventionally natural" (Culler, *Structuralist Poetics*, pp. 148-52) if we wish to indicate how naturalization occurs. To say that the text is an attempt to expose the conventions of the novel as mere conventions, as artifice, by showing how language leads to the creation of illusory meanings is overly reductive. While that subversive intent is, of course, present and important, as I have indicated, it is ceaselessly displaced from the center of the reader's attention by a convention that subsumes and transcends generic considerations: that of ludism. The topological metaphor, as it is assimilated by Robbe-Grillet from the cultural milieu out of which and for which he writes, points to the institutionalization of textual play, of shifting

Reading Nouveaux Romans

though arbitrarily related patterns of forms and meanings suggesting—paradoxically, given that very institutionalization—an infinite, and therefore liberating, range of possibilities.

THE READER AS FUNCTION

Sustaining this mobile pluralism are the fluid and interchangeable identities of narrator and narratee, scriptor and implied reader. Graphically illustrated by Robbe-Grillet's use of personal pronouns, this circulation of narrative roles makes it impossible to attribute the narrative to one or more recognizable narrators and consequently undermines selection of any narratees as possible intermediaries between ourselves and the text.[21] If we look beyond this confusion of narrative roles for a coherent implied author we come upon similar problems of attribution. On both levels, the *sujet parlant* or speaker is perpetually called into question, ceaselessly evicted from the originating center. Robbe-Grillet's concept of a mobile voice of narration is consistent with his redefinition of the implied author not in terms of identity, but as a function: "the implied author exists nonetheless. Only he displaces himself from character to character, from place to place, from gesture to gesture . . . all character is absent. And yet, there is an implied author . . . or, in any case, an authorial function (*une fonction scriptrice*)" ("Interview," p. 38). Correspondingly, the reader's understanding of and entry into the project of a novel like *Topologie* will depend upon his willingness not to assume a *persona*, as is customary, but to

---

[21] "The most obvious role of the narratee, *a role he always plays* in a certain sense, is that of relay between narrator and reader(s) . . ." Gerald Prince, "Introduction à l'étude du narrataire," *Poétique*, no. 14 (1973), 192 (emphasis mine). Robbe-Grillet's technique renders equally inoperative Gérard Genette's hierarchy of narrative levels with their attendant narrators and narratees. "Discours du récit," in *Figures III* (Paris, 1972), esp. pp. 265-66. Peter J. Rabinowitz's excellent classification of audiences in narrative literature rests on notions of belief and, above all, representation, that also make his categories inapplicable here. "Truth in Fiction: A Reexamination of Audiences," *Critical Inquiry* 4 (1977), 121-41.

Vicki Mistacco

become a function, his inscription in the text being susceptible to definition in Derridean terms as part of a structure of
generalized deferment. The text is thus transformed into a
topological surface, scriptor and implied reader approximating what Deleuze would call preindividual nomadic singularities whose separateness and identity are simultaneously maintained and denied. Ultimately this means the
reversibility of scriptorial and lectorial roles and points to the
self-realization of the reader as an active participant in a
salutarily open, dynamic process of production.

It also means that the communicative scheme elaborated by
linguists[22] involving interaction between two identities and
upon which are based theories of reading as precise and as
generally illuminating as those of Jonathan Culler, Wayne C.
Booth, Walter J. Ong, and Wolfgang Iser,[23] fails to provide an
adequate account of our experience of this type of narrative
and therefore renders those theories only marginally useful.
How does this breakdown occur?

From the perspective of linguistics, "je," like "tu," is an
empty sign, defined not referentially, but by its function in
the situation of enunciation and susceptible of redefinition
with each new speech-act.[24] Robbe-Grillet capitalizes on this
potential of the first person to deconstruct the subject and
disrupt narrative continuities by having it circulate among
different characters and even disappear entirely as it does in
the second space. Thus, while there seems to be some con-

[22] The classic contribution in this area is Roman Jakobson, "Closing Statement: Linguistics and Poetics," in Thomas A. Sebeok, ed., *Style in Language*
(Cambridge, Mass., 1960), pp. 350-77.

[23] Culler, *Structuralist Poetics*; Booth, *The Rhetoric of Fiction* (Chicago, 1961),
and *A Rhetoric of Irony* (Chicago, 1974); Ong "The Writer's Audience Is Always a Fiction," *PMLA* 90 (1975), 9-21; Iser, *The Implied Reader* (Baltimore,
1974).

[24] Emile Benveniste, "La Nature des pronoms" and "De la subjectivité
dans le langage," in *Problèmes de linguistique générale*, vol. 1 (Paris, 1966),
251-57, 258-66. Sylvère Lotringer takes Benveniste as a point of departure for
a brilliant demonstration of the breakdown of linguistic distinctions between
"I" and "he" in *Projet*: "Le Texte en fuite," in Rícardou, ed., *Robbe-Grillet:
Colloque de Cerisy*, 1: 231-36.

Reading Nouveaux Romans

tinuity between the somnambular archeologist who narrates
the "Incipit" and the "I" of the beginning of the first space,
the first person, already weakened by the incursion of the
pronoun "one," is eclipsed by a passage in the infinitive: "Ne
pas oublier, ici, de mentionner le barreau brisé. . . . Signaler,
tout à fait sur le devant, un caillou gros comme un poing . . ."
(p. 30) ("Don't forget to mention the broken bar. . . . Point
out, in the immediate foreground, a rock as big as a fist . . .").
With no personal or temporal deictics, the infinitive escapes
subjective appropriation in a communicative exchange between narrator and narratee, as well as referential limitation.
It deterritorializes the process of enunciation, and, particularly as Robbe-Grillet uses it here and in the section "Règle
du jeu" ("Rules of the Game," pp. 132-34), suggests language as the origin of language or, more precisely, the ideal
of a text engendered by the infinite play of words.

Dispossessed and deconstructed through the operations of
the infinitive, the narrative "I" can come into existence again
in the third space with a new identity, an unstable combination of detective, criminal, *metteur en scène*, and extension of
the D. H. or David H. upon whom the second space focuses.
In the fourth space, however, the single remaining element of
continuity with the initial narrator disappears when "I"
changes sex, emerging from "she" to materialize the dream
of a captive girl. Adding sexual instability to the imperma-
nence of narrative voices, Robbe-Grillet intimates, on a
higher level, a scriptorial/lectorial function that lies beyond
the realm not only of individualization, but of all forms of exclusion and contradiction, a dynamic topology allowing
sameness and difference, absence and presence, male and
female, to connect nonhierarchically and without dialectical
resolution.

By the time we reach the fifth space, "The Criminal Already on My Own Traces," a broad allusion to detective Wallas of *Les Gommes*, "I" asserts itself over a competitive "one"
(Paris ed., pp. 149-50). This narrator would seem to merge
with the sleepwalking archeologist-author of the opening
pages while retaining signs of his hybrid identity from the

Vicki Mistacco

third space. But lest this approximate fusion of diversity into one narrative voice return us to a traditional, integrative mode of reading, Robbe-Grillet has him decipher a text, a poor reconstruction of his own story, combining elements of the preceding pages and of the "Incipit." Here "I" becomes, paradoxically, the narratee of himself as another, narrating "I": "Et maintenant voici le texte: je me réveille. . . . C'est le matin, c'est le soir, je ne sais plus. . . ." (pp. 152-53) ("And now here is the text: I awake. . . . It is morning, it is evening, I no longer know. . . ."). In topological fashion, both sides of the narrative join in a continuous line.

As if this did not suffice to explode the subject, Robbe-Grillet also borrows the first person to make an obvious reference to himself as author of *Les Gommes*:

> ce problème particulier, le gommage d'une lettre et son remplacement par le signe suivant dans l'ordre de l'alphabet (soit, ici, l'effacement d'un G en faveur d'un H) [a] été traité de façon exhaustive dans le premier roman que j'ai publié jadis. (p. 98)

> this particular problem, the erasure of a letter and its replacement by the next sign in the order of the alphabet (that is, here, the obliteration of a G in favor of an H) was treated exhaustively in the first novel that I published long ago.

This intrusion by the author obviously breaks up the coherence of the narrative voice. But, above all, it has the paradoxical function of making the real author not the ultimate authority, the final referent for the text, but "a paper being and his life a *bio-graphy* (in the etymological sense of the term), an *écriture* without referent, matter for *connection*, and not *filiation*" (Barthes, *S/Z*, p. 217). The documentary figure of the author is thus turned into a "novelistic figure, unlocatable, irresponsible, caught in the plural movement (*le pluriel*) of his own text" (ibid.). The reader too is caught up in this movement. Projected into a larger intertextual space, he is afforded

Reading Nouveaux Romans

the possibility of yet other circuits and connections, a fact that broadens the principle of variable readings built into the individual text. Although this is the only intertextual reference presented by a narrative "I," the novel restructures countless elements from previous works by Robbe-Grillet as well as by artists (Delvaux, Rauschenberg, Magritte, Hamilton) and other writers (Proust, Baudelaire, Verlaine, Hugo, Mallarmé, Lewis Carroll). Fluidity is a function of literary, cinematic, and artistic competence: the more one brings to the text, the richer one's perceptions of the generators will be and the greater the possibilities for play. And because the link with *Les Gommes*, like most of the connections made by the narrator(s), is not quite exact since, given the Oedipal generators in that novel, it is H (for *les Hommes*, a deviant answer to the riddle of the sphinx) which is actually replaced by G,[25] no obstacle is posed to the reader's and the author's continued movement from text to text. Like the author, the reader is "unlocatable."

The pronoun "one" also guarantees the fluidity of narrative roles and contributes to the evacuation of the subject. Splitting off from "I" in the opening section and at several points in the fifth space, "one" suppresses the voice of narration and acts as focalizer.[26] Should a table be described as square or rectangular? "ici encore l'effet de perspective est trop marqué pour que l'on puisse en décider à coup sûr" (p. 21) ("here again the effect of perspective is too pronounced for one to decide for certain"). More profoundly, "one" does not simply substitute the subjectivity of an observer for that of a speaker, thereby obliquely reinstating the subject. As "fourth-person singular" (a term Deleuze borrows from Fer-

[25] See Robbe-Grillet's rejection of the cultural myth of *l'Homme* with a capital H in *NRHA*, 2: 161-62. Thomas D. O'Donnell discusses the *g/h* permutations and the hypothetical *les Hommes* in an unpublished manuscript, "Beyond *Topologie*: Robbe-Grillet's *métaphoricité fantôme*" discussed at the MLA seminar on "Le Nouveau nouveau roman," New York, December 1976.

[26] See G. Genette's distinction between voice and perspective in "Discours du récit," *Figures III*, pp. 203-67; and Mieke Bal's refinement of Genette's categories: "Narration et focalisation," *Poétique*, no. 29 (1977), 107-27.

Vicki Mistacco

linghetti in *Logique du sens*, p. 125), it stands for the preindividual nomadic singularities, for the potential that precedes the constitution of an individualized "I" "coextensive with representation" (ibid., p. 129). The interaction of "I" and "one," not unlike the interplay between "I" and the infinitive, therefore marks the inscription of an anonymous textual engenderment. The sliding between "one" and "I" is the sliding between a potential and an actualized text, a reminder of textual openness and a means of keeping the reader's role unstable.

Accordingly, "one" can assume a variety of functions. Like "I," the focalizer can slip into the position of narratee: "Cette lettre donne la série suivante, à laquelle d'ailleurs on devait s'attendre . . ." (p. 49) ("This letter yields the following series, which one should have expected moreover . . ."). Or the observer-narratee can vanish altogether: "le petit garçon et la petite fille se ressemblent trait pour trait, tels deux jumeaux, comme il fallait s'y attendre" (p. 68) ("the little boy and the little girl resemble each other feature for feature, like twins, as might have been expected").

"One" can also be actively taken over by a character as in a rather complex series of pronominal changes in the fourth space. Tenuously wrenched from the referential "she," the young captive's "I" is at first in tension with "one": "On dirait des moutons errant sur la lande. . . . Mais voici, maintenant, que se distinguent mieux les contours et les surfaces: c'est moi, tout simplement" (p. 124) ("One would say sheep wandering on the heath. . . . But here, now, the contours and surfaces are becoming more distinct: it is simply myself"). Thus engendered by the "one" of infinite possibilities, the discourse can begin to be personalized. The first person is now addressed to an ambiguous "you" (p. 126). Suddenly, however, personalized discourse gives way to the nonperson "she" (p. 127)[27] accompanied by a collective "one" ("les

[27] For Benveniste, "I" and "you" are a function of discourse and fall under the category of "persons," whereas "he," "she," "it," "that," have external, objective referents and are "nonpersons." *Problèmes de linguistique générale*, 1: 255-57.

Reading Nouveaux Romans

moutons . . . que l'on comptait pour s'endormir" [p. 128] ["the sheep . . . one counted to fall asleep"]) that appears, in the manner of free indirect style, to emanate from no clear situation of enunciation. The constant interchange of first and third persons already breaks down the habitual separation of pronouns upon which the logic of narration and representation is founded, but it is in the realization of all the possibilities of the pronoun "one" that the text most vividly reveals its madness, its movement in the domain of infinitely connectable noncontradictory meanings.

For we proceed from the collective "one" of little girls considered at a distance by an anonymous discourse, to a more personalized "one," associated with the voice of narration and alternately assimilable with a feminine singular "I" and a feminine plural "we," but not excluding the feminine singular or plural "you" of the narratee(s): "Si l'on est seule, il faut faire semblant d'être deux. Si l'on est deux . . ." (p. 131) ("If one is alone, one must make believe there are two. If there are two . . ."). Once this prescriptive sequence is over, the narratee fades away allowing "one," at first feminine plural ("I" and "she"), to be reduced to the singular and tell a story, thereby fully appropriating the discursive status of "I" (p. 136). With "one," then, "everything is singular, and thereby collective and private at once, particular and general, neither individual nor universal" (Deleuze, *Logique du sens*, p. 178), subjective and objective, discursive and referential, focalizing and narrating. Having once again fallen into the hole, as Robbe-Grillet would say, the first-person singular is free to pop up again later with a new narratee, a "tu," another captive in the sultan's harem to whom she tells *their* own story,[28]

[28] "Pour te consoler, je vais maintenant te raconter notre véritable histoire" (p. 140) ("To console you, I am now going to tell you our true story"). From here until the end of the fourth space, narrative "I" alternates with "we" and "one" (both representing, on the whole, "I" and "you" as female characters). However, in the first, third, and fifth spaces (e.g., pp. 51, 52, 55, 94, 152, 192), the first-person plural encompasses narrator and narratee and therefore plays a different role, entirely within the bounds, not of story, but of discourse. By creating a system of false or merely quasi-exact references to other sectors of the text, this "we" subverts the anaphoric function by which

Vicki Mistacco

thereby continuing the process of incessant transformation and exchange of narrative roles and assuring the permanent migration of writing.[29]

In a word, the sliding of pronouns in *Topologie d'une cité fantôme* reinforces and assumes what has now become a convention: that reading and writing are but two facets of the same activity, and that to read is to accept literature as "the proposition made to a subject to be all forms."[30]

REPETITION WITH DIFFERENCE

An aspect of ludism that has been widely theorized and so often highlighted in the *nouveau roman* that it approaches a critical cliché is the practice of repeating the same material (signifier, signified, or sequential configuration) but incorporating in the repetition an arbitrary factor of difference. The criticism of Ricardou, Heath, Barilli, Lotringer, and others suggests a remarkable convergence in this area between the theories of Foucault, Deleuze, Derrida, and Kristeva and the production of antirepresentational novelists. In fact, ludism's corollary *répétition différente* has permeated the intellectual climate to the extent of becoming a condition for reading and writing. If this feature appears all too familiar, it is because, as Jacques Leenhardt has stressed, it is now a standard means of naturalizing those texts: "The nouveau roman has accustomed us to considering as contradictory, or problematic, this type of duplication with difference . . . analysis must be made within a mode of readability instituted by a certain type of literature" (*Robbe-Grillet: Colloque de Cerisy*, 1: 439). The question

---

a novel creates "its own code of consumption and reading." Philippe Hamon, "Pour un statut sémiologique du personnage," in *Poétique du récit*, p. 124.

[29] Jean Ricardou gives an excellent account of how the migration of writing can represent literature as production and explains how reading as production may be inscribed in the text by using a given fragment as the basis, not for continuity, but for a change of direction, in Ricardou, ed., *Robbe-Grillet: Colloque de Cerisy*, 1: 158-61.

[30] Philippe Sollers, *Logiques* (Paris, 1968), p. 243.

Reading Nouveaux Romans

then is, How does Robbe-Grillet's novel program this mode of readability? Secondly, how do topology and other non-literary metaphors help clarify its conventions?

Reflecting the initial step of the reader's approach to any text, the dominant scriptorial and narrative function in *Topologie* is one of assimilation. "The work of reading," writes Todorov, "begins by bringing together, by discovering resemblance."[31] Resemblance, of course, insures meaning. We know that similarity may be discovered by the reader between the world of the text and a form of discourse that seems to approximate reality, or between elements within one or a group of specifically literary texts (Culler, *Structuralist Poetics*, pp. 140-60). *Topologie* calls for the kind of reading described by Leenhardt by taking up and subverting both kinds of assimilation. The narrative begins by establishing differences within the undifferentiated space of the phantom city, thereby setting in motion *signifiance*, the work of signification. These differences in turn are subjected to a double process of assimilation that does not yield meaning (*sens*) but rather blocks or displaces it.

Assimilation with the everyday world is impeded, paradoxically, by overuse of expressions such as "like," "as if," "recalling" and "analogous." These generally introduce gestures toward reality which prove spurious in the sense that, when totalized, they offer no grounds for a coherent representational construction by the reader. They are spurious contextually as well in that they are often used to multiply rather than reduce differences, setting both narrative and meanings in motion again, as in this seeming equivalence between two bedrooms:

semblable—dis-je—à ceci près, peut-être, que les fissures des parois, se ramifiant en un réseau complexe à la surface du plâtre au papier peint décoloré . . . deviennent ici, par endroit, de véritables crevasses où l'on passerait à l'aise une lame de couteau. (p.183)

[31] Tzvetan Todorov, *Poétique de la prose* (Paris, 1971), p. 247.

Vicki Mistacco

alike—I say—with this exception, perhaps, that the fissures on the walls, branching out into a complex network on the surface of the plaster with its discolored wallpaper . . . become here, in spots, veritable crevices into which one might easily slip the blade of a knife.

The function of "semblable" and similar expressions is therefore ultimately a ludic one; they serve as operators of the textual *glissements* resulting from the principle of "endless" association.

Analogous to these counterfeit gestures toward reality are gestures to this and other texts by Robbe-Grillet. Generally introduced by the phrase *déjà dit* ("already said") or some variant of it, they engage the reader in the process of assimilation. This device would seem to accentuate the movement of anticipation and retrospection that is an ordinary part of the reading process. Normally, this anaphoric activity preludes the development of a coherent configuration of meaning by the reader. In *Topologie*, however, it does not, since, after the first space, "déjà dit" usually signals not a true repetition but a contradictory variant or no repetition at all. In search of coherence, the reader is pulled back into the nonorientable space of the text only to be led forward as the pseudorepetition generates its own fiction and the promise of new meanings.[32] The following example is typical in its contradictory orientation:

Description des vitrines, les costumes en tulle blanc, les mannequins, la cabine d'essayage, le double fond et son fonctionnement, etc. Tout ce passage est déjà plus ou moins connu. Peut-être, cependant, reste-t-il un détail notable . . . il y avait une table en bois recouverte par une sorte de nappe qui retombait largement sur les quatre côtés; ce devait être l'étal d'un quelconque marchand de

[32] See Jean Ricardou, "La Fiction flamboyante," in *Pour une théorie du nouveau roman* (Paris, 1971), pp. 212-19, for a discussion of centripetal movement and various kinds of "fraudulent" or "relative" readability in *Projet pour une révolution à New York*.

Reading Nouveaux Romans

fruits ou de boissons, la tache rougeâtre qui souillait un des bords du rectangle ressemblant à quelque coulée de jus—grenade ou pastèque—ou bien à du vin. (p. 194)

Description of the store windows, the white tulle costumes, the mannequins, the fitting room, the false bottom and how it works, etc. This whole passage is already more or less known. Perhaps, however, there remains a detail worthy of note . . . there was a wooden table covered by a sort of tablecloth that hung down amply on four sides; it must have been the stand of some fruit or drink merchant, the reddish spot which stained one of the edges of the rectangle resembling some flow of juice—pomegranate or watermelon—or else wine.

Without claiming to be exhaustive, I should like to suggest some of the connections this text invites. First, it would appear to refer back to two widely separated passages: the description of a bridal-shop window above the site of the (ritualistic?) rape/murder of a young woman (pp. 113-15) and that of a watermelon stand where a mother accompanied by her boy and girl twins stops to buy a slice of the fruit for the girl (pp. 60-62). There is also an allusion to the title of the chapter, "A False-Bottomed Altar," which in turn may be associated with the ritualistic rapes that recur in the novel. On this very general level, then, the text displays its contradictory orientation by linking three distinct segments and by using one of these segments (the bridal shop) to lure the reader on to a "new" development (the merchant) that both repeats and transforms a still earlier passage. But the list culminating in "etc." creates a catalogue effect[33] and, along with the word *passage*, draws the reader's attention toward the nonlinear functioning of the text. Now the reader may discover that the two fictional segments brought together here are not so distinct, that they already show the concern for recombination of similar elements which governs the elabora-

[33] Jean-Claude Raillon in Ricardou, ed., *Robbe-Grillet: Colloque de Cerisy*, 1: 369-70.

Vicki Mistacco

tion of this passage and that, in fact, it is their relationship to each other which may explain their simultaneous reappearance and transformation here. Both contain, for example, a proliferation of p's and v's (pp. 60, 114) as well as reddish stains (watermelon juice at pubic level on the "immaculate dress" of the little girl, p. 62; red paint at groin level on the "formerly immaculate dress" of the bride, p. 115), which themselves "repeat" overall generators (p/v, violated virgins), thereby complicating even further the network of associations. Thanks to this play of resemblance and difference in the realm of signifier and signified, a perpetual "displacement of meanings"[34] is effected, causing the reader to traverse the text without finalizing a representational *or* a literal construction.

A similar process is exemplified by the manner in which Robbe-Grillet borrows and transforms material from a larger body of texts, freeing it from the semiotic order of unified significance that had checked its associative potential. This is especially evident in his playful parody of Freud's *Delusion and Dream*, a study of repression based on Wilhelm Jensen's *Gradiva: A Pompeian Fancy*.[35] Although the figure of Gradiva never appears in *Topologie* and her name is never mentioned, she is effectively "repressed" early on in the serial transformation of a group of letters that generate the story of the demigod David's birth: "divan—vierge—vagin/gravide—engendra—david" (p. 49) ("sofa—virgin—vagina/pregnant—engendered—david").[36] To put it in terms more consistent

---

[34] Robbe-Grillet sees this as a topological feature, in "Interview," p. 37. Alternatively, one might elucidate the functioning of pseudorepetitions by calling upon Deleuze's notion of transversality, the establishment of associative patterns that allow a work to cohere without betraying its multiplicity and fragmentation and without leading to a factitious, totalizing unity. See the chapter entitled "Anti-logos ou la machine littéraire," in *Proust et les signes*, 3rd ed. (Paris, 1971). His concept of "disjunctive synthesis" is equally pertinent.

[35] My references are to Sigmund Freud, *Delusion and Dream and Other Essays* (Boston, 1956). Jensen's text is appended to the volume.

[36] Robbe-Grillet suggests the relationship between this passage and the missing Gradiva in "Interview," p. 39.

Reading Nouveaux Romans

with my topological metaphor, like the missing Vanadian *V* in Danaé (p. 53), Gradiva has fallen into the hole and she reappears elsewhere in the text. As in Freud and Jensen, the repressed material does come out, but instead of closing off significance by providing a basis for the reader's discovery of resemblance over and above difference, it is disseminated, divided, pluralized. The intertextual relationship preserves resemblance *with* difference, frees the material from reassuring finality and allows it to enter new, equally "arbitrary" (a word neither Freud nor Jensen can abide),[37] combinations.

Thus, both a narrator in *Topologie* and Jensen's hero, Norbert Hanold, are archeologists. But whereas Jensen and, on a higher interpretive level, Freud, provide "destination" and "purpose" (*Delusion and Dream*, p. 34) for Hanold's aimless wanderings, Robbe-Grillet's narrator continues to wander at random among the ruins, never quite remembering what it is he is looking for (pp. 11-12). If, in Hanold's dream, Gradiva is buried alive by the eruption of Vesuvius, here a fraudulent Vanadé is mortally wounded during the volcanic eruption that destroyed Vanadium in 39 B.C. The stone that strikes her bears an engraved ("gravé," p. 40) *V*, adding an anagrammatic link with Gradiva. Hanold's involuntary designation of her peculiar gait as "lente festinans" (*Delusion and Dream*, p. 154) finds a covert echo in the "piétinement sans hâte" ("unhurried stamping," p. 55) of a crowd of spectators.

Freud is especially attentive to the presence of puns in *Gradiva*, and *Topologie* is, of course, dependent on them for connecting heterogeneous material in the reader's mind. Obviously intended as nonhierarchical, intratextual as well as intertextual puns assure the continued mobility and open plurality of the novel. Freud, on the other hand, inserts puns into the hierarchical, binary system of the sign, conceiving them as "compromises between the conscious and the unconscious" (*Delusion and Dream*, p. 110), and giving the latter

[37] See Freud, *Delusion and Dream*, pp. 51-52, and Jensen in ibid., p. 153. For an excellent discussion of Freud's drive to reappropriate through interpretation the "deterritorialized" semiotic features of the Gradiva story, see Sylvère Lotringer, "The Fiction of Analysis," *Semiotext(e)* 2 (1977), 173-89.

Vicki Mistacco

the privileged status of a signified, in a word, of truth. A similar binarism leading to dialectical synthesis governs the duplication of the Gradiva statue's special walk by the living Gradiva *rediviva* Zoë Bertgang in Jensen's novel. For Freud, Zoë's appearance restores meaning by projecting the otherwise senseless delusions and dream of Hanold into the realm of representation. Robbe-Grillet, however, borrows the Gradiva step and, by a double process of dissemination and differentiation, preserves it as "the 'decontextualized' kinetic element able to merge with all situations, gait outside of signification open on an ever-floating plurality of meaning" (Lotringer, "The Fiction of Analysis," p. 177). Thus we find it in the image of a young female victim running toward the missing part of a landscape (pp. 36-37), more discreetly in a girl's spectral gliding like that of an absent dancer (pp. 87-88), then in an absent, anonymous "suspended foot" (p. 149). Having been freed from subjective appropriation and the restrictions of intertextual antecedents, it can now be attributed to a little boy (p. 175) and finally even to the problematic male narrator (p. 190). The reader is again obliged to go beyond the temptation of interpretation (*Gradiva* as the "key" to *Topologie* in some sort of one-to-one relationship), to accede to the realm not of *sens* but of *signifiance* where male and female, mobile and immobile, absent and present, "representation" and "reality" coexist in disjunctive synthesis.

Overdetermination of the Gradiva elements is intensified by other intertextual references. If the landscape is reminiscent of the excavations at Pompeii, it also recalls the ruins of Ephesus, once the site of a famed temple to Artemis, or Diana, as the Romans called her, and whose anagrammatic relationship to Vanadé Robbe-Grillet does not fail to exploit either here or in his joint publication with the Belgian artist Paul Delvaux, *Construction d'un temple en ruine à la déesse Vanadé* (1975). The butterfly that alights on Zoë-Gradiva's hair may have something to do with the proliferation of *papillons* and *p*s in *Topologie*. But they also connect in the novel with the ambiguous sexual organs of the hermaphroditic David and, through him as well as by association with a kind of but-

Reading Nouveaux Romans

terfly known as "vanessa," with Vanadé, a transformation of the Norse Freya, surnamed Vanadis, goddess of love, music, spring, flowers, and fertility. Her name is akin to that of the Norse fertility god, Vanir, which brings us back to Gradiva, whose father, Hanold imagines, was perhaps a priest of Ceres, goddess of agriculture. Freud informs us, however, that the Gradiva relief described by Jensen is part of an ensemble portraying the Horae, goddesses of vegetation, and the related deities of the fructifying dew. Now the section of *Topologie* entitled "La Forêt magique" ("The Magic Forest") may in fact refer to vegetation rites . . . (O'Donnell, "Beyond *Topologie*"). By this seemingly interminable ramification, Robbe-Grillet blocks the kind of hermeneutic reading that Freud practices on Jensen and programs a mode of reading based on as many transformations of as many elements as the reader can render pertinent.

Mirrors are a figure for the principle of sameness with difference that determines such transformations as well as homeomorphic distortions and certain types of surfaces in topology. Robbe-Grillet uses them to provide the ultimate inscription of the reader's activity in the novel. In the fourth space, the novel's ludic organization is suggested by the games of the captive adolescents, in which mirrors play a major role. The captive girl dreams that her double in the mirror is an improbable lover, "other . . . and the same" (pp. 123-24). And in Lewis Carroll fashion, she fantasizes escape through the mirror to the other side (p. 124), "other" again becoming synonymous with "the same." In the aptly named section "Faire semblant"[38] we are told how to use mirrors to turn one into two and two into three, but "if one is more than three, it is better to make believe one is alone" (p. 131). Here is Robbe-Grillet's invitation to the reader to disseminate, unite, and disseminate again, to fragment then to bring together what is "impossible," only to break up the "synthesis" by realizing its potential for difference. Here is the inscription

[38] "Make believe," but "semblant" also suggests "resemblance" as well as "semblance" and therefore points to the factitiousness of denying difference in any assimilation.

Vicki Mistacco

of mobility, of the incessant circulation of matter within and among texts.

Mirrors help create a nonorientable ludic space by assembling irreconcilable opposites.[39] Uniting topology and reading, the final reprise of the motif transforms space into a virtual Klein bottle, where outside is inside and no representation is possible:

> Une grande glace, qui occupe toute la paroi visible derrière la table (toujours la même), renvoie l'image bleuâtre de la maison d'en face, comme si l'extérieur de la chambre se trouvait l'intérieur, selon un dispositif qui ne serait pas sans rappeler ce temple fanatique dont je reconstitue péniblement le tracé, jour après jour, à travers les redites, les contradictions et les manques. (p. 196)

> A large mirror, which occupies the entire visible wall behind the table (still the same one), reflects the bluish image of the house opposite, as if the outside of the room were the inside, according to an arrangement that would probably recall that fanatical temple whose layout I painfully reconstitute, day after day, through needless repetitions, contradictions and deficiencies.

In fact, it is only because, like the traditional reader, he is striving for a reassuring reconstruction of reality that the exhausted archeologist experiences this space not as a game but as a loss. In that respect, he points to something implicit in my discussion of topological space: the necessary *dédoublement* of the reader of a text like *Topologie*. For the kind of reading the text proposes is one whose effect depends on a sense of transgression. In order to enjoy the pleasures of *différance*, deconstruction, and topological sliding, the reader must also

[39] Cf. Jacques Derrida's reassessment of opposition: "one of the terms appears as the deferment of the other, as the other deferred in the economy of the same . . ." "La Différance," in Tel Quel, *Théorie d'ensemble* (Paris, 1968), p. 56.

Reading Nouveaux Romans

attempt what amounts to an impossible construction.[40] In short, the text must be read as a paragram (J. Kristeva, *Séméiotikè*, pp. 183-84 and passim) that takes monologistic discourse as the starting point for a productive network of connections. Pushed to the limits of monologism, the reader may become positively and productively schizoid.[41]

By stripping binary relationships of their dialectical force, *Topologie d'une cité fantôme* proposes a new mode of reading. The opposition of construction and destruction, sameness and difference, traditional and ludic reading, is preserved throughout, creating a new force which, in its defiance of synthesis, propels the reader through the text in *theoretically random* sliding motion. For, although Robbe-Grillet would seem to suggest chance as an ideal principle of connectivity by slipping a reference to Brownian motion (p. 104) and several allusions to Mallarméan *coups de dés* in the novel, it is the principle of repetition with difference, something very distinct from chance, that governs the production of meanings. Here, then, we have another convention of this type of fiction: just as we make believe that realistic novels "represent" reality, so must we believe in random movement as an ideal horizon of productivity. Rather than affording us an accurate description of the scriptorial/lectorial function, chance is a *conventional* designation for that which in the novel suggests the full range of possible connections, what Kristeva would call the geno-text. Or, to put it in Ricardolian terms, what we as readers participate in is not incoherence, but *discoherence*.[42]

[40] With characteristic humor, Robbe-Grillet reflects the reader's ambivalence by coupling every appearance of the word *construction* with *ruins* or with some variant of *destruction* or, at the very least, with the syllable *dé*.

[41] "The schizophrenic stands at the limits of capitalism: he is its developed tendency, its excess, its proletarian and exterminating angel. . . . Schizophrenia is desiring production (*production désirante*) as the boundary of social production." Gilles Deleuze et Félix Guattari, *L'Anti-Oedipe*, rev. ed. (Paris, 1975?), p. 43.

[42] See Jean Ricardou's remarks in *Robbe-Grillet: Colloque de Cerisy*, 1: 137-38, 143, 145, and in *Claude Simon: Colloque de Cerisy* (Paris, 1975), pp. 19, 24-25. Discoherence involves spatial, thematic, and other networks that are con-

Vicki Mistacco

Ludism, the reader-as-function, repetition with difference—we have finally acquired sufficient perspective on the nouveau roman to see these for what they are, no longer as irremediably alien instruments of an insidious subversion of traditional reading, but as conventions institutionalized by a veritable barrage of French critical, philosophical, as well as literary writing. In fact, the danger now would seem to be that of viewing those novels solely as illustrations of these conventions. At best, this would mean leaving criticism for the poetics of the nouveau roman, though only to reiterate conclusions already reached. At worst, this would entail ignoring the basic fact that, with the exception of mass literature, a literary work not only assumes the rules and conventions presiding over the body of texts out of which it grows, it also *transforms* them.[43] Resemblance over difference assures meaning, but also arrests it. All the more reason for a text conceived as theoretically limitless production, as a *texte scriptible*, to escape formalization by any set of rules, including its own. Each text should be thought of as a repetition—but with difference—of its own canon.[44]

If I have emphasized conventions here, it is primarily to point up the serious divorce between our approaches to these

---

tradictorily oriented. For Ricardou, it is a feature of many nouveaux romans. The affinities with certain topological surfaces are obvious.

[43] This point has been made in different ways by Culler (*Structuralist Poetics*, p. 160), Kristeva (*Séméiotikè*, p. 146), Iser (*The Implied Reader*, chap. 11, where he indicates that there are always elements which escape the coherent configuration of meaning arrived at by the reader), and, most forcefully, by Tzvetan Todorov, who suggests the comparison with mass literature in *Poétique de la prose*, p. 246, and *Introduction à la littérature fantastique* (Paris, 1970), pp. 10-11.

[44] This is perhaps why, despite the convention of deterritorialization or neutralization and despite a nagging malaise about slipping back into "referential illusion," some critics have begun to reconsider the diegetic material per se. See, for example, Susan Suleiman, "Reading Robbe-Grillet: Sadism and Text in *Projet pour une révolution à New York*," *Romanic Review* 68 (1977), 43-62.

texts as competent readers (including critics and practitioners of nouveaux romans as well as those who, like Barthes, speculate about reading *textes scriptibles*) and as general theoreticians of reading. For, however sophisticated theories of reading have become, they generally remain too tied to integrative notions of character, reception (a simple "I"/"you" opposition in the situation of enunciation), and representation to come to grips with the conventionality instituted by open novels like *Topologie*. It is not surprising, for instance, that Wayne Booth, who conceives of reading as communication between an implied author and an implied reader (that is, between a characterized sender and a characterized receiver) should offer only scant theorization of modern "unstable ironies" (*A Rhetoric of Irony*, chapters 8 and 9).[45] On the other hand, Wolfgang Iser comes close to formulating the convention of multiple connections and repetition with difference when he describes the ways in which the reader, especially of modern novels like Joyce's *Ulysses*, engages in a "process of equating and differentiating" that is "both disturbing and stimulating" (*The Implied Reader*, p. 228). However, Iser is much more concerned with situating the reader with respect to the text and with locating the "gaps" or "indeterminacies" that provoke the reader into active participation in the composition of the novel's (unfamiliar) meaning than with defining the *conventions* of that activity.[46] His theory rests, moreover, on the contested notion of a unified consciousness, in sum a character, struggling with the unintelligible and the problematic. It is Jonathan Culler (*Structuralist Poetics*) who has dealt most extensively with conventions of reading, and his work is to date the best point of departure for defining those conventions. But of his five levels of *vraisemblance*, only one, the conventionally natural, seems to

[45] Cf. Susan Suleiman, "Interpreting Ironies," *Diacritics* 6, no. 2 (1976), 20.

[46] Like Culler, he suggests that modern texts may often be assimilated by viewing as a consistent pattern their very resistance to the formation of illusion (*The Implied Reader*, pp. 284-85). However, the conventions behind that type of naturalization are not sufficiently brought into relief.

Vicki Mistacco

apply to nouveaux romans, and we have already seen the restrictive nature of that mode of naturalization.

Even the best theories of reading call for revision in the face of texts like *Topologie d'une cité fantôme*. Although there have been signs of great interest in the subject at Cerisy and wherever students of the nouveau roman have gathered, it remains for the practice of reading to generate a new theory.

Inge Crosman | Annotated Bibliography
of Audience-Oriented
Criticism

Since any reading—analytical, critical or interpretive—involves texts, readers, and their interaction, I had a wealth of material to choose from. It would be impossible to include everything; I chose those titles that seemed most relevant to our topic, and to the issues raised in this volume. For the sake of continuity, I adopted the categories of reader-oriented criticism outlined in the Introduction. Preference was given to recent developments in criticism, up to December 1979.

Assigning a category was not always a simple task, since some studies are informed by more than a single approach. Rather than repeat titles under all possible rubrics, I chose in each case what seemed to me the predominant one. Some of these choices were by no means clear-cut and could easily be revised.

The reader should bear in mind that entries, though under the same heading, are not necessarily of the same kind: there is, for instance, more than one structuralist or hermeneutic approach. Moreover, there are no absolute boundaries between categories. For example, since rhetorical, semiotic, and structuralist approaches all favor a context-centered text theory or model of communication, categories one and two might well be merged. Studies based on speech act theory, which I have put in the "Rhetorical" category, might as easily be included under the "Semiotic" heading, since semiotics pays attention to systems of signs and the contexts in which these signs are used.

Given our topic (the reader *in* the text), it is not surprising that most entries by far are under semiotic and structuralist criticism. Studies in this category pay special attention to how the audience is *inscribed in* the work, and to the reading strategies laid out for the reader who has "entered" the text.

I have created an additional category (seven) for special volumes and issues of journals dealing with texts, readers/ spectators, interpretation, and related topics. This seemed the best way to proceed, since these books and issues include essays that fall under different rubrics.

I have annotated important entries when their titles seemed insufficiently informative.

I. Rhetorical

This category includes studies with a primary interest in the situation of communication, its meaning, ideological content, or persuasive force. Includes speech-act theory.

Austin, J. L. *How to Do Things with Words*. New York: Oxford Univ. Press, 1962.

Blaicher, G. "Der immanente Leser in Byron's *Don Juan*." *Poetica* 8 (1976), 281-99.

Booth, Wayne C. *A Rhetoric of Irony*. Chicago: Univ. of Chicago Press, 1974. Examines the types of readings, reconstructions, and judgments readers are engaged in while examining a variety of texts from stable to unstable ironies.

―――. "Metaphor as Rhetoric: The Problem of Evaluation." *Critical Inquiry* 5 (1978), 49-72.

―――. *The Rhetoric of Fiction*. Chicago: Univ. of Chicago Press, 1961. Introduces the important concept of the "implied author," whose meanings and values are to be inferred and shared by the "implied reader." Booth's "rhetoric" studies the means of persuasion writers use in communicating with readers.

Bruss, Elizabeth W. *Autobiographical Acts: The Changing Situation of a Literary Genre*. Baltimore: Johns Hopkins Univ. Press, 1977.

―――. "L'Autobiographie considérée comme acte littéraire." *Poétique*, no. 17 (1974), 14-26. Applies speech act theory to the study of genres.

―――. "The Game of Literature and Some Literary Games." *New Literary History* 9 (1977), 153-72.

Annotated Bibliography

Describes reading as a situation of give-and-take between text
and reader: reading is a "game," with rules and strategies, in
which readers are equal, creative partners.

Charles, Michel. "La Lecture critique." *Poétique*, no. 34 (1978), 129-
51.

———. *Rhétorique de la lecture*. Paris: Seuil, 1977.

Argues that although reading is "rewriting," each text has inscribed within it its own reading strategies that "entrap" the
reader.

Crosman, Robert. "Some Doubts about 'The Reader of *Paradise
Lost*.' " *College English* 37 (1975), 372-82.

Questions Fish's "seventeenth-century reader" in *Surprised by
Sin*.

———. *Reading "Paradise Lost."* Bloomington: Indiana Univ. Press,
1980.

An application of the author's "reader centered" theory of the
production of literary meaning to a specific text. Differs from
Fish's *Surprised by Sin* chiefly in seeing the reader as primarily
"universal," rather than "seventeenth century" or "modern."

De Maria, Robert, Jr. "The Ideal Reader: A Critical Fiction." *PMLA*
93 (1978), 463-74.

Fish, Stanley E. "How to Do Things with Austin and Searle: Speech
Act Theory and Literary Criticism." *MLN* 91 (1976), 983-1025.

———. "Normal Circumstances, Literal Languages, Direct Speech
Acts, the Ordinary, the Everyday, the Obvious, What Goes
without Saying, and Other Special Cases." *Critical Inquiry* 4
(1978), 625-44.

———. *Surprised by Sin: The Reader in "Paradise Lost."* New York: St.
Martin's Press, 1967.

Gibson, Walker. "Authors, Speakers, Readers, Mock Readers." *College English* 11 (1950), 265-69.

Goodman, Nelson. *Languages of Art*. 2nd ed. Indianapolis: Bobbs-
Merrill, 1976.

Kamerbeek, J. "Le Concept du 'lecteur idéal.' " In *Expression, Communication and Experience in Literature and Language*. Ed. Ronald
G. Popperwell. London: The Modern Humanities Research Association, 1973. Reprinted in *Neophilologus* 61 (1977), 2-7.

Ong, Walter J., S.J. "Beyond Objectivity: The Reader-Writer Transaction as an Altered State of Consciousness." *CEA Critic: An
Official Journal of the College English Association* 40 (1977), 6-13.

Inge Crosman

Ong, Walter J., S.J. "The Writer's Audience Is Always a Fiction."
PMLA 90 (1975), 9-21.

Plett, Heinrich F., ed. *Rhetorik: Kritische Positionen zum Stand der Forschung*. Munich: Fink, 1977.
See in particular, Dieter Breuer, "Die Bedeutung der Rhetorik für die Textinterpretation," pp. 23-44; Klaus Dockhorn, "Kritische Rhetorik?" pp. 252-75.

Pratt, Mary Louise. *Toward a Speech Act Theory of Literary Discourse*. Bloomington: Indiana Univ. Press, 1977.
Puts forth a context-dependent theory of literature while pointing out that literary works, like other utterances, are addressed to an audience.

Rabinowitz, Peter. "Truth in Fiction: A Reexamination of Audiences." *Critical Inquiry* 4 (1977), 121-42.
Distinguishes between four different audiences: the actual, the authorial, the narrative, and the ideal narrative audience ("ideal" from the narrator's point of view).

Rader, Ralph. "Fact, Theory and Literary Explanation." *Critical Inquiry* 1 (1974), 245-72.

Ricoeur, Paul. *La Métaphore vive*. Paris: Seuil, 1975. In English, *The Rule of Metaphor: Multidisciplinary Studies of the Creation of Meaning in Language*. Trans. Robert Czerny. Toronto: Univ. of Toronto Press, 1977.
Discusses metaphor, and by implication texts, from different points of view. Takes the reader from classical rhetoric to semiotics, semantics, and hermeneutics, while metaphor is first considered as word, then as phrase and discourse, and finally as a paradoxical truth. Ricoeur's main point is that metaphor must be studied within the speech situation or text in which it appears, since it is primarily a contextual change of meaning.

Searle, John R. *Speech Acts: An Essay in the Philosophy of Language*. Cambridge: Cambridge Univ. Press, 1969.

———. "The Logical Status of Fictional Discourse." *New Literary History* 6 (1975), 319-32.

Todorov, Tzvetan. "The Origin of Genres." *New Literary History* 8 (1976), 159-70.

Verdaasdonk, H., and C. J. Van Rees. "Reading a Text vs. Analyzing a Text." *Poetics* 6 (1977), 55-76.

II. Semiotic and Structuralist

Studies under this heading are primarily concerned with the

Annotated Bibliography

analysis and description of texts, the process of reading, and the contexts in which reading and the construction of meaning take place.

Anderegg, Johannes. *Fiktion und Kommunikation: Ein Beitrag zur Theorie der Prosa*. 2nd ed. Göttingen: Vandenhoeck and Ruprecht, 1977.
   Studies fiction as a special type of communication between text and reader. Anderegg examines texts of fact and fiction, and discusses the relationship of text to reality.

Bakhtin, M. M. *Problems of Dostoevsky's Poetics*. Trans. R. W. Rotsel. Ann Arbor: Ardis, 1973.

————. *Rabelais and His World*. Trans. Hélène Iswolsky. Cambridge, Mass.: M.I.T. Press, 1968.

Bal, Mieke. *Narratologie*. Paris: Klincksieck, 1977.
   Defines narratology as the science that formulates the theory of the relations between narrative text, narration (*récit*) and story. Pays particular attention to narration and *focalisation*, description, duration, and the relationship between main and embedded stories.

Barthes, Roland. "Eléments de sémiologie." *Communications* 4 (1964), 91-135. In English, *Elements of Semiology*. Trans. Annette Lavers and Colin Smith. New York: Hill and Wang, 1978.

————. *Image Music Text*. Essays selected and translated by Stephen Heath. New York: Hill and Wang, 1977.
   These essays touch on a variety of subjects including structural analysis of narrative, the semiotics of photography, film, and advertising, the performance of music, and discussions on contemporary literary theory.

————. "Introduction à l'analyse structurale des récits." *Communications* 8 (1966), 1-27. In English, "An Introduction to Structural Analysis of Narrative." *New Literary History* 6 (1975), 237-72.

————. *S/Z*. Paris: Seuil, 1970. Trans. Richard Miller. New York: Hill and Wang, 1974.

————. "Sur la lecture." *Le Français Aujourd'hui* 32 (January 1976), 11-18.

Ben-Porat, Ziva. "The Poetics of Literary Allusion." *PTL* 1 (1976), 105-28.
   Studies the nature and function of intertextuality.

Benveniste, Emile. *Problèmes de linguistique générale*. Paris: Gallimard, 1966. In English, *Problems in General Linguistics*. Trans. Mary

Elizabeth Meek. Coral Gables, Fla.: Univ. of Miami Press, 1971.

Blessin, Stefan. *Erzählstruktur und Leserhandlung: Zur Theorie der literarischen Kommunikation am Beispiel von Goethe's Wahlverwandtschaften*. Heidelberg: Winter, 1974.

Brémond, Claude. "La Logique des possibles narratifs." *Communications* 8 (1966), 60-76.

Chabot, Barry C. ". . . Reading Readers Reading Readers Reading . . ." *Diacritics* 5, no. 3 (1975), 24-38.

Review article of Norman Holland's *5 Readers Reading*.

Chabrol, Claude et al. *Sémiotique narrative et textuelle*. Paris: Larousse, 1973.

Chatman, Seymour. *Narrative Structure in Fiction and Film*. Ithaca: Cornell Univ. Press, 1978.

In studying the nature of narrative, he distinguishes between story (plot, character, setting) and discourse (nonnarrated stories, covert versus overt narrators). See pp. 147-51 for definitions of "real" and "implied" readers, and "narratees."

———. "Towards a Theory of Narrative." *New Literary History* 6 (1975), 295-318.

Cohn, Dorrit. *Transparent Minds: Narrative Modes for Presenting Consciousness in Fiction*. Princeton: Princeton Univ. Press, 1978. Analyzes the techniques used in the representation of consciousness in the novel. Part i is devoted to consciousness in third-person contexts; part ii deals with consciousness in first-person texts.

Coquet, Jean-Claude. *Sémiotique littéraire*. Tours: Mame, 1973.

Corti, Maria. *An Introduction to Literary Semiotics*. Trans. Margherita Bogat and Allen Mandelbaum. Bloomington: Indiana Univ. Press, 1978. Translated from *Principi della comunicazione letteraria*. Milan: Bompiani, 1976.

See chapter 2 on "Sender and Addressee," which deals with internal and external addressees, relations among addressees, and the relationship between sender, addressees, and the work.

Courtès, Joseph. *Introduction à la sémiotique narrative et discursive: Méthodologie et application*. Paris: Librairie Hachette, 1976.

Crosman, Inge Karalus. *Metaphoric Narration: The Structure and Function of Metaphors in "A la recherche du temps perdu."* Chapel Hill: Univ. of North Carolina Press, 1978.

———. "The Status of Metaphoric Discourse." *Romanic Review* 68 (1977), 207-16.

Annotated Bibliography

Culler, Jonathan. "Presupposition and Intertextuality." *MLN* 91 (1976), 1380-96.

———. "Stanley Fish and the Righting of the Reader." *Diacritics* 5, no. 1 (1975), 26-31.

———. *Structuralist Poetics: Structuralism, Linguistics and the Study of Literature*. Ithaca: Cornell Univ. Press, 1975.

———. "Towards a Theory of Non-Genre Literature." In *Surfiction, Fiction Now . . . and Tomorrow*, ed. Raymond Federman, pp. 255-62. Chicago: Swallow Press, 1975.

Dillon, George L. *Language Processing and the Reading of Literature: Toward a Model of Comprehension*. Bloomington: Indiana Univ. Press, 1978.

Eco, Umberto. *A Theory of Semiotics*. Bloomington: Indiana Univ. Press, 1976.

———. *The Role of the Reader: Explorations in the Semiotics of Texts*. Bloomington: Indiana Univ. Press, 1979.

Fish, Stanley E. "Literature in the Reader: Affective Stylistics." *New Literary History* 2 (1970). Rpt. in Stanley E. Fish, *Self-Consuming Artifacts*, pp. 383-427. Berkeley and Los Angeles: Univ. of California Press, 1972.

———. "What is Stylistics and Why Are They Saying Such Terrible Things about It?" In *Approaches to Poetics*, ed. Seymour Chatman. New York: Columbia Univ. Press, 1973.

Fowler, Roger. "Language and the Reader." In *Style and Structure in Literature*, ed. R. Fowler, pp. 79-122. Ithaca: Cornell Univ. Press. Argues for a sequential reading and reexamines the concepts of "superreader," "ideal reader," and "literary competence."

———. *Linguistics and the Novel*. London: Methuen and Co., 1977. Chapter 5 examines the relationship between the novelist, the reader, and the community.

Frye, Northrop. *Anatomy of Criticism*. New York: Atheneum, 1965.

Gasparov, Boris. "The Narrative Text as an Act of Communication." *New Literary History* 9 (1978), 245-61.

Genette, Gérard. *Figures I, Figures II, Figures III*. Paris: Seuil, 1966, 1969, 1972.

———. *Mimologiques: Voyages en Cratylie*. Paris: Seuil, 1976. Considers the nature of language from different perspectives.

Inge Crosman

Opens his discussion with Plato's *Cratylus* (i.e., is language mimetic?).

Greimas, A. J. *Sémantique structurale*. Paris: Larousse, 1966.

——. "The Cognitive Dimension of Narrative Discourse." *New Literary History* 7 (1976), 433-48.

——. *Du sens: Essais sémiotiques*. Paris: Seuil, 1970.

Hamburger, Käte. *The Logic of Literature*. Trans. M. J. Rose. Bloomington: Indiana Univ. Press, 1973.

Hamon, Philippe. "Un Discours contraint." *Poétique*, no. 16 (1974), 411-45.

Hawkes, Terence. *Structuralism and Semiotics*. Berkeley and Los Angeles: Univ. of California Press, 1977.

Hutcheon, Linda. "Modes et formes du narcissisme littéraire." *Poétique*, no. 29 (1977), 90-106.

Discusses different modes of self-conscious fiction and the kinds of reading they entail. Considers the ontological status of such texts and readings.

Jakobson, Roman. "Closing Statement: Linguistics and Poetics." In *Style in Language*, ed. T. A. Sebeok, pp. 350-77. Cambridge, Mass.: M.I.T. Press, 1960.

——. *Questions de poétique*. Paris: Seuil, 1973.

Jameson, Fredric. *The Prison House of Language: A Critical Account of Structuralism and Russian Formalism*. Princeton: Princeton Univ. Press, 1972.

Janik, Dieter. *Die Kommunikationsstruktur des Erzählwerks: Ein semiologisches Modell*. Bebenhausen: Rotsch, 1973.

Jenny, Laurent. "La Stratégie de la forme." *Poétique*, no. 27 (1976), 257-81.

Killy, Walther. "Über das Lesen." In *Herkommen und Erneuerung: Essays für Oskar Seidlin*, ed. Gerald Gillespie and Edgar Lohner, pp. 11-25. Tübingen: Niemeyer, 1976.

Lange, Victor. "The Reader in the Strategy of Fiction." In *Expression, Communication and Experience in Literature and Language*, ed. Ronald G. Popperwell, pp. 86-102. Proceedings of the XIIth Congress of the International Federation of Modern Languages and Literatures. London: The Modern Humanities Research Association, 1973.

Questions the notion of the autonomous text, since reading is

Annotated Bibliography

shaped not only by structural features of the text but also by patterns of expectation. Discusses the importance of readers inscribed within a given text, since they provide us with a built-in interpretive system.

Lejeune, Philippe. *Le Pacte autobiographique.* Paris: Seuil, 1975.

Léon, Pierre R., and Henri Mitterand, eds. *L'Analyse du discours/ Discourse Analysis.* Montreal: Centre Educatif et Culturel, 1976.

Lintvelt, Jaap. "Modèle discursif du récit encadré." *Poétique,* no. 35 (1978), 352-66.

Lotman, Jurij. *Analysis of the Poetic Text.* Ed. and trans. D. Barton Johnson. Ann Arbor: Ardis, 1976.

――――. *Semiotics of Cinema.* Trans. Mark E. Suino. Ann Arbor: Univ. of Michigan Press, 1976.

――――. *The Structure of the Artistic Text.* Trans. Ronald Vroon. Ann Arbor: Michigan Slavic Contributions, 1977.

Lucid, Daniel P., ed. *Soviet Semiotics.* Baltimore: Johns Hopkins Univ. Press, 1977.

The essays in this volume give an overview of Soviet semiotics from the 1960s to the mid-1970s.

Matejka, Ladislav, and Krystyna Pomorska, eds. *Readings in Russian Poetics: Formalist and Structuralist Views.* Cambridge, Mass.: M.I.T. Press, 1971.

Matejka, Ladislav, and I. Titunik, eds. *Semiotics of Art.* Cambridge, Mass.: M.I.T. Press, 1976.

Metz, Christian. *Essai sur la signification au cinéma.* 2 vols. Paris: Klincksieck, 1968, 1972.

――――. *Film Language: A Semiotics of the Cinema.* Trans. Michael Taylor. New York: Oxford Univ. Press, 1974.

Monaco, James. *How to Read a Film.* New York: Oxford Univ. Press, 1977.

Muecke, Douglas. "The Communication of Verbal Irony." *Journal of Literary Semantics* 2 (1973), 35-42.

――――. *The Compass of Irony.* London: Methuen and Co., 1969.

Naumann, Manfred. "Auteur—Destinataire—Lecteur." In *Actes du VIè Congrès de l'Association Internationale de Littérature Comparée,* pp. 205-208. Stuttgart: Erich Bieber, 1975.

Nøjgaard, Morten. "La Fonction du narrataire, ou, comment les textes nous manipulent." In *Actes du 6è Congrès des Romanistes*

Inge Crosman

Scandinaves, Upsala, 11-15 August 1975, ed. Lennart Carlsson, pp. 197-204. Stockholm: Almqvist and Wiksell, 1977.

Peirce, Charles Sanders. *Collected Papers*. Ed. Charles Hartshorne and Paul Weiss. Cambridge, Mass.: Harvard Univ. Press, 1931-58.

Piwowarczyk, Mary Ann. "The Narratee and the Situation of Enunciation: A Reconsideration of Prince's Theory." *Genre* 9 (1976), 161-77.

Prince, Gerald. "Introduction à l'étude du narrataire." *Poétique*, no. 14 (1973), 178-96.

First extensive study of the "narratee," which is defined as "someone to whom the narrator addresses himself" (p. 178). He distinguishes between the narratee as opposed to the real, virtual, or ideal reader.

Quignard, Pascal. *Le Lecteur*. Paris: Gallimard, 1976.

Ray, William. "Recognizing Recognition: The Intra-Textual and Extra-Textual Critical Persona." *Diacritics* 7, no. 4 (1977), 20-33. Review-article. Extensive discussion of the "narratee" as described by Gerald Prince ("Introduction à l'étude du narrataire") and Mary Ann Piwowarczyk ("The Narratee and the Situation of Enunciation: A Reconsideration of Prince's Theory"), and Iser's "implied reader" (*The Implied Reader: Patterns of Communication in Prose Fiction from Bunyan to Beckett*).

Riffaterre, Michael. "Criteria for Style Analysis." *Word* 15 (1959), 154-74.

———. *Essais de stylistique structurale*. Paris: Flammarion, 1971.

———. "Interpretation and Descriptive Poetry: A Reading of Wordsworth's 'Yew-Trees.' " *New Literary History* 4 (1973), 229-56.

———. "Intertextual Scrambling." *Romanic Review* 68 (1977), 197-206.

———. "Paragram and Significance." *Semiotext(e)* 1, no. 2 (1974), 72-87.

———. "Paragramme et signifiance." *Semiotext(e)* 2, no. 1 (1975), 15-30.

———. *Production du texte*. Paris: Seuil, 1979.

———. *Semiotics of Poetry*. Bloomington: Indiana Univ. Press, 1978. A close study of the dialectics between text and reader, with

Annotated Bibliography

special attention to intertextuality and the overdetermination of poetic discourse. Shows how the meaning of a poem is determined by the text's own structures.

―――. "The Self-Sufficient Text." *Diacritics* 3, no. 3 (1973), 39-45.

―――. "The Stylistic Approach to Literary History." *New Literary History* 2 (1970), 39-55.

Roudiez, Leon. "Notes on the Reader as Subject." *Semiotext(e)* 1, no. 3 (1975), 69-80.

Rousset, Jean. *Forme et signification.* Paris: José Corti, 1962.

Schmid, W. *Der Textaufbau in den Erzählungen Dostoevskijs.* Munich: Fink, 1973.

Schmidt, Siegfried J. *Texttheorie.* Munich: Fink, 1973.

Scholes, Robert. "Towards a Semiotics of Literature." *Critical Inquiry* 4 (1977), 105-20.

Segers, Rien T. "Readers, Text and Author: Some Implications of Rezeptionsästhetik." *Yearbook of Comparative and General Literature* 24 (1975), 15-23.

Segre, Cesare. *Semiotics and Literary Criticism.* The Hague: Mouton, 1975.

Smith, Barbara Herrnstein. *On the Margins of Discourse: The Relation of Literature to Language.* Chicago: Univ. of Chicago Press, 1979.

Strzalkowa, Maria. "Entre l'auteur et le lecteur." In *Actes du VIè Congrès de l'Association Internationale de Littérature Comparée/ Proceedings of the 6th Congress of the International Comparative Literature Association,* ed. Michel Cadot et al., pp. 509-12. Stuttgart: Bieber, 1975.

Suleiman, Susan. "Ideological Dissent from Works of Fiction: Toward a Rhetoric of the *roman à thèse.*" *Neophilologus* 60 (1976), 162-77.

―――. "Interpreting Ironies." *Diacritics* 6, no. 2 (1976), 15-21.

―――. "Reading Robbe-Grillet: Sadism and Text in *Projet pour une révolution à New York.*" *Romanic Review* 68 (1977), 43-62.

―――. "Le Récit exemplaire: Parabole, fable, roman à thèse." *Poétique,* no. 32 (1977), 468-89.

Tamir, Nomi. "Personal Narrative and its Linguistic Foundation." *PTL* 1 (1976), 403-30.

Todorov, Tzvetan. *Introduction à la littérature fantastique.* Paris: Seuil, 1970. In English, *The Fantastic: A Structural Approach to a Literary*

Inge Crosman

Genre. Trans. Richard Howard. Cleveland: Case Western Reserve, 1973.

———. "La Lecture comme construction." *Poétique*, no. 24 (1975), 417-25.

———. *Les Genres du discours*. Paris: Seuil, 1978.

———. *Littérature et signification*. Paris: Larousse, 1967.

———. *Poétique de la prose*. Paris: Seuil, 1971. In English, *The Poetics of Prose*. Trans. Richard Howard. With a new foreword by Jonathan Culler. Ithaca: Cornell Univ. Press, 1977.

Traugott, Elizabeth. "Generative Semantics and the Concept of Literary Discourse." *Journal of Literary Semantics* 2 (1973), 5-22.

Uitti, Karl D. *Linguistics and Literary Theory*. Englewood Cliffs: Prentice-Hall, 1969.

Uspensky, Boris. *A Poetics of Composition*. Trans. Valentina Zavarin and Susan Wittig. Berkeley and Los Angeles: Univ. of California Press, 1973.

A study of point of view in narrative fiction. His main distinction is between internal and external points of view. Discusses four types of point of view: evaluative or ideological; the phraseological or stylistic; the psychological; the spatial and temporal.

Waldmann, Günter. *Kommunikationsästhetik I: Die Ideologie der Erzählform*. Munich: Fink, 1976.

Pays special attention to the author-text-reader relationship in studying the text-internal structures of literary communication. Part I is theoretical, part II analytical—with close analysis of a given text of war literature.

Weinrich, Harald. *Literatur für Leser*. Stuttgart: Kohlhammer, 1971.

A variety of essays on literary history and specific literary works. Chapter 3 calls for a literary history of the reader (pp. 23-34).

———. *Sprache in Texten*. Stuttgart: Ernst Klett, 1976.

Winner, Thomas G. "On the Decoding of Aesthetic Texts." *Studia Semiotyczne* 9 (1979), 43-62.

III. Phenomenological

The focus of these studies is on aesthetic perception, the role of the imagination, and the construction of meaning.

Annotated Bibliography

Hans, James S. "Gaston Bachelard and The Phenomenology of the Reading Consciousness." *Journal of Aesthetics and Art Criticism* 35 (1977), 315-27.

Husserl, E. *Erfahrung und Urteil.* Ed. L. Landgrebe. Hamburg: Claasen, 1948. In English, *Experience and Judgment: Investigations in a Genealogy of Logic,* revised and edited by Ludwig Landgrebe. Trans. James S. Churchill and Karl Ameriks. Evanston, Ill.: Northwestern Univ. Press, 1973.

Ingarden, Roman. *Das literarische Kunstwerk.* 3rd ed. Tübingen: Niemeyer, 1965. In English, *The Literary Work of Art: An Investigation on the Borderlines of Ontology, Logic, and Theory of Literature.* Trans. with an Introduction by George G. Grabowicz. Evanston, Ill.: Northwestern Univ. Press, 1973.

———. *Erlebnis, Kunstwerk und Wert.* Tübingen: Niemeyer, 1969.

———. *Vom Erkennen des literarischen Kunstwerks.* Tübingen: Niemeyer, 1968.

Iser, Wolfgang. *Der Akt des Lesens: Theorie ästhetischer Wirkung.* Munich: Fink, 1976. In English, *The Act of Reading: A Theory of Aesthetic Response.* Baltimore: Johns Hopkins Univ. Press, 1978. Studies how a literary work is "actualized" or "realized" during the reading process, and develops a theory of aesthetic response that pays attention to how textual features guide the reader's perception, imagination, and interpretation. This study is informed by more than one approach: besides drawing on phenomenology, it pays attention to speech act theory and historical-cultural contexts.

———. *The Implied Reader: Patterns of Communication in Prose Fiction from Bunyan to Beckett.* Baltimore: Johns Hopkins Univ. Press, 1974.

———. "Indeterminacy and the Reader's Response in Prose Fiction." In *Aspects of Narrative,* ed. J. Hillis Miller, pp. 1-45. New York: Columbia Univ. Press, 1971.

———. "The Reading Process: A Phenomenological Approach." *New Literary History* 3 (1972), 279-99.

———. "The Reality of Fiction: A Functionalist Approach to Literature." *New Literary History* 7 (1975), 7-38.

The material of this article is taken up again in *The Act of Reading* (listed above).

413

Inge Crosman

Ledebur, Ruth Freifrau von. "Überlegungen zur Ästhetik Roman Ingardens—an Beispielen neuerer deutscher Shakespeare-Rezeption." *Poetica* 8 (1976), 134-44.

Poulet, Georges. "The Phenomenology of Reading." *New Literary History* 1 (1969), 53-68.

———. "Point de vue du critique: Lecture et interprétation du texte littéraire." In *Qu'est-ce qu'un texte? Eléments pour une herméneutique*, ed. Edmond Barbotin. Paris: Corti, 1975.

Schütz, Alfred. *Das Problem der Relevanz*. Trans. A. v. Baeyer. Frankfurt am Main: Suhrkamp, 1971. In English, *Reflections on the Problem of Relevance*. Ed. Richard M. Zaner. New Haven: Yale Univ. Press, 1970.

Stierle, Karlheinz. "Position and Negation in Mallarmé's 'Prose pour des Esseintes.' " *Yale French Studies*, no. 54 (1977), 96-117.

———. *Text als Handlung: Perspektiven einer systematischen Literaturwissenschaft*. Munich: Fink, 1975.

———. "Was heisst Rezeption bei fiktionalen Texten?" *Poetica* 7 (1975), 345-87.

IV. Psychoanalytic and Subjective

The main interest of the majority of studies listed below is in how a reader's personality shapes reading and/or interpretation.

Barthes, Roland. *Le Plaisir du texte*. Paris: Seuil, 1973. In English, *The Pleasure of the Text*. Trans. Richard Miller. New York: Hill and Wang, 1975.

Black, Stephen A. "On Reading Psychoanalytically." *College English* 39 (1977), 267-74.

Bleich, David. *Literature and Self-Awareness: Critical Questions and Emotional Responses*. New York: Harper and Row, 1977.

———. "The Logic of Interpretation." *Genre* 10 (1977), 363-94.

———. *Readings and Feelings: An Introduction to Subjective Criticism*. Urbana, Ill.: National Council of Teachers of English, 1975.

———. *Subjective Criticism*. Baltimore: Johns Hopkins Univ. Press, 1978.

———. "The Subjective Paradigm." *New Literary History* 7 (1976), 313-34.

Bleich, David, Eugene R. Kintgen, Bruce Smith, and Sando J. Vargyai. "The Psychological Study of Language and Literature: A

Annotated Bibliography

Selected Annotated Bibliograpy." *Style* 12 (1978), 113-210.
An extensive bibliography of research in English that focuses on "language and literature as aspects of human psychology" (p. 113). Part I, "The Perception and Cognition of Language" (Eugene R. Kintgen); part II, "Subjectivity, Language, and Epistemology in Literature and Criticism" (David Bleich).

Crews, Frederick. *Out of My System: Psychoanalysis, Ideology, and Critical Method.* New York: Oxford Univ. Press, 1975.

————, ed. *Psychoanalysis and the Literary Process.* Berkeley and Los Angeles: Univ. of California Press, 1970.

Gibson, Eleanor J., and Harry Levin. *The Psychology of Reading.* Cambridge, Mass.: M.I.T. Press, 1975.

Harding, D. W. "Psychological Processes in the Reading of Fiction." *British Journal of Aesthetics* 2 (1962), 133-47.

Holland, Norman N. *The Dynamics of Literary Response.* New York: Oxford Univ. Press, 1968; rpt. Norton, 1975.

————. *5 Readers Reading.* New Haven: Yale Univ. Press, 1975.

————. "Hamlet—My Greatest Creation." *The Journal of the American Academy of Psychoanalysis* 3 (1975), 419-27.

————. "Literary Interpretation and Three Phases of Psychoanalysis." *Critical Inquiry* 3 (1976), 221-33.

————. "Literature as Transaction." In *What is Literature?* ed. Paul Hernadi. Bloomington: Indiana Univ. Press, 1978, pp. 206-18.

————. *Poems in Persons: An Introduction to the Psychoanalysis of Literature.* New York: W. W. Norton and Co., 1973. rpt. Norton, 1975.

————. "The New Paradigm: Subjective or Transactive?" *New Literary History* 7 (1976), 335-46.

————. "Transactive Criticism: Re-Creation through Identity." *Criticism* 18 (1976), 334-52.

————. "A Transactive Account of Transactive Criticism." *Poetics* 7 (1978), 177-89.

————. "Unity Identity Text Self." *PMLA* 90 (1975), 813-22.

Holland, Norman, and Murray Schwartz. "The Delphi Seminar." *College English* 36 (1975), 789-800.

Holland, Norman, and Leona Sherman. "Gothic Possibilities." *New Literary History* 8 (1977), 279-94.

Kintgen, Eugene. "Reader Response and Stylistics." *Style* 11, no. 1 (1977), 1-18.

Klinger, Eric. "The Flow of Thought and Its Implication for Literary Communication." *Poetics* 7 (1978), 191-205.

Inge Crosman

Lacan, Jacques. "Séminaire sur 'La Lettre Volée.' " In *Ecrits*, I, 19-75. Paris: Seuil, 1966.

Lesser, Simon O. *Fiction and the Unconscious*. Boston: Beacon Press, 1957.

Martindale, Colin. "Psychological Contributions to Poetics." *Poetics* 7 (1978), 121-33.
Comprehensive introductory article to this special issue of *Poetics* devoted to "Poetics and Psychology."

Mounin, Georges. "Devant le texte." *Etudes Littéraires* 9 (1976), 287-93.
Argues that literary studies should take account of the effects (emotional, intellectual, other) of texts on readers.

Roland, Alan, ed. *Psychoanalysis, Creativity, and Literature: A French-American Inquiry*. New York: Columbia Univ. Press, 1978.

Slatoff, Walter. *With Respect to Readers: Dimensions of Literary Response*. Ithaca: Cornell Univ. Press, 1970.

Spilka, Mark. "Unleashing the Third Force." *Novel* 9 (1976), 165-70.
Review article on psychological criticism.

Tompkins, Jane P. "Criticism and Feeling." *College English* 39 (1977), 169-78.

V. Sociological and Historical

These studies show a principal concern with the reading public at a particular time, within a given social and cultural context. Includes reception aesthetics (*Rezeptionsästhetik*).

Barthes, Roland. *Le Degré zéro de l'écriture*. Paris: Seuil, 1953. In English, *Writing Degree Zero*. Trans. Annette Lavers and Colin Smith. New York: Hill and Wang, 1978.

Brown, Steven R. "Political Literature and the Response of the Reader: Experimental Studies of Interpretation, Imagery, and Criticism." *American Political Science Review* 71 (1977), 567-84.
On Golding's *Lord of the Flies* and Burdick's *Ninth Wave*.

Cormeau, Christoph. "Zur Rekonstruktion der Leserdisposition am Beispiel des deutschen Artusromans." *Poetica* 8 (1976), 120-33.

Dubois, Jacques. "Théories et positions actuelles, IV: Sociologie de la lecture et concept de lisibilité." *Revue des Langues Vivantes* 41 (1975), 471-83.

Escarpit, Robert. *La Révolution du livre*. 2nd rev. ed. Paris: Unesco, 1969.

———. *Sociologie de la littérature*. 2nd ed. Paris: Presses Univer-

Annotated Bibliography

sitaires, 1960. In English, *Sociology of Literature*. Trans. Ernest Pick. 2nd ed. London: Cass, 1971.

Escarpit, Robert et al. *Le Littéraire et le social: Eléments pour une sociologie de la littérature*. Paris: Flammarion, 1970.

Goldmann, Lucien. *Le Dieu caché: Etude sur la vision tragique dans les "Pensées" de Pascal et dans le théâtre de Racine*. Paris: Gallimard, 1959. In English, *The Hidden God: A Study of Tragic Vision in the "Pensées" of Pascal and the Tragedies of Racine*. Trans. Philip Thody. London: Routledge and Kegan Paul, 1964.

―――. *Pour une sociologie du roman*. Rev. ed. Paris: Gallimard, 1965. In English, *Towards a Sociology of the Novel*. Trans. Alan Sheridan. London: Tavistock Publications, 1975.

―――. *Structures mentales et création culturelle*. Paris: Editions Anthropos, 1970.

Grimm, Günter. "Rezeptionsgeschichte: Prämissen und Möglichkeiten historischer Darstellungen." *Internationales Archiv für Sozialgeschichte der Deutschen Literatur* 2 (1977), 144-86.

Gumbrecht, Hans Ulrich. "Konsequenzen der Rezeptionsästhetik oder Literaturwissenschaft als Kommunikationssoziologie." *Poetica* 7 (1975), 388-413.

Hohendahl, Peter Uwe. "Introduction to Reception Aesthetics." *New German Critique* 4, no. 10 (1977), 29-63.

Jameson, Fredric. *Marxism and Form*. Princeton: Princeton Univ. Press, 1971.

Jauss, Hans Robert. *Ästhetische Erfahrung und literarische Hermeneutik*. I. *Versuche im Feld der aesthetischen Erfahrung*. Munich: Fink, 1977.

Develops a theory of the reader within the framework of a new literary history and considers aesthetic response.

―――. "The Idealist Embarrassment: Observations on Marxist Aesthetics." *New Literary History* 7 (1975), 191-208.

―――. "Der Leser als Instanz einer neuen Geschichte der Literatur." *Poetica* 7 (1975), 325-44.

―――. "Levels of Identification of Hero and Audience." *New Literary History* 5 (1974), 283-317.

―――. "Literaturgeschichte als Provokation der Literaturwissenschaft." In *Literaturgeschichte als Provokation*. Frankfurt am Main: Suhrkamp, 1970. Reprinted in Rainer Warning, *Rezeptionsästhetik*, pp. 126-62. Munich: Fink, 1975. See also in English, "Literary History as a Challenge to Literary Theory," trans. Elizabeth Benzinger. *New Literary History* 2 (1970), 7-37.

Inge Crosman

Jurt, Joseph. "Rezeptionsästhetik in Theorie und Praxis." *Schweizer Monatshefte* 55 (1975/76), 693-97.

Koch, Walter Alfred, ed. *Textsemiotik und strukturelle Rezeptionstheorie: Soziosemiotische Ansätze zur Beschreibung verschiedener Zeichensysteme innerhalb der Literatur, Studia Semiotica*. Hildesheim: Olms, 1976.

Leavis, Q. D. *Fiction and the Reading Public*. 2nd ed. London: Chatto and Windus, 1968.

Leenhardt, Jacques. *Lecture politique du roman: La Jalousie d'Alain Robbe-Grillet*. Paris: Editions de Minuit, 1973.

Lukács, Georg. *Die Theorie des Romans*. Darmstadt: Hermann Luchterhand Verlag, 1971. In English, *The Theory of the Novel: A Historico-Philosophical Essay on the Forms of Great Epic Literature*. Trans. Anna Bostock. London: Merlin Press, 1971.

Macherey, Pierre. *Pour une théorie de la production litteraire*. Paris: Librairie François Maspero, 1966. In English, *A Theory of Literary Production*. Trans. Geoffrey Wall. London: Routledge and Kegan Paul, 1978.

Mills, Gordon. *Hamlet's Castle: The Study of Literature as a Social Experience*. Austin: Univ. of Texas Press, 1976.

Naumann, Manfred. "Das Dilemma der 'Rezeptionsästhetik.' " *Poetica* 8 (1976), 451-66.

―――. "Literary Production and Reception." *New Literary History* 8 (1976), 107-26.

Naumann, Manfred et al., eds. *Gesellschaft Literatur Lesen: Literaturrezeption in theoretischer Sicht*. Berlin: Aufbau Verlag, 1973.

Probst, Gerhard F. "Gattungsbegriff und Rezeptionsästhetik." *Colloquia Germanica* 10 (1976/77), 1-14.

Purves, Alan, and Richard Beach. *Literature and the Reader: Research in Response to Literature, Reading Interests, and the Teaching of Literature*. Urbana, Ill.: National Council of Teachers of English, 1972.

Ricardou, Jean. "La Révolution textuelle." *Esprit* 12 (1974), 927-45.

Routh, Jane, and Janet Wolff, eds. *The Sociology of Literature: Theoretical Approaches*. Keele, England: Univ. of Keele, 1977.
See in particular David Coward, "The Sociology of Literary Response," pp. 8-17; Janet Wolff, "The Interpretation of Literature in Society: The Hermeneutic Approach," pp. 18-31.

Sartre, Jean-Paul. "Qu'est-ce que la littérature?" In *Situations II*. Paris: Gallimard, 1948.

Annotated Bibliography

Voloshinov, V. N. *Marxism and the Philosophy of Language*. Trans. L. Matejka and I. R. Titunik. New York: Seminar Press, 1973.

Watt, Ian. *The Rise of the Novel: Studies in Defoe, Richardson, and Fielding*. London: Chatto and Windus, 1957.

——, ed. *The Victorian Novel: Modern Essays in Criticism*. New York: Oxford Univ. Press, 1971.

Weimann, Robert. "Reception Aesthetics and the Crisis in Literary History." *Clio* 5 (1975), 3-35.

Zima, Pierre V. *Pour une sociologie du texte littéraire*. Paris: Union Générale d'Editions, 1978.

Zimmermann, Bernhard. *Literaturrezeption im historischen Prozess: Zur Theorie einer Rezeptionsgeschichte der Literatur*. Munich: Beck, 1977.

VI. Hermeneutic

Criticism in this category ranges from authority in interpretation to relativism, as in the work of the deconstructionists. Includes a number of articles on the debate of monism versus pluralism.

Abrams, M. H. "Behaviorism and Deconstruction: A Comment on Morse Peckham's 'The Infinitude of Pluralism.' " *Critical Inquiry* 4 (1977), 181-93. See Peckham below.

——. "The Deconstructive Angel." *Critical Inquiry* 3 (1977), 425-38.

Bloom, Harold. *Kabbalah and Criticism*. New York: Seabury Press, 1975.

——. "Poetic Crossing: Rhetoric and Psychology." *Georgia Review* 30 (1976), 495-526, 772-826.

On different contemporary approaches to poetry, poetics, and imagery.

Booth, Wayne C. " 'Preserving the Exemplar': Or, How Not to Dig Our Own Graves." *Critical Inquiry* 3 (1977), 407-24.

Cohen, Ted. "Metaphor and the Cultivation of Intimacy." *Critical Inquiry* 5 (1978), 3-12.

Culler, Jonathan. "Beyond Interpretation: The Prospects of Contemporary Criticism." *Comparative Literature* 28 (1976), 244-56. Claims that much Anglo-American criticism is harmed by a bias toward interpretation. In place of interpretation Culler offers a series of enterprises aimed at understanding, not individual texts, but literature in its relations to the variety of systems and discourses that are part of a culture.

Davis, Walter A. *The Act of Interpretation: A Critique of Literary Reason*. Chicago: Univ. of Chicago Press, 1978.

Inge Crosman

Shows how one might reconcile divergent readings of the same text.

Derrida, Jacques. *De la grammatologie.* Paris: Editions de Minuit, 1967. In English, *Of Grammatology.* Trans. Gayatri Chakravorty Spivak. Baltimore: Johns Hopkins Univ. Press, 1976.

———. *La Dissémination.* Paris: Seuil, 1972.

———. *L'Ecriture et la différence.* Paris: Seuil, 1967. In English, *Writing and Difference.* Trans. Alan Bass. Chicago: Univ. of Chicago Press, 1978.

———. "Le Facteur de la vérité." *Poétique,* no. 21 (1975), 96-147. In English, "The Purveyor of Truth." *Yale French Studies,* no. 52 (1975), 31-113.

Dilthey, W. "Die Entstehung der Hermeneutik" (1900). In *Gesammelte Schriften,* Vol. 5. Stuttgart: B. G. Teubner; Göttingen: Vandenhoeck and Ruprecht, 1968.

Fish, Stanley E. "Interpreting 'Interpreting the *Variorum.*' " *Critical Inquiry* 3 (1976), 191-96.

———. "Interpreting the *Variorum.*" *Critical Inquiry* 2 (1976), 465-85.

Gadamer, Hans Georg. *Wahrheit und Methode.* Tübingen: Mohr, 1960. In English, *Truth and Method.* Trans. Garrett Barden and John Cumming. New York: Seabury Press, 1975.

Goodman, Nelson. *Ways of Worldmaking.* Indianapolis: Hackett Publishing Co., 1978.

Graff, Gerald. "Fear and Trembling at Yale." *The American Scholar* 46 (1977), 467-78.

Grimm, Günter, ed. *Literatur und Leser: Theorien und Modelle zur Rezeption literarischer Werke.* Stuttgart: Philipp Reclam, Jr., 1975.

Hartman, Geoffrey H. *The Fate of Reading and Other Essays.* Chicago: Univ. of Chicago Press, 1975.
Includes self-contained readings of texts and reflections on the problematics of reading and interpretation. Hartman sees reading as a dialogic, creative, and assertive act.

———. "Literary Criticism and Its Discontents." *Critical Inquiry* 3 (1976), 203-20.

Hirsch, E. D., Jr. *The Aims of Interpretation.* Chicago: Univ. of Chicago Press, 1976.

———. *Validity in Interpretation.* New Haven: Yale Univ. Press, 1967.

Kincaid, James R. "Coherent Readers, Incoherent Texts." *Critical Inquiry* 3 (1977), 781-802.
Comments on Abrams, Booth, and Miller.

Kintgen, Eugene R. "Effective Stylistics." *Centrum* 2 (1974), 43-55.

Annotated Bibliography

Suggests a compromise between the "subjective" (Bleich, Slatoff, Holland, Ohmann, Fish) and "objective" (Jakobson, Sinclair, early Halliday) students of style.

Mailloux, Steven. "Reader-Response Criticism?" *Genre* 10 (1977), 413-31.

Discusses Stanley Fish's work in the context of four other reader-response critics: David Bleich, Norman Holland, Wolfgang Iser, and Jonathan Culler.

Man, Paul de. *Blindness and Insight: Essays in the Rhetoric of Contemporary Criticism.* New York: Oxford Univ. Press, 1971.

————. "The Timid God." *Georgia Review* 29 (1975), 533-58.

Michaels, W. B. "The Interpreter's Self: Peirce on the Cartesian 'Subject.' " *Georgia Review* 31 (1977), 383-402.

Miller, J. Hillis. "The Critic as Host." *Critical Inquiry* 3 (1977), 439-48.

————. "Stevens' Rock and Criticism as Cure, II." *Georgia Review* 30 (1976), 330-48.

Morawski, Stefan. "Contemporary Approaches to Aesthetic Inquiry: Absolute Demands and Limited Possibilities." *Critical Inquiry* 4 (1977), 55-84.

Nelson, Lowrie. "The Fictive Reader and Literary Self-Reflexiveness." In *The Disciplines of Criticism*, ed. Peter Demetz et al., pp. 173-91. New Haven: Yale Univ. Press, 1968.

Palmer, R. D. *Hermeneutics: Interpretation Theory in Schleiermacher, Dilthey, Heidegger and Gadamer.* Evanston, Ill.: Northwestern Univ. Press, 1969.

Peckham, Morse. "The Infinitude of Pluralism." *Critical Inquiry* 3 (1977), 803-16.

Comments on Abrams, Booth, and Miller. See Abrams above for a critical response.

Reichert, John. *Making Sense of Literature.* Chicago: Univ. of Chicago Press, 1977.

Ricoeur, Paul. *Le Conflit des interprétations: Essais d'herméneutique.* Paris: Seuil, 1969. In English, *The Conflict of Interpretations: Essays in Hermeneutics.* Ed. Don Ihde. Evanston, Ill.: Northwestern Univ. Press, 1974.

————. *De l'interprétation: Essai sur Freud.* Paris: Seuil, 1965. In English, *Freud and Philosophy: An Essay in Interpretation.* Trans. Denis Savage. New Haven: Yale Univ. Press, 1970.

————. *Interpretation Theory: Discourse and the Surplus of Meaning.* Fort Worth: Texas Christian Univ. Press, 1976.

Ricoeur, Paul. "Metaphor and the Main Problem of Hermeneutics." *New Literary History* 6 (1974), 95-110.

———. "The Metaphorical Process as Cognition, Imagination, and Feeling." *Critical Inquiry* 5 (1978), 143-59.

———. "Qu'est-ce qu'un texte?" In *Hermeneutik und Dialektik: Festschrift in Honor of H. G. Gadamer*, ed. Rüdiger Bubner et al. Tübingen: Mohr, 1970. 2:181-200.

———. "What Is a Text? Explanation and Interpretation." In David M. Rasmussen, *Mythic-Symbolic Language and Philosophical Anthropology: A Constructive Interpretation of the Thought of Paul Ricoeur*, pp. 135-50. The Hague: Martinus Nijhoff, 1971.

Said, Edward. *Beginnings: Intention and Method.* New York: Basic Books, 1975.

———. "The Problem of Textuality: Two Exemplary Positions." *Critical Inquiry* 4 (1978), 673-714.

Sherman, Carol. "Response Criticism: 'Do Readers Make Meaning?' " *Romance Notes* 18 (1977), 288-92.

Steiner, George. *After Babel.* New York: Oxford Univ. Press, 1975. See chapter 5, "The Hermeneutic Motion."

Todorov, Tzvetan. *Symbolisme et interprétation.* Paris: Seuil, 1978.

Wasiolek, E. "Wanted: A New Contextualism." *Critical Inquiry* 1 (1975), 623-39.

Watkins, Evan. *The Critical Act: Criticism and Community.* New Haven: Yale Univ. Press, 1978.

Wellek, René. "The New Criticism: Pro and Contra." *Critical Inquiry* 4 (1978), 611-24.

Discusses different ways of reading, describing, evaluating, and interpreting texts.

VII. Special Volumes

This category lists special volumes (books) and issues of journals dealing with texts, readers, criticism, interpretation, and related topics. Most of these include essays that fall under the various working categories adopted for this bibliography.

Amacher, Richard, and Victor Lange, eds. *New Perspectives in German Literary Criticism.* Princeton: Princeton Univ. Press, 1979. English translation of selected critical essays from five volumes of the German series entitled *Poetik und Hermeneutik* (Munich: Fink).

Doyle, Esther M., and Virginia Hastings Floyd, eds. *Studies in Interpretation*, vol. II. Amsterdam: Rodopi, 1977.

Annotated Bibliography

See in particular Richard Haas, "Phenomenology and the Interpreter's 'Interior Distance,' " pp. 157-65; Sheron Dailey Pattison, "Rhetoric and Audience Effect: Kenneth Burke on Form and Identification," pp. 183-98; David A. Williams, "Audience Response and the Interpreter," pp. 199-206.

Hartman, Geoffrey, ed. *Psychoanalysis and the Question of the Text.* Baltimore: Johns Hopkins Univ. Press, 1978.
Includes essays by Jacques Derrida, Geoffrey Hartman, Neil Hertz, Norman Holland, Barbara Johnson, Cary Nelson, and Murray Schwartz.

"In Defense of Authors and Readers: Wayne Booth, Wolfgang Iser and Others." *Novel* 11 (1977), 5-25. Special section.

Josipovici, Gabriel, ed. *The Modern English Novel: The Reader, the Writer, and the Work.* New York: Barnes and Noble, 1976.
Includes George Craig, "Reading: Who is Doing What to Whom?" pp. 15-36.

Kindt, Walther, and Siegfried J. Schmidt, eds. *Interpretationsanalysen: Argumentationsstrukturen in literaturwissenschaftlichen Interpretationen.* Munich: Fink, 1976.
See in particular Michael Kunze, "Probleme der rezeptionsästhetischen Interpretation: Überlegungen zu Hans Robert Jauss: 'Racines und Goethes Iphigenie,' " pp. 133-44.

Krieger, Murray, and Larry S. Dembo, eds. *Directions for Criticism: Structuralism and Its Alternatives.* Madison: Univ. of Wisconsin, 1977.

"Literary Hermeneutics." *New Literary History* 10 (1978).
Entire issue on this topic. Includes essays by Fr. D. E. Schleiermacher, *"The Hermeneutics*: Outline of the 1819 Lectures," by Peter Szondi, "Introduction to Literary Hermeneutics," and by Charles Altieri, "The Hermeneutics of Literary Indeterminacy: A Dissent from the New Orthodoxy."

"Literature and Psychoanalysis: The Question of Reading: Otherwise." *Yale French Studies*, nos. 55-56 (1978). Special issue.

"Poetics and Psychology." *Poetics* 7 (1978). Special issue.

Qu'est-ce qu'un texte? Eléments pour une herméneutique. Ed. Edmond Barbotin. Paris: Corti, 1975.
Contains seven essays on text theory, each presenting a different perspective: the point of view of the philologist, the linguist, the critic, the historian, the philosopher, the exegete, and the theologian. Chapter 3 deals with reading and interpreting literary texts (Georges Poulet, pp. 61-82).

Inge Crosman

"Readers and Spectators: Some Views and Reviews." *New Literary History* 8 (1976). Special issue on this topic.

"Reading, Interpretation, Response." *Genre* 10 (1977), 363-453. Special section.

"Rhetoric I: Rhetorical Analyses." *New Literary History* 9 (1978). Special issue.

> For a critical discussion of articles in this issue, see Jonathan Culler, "On Trope and Persuasion," pp. 607-18; and Marie-Rose Logan, "Rhetorical Analysis: Towards a Tropology of Reading," pp. 619-25.

Singleton, Charles S., ed. *Interpretation: Theory and Practice*. Baltimore: Johns Hopkins Univ. Press, 1969.

"Soviet Semiotics and Criticism: An Anthology." *New Literary History* 9 (1978). Special issue.

Valdés, Mario J., and Owen J. Miller, eds. *Interpretation of Narrative*. Toronto: Univ. of Toronto Press, 1978.

> Includes papers from a colloquium on Interpretation of Narrative held in Toronto in 1976. Essays range from the formalist to the hermeneutic approach, with specific attention to the role of the reader.

Warning, Rainer, ed. *Rezeptionsästhetik*. Munich: Fink, 1975.

> Contains essays by Ingarden, Jauss, Iser, Gadamer, Vodicka, Fish, and Riffaterre, representing various viewpoints ranging from semiotic, to phenomenological and historical criticism.

Weinrich, Harald, ed. *Positionen der Negativität*. Poetik und Hermeneutik VI. Munich: Fink, 1975.

Notes on Contributors

CATHLEEN M. BAUSCHATZ has taught at the University of Maine at Orono and at Bowdoin College. She has written articles on Montaigne and Du Bellay, and is currently writing a book on Renaissance conceptions of the reading process.

MICHEL BEAUJOUR is Professor of French at New York University. He is the author of *Le Jeu de Rabelais* and of the forthcoming *Miroirs d'encre*, as well as numerous essays on modern French literature and criticism.

CHRISTINE BROOKE-ROSE is a writer of experimental fiction and Professor in the Department of American Studies at the University of Paris VIII. Her critical works include *A Grammar of Metaphor* and *A ZBC of Ezra Pound*, as well as numerous articles on literary theory.

INGE CROSMAN is Associate Professor of French Studies at Brown University. She is the author of *Metaphoric Narration: The Structure and Function of Metaphor in "A la recherche du temps perdu,"* as well as many articles.

ROBERT CROSMAN has taught at Williams College, Trinity College, and Tufts University. He is the author of *Reading Paradise Lost*, and of articles on Milton, Joyce, Mailer, and critical theory.

JONATHAN CULLER is Professor of English and Comparative Literature at Cornell University. His books include *Flaubert: The Uses of Uncertainty* and *Structuralist Poetics*, and he has published numerous articles on poetry and critical theory.

NORMAN N. HOLLAND is the James H. McNulty Professor of English at SUNY Buffalo, where he founded the Center for the Psychological Study of the Arts. His books include *The Dynamics of Literary Response*, *Poems in Persons*, and *5 Readers Reading*.

WOLFGANG ISER is Professor of English and Comparative Literature at the University of Konstanz. He is the author of *The Implied Reader:*

Notes

Patterns of Communication in Prose Fiction from Bunyan to Beckett and of *The Act of Reading: A Theory of Aesthetic Response*, as well as other works.

JACQUES LEENHARDT teaches at the Ecole Pratique des Hautes Etudes in Paris, where he is Director of the Groupe de Sociologie de la Littérature. He is the author of *Lecture politique du roman: "La Jalousie" d'Alain Robbe-Grillet*, and of numerous articles on modern literature and critical theory.

PIERRE MARANDA is Research Professor of Anthropology at Laval University. His publications include *French Kinship: Structure and History*, as well as books and articles on myth, folklore, and computer applications to anthropological semantics.

LOUIS MARIN is the Jones Professor of French at SUNY Buffalo, and Directeur d'Etudes at the Ecole Pratique des Hautes Etudes. His books include *Utopiques: jeux d'espaces*, *Détruire la peinture*, and *Le Récit est un piège*.

VICKI MISTACCO is Associate Professor of French at Wellesley College. She has written articles and papers on Gide, Mauriac, Robbe-Grillet, and the nouveau roman.

GERALD PRINCE is Associate Professor of Romance Languages at the University of Pennsylvania. He is the author of *Métaphysique et technique dans l'oeuvre de Sartre* and of *A Grammar of Stories*, as well as numerous articles on modern fiction and literary theory.

PETER J. RABINOWITZ teaches Comparative Literature at Hamilton College. He has published articles on literary theory, modern opera, and Raymond Chandler, and is also an active music critic.

NAOMI SCHOR is Associate Professor of French Studies at Brown University. Her publications include *Zola's Crowds*, as well as numerous articles on nineteenth-century French authors.

KARLHEINZ STIERLE teaches in the Romanische Seminar, Ruhruniversität, Bochum. His articles on modern literature and literary theory have appeared in French, German, and American journals, and his books include *Text als Handlung*.

SUSAN R. SULEIMAN is Assistant Professor of French at Occidental College, and is a freelance translator. Her publications include the forthcoming *Fiction et persuasion: pour une poétique du roman à thèse*, as

Notes

well as numerous articles on twentieth-century French fiction and theory of narrative.

TZVETAN TODOROV teaches at the Ecole Pratique des Hautes Etudes and is an editor of *Poétique*. His many books include *Introduction à la littérature fantastique, Poétique de la prose, Théories du symbole*, and *Symbolisme et interprétation*.

Subject Index

addressee, in narrative, *see* audience, narratee, reader, reading public

allegory, 316-17, 332, 344-45

ambiguity, 65, 66, 98-99, 104, 135-44, 177-79, 194, 249ff., 345, 378. *See also* indeterminacy, meaning

anthropology, 4, 183-204 *passim*, 329, 330

antireferentiality, in literature, 18, 83-105 *passim*, 371-400 *passim*

audience, vii, 3-4, 190-92, 241-62, 327-28, 331-34, 340, 344-46; types of, 243-45. *See also* reader, reading public

author, 16, 20, 42-43, 75-76, 96n, 106, 120, 122, 145, 155-64, 323; and characters, 142-43, 258-62; and reader, 7-8, 50-51, 84, 106, 113, 243-44, 265-91; and reading public, 33-36, 206-209, 214, 327-28, 331-34; implied, 8-9, 11, 374, 379, 381; unlocalizability of, 384-85. *See also* authority, intention, subject of discourse

authority, of author or text, 9, 17, 20, 42-44, 158-59, 160-61, 182, 266-69, 289-91, 328, 342, 344-45, 374, 375, 384. *See also* author, text, validity

autoreferentiality, in art and literature, 89-92, 101-105, 251, 315. *See also* self-reflexiveness

biography, 120, 161

borrowing, in music and literature, 241-63; different types of, 246-49

capitalism, 34, 187, 397n

causality, in fiction, 74-75, 217. *See also* plot

characters, in fiction, 75-77, 81-82, 110, 116-17, 131-32, 142, 229n, 236. *See also* fiction

Christ, as model, 334-44

codes: in narrative, 11-21, 107, 109, 123-48, 227-35, 373, 374n; in painting, 293ff. *See also* conventions

color, in painting, 301-302

communication, literature as, 7-8, 84ff., 107ff., 207-209, 223-24, 237-40, 371, 373; linguistic model of, 7, 305, 310-12, 382. *See also* didacticism

competence: linguistic, 4, 49-50, 178, 366; literary, 50-52, 57-66, 87, 88, 122, 130, 227ff., 295, 371, 385, 398; pictorial, 294

context: relation to text, 12-13, 368; relevance in interpretation, 5, 44-45, 76, 150-55. *See also* cultural variables

conventions, of reading and writing, 11, 12, 15, 20-21, 45, 49-52, 57-66, 225-40 *passim*, 311, 371-400. *See also* interpretation: strategies of

"correct" reading or interpretation, 20, 23-25, 39, 43, 51, 149-64, 180, 225-27, 346-49

critical controversies, 16-17, 38-45, 149-50, 158-64, 362-70. *See also* interpretation

criticism, as a discipline, 46-56. *See also* theory, critical controversies

429

Index

cultural variables, in interpretation, 36, 76, 184-204, 215-17, 223

decoding, 8, 120-48, 167-82, 225-49 *passim*, 310-19. *See also* reading, interpretation

deconstruction, 40-43, 82, 361-62, 349, 364; in the nouveau roman, 371-400 *passim*

desire, reading and, 303, 342-49. *See also* fantasy, illusion

detective fiction, 134-35, 142, 238, 240, 359

dialogism, 142-44

diary, as fictional genre, 334ff.

didacticism, in literature, 266-91, 325-49

drama, modern, 241-49 *passim*, 247-63

ego psychology, 30, 31n, 55-56. *See also* psychoanalysis

encoding, 8, 21, 123-48, 225-40 *passim*, 325. *See also* codes

evaluation, of literary works, 36-37, 130, 256-62

exemplary novel, 336n, 344, 346, 349

exemplum, 336ff. *See also* didacticism

expectations, as part of reading, 23, 35-37, 86-87, 98n, 187, 284n, 372

experience, 28, 90-105 *passim*, 108, 278-91, 367. *See also* reading, response

fantastic, genre of, 135-43

fantasy, reading and, 28-29, 322, 329, 344, 348-49, 367. *See also* imagination, personality

father, as authority figure, 323, 326-29, 344-45, 356, 359. *See also* authority

fiction, 8-9, 18-19, 33, 67-82, 123-48, 211-24, 225-40, 350-60; and communication, 7-11, 84, 88-89, 92-93, 107, 112-19, 207-209, 223-24, 237-

40, 325-27, 371, 373; interpretation in, 78-79, 167-82, 237-40, 345; modern, 34, 81-82, 104-105, 131-34, 135, 241-56, 342-49; *vs.* pragmatic texts, 83-84, 92-97; and reality, 67-68, 83-88, 89-91, 97-98, 243-56, 375, 379, 389, 394, 397. *See also* characters, fictionality, narrative

fictionality, 88-97. *See also* representation

form, in literature, 48, 49, 103-105, 251-56

gaps, role of in interpretation, 24-25, 110-19, 171, 261, 399

grammar: generative, 4-5; of Port-Royal, 300-304. *See also* linguistics

hermeneutics, 16-18, 165-82, 183-204, 363; "positive" *vs.* "negative," 16-17, 20, 38-45; structuralism and, 17-18, 21, 165-68. *See also* interpretation, meaning

historical approach to reading, 32-38. *See also* literary history

historical painting, 298-324

iconic narration, 295-99

identity, *see* personality, self

ideology: in criticism, 158-64; in culture, 183-85; in literature, 145-47, 325-49 *passim*; in reading, 214-24; in research, 213. *See also* norms, stereotypes, values

illusion, literature and, 84-88, 95, 245, 247, 258-62, 343. *See also* imitation, representation

imagination, as factor in reading or interpretation, 111, 119, 171, 174, 285-86, 339. *See also* fantasy, personality

imitation: art and literature as, 67, 243ff., 266-69, 271; of models by

430

Index

the reader, 267-76, 334-45. *See also* didacticism, representation

implied author, 8-9, 11, 147, 374, 379, 381, 399. *See also* author

implied reader, 8-9, 11, 14-15, 98, 100, 169, 372, 381, 399. *See also* addressee, reader

indeterminacy, 24-25, 98-100, 102, 104-105, 110, 322; of narrative voices, 381-88. *See also* meaning

infantilization, of audience, 326-28, 333-34, 349

intellectualism, in interpretation, 357-60, 369-70

intention: authorial, 9, 25, 39, 42-43, 75-76, 121, 150-51, 155-64, 243-44, 259-62, 272-74, 324, 331-41; of the text, 83, 237-40

interaction, between text and reader, 106-109, 225. *See also* communication, reading, transaction

interpersonal relations, 107-109

interpretant, 44, 168-82

interpretation, 8, 11, 14-15, 16-18, 38-45, 47, 48, 50, 165-67, 183, 190-202, 249-56, 287-88, 358, 367; circularity of, 11, 30, 363; Freudian, 165, 352-55, 393-95; individual variations in, 51-52, 61, 66, 72-74, 159-60, 229-30, 239-40; inexhaustibility of, 96-97, 181-82, 317-18; represented, in fiction, 167-80; strategies of, 19-21, 44-45, 49, 57-66, 149, 161, 166; validity in, 16-17, 39-45, 47, 51-52, 153-64, 345-49. *See also* hermeneutics, meaning, reading, reception, response

interpretive communities, 20-21, 44-45, 149-64 *passim*

interpretive strategies, *see* interpretation: strategies of

intertextuality, 242, 384-85, 392-95

introspection, reading as, 282-86, 290

irony, 9, 60, 65, 128, 143-44, 256, 345, 378-79; dramatic, 257-58, 260

judgment, in reading, 94-95, 270-71, 276

linguistics, 4-5, 49-50, 202. *See also* grammar, communication

literary history, 32-38, 57, 76, 121, 170-82, 266ff., 325-49

"ludism," 122, 375, 388, 397, 398

meaning, 8, 11, 17, 39, 48, 49, 51, 59-66, 93-104, 113ff., 166-67, 171, 181, 221, 222; conflicting senses of, 149-51; indeterminability of, 322, 375-400 *passim*; modern refusal of, 40-41, 207-10; reader's role in creating, 106-19, 149-64, 362-70. *See also* ambiguity, interpretation

mental structures, in interpretation, 184-203, 221-24

metacommentary, 230-40

metaphor, cultural specificity of, 185-87, 196, 203

mimesis, *see* fiction, imitation, representation

mise en abyme, 169, 179, 380

modernity, theories of, 18-19, 81-82, 104-105, 207-209, 222-23, 328-29, 371-72, 397-99

monologism, 142-44, 397

morality, fiction and, 8-11, 344-49. *See also* values

music, modern, 47, 241-63 *passim*

myth: history as, 324; in literature, 249-56; social function of, 184-90, 192-93

narcissism, and interpretation, 169, 177, 190-91, 204

narratee, 13-15, 67, 169, 236-37, 272n, 372; indeterminability of, 381-88. *See also* implied reader, reader: encoded

431

Index

narrative, 3, 13-21, 225-40; first-person, 131, 330ff.; in painting, 295-99, 316-19, 414-15. *See also* fiction

narrator, 13-14, 70, 113, 131-32, 236-37, 244-45, 352, 359; deceptive or unreliable, 128, 138, 239, 245; indeterminability of, 381-88

naturalization, 19, 371, 380, 388, 399n

negation, 104-105, 119, 198-201; of the subject of discourse, 41, 209-210, 295-306, 322, 381-88

New Criticism, 5, 27, 28, 39, 45n, 55, 155, 362

nihilism, 9, 43

norms, in fiction, 26, 116-17. *See also* morality, values

novel, the, *see* fiction

nouveau roman, 134, 135, 143, 249-56, 371-99

Oedipus myth, 168, 249-56, 258-59

parody, 247, 379, 392

personality, role of in reading, 25-31, 54-56, 350-70

perspective: in fiction, 95-99, 113-16; in painting, 307-309, 313-14. *See also* point of view

phenomenological approach to reading, 21-26, 98-100, 106-19, 289

play, text as, 207-209. *See also* "ludism"

pleasure, in reading, 131, 182, 272, 286, 322, 324, 338-39, 346-49

plot, in fiction, 112-13, 233, 249, 251n. *See also* fiction

poetry, 43, 57-66, 104, 138, 144n, 151-54, 158-59, 193-202, 279, 330

point of view, in fiction, 69, 71-72, 115-16, 123, 128, 254-55

poststructuralism, 5-6, 19, 181-82. *See also* deconstruction

psychoanalysis: and interpretation, 107-109, 168-70, 352, 354-55, 393-95; Freudian, 28-31; Lacanian, 31n, 363

psychoanalytic criticism, 27, 28-31, 41n, 54-56, 350-70

psychographics, 188n

readability, 11, 12, 15-16, 18-19, 22, 43, 237-39, 376, 388-90

reader: active role of, in interpretation, 110-19, 149-64, 208-210, 265-91, 360-70, 381-82; actual or "real," 12, 16, 25-31, 53-56, 84-87, 95-102, 120, 128, 145-48, 243, 333, 346-49, 350-60; and author, 7-8, 50-51, 84, 106, 113, 243-44, 264ff., 282, 327-28, 331; encoded or inscribed, 12, 13-16, 121-48; fictitious or fictionalized, 113, 272n, 274, 333-34; historicization of, 25-26, 35-36; "ideal," 53-54, 121, 372; implied, 8-9, 11, 14-15, 98, 100, 169, 372, 381; in phenomenological criticism, 22-27, 98-100, 106-19, 121, 289; in rhetorical criticism, 7-9, 266-67, 346; in sociological-historical criticism, 32-38, 88, 205-24; in structuralist criticism, 11-21, 122-48, 225-40; in subjective criticism, 27-31, 54-56, 149-64, 290-91, 350-70, 372; represented, in the text, 167-82, 312-13, 318-19. *See also* audience, reading public

reading: act or process of, 8, 9, 22-31, 84-89, 92-103, 106-107, 110-19, 215-22, 225-30, 265, 271-72, 289-91, 304-310, 360-70; as collective phenomenon, 32-37, 53, 211-24; conventions of, 20-21, 45, 49-52, 57-66, 225-40 *passim*, 311, 371-400; "correct" reading, 20, 23-25, 39, 43, 51, 149-64, 225-27, 346-49; digestive metaphor for, 269-70; idiosyncratic, 23-25, 62, 153-54,

432

226; individual variations in, 25-31, 51-52, 61, 66, 72-74, 159-60, 229-30, 239-40; "naive," 85-89; as private experience, 27-31, 54-56, 149-64 *passim*, 282-86, 345-49, 350-60; of texts by themselves, 95, 230-40; systems of, 214-30; thematized, in fiction, 77-80. *See also* interpretation, reception, response

"reading interludes," 234-40

reading public, 32-37, 206-207, 211-24. *See also* reader, audience

reading subject, status of, 23, 25-26, 40, 41-43, 119, 381-82. *See also* reader

"realization" (*Konkretisation*), 22-25, 106

reception, 35-37, 83-89, 95-103, 107-19, 264-66. *See also* reading, response

redundancy, 16, 71; in reading, 217-18. *See also* repetition

referential discourse, 68-69

referential field, 114-19

referential function, of language, 89-90

referential illusion, 84-88, 95, 398n

referential reading, 84-88; *vs.* rhetorical reading, 65

repetition, 16, 71-72, 77, 135, 388-98

representation, 67-68, 83-91, 181; negation of, 322-24, 375, 379, 389, 394, 397; pictorial, 294-324. *See also* fiction, imitation

response, 24-31, 36-37, 86-89, 289-91, 360-70. *See also* reception, reading

Rezeptionsästhetik, 35-38, 365. *See also* historical approach, phenomenological approach

rhetoric, classical, 265-66, 335-36

rhetorical criticism, 7-11, 245-48, 325-26

roman à thèse, 325n, 329, 331, 332-33, 344-45, 348

schooling, role of in reading, 188, 208-209, 223, 329, 334, 342

science fiction, 84

self: as book, 280-87; different conceptions of, 30-31, 41-43, 55-56, 280-82, 360, 382-83; quest for, 343-44. *See also* personality, subject of discourse

self-reflexiveness, 4-5; in criticism, 38-45; in fiction, 167-82; in painting, 322-23

semantic charters, 185-90, 193ff.

semiotics, 5, 11-20, 39, 165-68, 177-78, 293-304, 334. *See also* structuralism

social class, as a factor in reading, 32-35, 206-207, 213-14

socialization: as semantic conditioning, 185, 188-90, 202-204; reading and, 208-209, 223, 326-27, 329, 345

sociological approach to reading, 32-38, 206-24

speech-act theory, 5, 10, 365

stereotypes: in literature, 86-87, 101n; in reading, 183-84, 201, 215-17

story, *vs.* discourse, 15, 295, 299, 313, 387n. *See also* fiction, narrative

structuralism, 5, 11-20; and hermeneutics, 17-18, 21, 165-68, 181-82. *See also* codes, semiotics

subject of discourse (*ego*): negation of, 41-43, 209-210, 299, 302-306, 312, 320-23, 381-88. *See also* author, reading subject, self

subjective criticism, 21, 27-31, 46, 54-56, 149-64, 289, 290-91, 350-70. *See also* personality, psychoanalytic approach

subversion, fiction as, 325-49, 380. *See also* transgression

"super-reader," 53, 122, 365

433

Index

symbolism, 128-30, 239, 316-24

symbolization (*vs.* signification), 72-73

teaching, and reader-oriented criticism, 27-28, 45n, 52, 148, 366-67. *See also* schooling

texts, literary and artistic, vii, 4; as communication, 7-8, 88-89, 107-19, 207-209, 223-24, 237-40, 371, 373; and context, 12-13, 368; role of, in determining interpretation, 23-25, 28, 29, 30n, 49, 68, 75-77, 94-95, 98, 100, 106-107, 110-19, 152, 154-55, 210, 220-22, 225-40, 265-67, 270, 345, 362-70; theories of, 18-19, 22, 40-43, 55, 58ff., 94, 120, 155, 207-209, 371, 398

"theme and horizon" (or theme and background), 97, 101, 102-103, 115-19. *See also* phenomenological approach

theory: *vs.* empirical investigation, 210-11; importance of, 46-56, 87-88; *vs.* individual description, 293-94

time, in narrative, 70-71, 123-30, 296-99, 324

topology: defined, 373n; topological space, 375-81

transaction, between text and reader, 30, 45n, 362-63, 365-70

transgression, in literature, 132-34, 222-23, 329-30, 347-49, 396

unity, textual: as a critical convention, 40, 58-64; negation of, 375-400 *passim*. *See also* texts

validity, in interpretation, 11, 16-17, 39-45, 47, 51-52, 153-64, 166-82 *passim*, 345-49. *See also* authority, intention, meaning

values: in literature, 8-11, 33, 116-17, 145-46, 325-49 *passim*; in systems of reading, 215-22. *See also* ideology

writer, *see* author, subject of discourse

writing (*écriture*), 207-10, 301, 321-24, 373, 376, 398. *See also* modernity

Index of Names

Abrams, M. H., 42, 43, 44n
Adams, Hazard, 60, 64
Adorno, Theodore, 166
Aeschylus, 258n
Alberti, L. B., 306, 307
Alger, Horatio, 252
Allais, Alphonse, 143
Alpatov, M., 314n
Althusser, Louis, 182
Andrewes, Lancelot, 366
Anouilh, Jean, 244, 252, 262;
    Antigone, 252, 252n
Antal, Friedrich, 205
Aristotle, 20, 267, 335
Arnheim, Rudolf, 114
Asp, Carolyn, 252n
Augustine, 265
Austen, Jane, 110

Babula, William, 262n
Bakhtin, Mikhail, 13, 134n, 142,
    142n, 144, 144n, 242n
Bal, Mieke, 385n
Balzac, Honoré de, 18, 19, 169n,
    174n, 225n, 230, 231n
Barilli, Renato, 378n, 388
Barrès, Maurice, 325, 330, 330n, 332,
    335, 344, 345, 347; *Un homme libre*,
    330-42, 345, 348
Barth, John, 241, 242, 245, 248, 255,
    257, 263
Barthelme, Donald, 31
Barthes, Roland, 6, 11-12, 12n, 13,
    18-19, 20, 21, 21n-22n, 34, 123,
    124, 128, 143n, 148, 166, 182, 228,
    228n, 265, 284-87, 326, 326n, 373,

373n, 384, 399; *S/Z*, 12n, 13, 18-19,
    123n, 144n, 228n, 374n
Bartók, Béla, 246
Bataille, Georges, 328, 329, 339, 348n
Baudelaire, Charles, 91, 122, 328,
    341, 385
Beckett, Samuel, 9, 25n, 257, 257n,
    262
Beethoven, Ludwig van, 263
Bellori, G., 320, 323n
Bely, Andrey, 246n, 250n
Benjamin, Walter, 96n
Benveniste, Emile, 15, 182, 295-96,
    299, 300, 302, 304, 320, 382n, 386n
Berio, Luciano, 241
Berlin, Normand, 258n, 262n
Bernheimer, Charles, 176
Betti, Emilio, 16
Bishop, Thomas, 253
Black, Max, 150
Blake, William, 57-65, 365n; "Lon-
    don," 57-65
Bleich, David, 21, 21n, 27, 29, 30-
    31n, 45n
Bloom, Harold, 39n, 61
Blunt, A., 293n, 314n, 317, 318, 320,
    323n
Bogdanovich, Peter, 242
Bonaparte, Marie, 354-55
Bond, Edward, 242, 263
Booth, Wayne C., 6, 7n, 8, 9, 9n, 10,
    14, 24, 42, 43, 44n, 128, 149, 244n,
    245n, 279n, 325n, 346-47, 372, 374,
    382, 399; *The Rhetoric of Fiction*,
    8-9, 346-47; *A Rhetoric of Irony*, 9,
    9n, 128n

Index

Borges, Jorge Luis, 263
Bourget, Paul, 345
Brecht, Bertolt, 246
Bremond, Claude, 13
Brooke-Rose, Christine, 15, 135n
Brooks, Mel, 242
Brunelleschi, Filippo, 307-308
Bruss, Elizabeth W., 10n
Burgess, Anthony, 263
Butor, Michel, 242, 253
Byrd, Max, 167n

Camus, Albert, 176
Carr, John Dickson, 238
Carroll, Lewis, 385, 395
Castiglione, Baldesar, 271n
Cato the Younger, 282
Cedergren, H., 202n
Céline, Louis-Ferdinand, 346
Chantelou, P. Fréart de, 324n
Charles, Michel, 10, 10n
Chernyshevsky, N. G., 247, 326,
   327-28
Chomsky, Noam, 5n
Christie, Agatha, 134-35, 238
Cicero, Marcus Tullius, 266
Cohen, Leonard, 189
Constant, Benjamin, 72, 76, 167, 341;
   Adolphe, 68-73, 75-76
Coppola, Francis Ford, 72
Coquet, J. C., 13
Corngold, Stanley, 166n, 177n
Crébillon, Claude-Prosper Jolyot,
   358
Crosman, Inge, 200-201n
Culler, Jonathan, 6, 13, 17, 21, 30,
   31, 45, 122, 149, 371, 372, 374, 375,
   380, 382, 389, 398n, 399
Curtius, Ernst Robert, 280n

Dante (Alighieri), 146
Davies, Peter Maxwell, 241
Defoe, Daniel, 33
Deleuze, Gilles, 173, 374, 382, 385,
   387, 388, 392n

Deleuze, Gilles and Guattari, Félix,
   397n
Delvaux, Paul, 385, 394
de Man, Paul, 5n, 6, 10-11, 39n, 167n
Derrida, Jacques, 6, 12n, 40-42,
   41n-42n, 44n, 149, 355, 356, 358,
   361-62, 364, 369, 370, 374, 388, 396
Descartes, René, 280n, 301-303,
   335-37, 338, 341; Discourse on
   Method, 335-37
Dilthey, Wilhelm, 16-17
Donne, John, 146
Dostoevsky, Fyodor M., 13, 134n,
   142, 142n, 144n, 174n, 190, 243,
   244, 247, 253; The Possessed, 243-
   44, 247
Doubrovsky, Serge, 170
Douglas, Mary, 202, 348n
Drieu la Rochelle, Pierre Eugène,
   145-47; Gilles, 145-47
Du Bartas, Guillaume de Salluste,
   146
Du Bellay, Joachim, 266, 269, 281,
   282; Deffence et illustration de la lan-
   gue francoyse, 266-67, 269
Duhamel, Joseph, 374n
Dumas, Alexandre, 225n, 233n
Dumont, L., 190n
Dunbar, William, 360

Eco, Umberto, 13, 102, 143
Edwards, Thomas, 61, 63
Eliot, T. S., 111n, 146, 157, 193
Ellison, Ralph, 142n, 231n
Eluard, Paul, 194-202, 203; "La Terre
   est bleue comme une orange,"
   194-202, 200n-201n
Escarpit, Robert, 32n

Faulkner, William, 142n
Fejes, Endre, 211n, 212, 215; Le
   Cimetière de rouille, 211n, 212, 215,
   217
Félibien, André, 316n, 320
Felman, Shoshana, 42n

436

Index

Ferlinghetti, Lawrence, 385-86
Fielding, Henry, 33, 115-17
Firges, Jean, 252n
Fish, Stanley E., 6, 10, 10n, 13, 20,
  20n, 39n, 45, 48, 48n, 55, 122, 149,
  161, 265n, 289, 365, 365n, 366, 374
Flaubert, Gustave, 34, 96n, 101n,
  103, 232n
Foss, Lukas, 241
Foucault, Michel, 44n, 287-88, 388
Freud, Sigmund, 31n-32n, 190,
  304n, 392, 393, 394, 395; *Delusion
  and Dream*, 392-95
Frye, Northrop, 47-48, 128, 360
Fuller, Edmund, 347

Gadamer, Hans-Georg, 16
Galletier, E., 321n
Gallie, W. B., 7
Gauclère, Yassu, 200n
Genet, Jean, 328
Genette, Gérard, 6, 10n, 13, 132n,
  167, 273n, 284, 289-90, 372, 374,
  381n, 385n
Gibson, Walker, 244n
Gillham, D. G., 60
Girard, René, 342-43, 348n
Glen, Heather, 58
Goffman, E., 109n
Goldmann, Lucien, 33-35, 34n-35n,
  205-207, 208
Gombrowicz, Witold, 325, 328, 345,
  346, 349; *Pornografia*, 325, 328-29,
  349
Graff, Gerald, 39n
Graves, Robert, 359
Green, André, 168
Greimas, A. J., 13, 167n, 332-33n
Grice, H. P., 150
Grossvogel, David, 250n
Guattari, Felix, 397n
Gurwitsch, Aron, 114n

Hamburger, Käte, 84
Hamilton, David, 385

Hamon, Philippe, 16n, 167n, 388n
Hartman, Geoffrey, 38-40
Hartwell, Hugh, 241
Hawthorne, Nathaniel, 235n, 248n,
  249
Heath, Stephen, 371-72, 388
Heidegger, Martin, 16
Heller, Erich, 166
Hemingway, Ernest, 76, 231n
Hirsch, E. D., Jr., 6, 16, 39, 60n, 63,
  121, 121n, 149, 150-51, 154-61,
  160n, 162, 365-66
Hobbes, Thomas, 157
Hoffman, Daniel, 353n, 357
Holland, Norman, 6, 27, 28-31, 30-
  31n, 39n, 46, 53-56, 243n, 265n,
  267, 284n, 289, 350-62 *passim*,
  367-70; *The Dynamics of Literary Re-
  sponse*, 28-29; *5 Readers Reading*,
  29-30, 54-55, 243n, 267
Homer, 241
Horace, 266, 271n
Hubert, H., and Mauss, M., 197n
Hugo, Victor, 235n, 385
Huxley, Aldous, 346

Ingarden, Roman, 22, 25, 25n, 95n,
  106n, 120-21, 121n, 148
Ionesco, Eugène, 259, 260, 262
Irving, Washington, "Rip Van
  Winkle," 123-30, 133, 138, 143, 147
Iser, Wolfgang, 6, 22-26, 25n, 27, 35,
  98-103, 265n, 289, 365n, 366, 372,
  374, 382, 398n, 399; *The Implied
  Reader*, 22-26, 98n, 99n, 169n,
  284n, 398n, 399
Ives, Charles, 248n

Jakobson, Roman, 7, 7n, 191, 311,
  382n
James, Henry, 135, 170-73, 174,
  174n, 181; *In the Cage*, 170-73
Jameson, Fredric, 39n
Jauss, Hans Robert, 6, 35-37, 35n,
  39n, 84n, 205, 222, 365n; "Literary

437

Index

Jauss, Hans Robert (*cont.*)
History as a Challenge to Literary
Theory," 35-37, 365n
Jensen, Wilhelm, 392, 393, 395;
Gradiva: A Pompeian Fancy, 392-95
Johnson, Anthony L., 144n
Johnson, Barbara, 42n, 369n
Jost, François, 371n
Joyce, James, 25n, 100, 105, 241, 399
Jozsa, Peter, 211

Kafka, Franz, 165-66, 170, 173, 176-
80, 254, 259; *The Trial*, 176-80
Kant, Immanuel, 94
Kennedy, Walter, 360
Klein, J., 314, 320
Kristeva, Julia, 222, 374, 388, 397,
398n
Kuentz, Pierre, 209n
Kuroda, S. Y., 304

Labov, William, 201n, 202n
Lacan, Jacques, 31n-32n, 41, 41n-
42n, 188, 189, 307, 351, 353, 355,
356, 358, 361-62, 364, 369, 370
Laing, R. D., 107, 108
Langland, William, 146
Lautréamont, 246
Lawrence, D. H., 146, 360-61
Leach, Sir Edmond Ronald, 202
Leavis, Q. D., 86n
Le Brun, Charles, 297
Leenhardt, Jacques, 21, 33, 37, 209n,
211, 388, 389
Lejeune, Philippe, 336-37
Lenin, V. I., 198n
Le Sage, Laurent, 242n, 250, 254, 255
Lesser, Simon O., 29
LeSueur, Eustache, 319n
Levenson, Jill, 257n, 260n
Levi, W. A., 5n
Lévi-Strauss, Claude, 4, 32n, 182,
184, 198n, 202
Lévi-Strauss, Monique, 200n
Levin, Harry, 348, 353

Lewis, Wyndham, 146
Liszt, Franz, 248n
Lotman, Juri, 13
Lotringer, Sylvère, 378n, 382n, 388,
393n, 394
Louis XIV, 33, 206
Loyola, Ignatius, 325, 334, 337-42,
345, 348; *Spiritual Exercises*, 334,
337-42

McGowan, Margaret, 272n
Macherey, Pierre, 102
McLuhan, Marshall, 280
Magritte, René, 385
Mallarmé, Stéphane, 104, 104n, 193,
385
Manetti, A., 307-308
Mann, Thomas, 103; *Mario the Magi-
cian*, 369
Mao Tse-tung, 198n
Maranda, E. Köngas, 192n, 193n,
198n
Maranda, Pierre, 184n, 185n, 187n,
192n, 198n, 203n
Marcuse, Herbert, 209
Marquez, Garcia, 91
Marvell, Andrew, 48
Mathewson, Rufus, 325-26
Maurer, Karl, 102n
Mauss, M., 197n
May, Georges, 326
Mehlman, Jeffrey, 32n
Mercier, Vivien, 242n
Meyer, Herman, 241
Michaels, Walter B., 5n, 41n
Miller, J. Hillis, 6, 39n, 43, 44, 181
Milton, John, 146, 158
Miner, Earl, 121, 121n
Minogue, Valerie, 250n
Mistacco, Vicki, 21n, 376n
Moldenhauer, Joseph J., 356-57n
Montaigne, Michel de, 264f.; *Essais*,
264-89
Moravia, Alberto, 248
Morgan, George W., 202

438

Index

Morrissette, Bruce, 251, 256n, 373, 379n

Nabokov, Vladimir, 248, 263
Nazareth, Peter, 252n
Neruda, Pablo, 146
Nezval, Vitězslav, 191
Nietzsche, Friedrich, 16, 17, 95n-96n
Nizan, Paul, 326n, 332-33, 345, 346

O'Brien, Flann, 131f., 141, 142; *At Swim-Two-Birds*, 131-34, 141, 142, 147
O'Donnell, Thomas D., 385n, 395
O'Flaherty, Kathleen, 242n
Ogden, C. K., 150
Ohmann, Richard, 365n
O'Neill, Eugene, 256, 258n
Ong, Walter J., 6, 169n, 244n, 266n, 272n-73n, 282n, 333n, 334, 382
Oriol-Boyer, Claudette, 371n

Palmer, R. D., 16n
Panofsky, Erwin, 295-96, 308, 314n, 316n, 319-20, 323n
Pascal, Blaise, 33, 206, 301
Pausanias, 315n
Peirce, Charles Sanders, 41n, 168, 168n, 181-82
Perec, Georges, 211, 215, 220; *Les Choses*, 211-12, 220
Piaget, Jean, 81, 119
Plato, 41, 265, 267
Poe, Edgar Allan, 42n, 135, 143, 231n, 350, 351, 352, 353, 354-55, 357, 360, 361-62, 369n; "The Black Cat," 135-41, 147; "The Purloined Letter," 350-62, 367-70
Pollock, Jackson, 301
Polybius, 315
Ponge, Francis, 105
Pouilloux, Jean-Yves, 272n
Poulet, Georges, 284
Pound, Ezra, 120, 146, 151-54, 154n,
155, 156; "In a Station of the Metro," 151-54
Poussin, Nicolas, 293, 297, 316, 318, 322, 323, 324; *The Arcadian Shepherds*, 293-94, 305, 306, 309, 310-24
Pratt, Mary Louise, 5n, 10n
Price, Martin, 61, 65
Prince, Gerald, 13, 15, 55, 169n, 230n, 244n, 372, 374, 381n
Propp, Vladimir, 129, 130
Proust, Marcel, 91, 103, 167, 170, 173-76, 174n, 230n, 284n, 350n, 385; *Un Amour de Swann*, 173-76
Pushkin, Aleksander S., 243, 249

Quintilian, 266

Rabelais, François, 13, 134n, 282
Rabinowitz, Peter J., 244n, 248n, 381n
Racine, Jean, 33
Raillon, Jean-Claude, 391
Raimondi, Marcantonio, 319n
Raphael, 319, 319n
Rasmussen, David M., 284n
Rauschenberg, Robert, 385
Rheingold, *Guest at Noon*, 248
Ricardou, Jean, 97n, 105, 207-209, 251n, 371, 372, 388, 388n, 390n, 397n-98n
Richards, I. A., 150
Richardson, Samuel, 33
Ricoeur, Paul, 17, 38, 193n, 194n, 284n
Riddel, Joseph, 39n
Riffaterre, Michael, 13, 18, 18n, 55, 122, 127n, 201n, 223, 242n, 365, 365n
Ripa, Cesare, 319
Robbe-Grillet, Alain, 143, 209n, 241, 246n, 249-51, 250n, 251n, 254, 255, 256, 371, 372, 373, 375, 376n, 379n, 380, 381, 382, 383, 385, 385n, 387,

439

Index

Robbe-Grillet, Alain (*cont.*)
389, 390, 392, 392n, 393, 394, 395,
397, 397n; *Les Gommes*, 249-51,
254-56, 383-85; *Topologie d'une cité
fantôme*, 371-400
Rochberg, George, 241
Rosenblatt, Louise M., 45n
Rospigliosi, Cardinal, 323, 324
Roudiez, Leon, 251n
Rousseau, Jean-Jacques, 185, 283
Russell, David H., 279

Said, Edward, 39n, 44n, 181-82
Sainte-Beuve, C. A., 341
Sankoff, G., 202n
Sartre, Jean-Paul, 34, 85, 258n, 332n
Sayce, R. A., 272n
Sayers, Dorothy, 238
Scheler, Max, 343
Scherer, Olga, 121n, 137n, 142, 142n
Schlegel, Friedrich, 96n
Schleiermacher, F.E.D., 16
Schmid, Wolf, 144n
Schoenberg, Arnold, 47
Scholes, Robert, and Kellogg,
Robert, 3
Schor, Naomi, 44
Schütz, Alfred, 115n
Schwartz, Murray M., 363n
Scott, Sir Walter, 249
Searle, John R., 5n, 121n, 150
Segers, Rien T., 365n
Seneca, 271n
Shakespeare, William, 121, 146, 248,
259, 260, 261, 262, 263; *Hamlet*,
241, 257, 259, 260, 261, 262, 263
Shklovsky, Victor, 222
Sidney, Sir Philip, 276, 281, 290
Simon, Claude, 105, 379n, 397n
Sinyavsky, André, 342n
Slatoff, Walter, 27, 28
Smith, Barbara H., 63n
Sollers, Philippe, 105, 388
Sontag, Susan, 165-66, 181-82;

Against Interpretation, 165-66,
181-82
Sophocles, 245, 254, 258, 259;
Oedipus, 254, 255, 258
Sparrow, John, 321n
Starobinski, Jean, 144n
Stein, Gertrude, 105
Steinbeck, John, 190
Stendhal (Marie Henri Beyle), 78, 79,
240, 333; *Armance*, 74, 78-80, 81
Sterne, Laurence, 131
Stierle, Karlheinz, 35
Stockhausen, Karlheinz, 241
Stoppard, Tom, 241, 242, 257, 257n,
258, 258n; *Rosencrantz and Guil-
denstern Are Dead*, 241, 257-62
Strawson, Peter Frederick, 150
Sturrock, John, 251n
Suleiman, Susan R., 9n, 10n, 16n,
121n, 145-47, 242n, 251n, 326n,
332, 333n, 336n, 398n, 399n

Tanner, Tony, 170n
Tate, Allan, 358n
Taylor, John Russell, 261n
Thackeray, William Makepeace, 249
Thomas, Dylan, 133
Todorov, Tzvetan, 6, 10n, 13, 16,
135, 167, 374, 389, 398n
Tolkien, J.R.R., 143
Tolstoy, Leo, 142
Trinquet, Roger, 272n
Trotsky, Leon D., 346
Tsepeneag, Dimitrou, 209n
Turgenev, Ivan S., 243, 247-49, 326,
327
Twain, Mark, 260n
Tylor, Edward, 202

Valéry, Paul, 97, 337
vanRossum-Guyon, Françoise, 371n
Verlaine, Paul, 385
Virgil, 266, 282, 321, 324
Viroux, Maurice, 246n

Index

Wasiolek, E., 5n
Watt, Ian, 33
Weinrick, Harald, 35, 208n
Weisbach, W., 314n, 320
Weisgerber, Jean, 242n
Whitehead, Alfred North, 163
Wilde, Oscar, 241, 256
Wilden, Anthony, 41
Willbern, David, 363n

Wind, E., 319n
Woolf, Virginia, 110, 110-11n, 111
Wordsworth, William, 152, 158, 159;
    "Lucy," 158-60

Yates, Frances, 266n

Zola, Emile, 169n
Zolla, Elemire, 329

LIBRARY OF CONGRESS CATALOGING
IN PUBLICATION DATA

Main entry under title:

The reader in the text.

Bibliography: p.
1. Reading—Addresses, essays, lectures.
I. Suleiman, Susan Rubin   II. Crosman, Inge
Karalus.
PN83.R4   801'.95   79-27619
ISBN 0-691-06436-9
ISBN 0-691-10096-9 (pbk.)